T0392256

Life Lifters

DEAN L GOSSETT

authorHOUSE®

AuthorHouse™
1663 Liberty Drive
Bloomington, IN 47403
www.authorhouse.com
Phone: 1 (800) 839-8640

Published by AuthorHouse 07/26/2018

ISBN: 978-1-5462-2703-8 (sc)
ISBN: 978-1-5462-2704-5 (e)

Library of Congress Control Number: 2018903645

ENDORSEMENT

I moved to California twenty-six years ago and I met Dean Gossett within the first few months of my arrival. Since that time, no one has consistently modeled their love and devotion to Jesus in my life more than Dean. Through his spoken and written words, Dean has a unique way of capturing the eternal truths of the Word of God in a timeless and creative manner. He captivates the young and the not as young in the same way - by describing the indescribable, immortal, incomprehensible God and His plans for humanity in a way that draws everyone around him to listen closely to whatever he's going to say next! Thank you for sharing your love for Christ and gift of communication with us all, Dean. God comes so close to us through you.

-Tim Barley

INTRODUCTION

As you read my articles in **Life Lifters** it is suggested that you may want to use them in order for daily devotions one by one, or do them at random. Each short article was inspired through over 60 years of seeking and walking with God. They cover just about every aspect of life, including Bible characters, prophecy, and miracle answers to prayers. They are inspired by God's word and real life stories. Some are dated. Others are not. Many of the articles are related to family, to Christian friends and to people in the news. If the article isn't mentioned as someone else's thoughts then it was written by myself. To God belongs all the glory for any encouragement or guidance you get from what I wrote. Lord Jesus, please use all that is said to encourage and lift up whoever reads these articles.

THE LAND OF BEGINNING AGAIN

There is a land I visit quite often called **The Land Of Beginning Again**. It's a land quite wonderful. Traveling down **Confession Highway** I see a hitch hiker beside the road. I think it might be you. "If you wish, get in please and join me on this journey."

We come to a cross road that leads us immediately to **Forgiven Lane**. Just beyond that we proceed over a bridge called **Reconciliation Bridge**. Crossing the bridge we glance below and see troubled waters left behind. Ahead a vast panorama of new wonders fill our view. The sign on the far side of the bridge says, "**You Are Entering The Land Of Beginning Again. Those Who Enter Here Find All Things Made New.**" We smile as we pass the sign. Entering this new land helps us leave failure behind. We realize that what is ahead promises new and rewarding experiences.

No wonder I visit this wonderful land quite often. I never tire of the fresh visions it gives me or of taking hitch hikers there with me. Hope you enjoyed the ride. Philippians 3:13-16

Triumph Over the Law

The law is good
Shows all that's Right,
But we are bad
Which faced, makes us sad.

It shows us how to act,
But we fail and that's a fact.
When we try to keep the law
It reveals our every flaw.

If we think we keep it better
Than most, it makes us boast
Then we become just
Legalistic toast.

Another law must suffice
The law of life in Christ.
We look to Him who paid our debt.
Our sins are gone, we need not fret.

What the law could not do.
Being weak through our flesh.
Christ did away with through His death
He died to make us pure and fresh.

Five Things Everyone Needs to Be Called, Justified, Bonafide, Sanctified, and Glorified

The Bible clearly teaches that anyone who truly comes to Jesus Christ for salvation is called by God and responds with belief. He or she is then justified, counted right before God. That person can say, "Justified, It is **just as if I'd** never sinned." Of course we all have sinned but Jesus paid sins debt through death to take away our sins. So He sees everyone who trusts His Son   as righteous and perfect.

Now in order to know you are truly right with God, you must be bonafide. That is God Himself must see your faith in His Son as genuine. Many people are called Christians who are not bonafide. They think they are earning salvation and heaven by being born into a Christian family or by doing good works. Of course that is totally wrong. It is "by grace that you are saved through faith and that not of yourself. It is the gift of God, not of works lest anyone boast." Eph. 2:8,9 So are you bonafide, for real?

If you are for real then the next reality that happens to you is that you grow in a life to be conformed to the image of God's Son. That is God's true, predestined purpose for every believer to grow more and more to be like Jesus. That growth process is an aspect of sanctification, set apart to become like Jesus, dedicated to love for God and others. Bonafide believers desire to be like Jesus. If you don't have that desire you are not bonafide. Get bonafide as quick as you can. Repent and believe. Like in the movie **Brother Where Art Thou**, I'm counting to 3.(-:)

Finally, God glorifies all who are called, bonafide, justified, sanctified believers. Romans 8:28-31 sums it up, "And we know that all things work together for good to those who love God, to those who are the called according to *His* purpose. **29** For whom He foreknew, He also predestined *to be* conformed to the image of His Son, that He might be the firstborn among many brethren. **30** Moreover whom He predestined, these He also called; whom He called, these He also justified; and whom He justified, these He also glorified."

To be glorified is to see Jesus fully as He really is. It is to be like Him forever.   1 John 3:2 sums it up**,** "Beloved, now we are children of God; and it has not yet been revealed what we shall be, but we know that when He is revealed, we shall be **like Him**, for we shall see **Him** as He is." "O that will be glory for me. When by His grace I look on His face. That will be glory for me!"

https://www.youtube.com/watch?v=-lOarryn9Ag>

Who Do You Listen To?

What you believe in life depends on who you listen to and believe. If you listen to and believe Mohammad, you become a Muslim. If you listen to and believe Buddha, you become a Buddhist.   If you listen to and believe   an evolutionist who claims everything has happened by chance, you become a person that leaves God out. In contrast if you listen to and believe Jesus Christ, you become a new-born-person in God's family. You then know the one who created all things and you know God as your eternal Father.

Let's think for a minute about believing Jesus Christ in contrast to believing other faith or non faith folks. Some examples only attributable to Christ: 1.Jesus birth in Bethlehem was prophesied(foretold miraculously) many hundreds of years before he was born. 2. Jesus as the ancestral offspring of Adam & Eve was prophesied thousands of years before his birth that he would defeat Satan which he is doing. 3. Jesus dying and defeating death and Satan was prophesied hundreds of years before he died. 4. Jesus prophesied a number of times when in his early thirties, that he would be rejected, crucified and rise from the dead three days later and it happened. 5. The Bible says he raised himself from the dead. 6. Jesus was seen by over 500 people, during a period of 40 days after he arose from the dead. Then he ascended alive back to his Father in heaven. 7. Before his death, Jesus did many miracles in about a three year period. He fed over 5000 people by multiplying matter. He fed them all with a kids lunch which consisted of only five loaves of bread and two fish. After he fed them there were many baskets of food left over. 8. Jesus said that he is the light of the world and proved it by giving sight to a blind man. 9. Jesus said that all power was given to him in heaven and on earth. He proved it in many ways, like telling a violent storm to stop and it did. 10. He told the apostle Peter to go fishing and find a coin in the fishes mouth to pay taxes and it happened; 11. He healed more than one insane man. 12. He walked on water. 13. He foretold prophetically the future of the world and his return. 14. He spoke of himself as the resurrection and the life, then he proved it by raising a man named Lazarus from the dead. 15. To add to his miracles, he saved me at age 20 and has kept his promise, for over 63 years, to never leave or forsake me. 16. He has answered over 49 miracle prayers asked by me and my wife. You can find the amazing facts about Jesus Christ by putting the key 14 facts underlined above in Google or Biblegateway.com and read them in the Bible. My last two personal underlined facts, number 15 & 16 are also based on John 3:16 and Hebrews 13:5 in the Bible.

There is so much more that Jesus Christ did that not even the world could contain all the books that could be written about him.

Now go back and look at all the religions of the world leaders and the atheists and agnostics. Have they done anything to compare with Jesus? No! A thousand times no. I choose to listen to Jesus who is God come in the flesh. He became a person in a human body. He alone promises me that because I believe in him and listen to him that he will come back and raise me from the dead. Best to throw all religion in the file-thirteen-waste-basket and listen to and believe the Son of God who exposes all false religious beliefs as a blind man leading the blind. Jesus said, "They will all fall into the ditch." So why not believe in the one who said of himself, "I am the way, the truth and the life. No one comes to the Father except by me." Seek him. Listen to him and receive the gift of abundant life which includes eternal life, love, forgiveness, joy, peace, faith, certainty, answered prayer, patience, gentleness, goodness, kindness, self-control and heaven forever. He won't cast out anyone who seeks him whole heartedly. He alone of all people who ever lived on earth should be listened to and believed. Go for it as you listen to this song:

https://www.youtube.com/watch?
v=PANivelKVX0>

John,

I'm praying for your emotional growth and for Jac & Sarah sometimes twice or more a day. Thanks for praying for me.

I woke up this morning thinking about the verse in the Bible that tells us what to think about. I'll share it below with the prayer that it enables you and me and Marsha to think properly bringing our thoughts and emotions into captivity to Christ. I pray every day for God to take away any spirit of fear you or Marsha or I might have and replace it with power and love and a sound mind-**right thinking**.

After 55 years I'm learning lessons I wish I had learned at 20. I'm getting a better handle on the power of proper thinking. The Bible tells us to "rid ourselves of imaginations that are improper, to reject every high sounding philosophy that has been erected against the truth of God and to bring every loose thought, emotion and impulse into captivity to Christ." Since God asks us to do that we must be able to do it. But how?

I'm going to meditate on and practice the following verses related to right thinking and right praying. My goal is to make it a life time practice which produces peace in my heart and and guards me against mental, emotional and spiritual immaturity. Perhaps you might want to do that too.

Take a look at the verses please.

Phil. 4:8 **Finally, brothers, whatever is true, whatever is noble, whatever is right, whatever is pure, whatever is lovely, whatever is admirable—if anything is excellent or praiseworthy —think about such things**. For example I can think on the lovely qualities in my wife, her love for God, her teaching others, her trim figure, her notes of encouragement she writes to others, etc. I can think of the admirable qualities in you trusting Christ, being kind to my grand kids and us all week, feeding us, taking Tyler shooting seeking to grow in emotional qualities. Those are all right thinking.

What is true? What is noble? What is right? What is pure? What is lovely? What is admirable? What is excellent? What is praiseworthy ABOut GOD? YOU? MARSHA? His Word,? others?, your past?, your position in Christ? etc.

Then How can we apply **these things to think about** to pray using Phil. 4:6 **Do not be anxious about anything, but in everything, by prayer and petition, with thanksgiving, present your requests to God.**
Phil. 4:7 And the peace of God, which transcends all understanding, will guard your hearts and your minds in Christ Jesus.

Reject anything that does not have these qualities. If its false reject it. If it isn't' noble reject it, etc. What do you think?

Let me know what happens.

I love you John, and pray that heaven will come down and fill your mind, emotions and soul.

Dean

Bethlehem Revisited
by Dean
Have you been to Bethlehem's manger?
Have you seen the child King?
Has your heart adored him?
Did you presents bring?

Have you pondered his family line?
Seen him as the promised one?
Royalty wrapped in swaddling clothes,
God's divine and human Son?

Have you thought of his conception?
How the angels dried the virgin's tears,
"The highest overshadowed her!"
Banished all of Mary's fears."

Have you imagined how he was formed
In secret in Mary's womb?
Come forth soon to build a temple
From an empty tomb?

Have you stood at Mary's side
As she nursed the Father of life?
Has your tongue extolled him
As did Joseph's wife?

Have you seen him as your Savior
Come to set you free?
Loosed your tongue in rapturous chorus
To the one who died for thee?

Have you been to David's city
Small and little though it be?
Seen the tiny baby as your king
Come to rule and set you free?

Have you heard the angel's singing?
Have you joined the joyous throng?
Have you praised him with the choir,
Echoed back the angel's song?

"Glory to God in the highest!
Peace on earth!
Good will to men!"
Sing it over and over again!

Have you walked with the shepherds
To the manger's dawn?
Wondered with them at their vision?
Told the world what went on?

Have you traveled with the wise men?
Seen his star afresh?
Bowed in worship near the Savior,
Seen him clearly as God in human flesh?

Have you seen his glorious future?
Sure to die but surer to live,
Soon to rule the world in splendor,
The perfect government to give!

Have you received God's gift from heaven?
Have you claimed him as your own?
Then you'll rule with him forever,
Seated on the Father's throne!

Listen, do you hear the angels'
Singing once again?
Are you joining in the chorus
Which shall never, never end?

Lift up your heart!
Make music with majestic tone!
Sing again of the earthly manger
Replaced forever with a heavenly throne!

Swaddling cloth no longer clothes him,
Royal robes enfold his form.
Every soul has room for Jesus,
Every heart toward him is warm!

Crown him afresh this Christmas.
Make him lord of all you are!
Follow him to Zion's glory.
Bow low again beneath his Star!

57th Valentine Reflection
for Gloria from Dean

You've come away to be my love
And we have shared the things above,
Where heights and depths of love divine,
United our hearts as they entwined..

We"ve rested in Him our true Rock
Who gently leads and feeds His flock.
By still waters where He leads
We"ve joyed in Him who meets our needs.

Though trials have come and trials have
gone
Our love in Him has thrived and grown.
And when we breathe our last on earth
We'll rise to heaven's joyous worth.

We'll Cross a higher threshold of love and
grace
Ours together as we gaze upon Jesus' face.
Love will come full circle without delay
In our final home in God's eternal day!

So come away once more and be my love
And we will exalt in heaven above.
Where heights and depths of love entwine
For I am yours and you are mine.

Well Dressed Windows Save Lives

I have a friend named Debra Griffith, who runs a business called "A Well Dressed Window." It brought to my mind well dressed windows in the Bible. One of those windows was on an outside wall in ancient Jericho.

The Israelite army led by Joshua marched around the walled city of Jericho seven times. As they did they could all see a scarlet cord hanging from one window. It was in the window of a ex-harlot named Rahab. Her home was on the wall. Previously two Israelite spies had entered the city of Jericho. The Jericho police sought to find them and kill them. Rahab who had come to believe in the God of Israel hid them on her roof top and they were not discovered.

Rahab then placed a scarlet cord out of her window, down to the ground. The spies climbed down the cord and escaped. Before they left, they told Rahab to leave the scarlet cord in the window and when the Israelites marched against Jericho and defeated it, she would be spared as long as the cord was hanging from her window.

By the time the Israelite army arrived at Jericho, Rahab had called her family and friends to come stay in her house. The armies of Israel marched silently around the city for seven days. All that could be heard was the tramp, tramp of feet until the last day's seventh time around. Then the priests blew trumpets and those marching shouted with a great shout. The wall of the city fell down flat except for Rahab's house. Rahab's mother, father, brothers, sisters and relatives inside the house were all spared. So her well dressed window with the scarlet cord helped the spies and Rahab's family and friends escape death.

Rahab, later married one of the Israelites named Salmon who may have been one of the original spies. She and Salmon became the great, great, great grandparents of David, King of Israel. She was also in the family line of our Lord Jesus Christ and is mentioned as such in Matthew 1:5,6. God's mercy to a converted prostitute started with faith and a well dressed window.

I'm reminded of a story about a father I heard walking with his son. As they walked the son asked what the gold stars in some windows meant. He was told that they represented sons who gave their life for our country. As they walked there was an open lot and the boy looked up and saw a bright star in the sky. He said, "Dad, did God give His Son for our country?"

The answer of course is yes. God put a star in a well dressed window of the sky that pointed to the birth of His Son. He grew up, gave his life, shed his scarlet blood for our sins and then rose from the dead. Now all of us who put our faith in the scarlet cord of Jesus' shed blood are forgiven and escape eternal death. It is simple but true. We, like Rahab, should invite our family and friends to join us in dressing the windows of our hearts with the cord of God's love given to us in His Son Jesus Christ. Whoever lets Jesus into their life will be well dressed in God's righteousness and fit for heaven. God saved a prostitute so no matter how bad you think you may be, you can claim the scarlet cord of God's forgiveness and escape eternal death. Here's a song to help you make sure the window of your heart is well dressed:

<http://www.youtube.com/watch?
v=qOnBFGAevks&feature=related>

Every Woman a Wonder Woman? Every Man A Superman?

The Wonder Woman movie was actually quite good though fiction. Believe it or not most every woman can be a true woman of wonder and most every man a true man of super strength. It all has to do with putting on the armor of God. Here is that armor if you are willing to wear it. It is available clearly for both men and women as shown in the Old Testament in *2 Samuel 22:36,*37 which says**,** "You have also given me the **shield** of Your salvation; Your gentleness has made me great." Then the armor of God is shown even more in the New Testament in Ephesians 6:12,13 which says, **"**Finally, my brethren, be strong in the Lord and in the power of His might. Put on the whole armor of God, that you may be able to stand against the wiles of the devil. For we do not wrestle against flesh and blood, but against principalities, against powers, against the rulers of the darkness of this age, against spiritual *hosts* of wickedness in the heavenly *places.* Therefore take up the whole armor of God, that you may be able to withstand in the evil day, and having done all, to stand,"

In the Bible 2 Samuel 22 and Ephesians 6 are rich with the Lord's shielding and spiritual armor against the Evil One and against all kinds of evil enemies. Take time today to read and heed all of 2Samuel 22:26-50 and Ephesians 6:14-18. As you read heed God's Word, **"A**bove all, taking the shield of faith with which you will be able to quench all the fiery darts of the wicked one." The true womder women and true supermen are those who defeat evil and fight the good fight of faith against spiritual wrong. They are often considered little men and women but they are gigantic in God's eyes. Hollywood often represents stardom falsely, while the true stars are those who walk with God winning real battles against evil.

God's armor also includes truth, a heart dedicated to right and readiness to share the good news of peace and faith. It also includes a mind set on salvation and filled with the word of God which destroys evil and pierces through to the heart like a sharp sword. The armor is kept powerful through persevering prayer and the bold application of God's Spirit to the needs of others

Are you one who puts on and keeps on God's armor every day? If so in God's sight you are a true wonder woman or a true superman because you are shielding yourself and others from evil and fulfilling the will of God!

Putting on armor takes a little time. So those who become wonder women or super men set aside time to tune into the Author of faith who equips us for our daily good fight of faith. Faith in Jesus, the world's greatest super man, and faith in is His Word empower us to defeat our greatest enemies, Satan and his followers. We win big time when one of Satan's human followers changes sides by coming to Christ and joining His side. If you haven"t, will you now trust Jesus Christ as Savior and join those on the narrow road that is a battle, but puts you on the road of right, leading to life eternal. Jesus will not cast out anyone who wants to be on the winning side by coming to Him. Do it today and become a wonder woman or a super man. In the movie Wonder Woman was not born but created out of clay. In real life a wonder woman or super man is first born then re-created. She or he is re-created by God's Spirit and all things become new. Read how that can become you in the Bible, in John 3, especially John 3:16 & 2 Cor.5:17. Please let me know if that re-creation has happened or happens to you now.

By the way, another fictional quality of Wonder Woman was that she could fly as could Superman. If you become a wonder woman or a super man in the Lord's army you will be able to fly someday. Jesus, our commander in chief, actually did fly away back to heaven after He died and arose. So all who follow Him will fly away as well. When Jesus returns He will shout and a trumpet will sound and those who know Him will fly away to meet Him and be with Him forever!   Sing about it here: <https://www.youtube.com/watch?v=192W0bhJNEg>

Jesus Death & Resurrection Started a New Covenant Hebrews 8:6-13

First Covenant -(Shadows)Given by God to Moses; Exodus 34:10

Hebrews 9:1-28 Old & New Covenant Compared

1. THE MESSIAH WOULD COME IN HUMILITY, NOT WITH POMP AND
    PRIDE.(Zechariah 9:9) (Matthew 21:1-9) (Matthew 11:29)
2.   THE MESSIAH WOULD BE DESPISED AND REJECTED BY MEN. (Isaiah 53:3) (Matthew 27:20-23) (Matthew 27:27-31).(Acts 4:27-28) (Matthew 27:3-10)
3.   THE MESSIAH WOULD BE BETRAYED FOR 30 PIECES OF SILVER. (Zechariah 11:12-13) (Matthew 26:14-16)
4.   THE MESSIAH WOULD BE INSULTED, BEATEN AND SPAT ON (Isaiah 50:6) (Matthew 27:26-30)
5.   THE MESSIAH WOULD SUFFER AND DIE FOR THE SINS OF OTHERS.(Isaiah 53:4-7) (1 Corinthians 15:3).
6.   THE MESSIAH COULD DIE FOR THE SINS OF OTHERS BECAUSE HE HAD NO SIN OF HIS OWN. (Isaiah 53:9).(1 Peter 2:22) Hebrews (10:12-14)
7.   THE MESSIAH WOULD DIE BY CRUCIFIXION. (Psalm 22:16) (Psalm 34:20)(John 19:18) John 19:31-34)
8.   THE MESSIAH'S CLOTHING WOULD BE DIVIDED BY GAMBLERS AT HIS DEATH. (Psalm 22:18) (Matthew 27:35)
9.   THE MESSIAH WOULD DIE IN THE COMPANY OF CRIMINALS.(Isaiah 53:12) (Mark 15:27-28).
10. THE MESSIAH WOULD BE BURIED IN A RICH MAN'S TOMB (Isaiah 53:9).(Matthew 27:57-60).
11.   THE MESSIAH WOULD RISE FROM THE DEAD. (Psalm 16:10) (1 Corinthians 15:3-7). (Isaiah 25:8).
12.   THE MESSIAH WOULD GIVE THE HOLY SPIRIT TO THOSE WHO BELIEVE IN HIM. (Isaiah 11:2; 44:3) (John 20:22). (Acts 2:1-18)
13. THE MESSIAH WOULD SEND HIS MESSAGE OF SALVATION TO ALL NATIONS. (Genesis 22:18) *(Isaiah 42:6-7; 49:6; 60:1-2;   V62:1-2)* (Matthew 28:18) (Mark 16:15)(Luke 24:47).(Acts 1:8)

All Roads Lead to Rome or Do They?
by Dean L Gossett

A lady, LAURA Love was walking down a narrow road when she saw across the way another person near where she was but on a broad, wide road. In fact there were many people on that road but one person caught her eye.

Hello, my name is LAURA Love. What's yours?

My name is LARRY, Larry Lost.

Where are you going, LARRY?

I'm on a road that leads to Rome. Don't you know that all roads lead to Rome?

Many people believe that, LARRY, and it seems right to them, but actually there's one road that doesn't lead to Rome."

How do you know that, LAURA?

Because I'm on it over here."

Yes, I can see it. But it's a very narrow road. Where is it going?

It's going to a very beautiful city."

Well, this road is going to a great city too, Rome. On the way I'm getting ready for my arrival.

How do you get ready, Larry?

Well I live it up with all the other people on this road. See how many of us are on our road. There are very few on your road. And we're having a blast. Some of us make out, and drink till were stoned. Others are religious. They do good things for people, worship gods of different kinds. In Rome you can pretty much live how you want. You know, eat and drink and be merry for tomorrow we die.

Are you really happy on the road to Rome LARRY?

Yeah, sometimes. I am for awhile. But after awhile I feel kinda of empty inside.

I know what you mean. I was on the road that leads to Rome once but I got off of it.

How did you do that LAURA, LAURA Love, that's your name, right?

Yes, that's my name but once it was LAURA Lost, like your last name, Larry. I'll tell you how my name got changed. The road I'm on now is a road of lasting love. My last name was changed from Lost to Loved when I got on this narrow road.

No kidding, Laura?

Yes, Larry, I was named LAURA Lost. Now my name is LAURA Loved. I got my new name when I changed roads. I switched from wrong,from addiction and from religion to right, to conversion, and to a new life.

How did you do it LAURA? How do I get off this road onto that road?

Here's how, LARRY. Go back to where you first got on the road to Rome. When you get to the beginning of the road, you'll come to a wide gate. The gate is locked. Search near it carefully and you will find a big book. Open to the heart of the book. Inside is a key in the shape of a cross. It is the key of faith. On the cross-key is written "The Key of Jesus Christ. On the horizontal top bar of the key are His words written there which say, 'I am the door, the way, the truth and the life. If I set you free you shall truly be free.'" On the vertical part of the key are more of His words which say, 'This key is a gift. It cost me my life to make this key for you but it is free to you if you want it. By it you can open the broad gate and go free.'"

Once you open the gate, look to the right. You will see another narrow gate. Take the key and put it in the lock of the narrow door and say and mean these words, "I want to get off the broad road. I want to enter the narrow way. With all my heart I believe the truth about myself and what the key says. With this key I enter into life."

LARRY put the key in the shape of a cross into the broad gate and it opened and LARRY LOST found his way out. Then He walked off toward the narrow gate. As he did he noticed that the sky seemed more blue. A rainbow suddenly appeared. There was something new in every hue that his eyes had never seen before.

LAURA watched as her new friend put the cross- key into the narrow gate. It opened and immediately he was on the narrow road with her. They embraced and walked on arm in arm on the narrow road. There was a look of joy on his face and hers. Love had lifted the load of emptiness off his back and his heart was full of joy.

He began to sing on the road less traveled. "I found joy, wonderful joy since I found the key of life. My sins are washed away. My night has turned to day since I entered the gate of life. I found joy, wonderful joy since I found the key of life."

You have a new name now LARRY. It is LARRY LOVED. Actually it has always been LARRY LOVED but you didn't realize it until now.

LARRY beamed with joy. All the people on the narrow road started singing with LAURA and LARRY, "We've left the road to Rome. We're on our way home. We're marching to Zion, beautiful, beautiful Zion. We're marching upward to Zion, the beautiful city of God."

Then Larry looked across from his joyous road and saw another person on the deceitful road to Rome and spoke to her. My name is LARRY LOVED. What's yours?
My name is ANNIE ADDICTION
Where are you going, ANNIE?
I'm in the way that leads to Rome. You know, don't you, that all roads lead to Rome? I'm on my way there. It's party time, time to revel, time to eat drink and be merry for tomorrow we all die. Right? It's the only way to go you know"
Oh no, ANNIE. There is another, best road. Let me tell you about it. It is an enlightened road of forgiveness, light and life. It is is best ANNIE. It is the way to Emmanuel's land. It is a sweet land of milk and manna-biscuits with honey. Come ANNIE . We are going to the place the Lord of this road said He will give us. It is a city that has lasting foundations whose builder and maker is God. Come join us on this road that ends in joyous life eternal.
How do I get on to your road, LARRY?
Larry started to tell her how and as he spoke the crowd on Annie's road began to mock him shouting out "All roads lead to Rome. Stay with us. Don't listen to those fools on that narrow road. Our road is full of people. Smart people go along with the crowd. Pay no attention to those crackpots!
ANNIE paused. She looked at both roads. The broad road was loaded with people. The narrow road was less traveled. Who will she listen to? There is a way that IS right and another way that SEEMS right. One ends in life and joy. The other ends in death and misery. Will ANNIE change roads? Which road are you on? Be wise. Take the one less traveled.
<https://www.youtube.com/watch?v=U8SsQTpTOAo>

Answering Pilate's Question to Jesus

John 18: **37** "You are a king, then?" said Pilate.

Jesus answered, "You say that I am a king. In fact, the reason I was born and came into the world is to testify to the truth. Everyone on the side of truth listens to me." **38** "What is truth?" retorted Pilate. With this he went out again to the Jews gathered there and said, "I find no basis for a charge against him."

After Pilate asked the question, "What is truth?" he then spoke a true statement, "I find no basis (fault) for a charge against him." Pilate did not get all the implications of Jesus coming into the world to testify to the truth but one thing he got. There was no basis for finding any fault in Jesus at all. The Bible says that Jesus didn't think any thing sinful, didn't do anything wrong or sinful and that his nature contained no sin or wrong.

So what? So he was the only person who ever lived who didn't deserve to die. Jesus had challenged everyone to find anything he ever did wrong saying, " I arrive on the scene, tell you the plain truth, and you refuse to have a thing to do with me. Can any one of you convict me of a single misleading word, a single sinful act? But if I'm telling the truth, why don't you believe me? Anyone on God's side listens to God's words. This is why you're not listening—because you're not on God's side." We each need to ask ourself, "Who's side am I on?" Am I on God's side?" We exist to seek the true God and find him and be on His side according to Acts 17:26,27

Once I was not on His side. I was driven and controlled by desires contrary to His will. Then on a Sunday 61 years ago I heard a message on how to be on His side. The speaker invited those present to come forward to receive Jesus as Lord and Savior. I wanted in my heart to come foreword but I felt helpless. I prayed, "God, I can't do this unless you help me."

The next moment I found myself walking forward all alone with tears running down my cheeks. After coming forward the speaker invited me to pray to accept Jesus as my Savior. I prayed and from that moment until now 61 years later I have been on His side and more important He has been on my side. He chose me and I chose Him. I listen to and believe all His truthful words. I know that my present and future life is secure in Jesus' hands and in my Father's hands. No one can pluck me out of their hands.

How about you? Have you come to Him? Will you come to Him today? Here's how. "Confess with your mouth Jesus as Lord, and believe in your heart that God has raised Him from the dead and you will be saved for whoever believes in Him shall not perish but have everlasting life. Ask Him to help you come today and He will not reject you. Then tell someone you came to Him. Listen to, learn and do what He says and and you will be blessed beyond your fondest dreams. This is life eternal that you know Him, the only true God and His Son Jesus Christ.

<https://www.youtube.com/watch?v=w2VrRk4pZHY>

Deception, Downfall & Destruction of Satan

Christians need a set of 3D Glasses to view the Deception, Downfall & Destruction of Satan. Lucifer started his deception in heaven seeking to be above God, deceiving 1/3 of the angels to follow him in his lust for glory! Shortly the first stage of his downfall commenced. He was banished from his position and cast down to earth where he became the old serpent in the garden of Eden. Using his cunning craftiness he tricked Eve into eating of the forbidden fruit. Her mate, Adam, quickly fell pray to his wife's deception and plunged the world into sin and death.

Since then the Devil has been the constant deceiver who seeks to control and destroy the destiny of all mankind He sought many times to wipe out Christ's ancestors, Israel, and later Jesus himself. Having failed to stop Jesus birth, he sought to snuff Jesus out in his youth. Then he sought to deceive him as he began his ministry, But the Devil failed and left Jesus presence in defeat.   Later Satan inspired the people of Israel and the Gentile Roman powers to sentence Christ to death upon a cross. Satan thought he was winning but actually through death Jesus destroyed him who had the power of death. On the cross Christ was bruised in his feet, then raised Himself from the dead crushing Satan's head and his power in fulfillment of Genesis 3:15.

Soon Satan will fall even further. He will be cast down into the bottomless pit for 1000 years. During his 1000 years in bondage the world will know its   most perfect golden age when   Christ will rule the world. Peace, prosperity and the knowledge of God will cover the world as the waters cover the seas. At the end of the 1000 years Satan will be released from his prison briefly and go out to deceive the nations for one final time. Surrounding God's Holy city and people, Satan and the deceived nations of the world will seek to wipe out God and His people. Then Christ will have had enough! He will destroy Satan under His people's feet as He casts him into the lake of fire, his final home prepared for him, the fallen angels and all his followers.

Thus Satan the deceiver, accuser and counterfeiter who sought to be above God was cast down to the earth, then to his defeat at the cross, then to his banishment to the pit of infamy and finally to his eternal downfall and destruction in the lake of fire. He who sought to lift himself up, up, up above God, above His plan and above His people will find himself cast down, down, down to slither, sulk and wander in the fires of hell. He who has eyes to see look through the 3D glasses of Biblical truth and learn the final fate of Pride's defeat, downfall and destruction.

My Books:
Journey Through the Bible: <https://www.ecsministries.org/Page_3.aspx?id=159972>
The Royal Ride: <http://www.authorhouse.com/Bookstore/ItemDetail.aspx?bookid=29837>
Beauty for Ashes: <http://www.authorhouse.com/Bookstore/ItemDetail.aspx?bookid=22613>
The Hair Angel: <http://www.authorhouse.com/Bookstore/ItemDetail.aspx?bookid=40178>

A Better Facebook
by DLG Aug. 16, 2015
Eventually we'll lose our friends on
Facebook
in one way or another.
But Jesus' friendship never stops.
He stays closer than a brother.
His love & mercy never run out on me.
They're mine for now and eternity.

God's Facebook is not a game- it holds no shame.
He'll never unfriend or blot out a true believer's name.
Forsake me? Never!
His love endures-Forever!
Face it-On Facebook we may lose a friend.
In God's Eternal Facebook friendship will never end!

Merry Christmas to My Gloria in **Excelsis Deo**!

We have shared 56 Christmases together. The first Christmas I got you under the tree in 1959. You came well wrapped, fully formed and huggable. My gift this year of 12 roses are given to remind you of the 4 dozen plus 8 Christmases we have celebrated over the years. When you look at the dozen roses, remember the dozens of delicious meals you have made for me and others. Remember the dozens of time you have cleaned the house, loved and hugged me, given me gifts, scratched my back, and put up with my faults.

How have you loved me? Let me count the ways.You loved me in the morning of our marriage when the days were shining bright. You me now in the evening of our lives when the night stars are still shining in our eyes. I love you because your love has taken me through all our Christmases. You have been an awesome, faithful wife and when we leave our home on earth we will be able to love each other even more perfectly with absolutely new, perfect bodies and heavenly motivated perfect love.

Each leaf on the 12 roses reminds me that in heaven the petals will never fade nor wilt. That is the way these roses I am gifting you this Christmas are now. They are hermetically sealed and preserved inside the glass to last for years.

Enjoy them and remember that
You My wife are like red, red roses newly sprung in June. You are like a melody sweetly played in tune. I thank God for roses But I thank him more for you, my red, red rose, My wonderful gift from God, Still blooming, still fragrant, still beautiful Still together growing younger in mind and mood In this our 56th year in our Christmas decrepitude!

The First Questiion Ever Asked

The first question ever asked on planet earth was asked by God. He asked Adam and Eve, "Where are you?"

God had given Adam and Eve permission to eat from every tree in the garden that he had made for them, except for one. They were not to eat of the tree of the knowledge of good and evil. Eve was deceived by the serpent and took of the tree and ate. So did Adam. Then in shame they hid from God putting on fig leaves for clothes and hiding behind trees.. God came to them and asked, 'Where are you?"

Adam admitted that he had eaten from the tree of the knowledge of good and evil and that he and Eve were ashamed and hid themselves in fig leaves among the trees of the garden. The consequences of their disobedience plunged the world into sin, disharmony, and death.

When my son was a little boy he sometimes got in trouble. When he did he would run in his room, put a pillow over his head and hide, but his little body hung out.

It is still human nature to want to hide when we are ashamed of our actions. But it is foolish to think we can hide from God.

Psa. 139:7   Is there anyplace I can go to avoid your Spirit?
             to be out of your sight?
Psa. 139:8   If I climb to the sky, you're there!
             If I go underground, you're there!
Psa. 139:9   If I flew on morning's wings
             to the far western horizon,
Psa. 139:10   You'd find me in a minute—
             you're already there waiting!
Psa. 139:11   Then I said to myself, "Oh, he even sees me in the dark! At night I'm immersed in the light!"
Psa. 139:12   It's a fact: darkness isn't dark to you; night and day, darkness and light, they're all the same to you.

God comes today and asks each of us, "Where are you?"

There are many fig leaves and trees behind which people still hide today?   Threre are leaves of religious good works. When confronted with their sins people often start telling God and others about their good works thinking that will make up for the wrong things they have done. It is the lie of believing that one's good works can outwegh one's bad ones. The problem with that is that no amount of good works can atone for bad works.

Another set of leaves and trees behind which people hide are participating in religious rituals or traditions thinking their actions or prayers will get rid of thieir sins. Again such behavior does nothing to remove sins or really solve the problem of guilt.

There are the leaves of atheism. Some people hide behind believing God doesn't exist . If he doesn't exist they think they won't be responsbile to him. The problem with this is that just believing something doesn't exisit does nothing to do away with its existence. The amazing thing is that some atheists pray every day.

There are the leaves and trees of false religion which say that all religions lead to heaaven.   The problem with that is that it is a broad road that leads to destruction. There is a way that seems right to some people but it ends in death. Jesus says of himself, "I am the way, the truth and the life. No man comes to the Father but by me."

There is the tree of chance or accident. Those who hide by such reasoning say there is no purpose in life. While it may seem wise to some it is a gamble that loses in the end. The Bible teaches that while some things appear to happen by chance, God knows about everything before it happens. To us there is chance but not to God.

So when God asks us today, "Where are you?" if we are wise we will admit that we have failed in our relationship with him. When Adam and Eve confessed their sinfulness and shame, God had them come out from hiding, take off the fig leaves of their own provision and accept his provision for their sins. He made the first sacrifice for sin, shedding the blood of an animal and making clothes for Adam and Eve. That sacrifice pre-figured the coming of his son to be the final and only true sacrifice to not only remove sins but to add to our lives his own righteousness. Jesus died, the rightesous for the unrighteous that we might be given the righteousness of God. The removal of our sins, our fig leave and trees behind which we hide is done by God for us. And when we receive Christ as our Savior he gives us his own perfection as a gift. Instead of hiding behind leaves and trees, we need to come to one who hung on a tree(the cross) for us. Sin came into the world by partaking of a tree. It led to hiding behind trees. And when we come out of hiding we are led to our Savior who is a tree of eternal life to all who believe. When we trust Christ God counts us as having died with Christ and being given new life and

righteousness as a gift. It is free to us but it cost God his Son. Where are you now? There is room at the cross(the tree) for you.   Milllions have come. There is still room for one. Are you that one? If not will you be tthat one right now?

A Man After Cod's Own Heart

1Sam. 13:14 But now your kingdom will not endure; the LORD has sought out a man after his own heart and appointed him leader of his people, because you(Saul) have not kept the LORD's command."

Acts 13:22 After removing Saul, he made David their king. He testified concerning him: 'I have found David son of Jesse a man after my own heart; he will do everything I want.

A man after God's own heart does what God wants him to do with a willing heart, rejoices in Him as He answers prayer, rejoices in His salvation, does not hide His righteousness in his heart but speaks of His love and truth to others, speaks sincere words from an upright heart, wants to meditate on what pleases God, keeps his mind on God continually causing Him to be glad and rejoice, trusts in God's unfailing love, delights in the Lord and has desires motivated by Him, takes the troubles of his heart to God to free him from anguish, wants God to examine his heart and mind, test him & turn him from any wrong, is confident when attacked when doing God's will, seeks God's face since God asks Him to,
 and leaps for joy because God is his shield, protector and defender.

A Mother's Love

A Mother Loves at all times,
When we're good and do the things we should.
When we're bad and make her sad.
No other care is as near to God's above
Than a mother's undying love.
It shines at birth with joy and mirth.
It grows through all life long,
Like a calm and soothing song.
It lifts a child in prayer to the Lord.
Every hurt pierces her heart like a sword.
When all is said and finally done
A mother's love is as life-giving as the rising sun!

A New Name for My Grandson

I pray for a new name for you my grandson, Tyler. May your great down-in-the-valley-affliction be a true wake up call. My daily study today was about the life of Joseph in the Old Testament. It inspired me to pray that you will, like Joseph, learn two great lessons in life. Joseph named his two sons after the events of his life. His first child he named Manasseh which means God made him forget the afflictions of his past and the loss of His father and home by a new and glorious home. His second son he called Ephraim which means God made him fruitful and victorious in a land where he once had been afflicted. So I pray that your affliction will cause you to be blessed by forgetting finally the past and going forth in fruitfulness empowered by God.

I pray this new name in my heart for you Tyler: Tyler M.E. Kline. Tyler=(of the valley(deep) M.=Manasseh(forgetting) E=Ephraim(fruitful). I pray that the new name I give you in my heart will characterize your whole future life, deep, forgetting, and fruitful.

My name, Dean, also means of the valley. A valley like all our lives takes time to carve out before it can be fruitful. It becomes fruitful after afflictions, wind, storms, and rain followed by sunshine! Listen please to this song called Down In the Valley. It was sung while its singer was down in the valley of Birmingham Jail. https://www.youtube.com/watch?v=8M_hLZykFw0> We are all in the jail of affliction until God's love lifts us out of it.

A New Spiritual Calendar for You! by DLG

After many years of slavery the people of Israel left Egypt set free on the first month of the Hebrew year in approximately 1447 BC. Their departure was the beginning of a new spiritual calendar for them, the month Abib(Nisan) which became throughout their history a time to be remembered for it was the month the Lord set them free from their bondage in Egypt.

Pharaoh who had resisted Moses plea to let Israel go free, finally relented after he and many other Egyptians lost their first born sons in a last terrible plague. The Israelites were told to kill a lamb and apply the blood to the doorposts in their home so when an angel of death came across the land of Egypt, the Lord passed over their homes and no one was hurt.

Pharaoh and the Egyptians who did not believe God put no blood on the doorposts. As the angel of death came to their homes every firstborn child inside died. Shocked, Pharaoh then let the Israelites leave Egypt. The Egyptian people were so eager to see the Israelites go that they "lent" them many treasures to take with them, a little back pay for building the Pyramids.

Thus the month Abib, the first month of the year, the year of Israel's first Passover, became a time to celebrate Israel's birth of freedom for generations to come.

In the New Testament Jesus is called our Passover. Jesus shed His blood upon the cross bleeding from the head, hands, heart and feet. Today Christians apply the blood of Christ spiritually to the door posts of their minds, hands, hearts and feet. In so doing they have a new birth of freedom, not from human slavery but from the slavery of sin. God's Son then passes over them and sets them free! At that moment, the date of their conversion, a new spiritual calendar begins.

That new spiritual calendar began for me when God's Son set me free on a Sunday in 1956 in Augusta, Georgia. As I stood there in a small chapel service an invitation was given to come forward and receive God's Son as my Savior. I stood with a hymn book in my hand as the congregation sang, "Be in time. Be in time. While the voice of Jesus calls you, be in time. If in sin you longer wait, you may find no open gate, and your cry be just to late. Be in time."

As I stood their tears began to flow down my cheeks and I prayed inwardly, "God I can't do this unless you help me." The next thing I knew I was walking forward like a magnet was pulling me, hymn book open in my hands, broken in heart. When I arrived alone at the front the Pastor directed me into a small room. There I prayed to receive Christ. As I emerged from the room I thought, "My life has been so messed up. How do I live this new life?"

A man approached me and without me asking he answered the question I was thinking, "If you want to have faith to live the Christian life, read this book." He held up the Bible and said, "Faith comes by hearing and hearing by the word of God. Believing this book will give you faith to live the Christian life." Then he said, "Romans in the Bible is a good book to begin."

So I read Romans over and over and over. One thing I discovered was that I had been born again having

God's Spirit come to live in me. Born once on May 8, 1935 I found my self with a new special calendar date being born again on Sunday in 1956 at the age of 20 shortly before my 21st birthday. My spiritual calendar began that day in 1956 and became the night of nights in which I was set free from spiritual bondage by the blood of Christ applied to my heart. It became the first month of the year for me spiritually

I wrote my mom a long letter telling what happened to me. At my mother's request, a chaplain called me into his office to talk to me. He wrote my mom and told her, "He has had a deep religious experience. It will all pass away in a little while." Well, 58 years have gone by and it still has not passed away. Why not? Because the Bible says, "He that began a good work in you will perform it until the day of Jesus Christ(Phil1:6).

How about you? Have you had a day when God brought about the good work of salvation in your heart? If you haven't had that new spiritual calendar start for you, you can have it happen now. Read Romans 10:9,10 and John 1:12-14 which tells you how to have that miracle date begin for you today.

Sing or read this song and believe it and this shall be the first month of the year, for you, the time of a spiritual rebirth of freedom: <http://www.hymnal.net/hymn.php/h/1043>

Judy,

Here is another poem, a Prayer Poem. I've added a stanza later about you. You will see it as you read through the poem.
Bless you! Dean

Prayer in the Night for Light
Dean L Gossett

Come Read my prayer though short on style
Still It will engage your heart and faith for a little while!

Tonight, at 3 AM as I lay upon my bed
This is what my longing heart said:

Lord Jesus, I look up to you upon Your Throne
My heart is reaching out and seeking You alone!

Hear my requests which are more than a few
Grant me faith to seek and find You too!

Be not far from my voice and my cry
Fill me with your Spirit or I'll die!

I want to be pure in heart so I can see your face
So I can keep in step with your Spirit"s pace!

Show me tonight your splendid glory

That I might proclaim love's greatest story!

Lead me to the Rock that is higher than I
To see you God now, not just bye and bye!

And what do I see as I look upon your forms?
I see a Father with outstretched arms
I see a Son with heaven's charms.
I see your Spirit strip me of all that harms!

I see love like a giant river of peace
Wash away my sins and cause them to cease!

I hear the voice of God in answer to prayer
"Fear not, I'll give you more than you ask or dare!"

So here now are my I requests-
They will be mine with your bequests!

Release dear Anne from torment in her mind
Help her son find salvation and peace divine!

Grant John and Marsha restored first love
That they might know the joy of heaven's Dove!!

Free dear Judy from dizziness and migraines
Loose her from all her aches and pains!

Help her husband Kent turn from unbelief
Grant him paradise like the repentant thief!
Work in my son's life 'til he walks with you
Fill him with Your Spirit-create in him all things new!

Help my daughter as she raises Kirsten and Tyler
Point them to You lifting them higher and higher!

Show my granddaughter and grandson
Paths of victory and salvation through Your Son!

Help my love for my dear wife
Grow in depth and light up her life!

Married in July, the firework's month of independence dances
Help us still send up skyrockets that burst into smiley faces!

Help my 19 year old neighbor Devin
Stop doing stupid things and open
His heart to heaven!

Help his life change for a long, long while
That his mom and dad might reconcile!

Bless Judy Chrysler in her heart and soul.
Grant that you may be her highest goal!

Grant me a pure heart to seek your face
That I may run with patience a godly race!

I've asked a lot of things from You in prayer
But you can do exceedingly, abundantly, above all
I share!

I ask, as you taught me to, in Jesus name
That His may be the glory and all the fame!

As I have asked today,
So let it be, I pray!

You've said " Call upon Me and I will show you
great and mighty things you know not!
So add to these prayers those mighty things that
escaped my thought!

I will praise you for all that you give
For it is in you that I Hope and live!

Your lovingkindness is better than life.
Stretching through time beyond earth's strife!

Thank you! Thank you! Thank you in advance
My feet and heart join now in a Holy dance!

My desire for all I ask is very strong
If you answer I'll join the angel's song!

Glory to God in the highest
Who brings peace and joy to the lowest!

We who are but dust and crashes
Expect you to give us beauty for our ashes!

So light up our lives and let them be
Shining lights and stars for Thee!

Since this was originally written my granddaughter Kirsten was converted and transformed. We are having a regular Bible study together. My 20 year old neighbor Devin asked to go to church with me which he did twice so far. We are having a rather intermittent Bible study together. Pray it will become regular. My wife and I have gotten closer. A new amazingly effective way to pray has opened up to me and others. Another neighbor, 16 years old asked to go to church with me. In all my life I've never had anyone who was not a Christian ask to go to church with me. It happened twice in one week. Kent mentioned in the poem was converted at the age of 81. Another man named Bob was converted in his late 70s. A couple whom we were counseling using the book Love and Respect both committed their lives to Christ. Three ladies were converted in jail with my cousin Marsha mentioned in the poem who lives in Wyoming. And God has done beyond what I thought blessing me through you at June's service. Also, a new way of praying that is more effective than anything I have ever been a part of came into my hands and has spread to about 20 people. AMAZING! And it is all because of His grace in response to PEP- Prayers given in Expectation and Persistence every day with a pact to never give up until the day I die.

If you have one person you would like seen converted, if you share his or her name with me and promise to pray for that person every day, expecting God to answer, with thanksgiving and praise for what God is going to do, I promise to pray with you. I'll agree with you to his or her conversion and promise to pray every day for that person. But you must agree to that prayer with me. It is God's will that no one perish but that all come to repentance so we can claim his answer together. You will need to let me know when he or she is converted. Let me know if you want to do that. Love, Dean

I wrote **Abraham's Search** below this to friends who because of the economy are going bankrupt. One of them told me they are packing their bags and going out "like Abraham who went out not knowing where he was going." But he did know what He was looking for. That is our whole point in life, to go to the place the Lord has prepared for us and win friends and family to go with us. Here is the poem which fits every person who trusts Christ for salvation. One friend told me she cried when she read the poem and is putting it in a special booklet she is keeping called Faith's Stones.

Abraham's Search is Ours
by Dean L Gossett Aug 17, 2015

Abraham went out not knowing where he was
going.
Leaving his path up to God to do the guiding.

Though he didn't know where he was going
He knew clearly for what he was looking-

He was looking for a city that has a lasting
foundation
Whose builder and maker is the Author of
creation.

He lived in tents, a pilgrim, one of God's
chosen
Everything as far as he could see was his, a
gift from heaven.

He was promised to be the Father of many
nations.
But had no son to bring about God's
declarations.

Childless he made his first recorded request
He asked God for a child to insure He would
be blest.

God answered Abraham's prayer
Promised him a son that he might not
despair.

Many years passed and no son arrived.
So he listened to what his wife desired.

"Have a son through my handmaid dear
Perhaps that is what God desires to take
away our fear."

It was a wrong choice thought right.
Along with it came their souls' blight.

Family troubles between her handmaid and
child.
Brought rivalry, and joy was defiled.

But God who always keeps his word
Visited Abe and Sarah and did the absurd.

He gave them a child in their old age.
They laughed when Isaac arrived on the
stage.

But God promised him much more than just a
little boy.
He promised land, and a multitude of
descendants to enjoy.

He promised Abraham a long life on earth.
With suffering and joy to build his worth.

He gave Abe proof of what He would do.
Through a sacrificial covenant which made it
true.

Abe's faith was tested which in the end gave
him joy
As he willingly sought to sacrifice his miracle
boy.

Abe thought if he offered his Son in sacrifice
God would raise him from the dead –that
would suffice!

But God stayed his hand –the deed was not
done.
Instead Isaac arose in figure pointing to
God's greater Son.

God spared Abe's son and let him go free.
But He spared not his own Son letting him
die for you and me.

Abe was called a friend of God as he saw
Christ's day
That friendship would continue till heaven's
foray(final victory).

Abe and those who would follow in faith's
way.
Would inherit a new earth and heaven some
day.

Wherever he went he built altars to His God.
He worshiped Him and trusted in His word.

While it gave him a place to stay, to live and
pray.
Earth's things were not enough to make his
day.

He, like you and I, look for something better
A New Heaven and Earth with all things
grander .

Abraham died upon this barren Sod
Then rose to see the face of God.

Now he walks the streets of gold
In the city with foundations of which we're
told-

A city with 12 gates of pearl and 12 jeweled
foundations

His spirit is now perfect as he realizes the promise of the ages.

Earth as we know it now was not his desire
Nor is it any wise person's place to aspire.

Only on a New Earth and New Heaven without alloy (mixture)
Only in the New Jerusalem will man find lasting joy.

For those who walk with God and see His face
All things are theirs whether time, or love or endless grace.

So go out my friend through this world of temporary residence.
Enjoy what you can but look beyond its decadence.

Look to God to lead you truly to your final Home
Where you'll hang your hat & crown never more to roam.

Add to Your Imperfect Hopes Some Perfect Hopes

The Bible tells followers of Christ to "always *be* ready to *give* a defense to everyone who asks you a reason for the hope that is in you, with the utmost courtesy." 1 Peter 3:15

There are different kinds of hope. There is hope that something might happen but it isn't certain. For example it looks like the Warriors may win the championship against the Cavaliers this year but it is not certain! A person may hope he is going to get a good grade on a test but it is not certain.

Biblical hope is certain. A person who believe in Christ as Savior is certain about having eternal life because God promises it and He always keeps His promises. We have been given to us exceedingly great and precious **promises**, that through these we may be partakers of the divine nature, having escaped the corruption *that is* in the world through lust. 2 Peter 1:4

Here are some of those promises that give followers of Christ perfect hope: "I am the door. By me if any man enter in, he shall be saved."John 10:9 Any man means you! "God so loved the world that He gave His only begotten Son that whosoever believes in Him should not perish but have everlasting life.John 3:16 Whosoever means you! "I will never leave you nor forsake you." Heb. 13:5 "He who believes in **the** Son has everlasting life; and he who does not believe **the** Son shall not see life, but **the wrath of God** abides on him."John 3:36 "Let not your heart be troubled. Neither let it be afraid. You believe in God. Believe also in me. In my Father's house are many mansions. If it were not so I would have told you. I go to prepare a place for you and if I go away will come again and receive you to myself that where I am there you may be also." John 14:1 "Which **hope** we have as an anchor of the soul, both sure and stedfast,Hebrews 6:19 "Blessed be the God and Father of our Lord Jesus Christ, which according to his abundant mercy hath begotten us again unto a living **hope** by the resurrection of Jesus Christ from the dead," 1 Peter 1:3 "I, Paul, am an apostle on special assignment for Christ, our living **hope**." 1 Timothy 1:1-2 For all the **promises** of God in Him *are* Yes, and in Him Amen, to the glory of God through us" .2 Corinthians 1:20 All of the promises above mean you with one stipulation. You must believe and receive them.

Here is a song to further enable you to experience perfect hope! https://www.youtube.com/watch?v=QVeHDun_oEQ>

Are You Afraid of Anything?

What are you afraid of? It is normal to fear some things but sad if you do not overcome them.

The Psalmist David says, "I sought the Lord, and He heard me, and delivered me from all my **fears**." Psalm 34:4

When I was twenty years old I heard the good news that Christ died for me. I was not a church goer but went to church at Bethany Chapel in Augusta, Georgia. The preacher invited people to come forward and trust Jesus Christ as Savior. I stood with the congregation with a hymn book open to a song about life being brief like the falling of a leaf. The song invited me to be in time and trust Jesus before it was to late. The preacher asked anyone there who wanted to, to come forward and receive Christ.

As I stood there with tears flowing over my cheeks, afraid, I prayed and asked God to help me. I told Him I couldn't do it without His help. The next thing I knew I was walking forward, alone, with the hymn book in my hand. I went into a private room up front and prayed with the preacher to receive Jesus as my Savior. God delivered me from my fear to accept Him and my life has been changed now for the better for 59 years. **The way to overcome fear I learned that day was to seek God's help, to be heard and to be delivered from it.**

After I came to Christ I was asked to share publicly what Christ did for me. I was afraid again but asked God to help me and His help enabled me to share what he did for me and could do for others who listened to my story. Over the years I have spoken thousands of times. At fist every time I preached I was so so tense that I perspired badly, so much that I had to have my suit cleaned after every sermon. After speaking in front of groups for about two years I finally got to the point that my trust in God stopped my fear and I quit perspiring. Trust in God delivered me from the fear of public speaking which is the number one fear of many people.

Sometime after I became a believer I sinned against God. I walked the streets alone crying and fearful because of what I had done. Then I read God's word that took away my fear. It said, "If we confess our sins, He is faithful and just to forgive us our sin and cleanse us from all unrighteousness." I John 1:9 What a wonderful verse. God said elsewhere that He blotted out my sins and would not hold them against me but forget them. So I confessed my sin and God kept His promise, forgave and cleansed me and delivered me from the fear that accompanies sin

and failure. The Bible says that anyone who says he has not sinned is a liar. He also promises to blot out and cleanse us from all sins when we admit them to Him because Jesus paid for all of them by dying on the cross for them and arose from the dead to forgive us and give us His righteousness.

I met my wife to be in 1959. She asked to ride with me on a singles snow trip. We fell in love and though I was a little afraid I asked her to marry me. She said, "Yes." And though a little fearful, six months later we were married. I joke and say, "Gloria snowed me on that snow trip and we lived happily ever after, for 56 years now. I sought the Lord in the midst of the small fear I had when we were married and He delivered me from it.

In 1972 I was asked to write a book about the Bible. I did and sent it to **Emmaus Correspondence School** in Chicago. For a long time I feared it would never be published. Then it was. Today my fears are gone as each week I correct the course I wrote called **Journey Through the Bible .** It has been revised and reprinted more than 14 times and completed by by over 1,000,000 people. No longer afraid to write, I have had four books published and almost twice a week write articles that go out by email, twitter, Google, Wordpress and Facebook.

The final fear God has released me from me is the fear of death. "...through death He (Jesus) destroyed him who had the power of death, that is, the devil, **15** and released those who through fear of death were all their lifetime subject to bondage." Heb. 2:14-16.

God has kept His promise and helped me time after time to conquer fear. There is nothing wrong with being afraid unless we fail to take our fears to God who will help us conquer them. David, mighty young man who defeated the giant Goliath, said it best, "Whenever I am afraid, I will trust in You." Psa. 56:3 If you haven't trusted Him you can right now as you sing this song: <https://www.youtube.com/watch?v=w2VrRk4pZHY> Please let me know if you do.

After Death What? by Dean L Gossett

There is one thing in the Bible that everyone agrees is true, "It is appointed to man once to die..." but everyone would **not** agree with the rest of the verse which says, "but after this the judgement(Heb. 9:27)." After death is the judgement! Judgement for what? The Bible clearly teaches that judgement after death involves rewards for true believers in Christ and punishment for those who refuse both to believe in Him and to believe what He says.

The verse following Heb. 9:27 which shows we will all die and then face judgement is followed by wonderful news in Heb. 9:28 which says, " So Christ was offered once to bear the sins of many. To those who eagerly wait for Him He will appear a second time, apart from sin, for salvation." So sin for the believer is not in question. Jesus comes for us who believe apart from sin.

The good news is that if you trust Him as your Savior who died for your sins and rose again then your judgement will be **salvation instead of damnation.**

Some people teach the erroneous lie that when we stand before God He will accept us if our good deeds outweigh our bad. Total nonsense and lie of the Devil. When we stand before God it will be because His good deed in sending His Son to bear our sins brought about our salvation. Salvation is the gift of God not or our works but of God's work. "This is the work of God that you believe on His Son." Why? Because Jesus paid it all, all that was necessary to make it possible for us to be forgiven and end up in heaven. The gift of God is eternal life.

No one can be good enough to earn heaven. If man's good works could save them, then they would brag about themselves, not God. Only God will get the credit for our salvation. He paid the debt of our sin. So quit being religious to try and earn heaven. Religious efforts to gain heaven are the Devil's Drugs. Instead of being drugged, be humble and joyfully believe in God's mercy and grace which alone can save you.

After death each one of us will be judged by what we did in reaction to the good news of Jesus, God's Son. If you reject Him your name **will not** be found in the book of life and Revelation says, "Whosever's name was not written in the book of life was cast into the lake of fire which is the second death."

On the other hand everyone whose name is in the book of life **shall have eternal life and overcome death and hell.** So what do you choose? Jesus bids you come to Him for rest in your soul. He bids you to come to Him and take freely the gift of God. The gift of God is eternal life. "For God so loved the world that He gave His only begotten Son that whosoever believes in Him should not perish but have eternal life."

So after death what will you experience? Eternal life or the second death? It is up to you. Sing this song and believe it and be rewarded eternally instead of punished forever. <https://www.youtube.com/watch?v=w2VrRk4pZHY>

Ali Keirn,
% Great American Melodrama
P.O. Box 1026
Oceano, Calif,
93475

Dear Ali,

Thank you for your kind note and the autographed photo. I'll but it above my desk on the mantel part where I will see it every day. I put you on my prayer list. I have over 200 people on it. Many are believers like you. Many are not. Since I started praying consistently and agreed with others who promised to do the same I have seen over 20 people commit their lives to Christ, many I have never met who live in various parts of the U.S. They got on my prayer list by people I came to know. I've been doing this for about a year and a half now. Because I am retired I have much time to devote to prayer and sharing Christ with others. I write a weekly illustrated news letter which goes out to a couple hundred people each month. It is designed to encourage people and point them to Christ. It takes about 3 minutes to read and is followed by a song I pick on You Tube that illustrates the theme for the article. If you would like to look at it I will send it to you. Just send me your e-mail to deanlgos@comcast.net and I will send it to you.

I know you would love my granddaughter, one of those who came to Christ in the last year. Her father committed suicide and it sent her into a tailspin of drugs and addiction. But a year and a half ago she gave her life to Christ and is totally free from all her addictions. She love people with a deep compassion and went to Rwanda Africa for 6 months as a missionary with YWAM, Youth With a Mission. We study and pray together once a week and she is so amazing, a great joy to my life. I know you would love her if you met her.

I was very pleased to find out that you are a baptized believer. Will you be doing the Melodramas in Oceano for a long time? Gloria and I hope to get down their again some time this year to see another Melodrama. We both agree that the plays there are the best we have seen anywhere.

I will pray these things for you:

1. That your life will be inspired by God and you will please Him in all you do.

2. That you might be filled with all the fulness of God.

3. That you will be ready always to give a reason for the hope you have in Christ.

4. That He will guide you in all your relationships.

5. That He will keep you filled with enthusiasm and joy in performing

One thing that really impressed me was that I could understand every word you said or sang. That is not true of some actors and actresses today.

God bless you and keep you and give you peace, Dean

Here is a song I wrote about God singing over those who are his. Lots of songs have been written in which we sing to God. I have not found one which shows Him singing to us. So I wrote one below. Can you imagine hearing God sing? Does He do all four parts at once? I hope it will encourage you because it is the way God feels about all his people that know Him and walk with Him:

Zeph. 3:17 The LORD your God is with you,
He is mighty to save.
He will take great delight in you,
He will quiet you with His love,
He will rejoice over you with singing."

God Sings Over Us
My Never Ending Ecstasy

I love you child with tenderness.
I love all you are to Me
I sing my love that set you free.
You are My eternal ecstasy.

I touch you now with gentleness
Love of My heartfelt tenderness.
You are My trophy for eternity
My never ending ecstasy.

I love you child with joyfulness
I joy in all you are to Me.
You are the life of My love
My ever lasting ecstasy!

I touch you now with gentleness
Love of my heartfelt tenderness.
You are my trophy for eternity
My never ending ecstasy.

You are My blood bought child
My love for you is gentle and wild.
You are Mine and I am yours
My ever lasting ecstasy.

I touch you now with gentleness
Love of my heartfelt tenderness.
You are my trophy for eternity
My never ending ecstasy

Rest now My tender love.
Quiet yourself my gentle dove.
We are one for eternity.
My ever lasting ecstasy.

I touch you now with gentleness
Love of my heartfelt tenderness.
You are my trophy for eternity
My never ending ecstasy

Three Rs That Don't Work & Three Rs That Do Work

Three Rs that people use to try to reach God that don't work are religions, rules, and rituals. Men have invented all kinds of religious systems to reach God. Even the Devil has a religion. He believes in God and trembles but it does him no good.

Men make up religious rules thinking it will get them into a right relationship with God and into heaven: Don't eat meat on Friday. Don't light a fire on the Sabbath. Keep the ten commandments which if one could do would work but no one ever kept them all except for Jesus. So if you want to get to heaven by keeping the ten commandments you are doomed because breaking one according to the Bible makes you guilty as if you broke them all. Some think they will be in touch with God if they keep rules like forbidding marriage and abstaining from certain food and drink.

Some think practicing rituals is the answer. So they count and recite religious prayers while fingering beads. They light candles, repeat memorized prayers over and over, touch or kiss the bones or hands of a 'Holy man." Jesus rejected man made religion, rules and rituals as unsatisfactory paths to God.

In opposition to religions, rules and rituals that don't work are three Rs that do work. They are **righteousness** received as a gift, **regeneration** of one's heart by God's Spirit and the **reality** of worshipping and serving God in Spirit and truth, **Righteousness plus true regeneration equals reality!**

One becomes righteous by believing what God says: Over 400 years before the ten commandments were given God counted Abraham righteous because he believed Him. The laws were given later not to save us but to show up our sin so we would come to God and believe in His sacrifice to take away our sins. **Jesus died once for all, the just for the unjust that we might be given the righteousness of God. He who works not but believes in Him who justifies the ungodly, his faith is counted for righteousness.** Finding God is a loving gift given by God to those who believe the record He gave us about His Son. **For God so loved the world He gave His only begotten Son that whoever believes in Him should not perish but have eternal life**. If you confess with your mouth Jesus as Lord and believe in your heart that God raised Him from the dead, you will be saved from death and hell and be given eternal life and heaven.

That belief imparts righteousness and regenerates the believer. **Whoever believes that Jesus is the Christ is BORN OF GOD.** That rebirth is based not on man made religion, rules, or ritual but on the redemptive, forgiving, transforming power of God's Holy Spirit. A person born into God's family worships God in Spirit and in truth. **'Old things pass away. All things become new**. He realizes he has a relationship with a person, a redeemer, God's Son, who not only saved him from sin, death and hell but also saves him to a new God-honoring life. He worships God, serves him and loves Him because God first loved and forgave him. He knows God not by religion, rules or ritual but through gifted righteousness, through a regenerated heart and through the reality of worshiping God in spirit and truth.

The 3Rs that don't work are a drag. The 3rs that do work are a dance. That dance is filled with His delight in you and your delight in Him.. On which 3Rs are you basing your life?

All is All We Need

There is a soap called "All" that makes our clothes all clean and sparkly. There is also an "All" that makes us clean, sparkly, acceptable and beneficial to God. It is the "all" of God's love to us and the all of our love to Him and others.

We are to love God with all our heart, all our soul and all our mind. If we do that we will have all we need. But how can we do that?

Only as we realize the all with which God loves us can we give him back all the love He deserves. Here is all the proof of God's love, not that we loved Him first but that He loved us first and pour out all His love to us. He does it through His Son who loved us and gave His all in dying for all our sins and rising from the dead to shower us with all His love

As for me, He has not dealt with me according to what my sins deserve but forgiven all of them. answered all my prayers, healed all my wounds, provided all my food, given me all my benefits, and given me all His love. He has poured upon me all the fruits of His Spirit, love, joy, peace, patience,gentleness, goodness kindness, faith, and humility, He bestows upon me all things that pertain to life, death, and the future to follow.

Once I was at the post office and a very beautiful woman was behind me. I went across town to an office supply store and was standing in line again. I looked and that same woman was behind me again. She smiled saying, "I'm not following you." I decided to call her goodness and mercy. Why? Because there are two beautiful ones who do follow me everywhere I go: They are called Goodness and Mercy. They follow me all the days of my life and I will dwell in the house of the Lord forever!

Due to His love for us, it isn't any wonder that you and I should return His love with all our heart, soul and mind!

Mary James, a radiant young woman for Christ had loved ones who put on her Tombstone , "All For Jesus." I've never met her but I love her and will see her someday!

She wrote this song: <http://www.youtube.com/watch?v=kkhTYvFpKlc>
Here is another song called All for Jesus in Hawaian Form:
<http://www.youtube.com/watch?v=6ClQyxxiAWw&feature=related>
Love to you, Dean

Amazing Day

PIE, One Secret to Success

My wife and I had an amazing day with William Osser, a student I had in 1st and 2nd Grade in 1973,74 at Palomares School in Castro Valley, Ca, He came with his wife, Heather and two children, Griffin and Jasper.. Billy as he was known in the days when he was in my class was a brilliant student. By 3rd grade he had finished four math books and then skipped a grade. He graduated from college at age 17. At dinner with them we provided barbecued tri-tips. He and his wife provided good conversation, good appetites and peach pie! PIE makes a nice acrostic which was Billy's and other's in my class secret to success. The P in PIE stands for Prayer. The I in PIE stands for Individualize. The E stands for Encourage and Excel. That was the approach I took to teaching which is a secret for success. I prayed for each student. They learned both math and reading at their own individualized pace. And they were awarded prizes for excelling.

I made it my goal for each child to grow in one year at least two years in their reading ability. The first year I followed the PIE formula a child, J.W. grew 21 months in 9 months. One child who scored Zero at the beginning of the year in comprehension scored 49 months growth over a period of 9 months which meant his reading ability was beyond 4th grade in 2nd grade.

What motivated me to do the PIE approach to teaching was partly because of two encouraging teachers I had. In sixth grade I was "given the benefit of the doubt" and passed by a teacher who continually criticized me. In 7th grade my teacher, Mr. Manford, constantly encouraged me. One example was the day he came down and encouraged me during a baseball game. He took time with me. That day I hit three home runs. I got the best grades in his class. In high school I had a track coach who took time to encourage me. At one meet he came over, told me to snap my foot when i high jumped because my trailing foot nocked the bar off. He rubbed me down and that day I jumped the highest I had ever done, 5 feet, eight inches. Then when I became a Christian at age 20 I was blessed by encouragers who met with me, ate with me, had me to their homes and I learned the scripture that tells us to encourage one another.

Each year my students excelled in their individualized reading to the point that the Miller Unruh reading specialist said to me,"I don't know what they are doing but keep it up." I told her. She told me she never thought of prayer.

Over the years children did so good in reading and math that my principal Mrs. O, said she wasn't going to let me test them one year. She would do it. That was rather embarrassing because it meant she might think I was cheating. So she tested them and they still excelled. This PIE acrostic, Pray, Individualize and Encourage worked for me and my students and it will work for you. God's plan in the Bible is individual. He seeks people to trust Him one by one. At our table for dinner Will's(Billy")s) son read a verse from the Old Testament that says to seek God with all your heart and you will find Him. That is the most wonderful individualized plan in the world. It fits all of us.

When Will(Billy) was in my class I use to tease him with a song, "Can you bake a cherry pie, Billy Boy, Billy Boy. Can you bake a cherry pie charming Billy?" Amazing thing is Billy has become an avid pie baker. He brought us his peach pie which was delicious. What I marvel at is what a good taste it and the day had. I marvel at what the PIE formula, Pray, Individualize and Encourage, did in the lives of my students.. God, not me, gets the glory for any success. After all, He designed us to enjoy PIE right now as well as in heaven bye and bye. You might want to try out the PIE formula. It works with anyone who tries it. Taste and see that God is good.

Here is Billy's response to our day together with him and his family. "Our visit with you and Gloria yesterday was sweeter than any pie I've ever made. And what a thrill it was to discover my memories of you and the teacher you are have remained accurate. I learned so much from you.". Sing about it here: https://www.youtube.com/watch?v=cfyM7PYpE6I>

Amillennialists Right or Wrong

Amillennialists do not believe the 1000 year reign of Christ mentioned in Revelation 20:4-6 is a thousand years. It is supposedly a symbol which they interpret as meaning "a while or indeterminate" time. They say we are in that "thousand year reign" now. Christians are supposedly now reigning with Christ.

The problem with that interpretation is that it is totally disproved by the rest of scripture. Scripture tells us that at the same time the 1000 year reign is going on Satan is bound and can't deceive the nations until he is loosed at the end of the 1000 years. Well, the Apostle Peter didn't believe the nonsense that the church was in the "1000 year reign now." He says in 1Peter 5:8 that the Devil goes about like a roaring lion seeking whom he may devour. Paul didn't believe the day of the Lord's return to reign had occurred yet either as he states in 2Thessalonians 2:1-12.

Here's a no brainer: How can the Devil be bound and yet go about seeking whom he may devour? We are told not to let Satan get a foothold in our lives. How can he get a foothold in our lives if he is bound during the 1000 years of Christ's reign which Amillennialists say is now. The answer is, "He can't!"

He is not bound and the church is not yet reigning with Christ.

Probably the reason Amillennialists believe the 1000 years does't mean a 1000 years is because more than a thousand years has passed since the church began. So it doesn't fit their interpretation of a 1000 years meaning a time of completion. Confused? Let Amos and Andy help you out.

Amos: Andy, if we is in the thousand year reign of Christ it is is sure a lousy reign!

Andy: Why do you say that, Amos?

Amos: Well, during the reign of Christ, the lion is suppose to be lying down with the lamb, yet lions are still eating lambs. Also the earth is suppose to be filled with the knowledge of the LORD as the waters cover the sea. And right now there are 20 major religions and many minor ones most of whom do not honor the LORD of the Bible. Also, during Christ's rule people are suppose to live as long as the life of a tree and anyone who dies at the age of 100 during the reign will be considered a child. Also, weapons of war are suppose to cease durning that time. Also people are suppose to go up to Jerusalem too honor Jesus and if they don't they will not have rain in their land. None of that is happening, Andy.

Andy: Hey Amos maybe the 1000 years means a thousand years and hasn't happened yet.

Amos: You got it Andy!

Looking forward to that day when Christ will rule for a thousand years and to the eternal day when He will rule forever! God bless you. Dean

Wayne & Joan,
Thank you for your encouraging card. We had a great day of fun, food, fellowship and sharing. for my big 80. We missed you. I shared the thoughts below with everyone.
Dean & Gloria
PS Be sure to listen to the song at the end.

Parts of Us Never Grow Old

I just turned 80 years old but thanks to God parts of me are much younger because God continually recreates them. My liver is only about 5 months old, my taste buds are only about ten days old, my heart is about 20 years old, my lungs 2 to 3 weeks old, my skin about 2 to 3 weeks old, my bones about 10 years, my intestines 2-3 days, my nails 6 -10 months, my red blood cells about four months, and my hair 3 years old.

Only my brain cells and certain cells in my eyes are 80 years old. We keep most but not all of our near 100 billion braincells from birth to death. God is recreating our body continually without us even hardly thinking about it. There is an unseen but real power in the universe, intelligent, personal, creative and real. He remakes and repairs our bodies with the use of DNA, blood, and all the body systems He designed.

God is in the business of recreating our bodies moment by moment. "Thank You for making me so wonderfully complex! Your workmanship is marvelous—how well I know it."Psalm139:14

I joke now as I get older and often say, "As I grow younger I seem to forget some things more easily." Part of me and you **IS** younger than our age. Though our outward man is perishing, our inward man is enabled to be renewed day by day. However it's possible for our brain to lose some of its near 100 billion cells which are not regenerated so forgetfulness and sometimes dementia can occur.

Our physical body is mostly very young though outwardly it ages. Scientists can not explain why our body slowly dies; but God explains that it is because of sin that entered the world.

When we do die there is a part of us that does not die. We have a spirit which lives on forever with or without Christ. Every Christian has the Spirit of God indwelling them. God's Spirit enables us to be renewed so that our spirit never grows old.

There is constant change inside us as our spirit is in touch with God's Spirit. We behold partially as in a mirror the glory of the Lord being changed from glory to glory. At age 20 I received the Lord Jesus Christ as my Savior. At that moment I was born of the Spirit. Since then God has graciously worked in my life, forgiving me when I allow my old self to be in control and changing me when my new self trusts and obeys Him. The root of the Spirit produces the fruit of the Spirit. We enter this world by being born with a physical body that dies. We enter the kingdom of God by being born a second time, by the Spirit of God. Those who know Jesus as Savior will eventually receive a new spiritual body that will never die. Jesus said, "Who ever believes in me, though he were dead, yet shall he live and whosoever lives and believes in me shall never die." Then he said, "Do you believe this?"

I do. How about you?

My first birth was brought about by my parents. My second birth by God will and Spirit joined to my will and spirit. Since my second birth sixty years have passed. I wonder if we will celebrate our first or second birth in heaven? If so after a few thousand years we will sure have a lot of candles to blow out.(-:) Here is a song about a land where we can have endless years and never grow old. https://www.youtube.com/watch?v=B0d7RliBznE>

Best New Year

Israel's civil calendar and Israel's spiritual calendar are different. When God determined to free Israel from its bondage in Egypt, He did something amazing. God instructed the people to kill a first born lamb during the month Nisan, the fourteenth day of what God called Israel's first month. "This month *shall be* your beginning of months; it *shall be* the first month of the year to you." Ex 12: 2.

God's instruction to Israel meant He would free them from their bondage as slaves in Egypt. They obeyed God and put blood on the doorposts of every home with a firstborn child in it.

God passed through the land and everyone who had no blood on their doorposts had any firstborn children die that night. Even Pharaoh's son died. It was a final plague on Egypt that convinced Pharaoh to let Israel go free.

That night was created and guided by God and was called by God the first month of the Israelite's year. After it happened Israel left Egypt as a new nation. The nation had a civil calendar which marked them out before but then God caused them to have a new spiritual first month based on their deliverance from Egypt and bondage. For Israel it was called The Passover.

That true story can have a marvelous application to you and me.

To me, I was born physically under the civil date of May 8,1935. My spiritual birth calendar happened twenty years later. I heard about the Passover story when I was 20 years old. In the New Testament Jesus Christ is called our passover. "For indeed Christ, our **Passover**, was sacrificed for us." ! Cor. 5:7

As Israel had a new beginning with the death of a firstborn animal whose blood was put on the door post of Israel homes, I had a new beginning on the day I believed in God's firstborn Son's death for me. I was born again which became my first day free from the slavery of sin. Christ knocked on the door of my heart applying His blood shed for me on the cross as I invited Him into my life " Jesus says to all, "Behold, I stand at the door and **knock**. If anyone hears My voice and opens the door, I will come in to him..." Rev. 3:20. I listened to His knock and His voice. I opened and as my Passover, He paid for my sin and set me free from my bondage to sin.

Without Israel's Passover Lamb Israel would not have been set free from bondage in Egypt. Without Jesus death and blood applied to the door of my life I would not have experienced new life including being set free from slavery to sin.

I believed God and a new spiritual calendar celebrates my release from sin's bondage. Physically I'm 81 years old. Spiritually I'm 61 years old.

As you begin the year 2017 have you experienced the best New Year possible? You can today. Whoever receives Christ is born anew and set free forever! If you trust Jesus today as your Passover you will experience a truly New Year? I have had the best new year of my life ever year because 61 years ago I opened the door of my life to Him and He set me free to be an eternal citizen of His heaven. How about you?

<https://www.youtube.com/watch?v=i1hSRerQ60c>

Animal Facts & Fun In The Bible

In the beginning of creation, at first, before the flood, people and animals were primarily vegetarians. After the flood God allowed eating of certain clean animals,. The first animal ever killed was a sacrifice by God who made animal-skin clothing to cover Adam & Eve's sin. It was an offering that pointed through time to illustrate that the death of Christ, makes possible the removal of sin and the gift of righteousness, to be clothed in God's gift of forgiveness and perfection! The first sacrifice of an animal and the final sacrifice of Jesus, the Lamb of God, are both brought about by God. He is the author and finisher of our salvation.

Meanwhile between the time of creation and now animals are to be treated as God instructs us. Some for food; Some to enjoy; Some to die as illustrations of Jesus final death for us.

The Bible clearly has commendable words for those who treat their animals and pets properly. Feed them. Help.them. Enjoy them. Protect them. Rescue them. God makes us humans responsible for ruling rightly over His creation of plants and animals.

It is clear that there will be animals during periods of future history when vegetarianism will become again the practice of people. Even creation will be altered and "The lion will lie down with the lamb."In other words animals will also be harmless vegetarians. Children will play with snakes with joy. Moms will let them play with animals once dangerous but no longer to be feared. God has made His creation to be beneficial to us and someday it will be delivered into great freedom to be no longer fearful of other creatures or of mankind.

In eternity when creation is changed will there be animals? Revelation makes clear there will be animals in eternity.

I remember a Sunday School teacher saying," None of your pets that die will live on again because they have no soul." That is pure heartless speculation! It is within the power of God should He desire, to amaze us with the restoration of our pets to enjoy. Is that speculation? Of course it is but I think it is speculation reflecting God's kindness and love for His people and for His creatures. "The Bible in the book of Job indicates that even God enjoys and plays with his creatures. He, like us, gets delight and pleasure from his animal creation.

Since no good thing will He withhold from those who walk up rightly should we not expect to enjoy all aspects of His new heavens and earth. Imagine the joy we will have with what He has prepared for us. Wouldn't you love to pet a lion, or an Eagle or ride a whale all of which would be totally full of affection and playfulness? Maybe we will find our once earthly pets that died risen and running up to us with joy? I'll take that possibility and hope any day over the tactless conclusion that says. "Sorry little One, you'll never see your pet again because it has no soul!"

Once I was at my wife's grandmother Minnie's memorial service when I noticed off to the side of the grave, a sparrow dead, lying on its back with its feet pointing up to the sky. For a moment I wondered if the preacher put it there? Then I remembered Jesus words, "Are not two sparrows sold for a copper coin? And not one of them falls to the ground apart from your Father's will. But the very hairs of your head are all numbered. Do not fear therefore; you are of more value than many sparrows." Matt. 10:30,31 Animals are important. God values them and enjoys them. So should we. We don't know for sure if God will raise any animals from the dead but we do know that humans who confess Him as Lord and Savior will rise from the dead to enjoy God's new heaven and earth. So let us treat and value animals with joy, but let us value people even more as Jesus does, who died to free us for sure from death and hell to eternal life and heaven. Amazing wonders are yet to come which will include animals of His creation, possibly even risen pets. What joy and fun will be His and ours! Sing about Animals: <https://www.youtube.com/watch?v=8zJe_KSg1SQ>

For Gloria On our 57th Anniversary From Dean
Celebrating At Paradiso Restaurant In San Leandro
On this our special anniversary you are my Gloria Blanche bride, palintine. So I

lift my voice in thanks that I am yours and you are mine! You are my Gloria, a gift of glory from God to me. You are my Blanche which means pure, untarnished beauty.

On this our 57th anniversary I can truly say that you have been fully God's gift of glory, purity and beauty to me.

Creative Bible leader for more than 32 years, giver of gifts too each of your many friends, writer of notes with noble ends. Crafty creator of collages for wedded couples, & children's births, still adorn the walls of countless homes and nooks.

Master gardner, consummate home maker, sewer and tailor of clothes for both young and old, I've watched over the years your talents unfold!

My Lover and friend, my back and hair caresser showing me affection that causes my heart to mend. Prayer partner, valued companion daily, as we read, share and discuss God's truth. Helper, comforter and forgiver in sickness and in health.

In our older age because of a slight decline at times in our energy we can not show the youthful love that once was ours in fulness. But we still cherish the memories and know that God in His grace still enables today each deeper, kind and loving embrace.

We have entered a new golden era, a time when by God's grace we know a deeper, different side of loves gentle face. So God grows our love in a new and lasting way until that day when the weakness of earth's short stay will break forth into our final brightest day!

Until then when the shadows flee away I wish you Gloria, my deepest love on this our special day!

After this poem with tears in my eyes Gloria added to my bliss a sweet and tender kiss.

Summing Up Our 57th Wedding Anniversary

It all started in my 1938 Dodge as Gloria laid her head on my shoulder.
Naturally I returned the move and got bolder.
Fifty-seven years of wedded bliss
All started with a well placed kiss!

We started out with a coffee can filled with forty bucks
In spite of that our Yosemite honeymoon was deluxe.

We held hands and hiked the trail to the bridal falls
Enjoying first love with all its thralls!

I rejoiced then with the wife of my youth.
Her love satisfied me and that's the truth!

I fished for hours in Yosemite river
While Gloria waited on a rock with restrained ardor.

We never saw a soul at the river all that time
If we had I couldn't have made up this rhyme.

We watched the fire-fall from up above
It's falling embers as hot as our glowing love!

The fire-fall at Yosemite has long been canceled.
But our love goes on still unbridled!

After that life then took on a great deal more formality.
We returned home to work, school and family reality.

Then 1+1 before long brought us to four
Caused by the fruitfulness of me and Glor

First there was Glenda with her golden hair
With Her sweet smile and her face so fair!

Then their was Ken who couldn't sit still.
Now he's as calm as a sleeping pill!

Then four turned to six

It's all part of the matrimony fix.

There's grand kids, Kirsten who never does slow.
And Tyler sensitive and caring, daring to grow!

Today Gloria and I are back to 1+1 and that's no pun
I can say with joy, the empty nest syndrome is lots of fun!

We were married you know in July the month of fireworks.
And believe me it has had its perks as well as quirks!

After fifty years we still send up skyrockets to high places.
And to our joy and amazement they burst into smily faces!

Thanks to God's grace after all these years
Our love for each other still adheres!

Gloria was the wife of my youth whom I pursued.
Now she is the wife of my decrepitude.

As the wife of my youth and old age
Together were still on the same page-

A page of love that lasts till its final perigee
(lowest point, death's short separation)
When love divine love lifts us to heavens apogee!
(highest point)

We'll meet again where we'll never shed a tear
Together forever in eternity, the final Frontier!

Can we improve as we stay upon our journey.
You bet, but this I can say clearly-

God , our perfect hope and trusted guide
Has kept us all these years on a Royal Ride-

A Ride that ends in glory
Where if you believe, you'll hear the rest of this story.

Until that day dawns and shadows flee away.
Thanks for joining us on this our special day!

Gifts to Gloria On This Our Special Day

I gave my wife Gloria a golden coffee can filled with stimulus bills and other girts.   Here is what was in the golden can.

1. Eight $5 dollar bills. 8 is the number of a new beginning in the Bible.
Fifty is the number of a new beginning, too. Pentecost was on the fiftieth day after Jesus resurrection when God started something new, the church which started out **Glor**iously! In Israel the Jubilee came every fifty years. All debts were forgiven, property returned to its original owners, slaves were set free and there was a big celebration! Gloria, my queen, that makes me a king, I hereby forgive all debts and acknowledge all believers in Christ set free!!

2. Gloria's engagement ring, wedding ring and ruby ring all soldered together
with gold. Looks like our marriage has stuck. Though our faith has been tried
as we have grown old, our commitment is as good as gold!

3. A set of sunflower coasters.   Sunflowers are Gloria's favorite flowers.   She is my favorite flower! Because we share mutual faith in God's Son who created the flowers, we can say together: The Best is Yet to Come!

4. A fancy flowered wine cork which says, "Aged to perfection." That's her!

5. A golden book mark with a swan swimming across the top.   You can read into that whatever you wish. Just remember to keep it graceful like
 the swan.

On the side of the golden coffee can with the golden ribbon on top it
says: Yuban. Lord may You ban from our life all the displeases you. Banthe Devil and his schemes. Ban all lack of faith and trust. Replace them all with a close walk with you and love for reach other until death
do we part.

The gifts in the can replace the caffeine stimulus with 5 other stimulaters already mentioned. Instead of getting on our nerves may those gifts stimulate us to gratitude and relaxation in God.

It also says Organic. Organic means pesticide free life. Stimulates us with Your life more abundantly and keep away the pests and Satanic pesticides!

In order to come out good the coffee has to be ground and to go through fire and heat. Help us as we grow old though tried and tested to come out as gold!

It is premium coffee. We thank you for the premiums of the Christian life. All blessings are ours in Christ!

The can container is made from recycled materials. How often have our bodies been recycled and renewed. Someday they will receive a final recycling to come out transformed, incorruptible, immortal fashioned like Jesus' risen glorious body. Let it be! Amen

It also says on the can, "Taste the Difference...Make a Difference." As we taste and see that You Lord are gracious, change us that we may makea difference for You and for the benefit and blessing of others." Thank You Lord!

As coffee actually has a better aroma than taste, may our love be an aroma for you Lord in every place.

Annihilate Anxiety

Hi Mackenzie, saw your feeling of anxiety and depression. Of course we all feel anxiety at times. What to do with it? Try reading and following the cure for anxiety as found in the Bible in Philippians 4:6-9.

Try this. Tell God about your anxiety. Believe that as a follower of Christ you can annihilate it. Don't focus on felling sorry for yourself but focus on how much God loves and cares for you, how he sees you as being counted perfect forever! Having loved you to the uttermost dying for you and rising to live inside you. Focus on His love and His interceding for you. Be like a person I heard about sitting beside the road with a look of peace on his face.

Someone asked him what he was doing. He said, "I'm just letting God Love me."

Remind yourself that God loves you to the uttermost dying for you and counting you perfect. "By one offering on the cross He made you His own, His very own child, He set you apart to Himself and counts you perfect." Focus on how he took away all your sin and sees you as perfect as His Son. Then thank God for what He has done and for hearing your prayer and thank Him for what He will do. The result will be annihilation of your anxiety replaced with the peace of God which is wonderful beyond your understanding but real. It will calm your heart and mind through Jesus Christ.

Then things get better. You have the peace of God. Now you need to add to that the God of peace. How do you do that? Focus on what is true. The peace of God is yours. God gave it to you. Tell Him honestly you believe that He is just and has justified you. Tell Him his death for you makes It become "just as if I'd never sinned." Think about whatever is pure. He is pure. He has bathed you in His love and you are pure! Think about whatever is lovely, He is lovely. So are you. Think about whatever is good, even God Himself and you because He has regenerated you as good! Thank Him for giving you His virtue. Praise Him for everything. Praise Him for what you have learned, received and heard and seen in people who love Jesus The result will be double peace as the God of peace Himself shall join you as you experience the peace of God. God's peace and presence will annihilate your anxiety.

Then sing this song. <https://www.youtube.com/watch?v=LdjcuHb7J7U> My guess is you won't be able to sing it without tears of gratitude as I am shedding now as i write this. What happens if your anxiety returns? Read and practice Phil.

4:6-9 again and sing the song again, Christ lives in me1

Did Jesus Teach That We Are All Children Of God?

I just heard on the news a religious leader say that we are all children of God. Was he right? Please read the following which Jesus said to religious people in the temple in Jerusalem in the Bible in John 8:37-44 "I know that you are the offspring of Abraham: but you seek to kill me, because my word has no place in you. I speak that which I have seen with my Father: and you do the things that you have seen with your father." They answered, and said to him: "Abraham is our father." Jesus saith to them: "If you are the children of Abraham, do the works of Abraham. But now you seek to kill me, a man who has spoken the truth to you, which I have heard of God. This Abraham did not. You do the works of your father." They said therefore to him: "We are not born of fornication: we have one Father, even God." Jesus therefore said to them, "If God were your Father, you would indeed love me. For from God I proceeded, and came; for I came not of myself, but he sent me: Why do you not know my speech? Because you cannot hear my word. You are of your father the devil, and the desires of your father you will do. He was a murderer from the beginning, and he stood not in the truth; because truth is not in him. When he speaks a lie, he speaks of his own: for he is a liar, and the father thereof."

Though some religions teach that we are all children of God, the Bible does not. It teaches that we all are created by God and he loves us but it doesn't teach we are all God's children. The first person to clearly have the Devil as his father was Cain who killed his brother Abel. Why did he do that? Because the Bible says, "he was of the wicked one." His father the Devil motivated him to murder his brother Abel whose Father was God.

At age 20 I was not a child of God. My life was being motivated by the Devil, not God. I realized that and in tears admitted my sinfulness and came to Jesus Christ and received Him as my Lord and Savior who died to take away my sin and arose to make me His child. Without that rebirth the Devil was calling the shots in my life and he was my father. But once I trusted Jesus as Savior I was born of God and He became my Father.

The Bible tells us how to become children of God in John 1:11-13: "He came unto his own, and his own received him not. But as many as did receive him , he gave the power to become the sons of God, to those that believe in his name. Who were born, not of blood, nor of the will of the flesh, nor of the will of man, but of God." So to become a real child of God, Jesus says we must believe in his name and be born not of a natural birth by the will of man, but be born of a spiritual birth by the will of God.

If you are not sure you are a child of God you can be sure today. The gospel(good news} is that "whosoever believes that Jesus is the Christ is born of God." 1John 5:1 Believing in Christ sent by God to die for your sins is what will take you out of the Devil's family and places you into God's family. Believe that today and you will become a member of Jesus Christ's church, made up off all who are born again. Regeneration, not religion is what is necessary to become a child of God. If you receive Him today you will be regenerated, born a second time? Those who are members of His family will enjoy singing about it here:

<https://www.youtube.com/watch?v=Fd3gVGUMvDU>

Are you a Berean or a Thessalonian?

In the Bible Bereans and Thessalonians were people who lived in ancient cities of Macedonia. Both cities had Jewish synagogues. The apostle Paul visited the cities and preached to the Jews there about 19 years after Jesus death, resurrection and ascension. Quite a few Thessalonians believed Paul's preaching about Jesus as their Messiah but the synagogue leaders had closed minds and rejected what Paul taught. They opposed him so strongly that Paul obeyed Jesus words and quit casting pearls of truth to those who wouldn't listen. He left and made his way to Berea, a three days walking trip from Thessolonica.

Arriving in Berea he taught in the Berean synagogue. The Bereans had open hearts, and were fair minded which enabled them to search and to validate the truth Paul preached. They were more noble than some who lived in Thessolonica who were closed minded, not ready to search to find out the truth.

When the Bereans heard Jesus Christ preached as the Messiah they listened and searched the Old Testament scripture to see if what Paul said was true. Paul told them Jesus fulfilled the Old Testament prophecy proving Jesus is both their Messiah and Savior. They validated what he said that Jesus came to be a servant, to perform miracles, to heal the sick, to die for their sin and to rise from the dead. When they heard these things, they searched the Old Testament and found that what was said of Jesus is true and many believed in Him as both their Messiah and Savior.

I talked to a man recently using scripture about Jesus . He said that all writers of scripture are dead so we can't cross examine them to tell if what was said is true. Using that weird reasoning nothing is valid that anyone wrote who has died because we can't cross examine them. Totally illogical! That is an unfair response to truth.

We can be assured that of all books ever written we can trust what the books of the Bible say because whatsoever was written down in them was inspired by God. They are valid, written for our learning, encouragement, comfort, and assurance so that we can have hope now and know what is to follow after we leave this life.

Are you noble like the Bereans with a mind ready to listen and search until the truth sets you free? Jesus said that those who believe His word are His disciples for sure and continuing in His word they will know the truth and the truth will set them free. Bereans didn't abandoned their thinking but transformed it by opening their minds as well as their hearts to the truth. Are you a Berean, open and fair minded? Or you one of the closed minded Thessalonian leader types? If you believe the facts about Jesus you are both noble and saved by Jesus Christ. I'm a Berean. Are you? If you are a Berean you will love this song: <https://www.youtube.com/watch?v=4XJu0mnn_b4>

Are You One of God's Chosen?

The Bible speaks of the those chosen as the elect of God. It also says "many are called but few are chosen." If sides are being picked for teams we all know what it is like to be chosen. How can a person know that he or she is chosen by God? Jesus says, **"Whoever comes to me I will not drive away."** So being chosen depends on God's grace in allowing anyone to come to Him for salvation.

Isaiah 46:10 tells us **"God knows the end from the beginning."** So He has to know who will come to HIm and be with Him in heaven. BUT that does not take away our ability to choose or not to choose Him," **Whosoever will, let him come and take the water of life freely."** We have a choice when called to either accept or refuse what God offers. So how do we know for sure? Because God who cannot lie makes promises and keeps them. He is not a politician making unkept promises. **All the promises of God in Jesus are "Yes and Amen."** In the final analysis our trip through life to make it to heaven or hell is based on our response to God's call. Jesus said, ""no man comes to the Father unless the Father draw him." He also said, "If I be lifted up I will draw all men to myself. He draws and calls us to Himself. All ll who do His will by coming to Him through grace by faith and continue by grace to trust Him are the chosen or elect of God.

Here is a short true parable which illustrates our ability to choose and God's foreknowledge of who will come to Him. Jesus is the door to heaven. A sign over that door says,**"Whosoever will let him come and take the water of life freely!"** Then if you go to Him through the door you turn around and look at what is written on the sign on the backside of the door. It says, **"Chosen in Him before the foundation of the world."** Selah(Pause and think about it.) That sums up the meaning of free will and election. How do we reconcile election and the right we have to choose? God elects those he knows will come to him by His grace and foreknowledge. But still from our point of view it is somewhat of a mystery.

How do we deal with this mystery that is revealed but we don't fully understand? About 2000 fulfilled prophetic truths prove beyond a shadow of a doubt that the Bible is true. Also Christ said, "If I do not the works of my Father, believe me not. But if I do, though you believe not me, **believe the works:** that you may know, and believe, that the Father is in me, and I in him." So Christ's works and Bible prophecy together seal for sure the absolute truth of the Bible. **So when the Bible reveals things we can't totally understand, we know they are true because of the things we can understand. "The secret things belong to God but those things which can be understood belong to us and our children forever."**

We wouldn't have a clue about what life is like after death if Jesus and God's Word hadn't revealed it to us. We, who have chosen by God's grace, power and choice to come to Christ, know we shall die and rise again because Jesus is a gentleman who **never lies.** He is the way, **the truth** and the life. So why not believe Him and throw what you can't understand into file 13(the waste basket). Then major on what you can understand. That means believing absolutely the secrets God shares with you. Perhaps believing God **IS UNDERSTANDING** on the highest level. **Even our ability to think, choose and believe is a gift of God. Therefore** if we choose to receive Christ as Savior, even our choice is His gift. So salvation is ALL of Him.

What do you think? So are you among the elect, the chosen? You can be sure. God has chosen you if you by His grace choose Him and His Son as your Savior. Listen to this song and do what it says by God's grace and you will know that you are God's chosen?

https://www.youtube.com/watch?v=w2VrRk4pZHY>

Ascending & Descending
Teeter Totters of Glory

When I was a kid I loved to ascend and descend on rides. What kid doesn't enjoy those ups and downs? Now that I'm older I still enjoy ascending and descending but on a much higher level.

Sitting in my backyard I am enabled to enjoy the heights and depths of God's creation. In my mind I go down to the sea and ponder some of God's wonders in the deep like a mighty whale and a lowly clam inside of which I found a large pearl. God's wonders of the deep are inexhaustible. Scientists still have not discovered all the wonders of the ocean depths.

Besides creation's heights and depths, the Bible illustrates the heights and depths of life. Jacob in s dream saw angels descending and ascending a ladder with God at the top who promised to watch over him. Of course angels watch over all the heirs of salvation. They help fulfill God's promises to all who trust Him.

Jesus also left the heights of heaven descending to earth to fulfill God's promises to all who are heirs of salvation. Though higher than angels Jesus took upon himself a human nature lower than angels. His descent into humanity meant continual "ups"for others whom he taught and healed. Then his descent into death for your sins and mine caused Him great sorrow and suffering, so much so that an angel came to strengthen Him as He faced death. He defeated death destroying Satan's power over it thus enabling us to ascend into His presence.

A time is coming when all who know Christ as Savior will ascend into God's eternal, capital city, Mount Zion.   That ascension into His presence on the mountain of the Lord is only made possible because Jesus descended into the lowest parts of the earth. There He took captivity, captive, releasing and removing those imprisoned to ascend into a final eternal paradise in heaven.

Someday Jesus will descend from heaven with a shout, then all who know Christ will ascend, caught up to meet Him in the air and so we shall ever be with Him in endless glory! Our seesaws of life will thankfully end in an "up position" from whence the view will be breathless!   Sing about it. "Oh that will be glory for Me, glory for me, when by His grace I gaze on His face, that will be glory, be glory for for me."   https://www.youtube.com/watch?v=FKEv1fGDii8>

The Fate of Babylon the Small, the Medium and the Great

In the Bible Babylon is always spoken of in an evil sense. The first Babel took place during the days of Nimrod who was a leader and inspirer of those who sought to reach into the heavens by building a large tower. It was associated with astrology and a false attempt to either reach God by self effort or to become above God through a unity of purpose.Whatever their intent it was evil because God Himself put a stop to it by confounding their communication with one another.Their languages were changed so that they quit their work and in confusion were dispersed.

Another Babylon is that of Nebuchadnezzar's time. In his case he is instructed by the prophet Daniel that God had made him a great ruler of the then known world. Nebuchadnezzar lost his rule for seven years. He was an evil king until God changed him. After a period of madness, he humbled himself before the true God and was restored to power. He was converted and denounced the false gods of Babylon.

Nebuchadnezzar's grand son became ruler under his father Nabonidus and in pride had a feast where he took the sacred vessels of Israel, drank wine from them and joined in a drunken orgy of mockery of the true God. He lost the kingdom in one night after seeing handwriting on the wall that condemned him. He died when Babylon was defeated that night by Darius and Cyrus, Medes and Persians.

Babylon appears again as a world power in the book of Revelation. There we read of Babylon the Great. It is a combination of evil religion and economic power. For 3 1/2 years a trinity of evil beings rule the world. They are called the beast, the false prophet, and the Dragon who has a Whore riding on his back. Their evil is judged by God who pours out his wrath upon them by destroying the Dragon's great whore of false religion, by wiping out the beast and false prophet and by destroying Babylon the Great in one hour. In the end the evil ones are all cast into a lake of fire and the Dragon(Satan) is bound for 1000 years. Then Christ and His followers rule over the earth during that 1000 years. It is the golden age of earth when war ceases, and the Devil does not deceive the nations. After evil has been kept in check with peace abounding for a 1000 years, the Devil is released from his prison in the bottomless pit. In a short time he deceives the nations again. He gathers those opposed to God from the four corners of the earth to go and fight against Christ and His people who have ruled justly for 1000 years. The Lord Jesus Christ, the rock of ages smashes them all in a moment of time. He creates a New Heaven and a New Earth filled with perfect peace and righteousness forever.

Thus Babylon the Small, the Medium and the Great and all evil doers are barbecued in a lake of fire. God is triumphant and never again shall Babylon raise its ugly Satanic head. This is the "shema" the witness of scripture regarding Babylon. We are to come out from her and praise God, honoring Him forever for His glory, power and kingdom. Amen

Listen to this "Shema" presentation on You Tube.

<http://www.youtube.com/watch?v=8gqWZqQZLxw>

BAPTISM

READ these scriptures in your Bible - to help to understand baptism.

I.   Who Should be Baptized?

A.   The only requirements for Baptism are the requirements for salvation; found in - Romans 10: 9-11…

1.   Heart belief in Jesus Christ as Lord and Savior. 2. Confession of heart belief that He is Lord and Savior.

B.   The clearest case of an individual's baptism in the Bible is the Ethiopian eunuch in - Acts 8: 26-39. In verse 36, the eunuch asked, "…what doth hinder me to be baptized?" Philip then answered with the condition of baptism in verse 37, "If thou believest with all thine heart, thou mayest." The eunuch's response then sealed the matter, "I believe that Jesus Christ is the Son of God."

C. There are NO examples of baptism in the New Testament of anyone but believers.

D. Two other examples of baptism immediately after salvation include:

1. Acts 18: 8 2.   Acts 8: 12

11. What is the Method of Baptism?

A.   Again, Acts 8: 26-39 gives the clearest example. In - Acts 8: 38-39, BOTH Philip and the Ethiopian eunuch went down into the water and came up out of the water.

B.   In - Mark 1: 9-10 Jesus was baptized in the same manner.

C.   Baptism is a picture of death, burial, and resurrection. The only way to bury someone is to put them completely underground. The method of Baptism is to put them completely underwater.

III What is the Purpose of Baptism?

A. There are 7 - types of baptism mentioned in the whole Bible. In each case, physical baptism is a picture of a spiritual truth. The important point to consider is the picture portrayed by baptism.

B. There are 2 - types that pertain to the New Testament believer…

1.   Holy Spirit Baptism; As found in - Ephesians 1: 13 and John 14: 16-17,

And the basic purpose is as found in - John 14: 25-27 and I Corinthians 2: 9-14.

2.   Water Baptism; This is as was previously discussed. The purpose is as found in Romans 6: 1-7, to show the death, burial, and resurrection of Jesus Christ IN the new believer. Sprinkling does NOT picture or communicate death. This also pictures the individual becoming a new creation in Jesus Christ, passing from the old person to the new - 2 Corinthians 5: 17.

IV.   How Important is it to be Baptized?

A.   It is NOT essential for salvation. Ephesians 2: 8-9 makes very clear that a person is saved by Grace through Faith WITHOUT works of any kind or type, including Water Baptism.

B.   It IS essential for service and spiritual growth. The "Great Commission" as found in - Matthew 28: 18-20 proves that it is essential. Baptism is an integral part of the Great

Commission and it is found in verse 19 preceeding teaching in verse 20.

C.   Before anyone can be taught to follow Jesus Christ, they must be willing to submit to the "First Act of Obedience". If a person refuses to obey the Lord in the first point, they will not obey Him in future points.

V.   Why Does God Instruct us to be Baptized?

A.   Baptism is the First Act of Obedience in service to the Lord.

B.   Jesus set the example Himself by submitting to baptism before He began His public ministry - Matthew 3: 13-15, "to fulfill all righteousness." This point of submission and obedience is the single most important thing to realize regarding Baptism.

C.   It is a public testimony of the new convert's identification with Jesus Christ through the death, burial, and resurrection. It identifies the new child of God with the Lord Jesus Christ - John 1: 12-13.

D.   Three examples of people in the Bible who submitted to Baptism after salvation:

1. The Apostle Paul - Acts 9: 10-18.

2. The Philippian jailer and his household - Acts 16: 19-33.

3. The Ethiopian eunuch - Acts 8: 26-39, as previous discussed.

Now we see clearly that Baptism is most important, by the examples God has given us in His Word.

VI.   There is much false teaching among religious groups concerning Baptism. Three examples are;

A.   Man must be baptized in order to be saved.

B.   Babies should be baptized into God's family, or into "the church".

C.   Baptism by being sprinkled is just as meaningful as immersion.

VI I   Your Baptism-Baptizer(s) Albert, Tom. Walt. Pray for You-Dean

Be ready when in the tank before the micraphone to

A. share your testimony of how you came to know Christ

B. share how your life has changed.

C. share who influenced you to know the Lord

D. share a couple of favorite verses you have learned.

E. share what you would like one who prays for you to ask God for you.

Be Prepared

Prepare now to believe on the Great Things God has prepared for you.
Jeremiah 33:3 (NKJV)3 'Call on Me, and I will answer you, and show you great and mighty things, which you do not know.' He is prepared   to call you to hImself, to enable you to look for an eternal city, to justify you, to answer your prayers, to be obedient to his calling,to worship Him, to glorify you-to give you a new body, to give you a great Inheritance and to be with hIm and see him forever.   His preperations for you are based upon his promise to you, "Call upon me and I will show you great and mighty things which you do not know."

Sing about it here: <https://www.youtube.com/watch?v=-15v9iworAU>

Oil is Power - Are you Well Oiled?

The first oil well that led to the proliferation of oil in the world was drilled in 1859. It was called "Drakes Folly."

Along with the refining of oil by chemists that first well led to the power that oil is today throughout the world. The uses of oil today are many. A few of those uses are soles for shoes, color crayons for kids, gas for you car, fluid for your lamps and candles for a romantic evening. He who controls the oil controls the world or least that is how many see it.

There is a kind of oil that is special beyond all others. In the Bible it is called "the oil of joy." Oil in the Bible represents the Holy Spirit. When David was anointed king, he had scented olive oil poured on his head and He was filled with the Holy Spirit. He was given a new source of power and joy in his life.

Oil shines and gives light when burned. When mixed with spices as it burns it give off a pleasing aroma. So a person in whom God's Spirit dwells lights up the world and gives off an aroma of God's fragrant Spirit. Jesus said of those who are His own. "You are the light of the world." Some oil in the Bible flowed through a seven branched candlestick in the tabernacle and lit up the room. Oil not only gives light and can perfume the room, it was used in healing in the Bible. Still today oil is part of many medicines used in the healing process.

How does one procure the oil of the Spirit so that he or she can shine for God, can be a healing influence on others, and spread a fragrance of joy? Jesus tells us clearly how to be filled with His Spirit, "If you being evil know how to give good things to your children, how much more will your Father in heaven give the Holy Spirit and good things to them who ask."

Oil today is very expensive but the oil of the Spirit is a gift. He gives the Spirit and good things to those who ask.

If you believe in Jesus Christ as your Savior from sin and ask He will give you His Spirit to empower you, to heal your heart, to make you creative, to fill you with joy and to make your life a fragrant blessing to others. So, why not ask today? !

"Give me oil in my lamp, keep me burning. Give me oil in my lamp I pray. Give me oil in my lamp, keep me burning. Keep me burning till the break of day." Be well oiled for Jesus!

Love to you,

Dean

Beat the Devil Day

The real path to good success is: "What ever Jesus says, do it." Fill up the empty water jar of your life with the water of His word. Then pour it out to others and watch it turn into the spiritual wine of heaven. Wise people will know It is the best! Then you will know because you did what He said that you had good success instead of the bad success of a life filled with the empty air of the Prince of the power of the air, the Devil. It's defeat the Devil Day! Let's do it by doing what Jesus says!

Moses did what God said even through he didn't feel like it. Faith he exercised! Feelings he made obedient to His will. Joshua had God's word on the tip of his tongue and in the center of his heart and actions.He had good success and God made His ways prosperous.

The servants took Mary's sound advice at the wedding of Galilee, "Whatever he,Jesus says, do it." So at His bidding they filled empty water pots up to the brim with water. They could have said, "Hey, what the sense of filling the jars with water. We need wine! Besides we have more important things to do. Those water pots are for purification, not for drink at a wedding." But they didn't say that. Instead they did what Jesus said and had good success. As they watched in amazement,the water turned to wine, the best wine. We have the treasure of heaven"s wine in earthen jars, bodies of clay that the glory may go to God and not us!

Noah did all that God commanded him resulting in a life that led to building a boat that rescued him and his family from the fate of drowning with the rest of the world. The secret of life is "DO WHAT GOD SAYS." If we do we will find prayer filled revival, families saved, enemies converted,and believers restored. One drink from the hand of God is worth a thousand at the Devil's dull handouts. So lets drink deeply saturating ourselves with the water of His His words. Let's join together in Beat the Devil Day!

Abraham beat the Devil by believing God and God counted him righteous. David believed God and beat the Devil's giant buddy. Jesus believed His Father and beat the Devil through death, destroying him who had the power of death. Let's make Beat the Devil Day, every day! Dare I say and hear a Hip! Hip! Hooray!

The Best Ways to Learn Not to Lie

I taught school for 33 years and the Bible now for about 52 yearrs. It hit me with new insight and clarity that the best ways to learn about living are the most interesting, reasonable, and helpful and based on real life stories.

Let's think about learning not to lie. Most parents and teachers teach their children not to lie. Basically, they say "don't lie or you will get in trouble." True, but not very life changiing.. I suggest a better way. Instead of a direct command not to lie, share stories of what happens to people who lie and what happens to people who are truthful. Both tthe Bible and the daily news are full of stories about people who lie and the results of their lying.

God did not give the 10 commandments, which include not lying, until thousands of years of Biblical history had revealed the results of lying. Satan lied. Adam lied.by blaming Eve. Eve lied by blaming Satan. The world was full of lying just before the flood. Aftter the flood lots of lies were told befroe the 10 commandments were given. Sarah lied. Abraham lied. Jacob lied. Joseph's brothers lied. God had shown the world the consequences of lying before He gave the commandment not to lie. That is the best

way for us to learn and to teach our children. Show the consequences, then give the command. Even ask a child to act like he is an adult for a moment and decide what command he would give his children after hearing the results of lying. Then after he comes up with the right answer, tell him he is wise because he agrees with God.

Potiphar's wife lied and an innocent man went to jail. Tell the story then ask them what they think about what happened because of her lie.

Modern examples of the consequences of sin abound. One iexample is a lie I told in hte eighth grade. I had a little plastic viewer on a chain. Look inside and there was a naked woman. My teacher caught me with it. I was in trouble. In order not to get in too much trouble I lied and told her that her son gave it to me. He may have gotten in trouble because of my lie. I just now realized I never confessed that sin to God so i did it just now.

After telling stories like these we need to ask our children and our selves, what were the results of lying in these stories?. What do you think about lying? Why do you think God made a commandment not to lie? Have you ever lied? What should you do if you have lied. Then let your chilld express his understanding about lying. The consequencces he hears in the story will be much more influential in his life than just being told not to lie.

But we need to get beyond the consequences to the fact that everyone of us has lied or done wrong in some form or other at times. Is there any way to alleviate or liff the burden of guilt off our backs if we lied or did something wrong? Oh Yes. Praise God for that.

There is forgiveness for lying. Jesus died for our lies so we can be forgiven. God hates a lying tongue but he loves the lier. And He has made a way for us to be forgiven. So let us confess our lying, be forgiven and seek to be truthful. I John 1:9 is the Christian's bar of soap and we need to wash every day. The truth sets us free as we admit we lied and the blood of Christ cleanses us from all sin as he forgives us.

Is that the way you were taught not to lie as a chilld? i wasn't. I learned it as an adult. Have you learned from these stories not to lie as an adult?

The best way to learn is God's way. He tells us to teach our children about what He has said in His word every chance we get while we walk, when we are standing and when we are sitting. As adults we must live out what we learn enabling us to be examples to our children and to others. Lying causes misery. Truth imparts freedom and blessing.

The opposite of lying is being truthful. May God helps us learn from the mistakes of others so we may not have to learn from our own. Love to you, Dean

Better Than Winning Powerball

When the Powerball lottery was over a billion dollars, we all knew what a lot of people were thinking. They were thinking what they would do if they won. Some thoughts were noble like the person who said he would devote his winnings to helping the poor, healing the sick, giving it all away to honor God. Others were not noble like the guy who said he would spend it on call girls and cocaine.

Good news. You can win way bigger than any lottery jackpot. There is a treasure that awaits you every day. It is God's gift of his Son to you if you will believe him and receive him. He had come to earth and in him the Bible says were"hid all the treasures of wisdom and knowledge." He came to earth to shed his blood, die and rise from the dead for you. Why? So that you might have and endless treasure of wisdom, love, eternal life, the joy of having all your sins forgiven, and the certainty that when you die you will live forever with him. Coming to Christ and receiving God's gift ensures heaven for you someday and an abundant life now. How do you get this gift from God? You can't buy or earn it. To think you can earn it is an insult to God. If you could earn it you would boast in yourself and not God. False religion says you can work for and be good enough to earn the gift, a total lie.

The truth is you must receive Jesus as your Savior and by God's grace the gift will be yours. You must humble ourself and receive the gift of God by faith or you will never have it. And what a gift it is, so much better than Powerball millions. Why? Because everyone who ever won a lottery took nothing with themselves when they died. But anyone who receives God's gift lives forever getting a new, perfect body, getting a new perfect home, getting an inheritance that never fades away or stops, and getting the everlasting riches of heaven. Powerball may make a person a winner or conqueror for a while but it is powerless to win forever. The good news of Christ is the gift of God is the power of God to salvation that makes every believer an eternal winner.

So what will you do about God's gift? It is the gift of gifts, all other gifts surpassed. Have you or will you receive God's gift today? Here's how to receive it; "If you confess with your mouth Jesus as Lord and believe in your heart that God has raised him from the dead you shall be saved." Rom. 10:9,10 Then through Jesus, you will get the best gift and win the greatest victory of your life. That is power that will keep you on the ball forever! <(https://www.youtube.com/watch?v=PBqUwpCvCL8>

Hi Betty,
I suppose you are settled into your new home by now. While praying for you today the 23rd Psalm came into my mind in a new way. Thought I'd share it with you and pray that it will bless you. Our days on this earth are limited no matter how long we live. But the Lord our Shepherd is not limited. So even though now we may not fully realize it, we never lack any good thing.

The Lord is your shepherd Betty, so you will never lack a thing.
You will never lack rest and refreshment,
For He makes you lie down in green pastures.
He leads you beside quiet waters.
You will never lack spiritual nourishment,
For He will feed your soul.
You will never lack direction.
He will guide you along right paths to glorify His name.
You will never lack courage to overcome fear and worry,

Even though you walk through the valley of the
shadow of death,
For that shadow will flee away in a moment,
In the twinkling of an eye,
In the Light of His presence,
All fear of evil will be removed forever!
The Lord's words to you are: You will never lack
My presence,
I am with you and you are with Me.
I will never leave you or forsake you.
You will never lack protection and care,
for My rod will comfort and shield you,
My staff will remind you that I number you among
my own,
It will lift you up when your strength fails.
You will never lack peace.
Even when surrounded by Satan and his
threatening enemies,
I will prepare a secure table for you as they look
on in helpless defeat.
You will never lack my healing presence.
I will tenderly sooth your wounded thoughts with
the oil of My Spirit.
And your response Betty will be,
"Lord how grateful I am! You have filled up My
cup until I overflow with joy.
All my days, even when I was not aware of it,
I have never lacked any good thing.
Now I see it,
Your goodness and love followed me everywhere
I went.
Then I will see it all so clearly,
You were always good to me and loved me.
Even though I moved from home to home on
earth,
I will dwell in my final home in Your house Oh
Lord
I will behold and enjoy your beauty forever!
I will say to you my Shepherd King-
I never lacked a thing!"
Love, Dean

Beneath the Cross of Jesus I fain would take my
stand,
The shadow of a mighty rock within a weary land.
I take Thy cross Oh Jesus for my abiding place.
I need no other sunshine than the sunshine of Thy
face.
Content to let the world go by to know no gain nor
loss.
My sinful self my only shame, my glory all the
cross!

Bible Firsts and Lasts

And so it is written,
"The first man **Adam** became a living being."
 The **last Adam** *became* a life-giving spirit.
That was not first which is spiritual, but that
which is natural; and afterward that which is
spiritual. The first man was of the earth, made of
dust. The last Man is the Lord from heaven. As
was the man of dust, so also are those who are
made of dust; and as is the heavenly Man, so
also are those who are heavenly,And as we have
borne the image of the man of dust,we shall also
bear the image of the heavenly Man." ! Cor.
15:45-49

How many things came first in the Bible and how
many came last?
    One example: We are born naturally first. Our
bodies are made out of the dust,elements of the
ground. If we become a true follower of Christ we
are born of God and become new creations with
God's Spirit dwelling in us. Our lives then become
spiritual as well as natural. First natural birth
without understanding of the spiritual world. Last
spiritual rebirth with entrance to and
understanding of the kingdom of God(the sphere
of God's rule, wisdom and control.) First the
natural and then the supernatural. I will share
other examples of first and last things in the Bible
in coming articles. Meanwhile if you are a true
follower of Christ, rejoice in the fact that you are a
new creation in Christ. Old first things are passed
away and all thing have become new for you. 2
Cor. 5:17 Old things have passed away but God's
love for you will never pass away! If you look at
this song as meaning Jesus it captures at its end
what was just shared: https://www.youtube.com/
watch?v=bwzDxp2TC7l>
Bible Firsts and Lasts
That was not first which is spiritual,
but that which is natural;
and afterward that which is spiritual. !Cor.
15:45-46

    Of the many examples of Bible firsts and lasts
are the first and last heaven and earth. Genesis 1
tells us about the First Heaven and Earth, "In the
beginning God created the heavens and the
earth."
    Revelation 21: tells us about the Last New
Heaven and Earth- "Now I saw a new heaven and

a new earth, for the first heaven and the first earth had passed away."

The first heaven and earth had a sun, moon, stars, oceans and people with temporary lives. In the last new heaven and earth there is no need for the sun, and moon since God is its light. Also there is no more sea, nothing to divide continents or people. The first heavens and earth were temporary. When they disappear in a giant explosion, the new heaven and earth is formed from its melted state. It still has the same name, heaven and earth but it is a last creation that is forever. It contains a special city whose builder and maker is God. In that city there will be no more curse, no more death. no more tears. no more sin. The temporary is gone. The eternal has arrived. All will be well forever for those who inhabit that last new heaven and earth.

Are you among those who will be a part of the last heaven and earth? All who truly trust God and His Son will be a part of it. That is what we are told in Hebrews 11:13-16, Those who know the Lord have "embraced God's promises and confessed that they were strangers and pilgrims on the earth. For those who say such things declare plainly that they seek a homeland. And truly if they had called to mind that *country* from which they had come out, they would have had opportunity to return. But now they desire a better, that is, a heavenly *country.* Therefore God is not ashamed to be called their God, for He has prepared a city for them. Will you be there? Make sure. Embrace God's promises in John 3:16 and Romans 10:9. If you do embrace them you will be there for sure! Click below and sing about it.

https://www.youtube.com/watch?
v=IofNq0U2xk0>

https://www.youtube.com/watch?v=cq831p4uM-
g>

Can you list other **things in the Bible that are first** and then contrast them with that which is later or last?

First Work of God-All things were made by him and for him and without him, Christ, nothing was made that was made. John 1:2 The First Work of Man is told in Genesis 1:15. "Then the Lord God took the man and put him in the garden of Eden to tend and keep it." **Genesis** 2:**15** Out of the ground the Lord God formed every beast of the field and every bird of the air, and brought *them*

to Adam to see what he would call them. And whatever Adam called each living creature, that *was* its name. Gen. 1:19 So God created man in His *own* image; in the image of God He created him; male and female He created them. Then God blessed them, and God said to them, "Be fruitful and multiply; fill the earth and subdue it; have dominion over the fish of the sea, over the birds of the air, and over every living thing that moves on the earth."Gen. 1:26-28 So first came tending the garden of Eden, naming the animals, and having dominion over every living thing on earth.

What is mankind's work today? Men and women's first responsibility is to seek God and find him. Then once found by God the main work of a redeemed, Spiritual person is to serve God and others in all he does and to share Christ with in word and prayer. We are to go into all the world and preach the good news. What kind of work do you do today, God? "This is the work of God that you believe in Him whom He has sent." And he uses redeemed people to do that work.

First Man Adam & His bride Eve. Created, not Born. And the Lord God formed man *of* the dust of the ground, and breathed into his nostrils the breath of life; and man became a living being Gen:2: And the Lord God caused a deep sleep to fall on Adam, and he slept; and He took one of his ribs, and closed up the flesh in its place. **22** Then the rib which the Lord God had taken from man He made into a woman, and He brought her to the man.
23 And Adam said:
"This *is* now bone of my bones
And flesh of my flesh;
She shall be called Woman,Because she was taken out of Man." Gen. 2:21-23 Last Adam, Jesus through death and resurrection creates bride through supernatural birth.

First Lies On Earth by Satan. Last Lies After 1000 Years of Bondage.

Adam & Eve, First Disobedience. First shame. First Hiding. First Confession. First Fig Leaf Clothing. First Sacrifice& Forgiveness, Clothing By God for A and E.

First results of sin- Death, Curse of Ground, Hinderances to man's work. First pain in childbirth. First promised crushing of Satan. Last

Death Defeated. Adam & Eve Restored to Garden and Tree of Life. Last, no child bearing. No pain. No Curse.

For as in Adam all die, even so in Christ all shall be made alive. **1 Cor 15:22** There is a natural body, and there is a spiritual body. **45** And so it is written, "The first man Adam became a living being." The last Adam *became* a life-giving spirit. 1 Cor. 15:45

First Disobedient and Obedient Child: Cain and Abel
First obedient and disobedient genealogies. Cain's. First ungodly families & Offspring. First Destruction of Cain's family line.
Seth's obedient genealogy with faith displayed. First destruction of Mankind. Then First Ark of Escape. Last ark Jesus Christ.

Happy Birthday
Dear Anne,
In Sunday School we use to sing this song with kids. Happy Birthday to You. Happy Birthday to you. Happy Birthday Dear "Anne" Happy Birthday to you. Only one will not do. Only one will not do. Born again means salvation. How many have you?

I want to wish you a happy birthday and a joyous day. I was thinking about birth the other day with two 20 year olds, with which I was having a study of Nicodemus. Jesus told Nicodemus that he couldn't see the kingdom of God unless he had another birth. I explained to the two ladies that God's kingdom is invisible but real. He is king and those who trust him are part of his kingdom.

Jesus said that Nicodemus could not enter the kingdom unless he had another birth. So it is necessary to both see and enter or become a part of the kingdom of God through the new birth. You can read all about this in John 3.

Nicodemus didn't get it. He asked Jesus if he could go back into his mothers womb. Jesus explained that two kinds of births are necessary. One is of water and the other of the Spirit. Some say Jesus was talking about baptism but the context doesn't fit. If Jesus really answered Nicodemus' question then water referred to his first birth. He was born of water when his mom's water broke and he came into this world. One can not

have a second birth unless he or she has a first birth.

Nicodemus has had one birth. Now he needed another but not one of water, not a natural birth, but a supernatural birth. He needed to be born of the Spirit. Jesus further explained that birth by explaining it as being like the wind that blows in the trees. You can hear the sound of the wind among the leaves but you can't see it. So is everyone one born of the spirit. In other words it is invisible but real and once the birth takes place we can tell it has happened by the effect it has on the person. The person passes from death to life and endures as Moses did by seeing the invisible God. The person enters into the Kingdom of God and that spiritual realm becomes real.

Jesus used earthly examples to lift us to the spiritual world. One example is the wind. We under stand invisible wind and its power and results.

When we are born the first time "wind" or air enters our lungs. God breathed into Adam and Eve the breath of life and they became living souls. Without wind or breath we die. There is a greater breath, the breath of God's Spirit which breathes eternal life into our being. At that moment we have a second birthday. It is more glorious than the first birthday that fits us to this life. The second and last birth fits us for the real, eternal spiritual world. When that happens old things pass away and all things become new. Jesus becomes our Savior from our sin and God whom we didn't really know becomes our Father.

That new birth is brought about by our reception of God's will and work as displayed in His Son. The Son of man, Jesus, is lifted up on the cross to die and take away our sins. Then after burial he rises to an endless life in a new and glorious body. If we look to Him and believe in Him on the cross, the poison of sin is removed. It is brought about not by water baptism but by God's Spirit, by Spirit baptism. John the Baptist baptized in water. Jesus baptized by the Spirit. John's baptism prepared people for the greater experience of having God"s Spirit come into them bringing about a new birth. The word baptize has caused many people to misunderstand salvation. It simply means "to put into". Greeks baptized their dishes. When a person receives Christ the Holy Spirit is put into him or her. It is simple yet profound. Christian baptism in water always followed belief in Him in the Bible. It was an outward symbol of an inward reality.

Not once in the N.T. can you find any baby every baptized. But you can find all kinds of adults who were baptized because unless one truly believes in Christ in his or her heart water baptism does nothing but get someone wet. It is a symbol which when understood points to the greater reality of the indwelling Spirit being put into someone by God Himself. A person must believe in Christ for that to happen That is Crystal Clear as indicated in John 3:16, the Bible in a nut shell: "For God so loved the world that whosoever believes in Him should not perish but have everlasting life." So clear that philosophers stumble over it but simple people get it.

I will be celebrating my first birth in May, 2011, at 76 years. I enjoyed having had a second birth at age 20. I will be celebrating my second birthday for the the 56th time in 2011. While I value my first birthday and celebrate it every year, I treasure my second birth because it enabled me to see and enter and understand the kingdom of God. It changed my life forever!

Anne, I wish you a wonderful birthday on this September 20th. And I wish you a second birth to transcend your first. Happy birthday to you! Happy birthday to you. Happy Birthday dear Anne, Happy Birthday to you. Only one will not do. Only one will not do. Born again means salvation. How many have you?

Blessings in Your Own Backyard

Did you hear about the guy who traveled all over the world searching for diamonds? Finally he returned home unsuccessful. Then, after a while, he found diamonds in his own property. An article was written about it called *Diamonds in My Own Back Yard.*

I have lived in my home for many years. One day seated in my backyard I looked down and spotted a ring. It was a wedding ring made of platinum. Needless to say I was happy about my find. It had been there many years but I never knew till then that such a blessing was in my backyard.

Do we have to travel the world to find God or is He as near as our backyard? The Bible says that "he is not far from us and that In Him we live and move and have our being." He is as close as an open heart, as near as an open door, as big as an open sky, more vast than a star studded night, as real as a gentle wind, as present as a pleasant perfume, more beautiful and lasting than a hair dresser's temporary permanent, more elevating and lifting than a powerful whirl wind, and as near as a whispered prayer. So maybe you would like to join me in this prayer: Lord, help me let go of doubt and hold on to faith in who and what You are here, right now. I open up to You. You are the ring of perfect, endless love. You are the giver of every perfect gift, the forgiver and unchanging sustainer of my soul! Lead, help and guide me today. In Your Son's name, Amen!

<https://www.youtube.com/watch?v=_2eSfKqMRbA>

Blindfold Removal

Why is it that so many people are on a broad road that ends in destruction when they could be on a narrow road that leads to life?

It is because the god of this world, called Satan, has blinded their spiritual eyes to keep them from experiencing the light of the glory of God shining into their hearts. If that is your condition you can humble yourself and cry out to God to snip away the blindfold that keeps you from seeing the glory of God. If being blinded spiritually isn't your condition pray for anyone who reads this to have Satan's blindfold removed.

If you do cry out to Him in true belief He will hear you, destroy and remove Satan's blindfold. He will command the light to replace your darkness and shine into your heart and mind to reveal the glory of God's love, forgiveness and peace for you in His Son, the Lord Jesus Christ.

His Son's death for you believed allows Him to remove the darkness of your sin and fill you with the light of His life as you see your sin wiped out and are filled with the gift of His Spirit and His Son's risen perfection and righteousness.

Will you ask Him today to remove Satan's blindfold? Then you will with all who know Him be enabled to see the light of the glory of God in the face of Jesus Christ.

When it happens you will never be the same again. You will begin as a new creation to worship your Creator and Savior. How can you know this to be true?

You will know it is true when you cry out to the true God and seek and find Him and it will be the beginning of a new life for you. Read the Bible and do what the Lord Jesus Christ tells you to do in John, chapter 3, especially verses 14-21 where Jesus tells you to come to the light in verse 21.

If you believe Jesus and do what He says, old things will pass away and all things will become new. It will be a new evening and morning, a first day new-birth-revelation and an understanding of the division between the darkness and the light. When God removes the blindfold the light of a joyous, fruitful future will begin for you! You will call that day what God called His creation, "Good!"

Sing about God's goodness: <https://www.youtube.com/watch?v=cbLNVAIquml>

Totally Whole
by DLG
God knows the end from the beginning.
He's got it all figured out.
He knows those who will come to Him for life.
He draws them by His Spirit through trials and strife.

The way may sometimes be sad and dreary.
Yet He speaks a word in season to those who are weary.
This world has many laughs as well as tears.
But it is not our final home where we'll know no fears

Today I am both happy and sad.
For one I love has treated me bad.
Not a word of soothing love is said to me,
Just one tender word could set me free.

O what a kind word would do for my soul.
It would banish my grief and make me feel whole.
But no word is spoken. My friend is to busy for me.
So I grieve in my heart awaiting a kind word to be.
But alas all is silent.
Not a word is spoken though time is given to others.
I am a friend that silence smothers.

But I know a day will come when all walls will fall down.
And we will be one in wearing a crown-
A crown that makes us totally whole.
Never to hurt each other in God's Holy fold.

We will always have time for one another then.
For we will be together to care without end.
At last we'll be engulfed in kindness set free,
Free to show affection through all eternity.

Broken Friendships & Lost Loves Restored

Silently my brother and I watched as we poured the ashes of our mom and dad into the crystal stream. Once our parents had been in love. Then sins blight broke their bond. Divorced for many years they passed away. Now their ashes blended together in the flowing stream. "One son thought,"What will be for them is more certain than a magnificent dream!"

Each of their parents after years of divorce found the Savior. They knew themselves forgiven for their past behavior. What will their future be? In heaven Jesus tells us their will be no marriage, thus the divorce problem for God's forgiven people will not exist. They will be united as all believers in an unimaginable bliss. What of others who lost friendships or loves?

On occasions one seek to show love to a friend only to find it broken seemingly without the possibility on earth to mend.

At first there was sharing from the heart, agreeing together on a friendship they promised would never depart. Then gradually not being able to restore it the friendship begins to die. So enter broken hearts, aching with grief because their joy has been robbed like a thief. Searching for the reason why, all that is left is a broken heartache and sigh. Only in eternity will broken friendships, divorces, misunderstandings, and jealousies be removed for those who know the Restorer and Redeemer of all God"s own.

All will be made right with the banishment of sin's blight.. There will no longer be the evil of night. All will be bright and filled with light. Sins will be gone as the Savior makes all things new. No more sighing! No more crying! No more parting! Such is the destiny of God's once broken family.!

Change the Past Or the Future?

Someone asked a question on Facebook which warrants a reply. "If you could go back in time and change one decision what would it be and why?"

Is there any one of us who would not go back in time and change one decision? Of course we would if we could but we all know we can't. As I look back on my life I regret things I blurted out which hurt others as well as myself. The apostle Peter did that, miss spoke, when he rebuked Jesus for saying "the Son of man(meaning Jesus himself) must suffer many things, and be rejected of the elders, and of the chief priests, and scribes, and be killed, and after three days rise again." Peter then began to rebuke

him. But when Jesus had turned about and looked on his disciples, he rebuked Peter, saying, Get you behind me, Satan: for you savor not the things that be of God, but the things that be of men." Luke 8:31-33 Peter meant well because he didn't want Jesus to be killed but he was dead wrong because God's will was that Jesus die for Peter's sins so he would be forgiven and he would be enabled to have a new life and go to heaven.

What have I done in my life which I thought was right but was wrong or that I clearly knew was wrong and said or did anyhow? Too many things unfortunately. But the wonderful thing is that I, like you, am a work in progress. While I can't look back and change bad decisions, I can look back and thank God I learned from them to admit my wrong, confess my sin and believe God's wonderful promise to me in the Bible, "If we confess our sins, he is faithful and just to forgive us our sins and cleanse us from all unrighteousness." I John 1:9 Followers of Christ sin less but they are not sinless!

The question then really is not to look back in time and just regret our sinful decisions but to learn from them. By God's grace I have learned to abandon the things I have done and said that were sinful. So now I can live forgiven, successful and joyful. I haven't arrived fully to what I should be but there has been progress. if we learn from past failed decisions, we can enjoy present successes. These two songs help make spiritual success real:

Only to be what He wants me to be
Every moment of every day
Yielded completely to Jesus alone
Every step of this pilgrim's way
Just to be clay in the Potter's hand
Ready to do what His word commands
Only to be what he wants me to be
Every moment of every day.

Then there will be Just a Closer Walk with Thee
https://www.youtube.com/watch?v=OOKaircCiGl>

December, 2014
Christmas Eve & Adam

On Christmas Eve, Adam and Eve looked down on earth from heaven.
It had been thousands and thousands of years since their glorious promise was given. Eve thought how wonderful it was that God gave to them the first promise of God's coming Son. Every time a child was born they wondered, "Is this the promised one?"

Year after year for hundreds of years they waited, looking for the Son who would come and crush the Wicked one They both died not having received the promise. But they awoke in spirit in a beautiful paradise-A paradise that filled each day with righteous men and women who had trusted God His way.

Then one bright day there came into the garden God's risen Son that He sent. He gathered Adam & Eve together, made them perfect in Spirit, and took them into heaven. As they left they looked down on Satan's ugly head. It had been crushed by their promised child just as God had said. That child born on Christmas day grew to do in Satan who had hell to pay.
That sight each Christmas Eve night is Adam & Eve's greatest delight!

Christmas Comes But Once a Year
   by Dean L Gossett

Christmas Comes But Once a Year
Filling hearts with love, hope and cheer.

Flowing o'er the hills of time
Inspiring anew words of glorious rhyme.

Mary births her baby Son
Her Pain releases God's Holy One

Counting each perfect tiny finger and toe
She forgets her past painful sorrow

The baby cries in His manger bed.
'Til Mary nurses him and He is fully fed.

Shepherds come to pay Him proper respect.
Joseph and Mary look on wondering what next to expect.

This Child so small will grow to be a Savior and King.
His hands full grown will feel the nails our sins shall bring.

His lips will reveal secrets unknown from the beginning of the ages.
His words and teaching will exceed all the wisdom of the sages.

He fulfills all the prophecies of old
As wise men bring gifts of myrrh, frankincense and gold.

He is set for the fall and rise of many in Israel's land,
His glorious return will gather His own all into a Holy band.

That tiny babe grown tall
Finished the work to save us all.

He'll come back some day to create a new heaven and earth.
Filled with those who have known a second birth.

Forever He will wipe all our tears away,
For His new heaven and earth will be here to stay.

We'll hang our crowns in our eternal home
Prepared by this child, now grown, and on His throne!

All glory will be His as King of Kings and Lord of Lords.
We'll praise Him with new harmonious vocal chords.

Heaven's music shall fill His universe
As angels, men and women burst forth in endless chorus.

Who can match this child of Christmas,
Grown tall to always love us?

The answer, "He is matched by none!"
God's Son alone is the matchless One!

For who in the heavens can be **compare**d to the Lord? *Who* among the sons of the mighty can be likened to the Lord? Psalm 89:6 The answer is Jesus alone, as He said, "He that has seen me has seen the Father." John 14:9

Gloria **and I want to wish you a nice Christmas with your family and friends. I wrote the following article which if practiced by anyone would heal relationships, empower Biblical marriages and help change not only us but the world. I pray that you will find it helpful to love God and to love others. Since love is the greatest thing on earth, I seek to make that the goal of my life.**

God bless you,
Dean
PS

I pray for you daily. Anytime you want to share something to pray for let me know.

Seeking, Finding & Displaying The Greatest Thing in the World-<u>True Love</u>

By God's grace I will love you with the love God wishes. That is I will be patient with you. I will not envy you. I will not be irritable, arrogant, rude or resentful toward you. I wont rejoice when you do or say something wrong but I will rejoice with you when you do right and speak the truth.

I will not force myself on you. I won't fly off the handle at you. I won't keep score of your sins but forgive them. I won't be happy when you feel bad. I'll put up with anything even to the point of dying for you.

I will always look for and encourage the best in you. I will trust God always to help me show this love toward you and everyone I know. I will forgive and forget any hurts inflicted on me by your actions and keep seeking to grow in God's kind of love for you.

Because this kind of love is supernatural, I will cultivate it through prayer and beholding God's love in the face and life of His Son and those who follow Him. This love He and His followers show both to those who practice His love and to those who do not. God as Father, Son and Spirit rains His blessings on both the just and the unjust. So must I.

Three things really help us live as we should. They are faith, hope and love. I believe God now without seeing HIm. Faith will pass aways and give place to sight. I have a perfect hope in the future to be with Him and be like Him. Both faith and hope will be realized and no longer needed in the next life, but love will go on forever. So with God's help that is my chief goal in life, to major on what is most important not only for now but forever. When love is fully realized in the fulness of His presence then I will know fully how necessary it is and shall always be.

While this love now is not so called romantic love, it shines high above it and binds those who practice it in marriage to the highest possible marital bliss. This, God's love, is meant to be shown not only to my wife and family but to you and to everyone I know. This is my high calling, to seek to love God and you with love that is true and not the myth of love as corrupted by much of the world, by the natural man and by the Devil's religion.

True love is God's love experienced and created afresh in the hearts of those who know Him. Without Him no one can really love as He loves. With Him all things are possible, even true love. Jesus says it best, "By this shall all men know that you are my learners because you love one another." I then can love through Christ who strengthens me to love as He loved. Finding true love and displaying it is not only admirable, it is accessible, authentic, adorable and the apogee of Divine experience.

May we each receive and realize this Christmas the greatest present of all, the presence of His love in our hearts.

Christmas Packages
by DLG

Every Christmas God Sends Packages
Wrapped in Love,
All kinds of packages sent from Above,
Packages of sunlight and snow-flake
lace,
Of family and friends who light up our
space.
Packages of fruits and all kinds of
sweets.
Fill our Christmas with heavenly treats.
Packages of music to heighten our joys.
Packages of play things, all sorts of toys.
Yes each Christmas God Sends
Packages from above.
His very best gift, the Son of His Love.
In Him are Packages of forgiveness and
life
He Banishes our sin and buries our strife.
With out stretched arms and pure grace.
He opens His arms to receive our
embrace.
So be wise through and through.
Take the gifts He gives to you.
Accept them all, especially His Son,
For He is the "gift of gifts, all other gifts in
one."

Many Christmases
For Gloria and All!
by Dean

Many Christmases have come and gone
Since our first wedding song
Our first was just family and us two.
We enjoyed each other through and
through.

Then came Glenda and Kenny
And our first tree which they enjoyed with
glee.
We pointed them to the Savior who hung
upon a tree.

And told them each Christmas how he
came to set them free.

This year we celebrate our 54th
Christmas with many.
The family has grown over the years
aplenty
Now we have grand kids, nephews, and
in laws so dear
And all the kids enhance and fill our
Christmas with good cheer.

For years we had George's chili
Which tasted fine for a long time.
Then grew less tasty to eat.
So we changed to ham and choice meat.

There have been a few very sad years.
We have had our share of hurts and
tears.
But God in grace and love
Has banished all our fears.

Frannie, Carl, George, June, Ina, my dad
Ken, and Greg have gone.
We hope they celebrate a finer Christmas
in heaven's dawn.
One day our Christmases on earth will
also be done
We'll graduate to a greater feast with
God's Son.

We will eat the marriage supper with the
lamb.
We'll sing and shout to beat the band.
We'll hug and kiss and jump for joy.
In a final Christmas without alloy.

So let's celebrate again this year.
Let's think of Christmases that have
come and gone.
Let's rejoice with good cheer.
Let's thank God for all that is to come and
all that He has done.

Kiss the Son Psalm 2:12

O Bethlehem!
Little town,
Yet of God
Given such renown!
Of Judah's thousands
Very small,
Yet in gift of grace
You outshine them all!

Son of sorrow
Son of might
Was born in you

That Christmas night.
Perfect judge,
Just in all His ways,
To be smitten by man,
That fruit might grow
From you, O Bethlehem
Bethlehem!
So richly spread
with table of redemptive bread;
We feast on you,
Our souls with love
And kindness fed.

He came a shepherd King,
A tiny Holy thing,
A sacrifice,
A tender lamb,
That forgiveness might be mine
From Bethlehem!

A well of water
Springs from you,

Eternally fresh,
The river of God
Incarnated in human flesh.

A remnant born to you
Lives on O Bethlehem
Who find enshrined
In your gentle slopes
The beginning and end
Of all their highest hopes.

O Kiss the Son born this Holy day
Adore the rising Son
Kneel and pray
Worship and rejoice in Him
Who took all your sin away

I would be a Bethlehem
O Lord this Christmas day,
That Christ might fill
My little heart,
And coming in with power
Rule as King my every hour!

A Christmas Poem
for My Precious Family & You:
Christmas Through Time

Many Christmases have come and gone
Since we first saw the light of dawn.
There were the days in our childish youth
When Santa was "truth."

Then there was Christmas in our teen age
When partying was a rage.
Then came early married years
When our children joined in with cheers.

There came a time we realized its true
meaning
When Christ saved us from all that is
demeaning.
We realized the true meaning of Christmas
Jesus was born to die to save us.

Now is a time in our golden years
When possible death might bring us fears
But those fears are banished away
As we know Christmas points to a brighter
day.

It will be a day when we understand
Christmas best of all.
When in heaven at His feet we'll fall.
We will have the greatest present of all on
that day.
For all sin, sorrow and death will have passed
away.

His presence will be the best present of all.
Lifted from earth's darkened pall
Into heaven's endless treasure hall.
Our Savior will make us feel ten feet tall.

We will see the diapers fully unwrap

When we awake from earth's dark nap.
The baby in the manger fully grown
Will hold us in His lap upon His thrown!

Our greatest desires will be met.
Our hearts will no longer fret,
Gazing on Heaven's greatest gift.
Jesus fully grown in our midst.

Earth's wrappings are left behind,
As that moment floods our mind.
We'll know as we are known
Then proclaim this with joyous tone:

"Our Christmases on earth so small.
Have grown to be our all.
What started as children on earth.
Has grown to endless worth.

Christmas like life, unfolding through time
Has elevated us to all that is sublime.
Lifting us from earth's lowly stall
To the Lord, best present, our all in all.

So again on earth we celebrate His birth.
Waiting the day when we realize its endless
worth.
If your heart the Grown Child has won.
Then under the mistletoe kiss God's Son
Show Him gratitude for all He has done!"

Sing About Mary Did You Know? https://
www.youtube.com/watch?v=ifCWN5pJGIE>

Suggestions For Preachers

Your ministry is special and I thank God for you. My time here on earth in limited and I would like to make a suggestion. I've noticed over the years that emphasis on ministry has shifted some from an evangelistic clear call to come forward to receive Christ at the end of the service to an emphasis on ministry to believers. Both are important but how are we doing making clear a call to salvation?

Of course people come to Christ through individual acceptance of Christ with a witnessing believer like Philip leading the Ethiopian Eunuch to Christ and other different examples like thousands converted due to Spirit inspired preaching at Pentecost and group meetings.

I am a strong believer in making sure people are clearly invited to come to Christ. I have spoken and written the word of God thousands of times over the past 62 years. I almost always close when I write or speak inviting people to come to Christ. At camps where I spoke for 30 years and at churches many came to Christ in a group setting after a clear invitation.

Both myself and Gloria were born again by going forward in response to a clear invitation to come to Christ. Gloria at age 23 came forward at a Billy Graham clear invitation in S.F.

I accepted Christ after an invitation at Bethany Bible Chapel in Augusta, Georgia at age 20. Asked to come forward to receive Christ, I was frankly a little scared. I told God I couldn't go forward without His help. He helped and all alone pulled me forward like a magnet to receive HIm. Then he preacher took me aside and showed me how to pray to accept the Lord.

After I walked out of the room my first thought was, "How do I live this life?" Someone came up to me and answered my question I was thinking inside but did not ask out loud. He held out a Bible and said, "To live your new life you must study this book." So I have studied it for 62 years now and it has worked.

So while many people are saved in various ways, the emphasis of scripture is on preaching the good news to any we can but it happens mainly through hearing the message through many hearing it all at once, and one or more making a public confession of Christ.

Our emphasis at VBC through the years is to emphasize believers leading others to Christ individually which it should but the larger church group type invitations are not emphasized as much today as they were originally. Salvation is not a one man show but a team effort by the Spirit through sowers, waterers and reapers. Reapers call clearly to come to Christ.

I purposely almost never preach or write articles that fail to give a clear invitation for those present to come to Christ. How many people in the Bible came to Christ in groups verses friendship evangelism? How many clear examples from the Bible can you think of that resulted from one on one friendship evangelism conversion? How many can you think of as a result of group meetings?

I would like to suggest that those preaching give clear invitations often, not seldom. People need to be told clearly by the speaker, "if you have never received Christ as Savior, we encourage you to come forward today to receive Him. Slip out of your Chair and go to either side of the stage and tell those who will pray for you," I would like to

receive Christ today." Or "You may may come to me(the speaker) and I will help you come to Christ. If you have anything else you wish to pray for we will be here for that prayer as well." Those who preach should stay up front to talk or pray for anyone seeking help.

Evangelism in the N.T. was done in a variety of ways,sometimes friendship evangelism but many were done in groups, large and small, listening and believing or rejecting the message. Salvation is the believing response to God's supernatural Spirit led message of good news.

Let's continue to do what Jesus says," Mark 16:15-16(NKJV) **15 And He said to them, "Go into all the world and preach the gospel to every creature. 16 He who believes and is baptized will be saved; but he who does not believe will be condemned." Acts 17:9. And you shall receive power when the Holy Spirit has come upon you; and you shall be witnesses to Me in Jerusalem, and in all Judea and Samaria, and to the end of the earth."** Most likely every week there are a number of people present at VBC who have never yet received Christ.

Love you,
Dean

Let's Go Climb and Move Mountains

Join me today climbing and moving mountains. Caleb, in the Bible, at 85 years old asked for a mountain in the hills of Hebron. It was inhabited by scary giants. Caleb looked beyond the puny giants to God who eclipsed them in size and power. So God granted him the power to win that mountain because of his faith. It became his inheritance.

I am 79 years old now, 59 years after my conversion I am am looking forward more than ever to climbing and moving mountains. I pray for mountains of unbelief in people's lives to be cast into the sea. I pray for unconverted family members and friends to exchange their unbelief for faith. Some are T, K, G, J, H, M, D, T, D, J, R, A,S, J,M,T, T, O, the first initials of those who need unbelief turned to belief. By faith I say, "Mountains of their unbelief be cast into the sea of God's forgiveness and forgetfulness. Draw them to faith in You in Jesus name."

Dawson Trotman went up on a mountain after his conversion with a map. He marked it with places all over the world and prayed that God would win people to Christ at every place. He started the **Navigators** who spread the word of God on ships and on land all over the world. Guess what? His prayers were answered. Dawson's mountain top experience grew to win folks world wide to the Lord Jesus. He delighted himself in the Lord and the Lord gave him the desires of his heart.

Phil Wagner and I prayed on our knees at Fairhaven Bible chapel in San Leandro many years ago to touch the world through his ministry, which had not yet, but would be born. Today his ministry called **Set Free** is touching and saving prisoners and all kinds of people all over the world. We are all capable of digging up and moving mole hills. God is able and can also help us move mountains! Want to be enriched? Study all the mountains of the Bible. Then go out with God's blessing and be a mountain climber and mover.

In 1972 I was asked to write a correspondence course about God's plans. I prayed about it and did it and **A Journey Through the Bible** was published in 1973 and has been revised and reprinted many times. It has been done by over a million people. If God can do that with me, an ordinary forgiven sinner, He can move mountains for you.

Lord, help those who read this to move mountains of fear, mountains of bitterness, mountains of unbelief, mountains of sin and replace them with valleys of love, valleys of faith, valleys of forgiveness, and valleys of righteousness. "Every valley shall be exalted, and every mountain made low; and the crooked shall be made straight, and the rough place smooth; and the glory of the Lord shall be revealed..." (Isaiah 40;4,5)

Move every mountain, cross every stream, follow all of God's rainbows until you find your dream! Let's sing about it here with Julie Andrews: https://www.youtube.com/watch?v=U4lJUzrgSJA>

Poem Story
From year one to 56 for My Gloria

In our first year you came away to be my love
And we have shared the things above,
Where heights and depths of love divine,
Caused our joyful hearts to entwine.

We've rested in Him our true Rock
Who gently leads and feeds His flock.
By still waters where He leads
We've joyed in Him who meets our needs.

Though trials came and tears were shed
Our love in Him has soothed our dread.
And when we felt hurt on earth
We arose to see heaven's birth,

A new birth of love and grace
Became ours as we gazed upon His face.
Love will come full circle and never go away
In our final home in God's eternal day!

These 56 years you have been my love
We have rejoiced on earth and in heaven above.
Heights and depths of grace divine
Have made us one for I am yours and you are mine!

Come Out! Come In! Look Up

Come Out! Come Out! Come out!
Trust God now and seal your fate.
Don't leave Babylon to late.

Come Out! Come Out! Come out!
Don't call evil good or bright.
Leave Babylon! End up right!

Come Out! Come Out! Come out!
Escape the end of Babylon's blight.
Come in to God's truth and light!

Come in! Come In! Come In.
Come to Christ and then you'll win.
He'll see you through thick and thin.

Come in! Come In! Come in!
To all He has just for you.
Count on it! His way is true!

Come in! Come in! Come in!
Leave behind all of your sin.
He's open wide. Let Him in!

Look up! Look Up! Look up!
Beyond the hills to our God.
Be blessed by His shepherd's rod.

Look Up! Look Up! Look up!
Trust Him in trials and strife.
He'll walk with you all your life.

Look Up! Look Up! Look Up!
He will fill your empty cup.
He'll come back to take you up.

Up! Up! Up! Up! Up! Up!
To your heavenly home
To sit with Him upon HIs throne!

Come Out! Come To! Come In!

In The Bible God calls His people who trust Jesus as Savior to come out from all that is evil and come to the Lord and rejoice in all that is right. 2 Corinthians 6:17,18 says "Come out from among them and be separate, says the Lord. Do not touch what is unclean, And I will receive you. I will be a Father to you, and you shall be My sons & daughters,Says the Lord Almighty." "Revelation 18:7 says "I heard another voice from heaven saying, "Come out of her((Babylon the Great), my people, lest you share in her sins, and lest you receive of her plagues."

If we recognize wrong, evil and sin for what it is and we want to come to the Lord, we will come out of them and He will receive us. In the end-times an evil agent of Satan called Babylon the Great, a prostitute riding on a beast, will fool most of the world to follow her insidious ways even calling evil good. Some who know Christ may possibly be caught up in her economic, religious and sensual sin. So God says to them," Come out of her my people."

What are we told to come out of?   Clearly we are to come out of her 1. demonic influence. 2. lawlessness. 3.darkness. 4 idol worship. 5. unbelieving fellowship 6. fornication. 7. sinful luxurious abundance. 8. iniquities. 9. self righteous works. 10. torment. 11. sorrow. 12. self glorification. 13. her false belief in expected freedom from sorrow. 14. her being burned up. 15 her .judgement by God. 16. weeping and lamentation. 17. destruction in one hour. 18. torment. 19. desolation and eternal loss. 20. sudden, sinking demise. 21. her murders. Coming out of her to the Lord, insures that we won't be a part of her great unending loss.

What will we come to if we come out of her? We will come to 1.the Lord who receives us. 2. to rejoicing over His vengeance and removal of her, Babylon the Great. 3. to singing Hallelujah to God for His just judgement of the great harlot whose destruction is forever and ever. 4. to join the twenty-four elders and the four living creatures representing all creation falling down and worshiping God seated on HIs throne saying, "Amen! Hallelujah! 5. to a voice from God's throne calling out, " Praise our God, all you His servants, and those who fear Him, both small and great!"   7. to a glorious wedding: Let us be glad and rejoice and give Him glory, for the Marriage of the Lamb is come, and His wife has made herself ready." 8. to be "blessed when called to the marriage supper of the Lamb!"

We are called out from Babylon the Great Harlot bride of Satan's destruction, and to come in to the true, pure, indestructible Bride of the Lamb, to be a part of His marriage supper. Such is the glory to come soon for all of the Lamb's people who are cleansed and made holy by His blood. All will be lost forever for Satan's Bride, the Great Harlot and her followers while all glory is found forever by those who came out of her to be part of the marriage supper of the Bride and the Lamb! "These are the true sayings of God." Let us look up to Him and fall down and worship only Him. Amen! https://www.youtube.com/watch?v=IUZEtVbJT5c>

Come in! Come in! Come in!
Leave behind all of your sin.
He's open wide. Let Him in!

Look up! Look Up! Look up!
Beyond the hills to our God.
Be blessed by His shepherd's rod.

Look Up! Look Up! Look up!
Trust Him in trials and strife.
He'll walk with you all your life.

Look Up! Look Up! Look Up!
He will fill your empty cup.
He'll come back to take you up.

Up! Up! Up! Up! Up! Up!
To your heavenly home
To sit by Him upon HIs throne!

Come Out! Come In! Look Up!
DLG

Come Out! Come Out! Come out!
Trust God now and seal your fate.
Don't leave Babylon to late.

Come Out! Come Out! Come out!
Don't call evil good or bright.
Leave Babylon! End up right!

Come Out! Come Out! Come out!
Escape the end of Babylon's blight.
Come in to God's truth and light!

Come in! Come In! Come In.
Come to Christ and then you'll win.
He'll see you through thick and thin.

Come in! Come In! Come in!
To all He has just for you.
Count on it! His way is true!

Concerned About Your Children? God is too!
Isaiah 41:21

In prayer for your children, "Present your case," says the Lord. "Bring forth your **strong *reasons*,**" says the King of Jacob.

God has promised us salvation for our children in Isaiah 49:25. "for I will contend with him who contends with you, and I will save your children." Who contends with you? The world, the flesh, and the Devil. God has and will overcome the world's allures, the fleshes' lusts, and the Devil's deceptions!

This is just one of about 3573 promises in the Bible and unlike politicians God keeps every promise. Not one word has failed of all the good things that the Lord your God has promised concerning you. All have come to pass for you, not one of them has failed" Joshua 23:14

"All the promises of God in God's Son Jesus Christ are Yes and in Him Amen to the glory of God..."2 Cor. 1:20

How many promises do you know? Share them with me if you wish.

Sing about them: https://www.youtube.com/watch?v=IofNq0U2xk0>Constant Confidence Going and Coming!

Constant Confidence
Psalm 121

Yesterday my wife Gloria and I went to San Francisco to the Aveda Institute for hair stylists. My granddaughter Kirsten invited me to come and be her first male model to cut my hair. I wanted to go to encourage her but I was a little concerned about going up and coming down escalators and stairs now that I'm "growing younger," almost 81. I find myself being very careful to hold on to the rails and watch my step.

So I read and prayed that Psalm 121 would be my experience. It promises to help a person not lose footing or slip in verse 3. Well, all went well in spite of possible hazards on the way to SF and back, both going and coming.

Going in to get my hair styled and cut, by my granddaughter Kirsten, was a great experience. She did an outstanding job. In fact she made me look so good that coming out, when we got on Bart and sat in the "old folks section," a lady, standing, asked us how old we were. We said 80, almost 81. She told us she knew people who were in their 60s who looked older than we did. True or not, it encouraged our day.

God makes some wonderful promises in Psalm 121 to always be with our going and coming. If we look beyond the hills to the Maker of heaven and earth those promises can be ours, every day. He promises us help and strength no matter whether young or old. God promised to a guy named Asher in Deuteronomy 33:24-26, "As your days are so shall your strength be." And God promises in Isaiah 56:4 that "even to your old age and hoar hairs (gray hair) I will carry you, and will deliver you." And in Psalm 92:14 He promises "You shall bring forth **fruit** in old age; " So constant confidence in God's continual help is ours by believing and doing what we are told to do in Psalm 121. Read it, believe it and rejoice!

Psalm 1:121 tells us to look beyond the hills to the maker of heaven and earth because our help and strength comes from him. So if we look to him we can be continually confident that He will watch over us. Since He never slumbers or sleeps, He watches over us at all times to help us keep our spiritual footing. He is our keeper, and our preserver keeping and preserving us from all evil. We can be constantly confident that He will be with us both going and coming, and even finally when we go out of this life and come in to the next. Life is all about going and coming and God wants us to trust Him through them all. As we do look to Him we can be confident that He will be with us through all our "going out and coming in from this time forth and forever more." I think I'll sit down and listen to Andrea Crouch singing *Through it All* while I drink a cup of Constant Comment tea and thank the Lord for being my Constant Confidence!

Join me here if you wish: <'https://www.youtube.com/watch?v=iB2pPCydEjs>

Copies and Originals-Pictures and Realities

In the Old Testament we find the Bible full of copies and pictures and in the New Testament they are replaced with originals. Which would you rather have, a copy or an original?

Moses was told to make a tabernacle that was to be carried around in the wilderness and was the center of worship for Israel. That tabernacle, pictured above, was a copy of what God revealed from heaven.

Every aspect of that portable tabernacle was a copy or picture of the Lord Jesus Christ. It is even said of Jesus that "the Word was made flesh and he **tabernacled** among us." There was one entrance to the tabernacle and those who entered it came with an animal sacrifice which was offered on an altar. Blood was put on the horns of the altar and the animal was burnt up. The one door to the tabernacle is a copy or picture of the Lord Jesus who said, "I am the door. By me if any one enter in he shall be saved." The burnt offering is a picture of Christ's offering which alone pays the debt for our sins and fits us for heaven.

Inside the tabernacle was a room called the Holy Place where were articles, each of which was a copy or picture of Jesus Christ. There is a table of shewbread which reminds us that Jesus "is the bread that comes down from heaven" to fill our spiritual hunger. There is an altar of incense which reminds us that our prayers go up like perfume to God through His Son. There is a lampstand menorah continually lit by olive oil which is a picture of Jesus and his people being the light of the world.

Inside the main room of the tabernacle, called the Holy of Holies, there was an ark in which were the ten commandments, Aaron's rod that miraculously budded, and a container of manna. On top of the ark was a mercy seat, a lid where a priest once a year put blood. Overlooking the mercy seat were angels, one on each side.

The ten commandments inside the ark picture Christ who said, "In the volume of the book, it is written, I come to do Your will. Your law is in my heart." He is the only man who ever lived who ever kept the law perfectly. So he didn't deserve to die. The blood put on the mercy seat was was a picture of the fact that Jesus would die for us so that we could find mercy, be forgiven and be counted perfect. The angels represent the heavenly beings who watch and see the wisdom of God in providing a way for sinful man to be counted sinless.

Once a year only the high priest of the Old Testament went into the main room, the Holy of Holies and placed blood on the mercy seat. No one else had that privilege and responsibility. When Jesus came and died he went into heaven itself offering his own blood as the final payment for sin. When he died the curtain between the outer and inner room was ripped open from top to bottom. So now all of God's people are priests and can go directly into the presence of God to worship and receive grace and mercy to adore, honor and serve him.

So the copies and the pictures are no longer needed except to point to Christ. We now have the originals and the realities which are far better than the Old Testament temporary copies and pictures being only shadows of the best which are the lasting originals and realities of God seen in his Son. God makes good copies and pictures but his originals and realities are the ultimate in satisfaction.

Sing About It <http://www.youtube.com/watch?v=hk7nXZOOTBs>

The Voice of Creation-
Do Your Eyes & Ears See & Hear?

The heavens silently shout the glory of God. Yet, many who have eyes to see the starry hosts do mot have ears to hear them. Instead some look up at the majestic night sky and declare that it all happened by chance.

My wife and i went to the Grand Canyon on a bus and a video was playing explaining how the it supposedly came to be after millions of years. Someone at a convention had earlier given me a book on the Grand Canyon with much proof that it happened over a much shorter time. I took it on our trip and was reading it. One proof that it didn't happen over millions of years of time is fossil evidence. Fossils to be preserved must be buried quickly or they will deteriorate over time. Their are millions of fossils in the sediment layers in the Grand Canyon. It is more likely that it occurred quickly due to a gigantic flood and upheaval of subterranean waters.

However the video on the bus emphasized that it all happened by chance natural causes over a huge period of time. It also made no mention of God, our Creator. When we arrived at the canyon, we all got out of the bus and went to the canyon rim. As we stood there looking at the breathtaking sight, I asked, " How many of you think this happened by chance?" No one said a word. Then I said, "How many think God created it? A few near me said, "God created it." They had eyes to see beyond the Grand Canyon's grandeur to the glory of the God who brought it into being. The canyon silently declares the glory of God to those who have eyes to see and ears to hear.

While no sane person claims that there are not natural causes at work in creation, it is insane to think that the vast starlit heavens and the immense Grand Canyon came into being by chance apart from our Creator.

The Bible confirms the fact of creation. He "made all things and upholds all things by the word of His power.". Heb 1:3 "Know this: GOD is God, and God, GOD. He made us; we didn't make him..."Psa. 100:3 And it even claims His creation more emphatically in Romans 1:19,20: "But the basic reality of God is plain enough. Open your eyes and there it is! By taking a long and thoughtful look at what God has created, people have always been able to see what their eyes as such can't see: eternal power, for instance, and the mystery of his divine being. So nobody has a good excuse."

Do you acknowledge God as your Creator and the Creator of heaven and earth? It is the first step in having eyes to see and ears to hear. It also means that you may if you wish go further in knowing Him. " It's impossible to please God apart from faith. And why? Because anyone who wants to approach God must believe both that he exists and that he cares enough to respond to those who seek him."Heb. 11:6 God is silently shouting to each one of us through His creation." Are you listening? Do you hear Him? Do you know Him? Are you responding to Him. Is He responding to you?

"The heavens declare the glory of God; the skies proclaim the work of his hands. Day after day they pour forth speech; night after night they display knowledge. There is no speech or language where their voice is not heard. Their voice goes out into all the earth, their words to the ends of the world..." Psalm 19:1-4

Lord help us all have eyes to see and ears to hear Your voice.

Love, Dean

Evil in the World? Dealing With It

A man breaks into a house, rapes a woman and kills one of her children. Is that evil? An Islamist terrorist cuts a man's head off in the name of Allah. Is that evil? A little girl or boy steals money out of her mom's purse. Is that evil? Only a fool would deny that such evil exists? The word evil is found over 700 times is the Bible and sin 1150 times. Sin is the result of evil. It is anything that doesn't please God and is not His will. We are all guilty of evil and sin. They are part of our nature. Not everything we do is sinful or evil because we are also created in the image of God. Jesus said, "If you being evil know how to give good gifts to your children, how much more will God give good things to them that ask." We all are evil when compared to our perfectly good God.

So where and how did evil begin? The Bible gives the only satisfactory answers to the problem of evil. It tells us that evil began before the creation of heaven and earth. It began with a vile being called the Devil. Interestingly enough the Devil's name has evil in it in English. Take the D off of Devil and evil is left. The Devil, or Satan or The Old Serpent, or Apollyon(the destroyer), as he is called, is the first one to practice evil and the destroyer who influenced the first woman, Eve, and the first man, Adam, to practice evil destroying their and our relationship with God.

Misery loves company. The Devil had deceived one third of the angels to rise up against God with him at the head of the rebellion. Then he added Adam and Eve temporarily to his flock. God had given Adam and Eve permission to eat of every tree in the garden of Eden but one tree, the tree of the knowledge of good and evil. He told them they would die if they ate it. The Devil, the serpent lied, telling them a half truth. He said they would not die but they would become like God knowing good and evi. Tha they would become like God knowing evil was half true. Beware believing a half truth because you will get the wrong half! The Devil's deception brought evil into the world. First he messed up part of heaven. Then he began messing up earth. It is called sin. It caused Adam and Eve to momentarily die spiritually. They tried to hide their sin by covering their open nakedness with fig leaves. It didn't work.

God came to them and asked them the first question ever asked 'Did you eat of the tree of knowledge of good and evil?' Eve said, "The serpent deceived me and I ate." So How did God deal with their sin and how do we deal with wit our sin? God then did a marvelous thing for Adam & Eve. He sacrificed an animal and from it made skins of clothing to cover them. Adam and Eve got rid of their fig leaf clothes and dressed in God's special clothing designed to cover their sin until God's final sacrifice. His Son would come someday not to cover sin but eradicate it through His death for them.

God in HIs mercy has provided a means of forgiveness and removal of sin and evil for us today through His Son. "God so loved the world that He gave His only begotten Son that whosoever believes in Him should not perish but have everlasting life." Sin brings death. No one except God has clearly told us why we have to die. He says, "T**he wages of sin is death** but the gift of God is eternal life through Jesus Christ"

A person's sin and evil problem is solved through accepting Christ and being forgiven. Then a marvelous change takes place. That person knows he is loved by God.. "Here is the proof of love, not that we loved God but that He loved us and sent His Son to be the propitiation(payment) for sin." His death and resurrection purges a believer's sin away. "Through one offering He has perfected forever those sanctified, set apart to Him."

Through Christ's offering a believer begins to love God back. "We love God because He first loved us." Though those who truly believe God are counted perfect by God, we don't always act perfectly but that is our goal. God has provided for our failures by telling us that "If we confess our sins He is faithful and just to forgive us our sins." Why? Because "the blood of Jesus Christ cleanses us from all sin." He is just(right) to

forgive us all sin when we confess it because God has forgiven all our past, present and future sins. A believe doesn't confess his or her sins to get to heaven but to restore fellowship with God. It is like a child in a family. The child does something wrong. It is pointed out. The child realizes his wrong doing. His parents reject his bad behavior but don't reject him. Jesus promises every born again believer, "I will never leave you or forsake you." A believer can't be unborn! Jesus was forsaken to solve the sin problem but arose from the dead never to be forsaken again by His Father. Now He promises to never forsake us. Do you believe Him? If so you know how He solved the problem of evil to make you right in His eyes forever! Isn't that good news? O yes!---if you believe it!

Dealing With Grief Honorably

Losing loved ones is a hard thing for all of us. One vivid example in Scripture is the loss of Aaron's sons. Two of his sons, Nadab and Abihu were priests who died during Old Testament days. Here is what happened: The two brothers thought that they could worship God their way. So they took their censers, special metal containers with incense in them, to offer to God.

There was a problem with their approach to God. They failed to get the fire to light their sensors from off the altar of burnt offering. Instead the Bible says they offered strange or profane fire. The only way to approach God is his way which was represented by the fiery altar which pointed forward to Jesus Christ's death through whom we find salvation. If we seek to come to God another way instead of His way we will be rejected. The Bible says that fire came out of the main sanctuary and killed both Nadab and Abihu.

You can imagine how Aaron's family felt because they lost Nadab & Abihu Then God told Aaron and his two living sons to not mourn their death outwardly by tearing their clothes or uncovering their heads. He said that the congregation outside of the court of God's presence could mourn the death of Nadab and Abihu, but none of the priests inside the court were to express outward sorrow. Why not? **Is it because when God does something it's always right. Those who represent God must not show outward grief for what He does**.

Then God told Aaron that his other two sons, Eleazar and Ithamar, to offer sacrifices and approach God the right way which they both did. **They trusted and obeyed. Lesson learned!**

But they left out one thing they were to do. The rule was that priests were to eat the edible parts of their offering. That speaks of the sacrifice of Christ who said,"Unless you eat my flesh and drink my blood you have no part with me." Of course He was speaking spiritually saying we must accept all of Him into our lives. The offering of Eleazar and Ithamar brought God's way benefited them because it brought them forgiveness but part of it was to be eaten.

Well, they didn't eat it, so Moses came to Aaron their father and was angry. Aaron responded to Moses anger by telling him that they showed no outward mourning though they felt it inwardly. They didn't feel like eating anything having lost their brothers.' Moses accepted their excuse.

The lesson here is that when things happen to us that aren't good that we may grieve inwardly but we should never blame God as if it is his fault. God is always just, good and pure. So instead of getting mad at God or feeling anger toward Him, we should except our lot in life. It hurts when we lose a child or a loved one but we should respond like Job who though grieving said, "The Lord gives and the Lord takes away. Blessed be the name of the Lord!" We can not understand everything that God does or allows but one thing we must do. We must realize that He does nothing wrong and we should worship Him in spite of our grief. We can feel grief and still worship God!

This song sums it up: https://www.youtube.com/watch?v=TDpqBEEY6as

Death a Shadow?

Winter 2018

Last week I had to go to the hospital for three hours. I was given pain killer for extreme pain. It worked. Then I had a CAT scan and they discovered a kidney stone almost passed. I was given pills and sent home. The pain never returned. It was awful but wonderful when it was all over.

I likened the pain to dying, not good to go through, but when it was over it was wonderful! If you know the Good Shepherd, the Lord Jesus Christ, once death is over it WILL be wonderful! I shared that with one doctor who said he never heard anyone say that before. His name was Dr. Marshall. Please pray for his salvation.

Death. to one who has Jesus as his shepherd, is like a shadow. The last thing my dad said to me before he died was from Psalm 23, "Yea, though I walk through the valley of the shadow of death, I will fear no evil for You are with me...surely goodness and mercy shall follow me all the days of my life and I will dwell in the house of the Lord forever."

A shadow is scary but can't hurt anyone. Death, like a shadow, is scary, but afterword it is magnificent for all who know the Good Shepherd. He gave His life for us sheep who had gone astray so we can dwell in the house of the Lord forever!

Have a great thanksgiving everyone! "In everything give thanks for this is the will of God in Christ Jesus concerning you." Thank you Lord that death is a shadow that will usher me and all who know you into your presence forever! That is God's promise and He never lies. Count on it 100%!

Love to all, Dean

Hi Rich.

The word **pray** occurs 313 times in the Bible and basically means to ask both people as well as God for something. Often it means to ask another person. Moses asked his father in law , "Let me go, I pray thee(ask you) and return to my brethren in Egypt."

To ask God: O my Lord, send I pray thee(I ask you) by the hand of him whom you will send." Moses asked God to send someone else. God didn't grant his request. He sent Moses to free the Israelites.

The word Prayer occurs 114 times almost always talking to God, asking him for something.

Intercession is a form of prayer. It usually means to ask God for something for someone else instead of oneself and to be willing to give one's all on behalf of another, even to the extent of suffering for someone else. It sometimes means willingness to perish to save someone else, like Esther. She interceded for Israel willing to perish for the nation if need be.

Example: "Lord save my son Ken even if it takes my death to bring it about." Other forms of prayer:

Supplication and fervency seem to mean asking with humility and great desire.

Petition is something asked for specifically.

Thanksgiving is a prayer of gratitude.

Confession is admitting sin and being forgiven for it.

Cleansing takes place after confession and removes unrighteousness.

Forgive means to lift a load off of one's back, to take away sin.

Belief in prayer means you expect God to do what you ask without doubting.

Strong reasons in prayer are based upon God's promises or desires. We must remind Him of his own desires and will in matters.

Prayers of overzealous dedication are often rejected. Moses asked God to blot him out of His book to spare the people. His request was rejected.

Paul wished himself accursed that his people might be saved. God didn't answer his prayer and curse him. However in a future day his desire for Israel to be saved as a nation will be answered but not by cursing Paul.

The only one it seems that God cursed to set us free was His Son but he knew that Jesus would rise again after the curse fell upon Him and thus defeat the devil.

A broken and contrite heart in prayer is not despised by God. Tears of compassion seem to water prayers and make them more effective. Jesus wept over Jerusalem, over Lazarus, over rejectors. It hurt Him that people didn't respond to His love and teaching.

I hope and pray what I have just shared will help your prayer life.

Thanks for your participation in the class. I need your prayers to be filled with the fulness of God so I can truly be effective when I teach or share the word. Your prayers help me on Sunday as well as others you are praying for.

Love you Rich in our Savior,
Dean

Divine "I"phone

Father
How sweet your love
Streaming from above.
Grace lights up my grateful face.
Wraps me in your forgiving embrace.

My ears fill with heavens ringtone.
Echoing from loves highest throne.

Your mega "I" phone
says I'll never be alone!
Bought with a price of caring pain
I sing now this divine refrain:

Loved with love so fine.
I am yours and you are mine.
Yes, Loved with love divine
I am yours and you are mine.
Loved by Christ and loved forever.
To the utmost heaven imparts.

Dependent or Independent

Have you thought about how dependent God became when He became a human? The Word, (Jesus Christ) was made flesh and lived among us. As a baby he was completely dependent on his mom and dad. Mary must have thought deeply while nursing him about what was said at his birth. She had been told that he was 1. King of the Jews. 2. She saw him Worshipped by shepherds and wise men. 3. She was told he would bring about the fall and rise again of many in Israel. 4. She was told a sword would pierce her heart. 5. She knew his name meant he would save her, Joseph and his people from their sins.

If you had been in Mary & Joseph's shoes would you not have pondered often or constantly the 5 prophecies just given about Jesus. As a baby he was completely dependent upon his mom and dad. As a boy of 12 he was brilliant in his dependence and understanding of scripture that he learned at home. Growing up in Nazareth he was dependent upon Joseph to teach him carpentry. During his miracle teaching and ministry he depended on his apostles and women to help care for his needs. Then Mary realized at his death what was meant when she was told that a sword would pierce through her heart. She stood in grief watching Jesus as he hung upon the cross and the sword that pierced his heart pierced hers. Jesus final dependence upon his true Father enabled him to raise himself from the dead. Jesus died for Mary's sins as well as Joseph's and all our sins. Through his dependence upon his Father, he became the one on whom we totally depend for forgiveness and everlasting life. So he who had lowered himself to depend upon his parents and others in the end had them all depend completely upon him to be saved.

To be totally independent from loving and serving God and others is a disaster.

Divine Perfume
by DLG
From whence comes this sweet perfume?
There are no flowers in the room!
Then spoke the One who made me whole.
It is I. I've blossomed in your soul.

May that experience be yours as it has been for me and a woman I once read about from India who had a dream and awoke to the odor of a sweet fragrance in her room. It was strange because there was nothing in her room to cause the aroma..

In her dream she was directed to go to a house of missionaries in India who would explain someone in her dream called John the Baptist. She went and was dramatically

led to a genuine relationship with God's Son to whom John the Baptist pointed. The book I read about her was called, "I DARED CALL HIM FATHER" It refered to God who the Muslims will never call Father. Some sought to take her life because of her conversion to Jesus with God becoming her Father in Heaven!

I read her story. Then later after I read it,wrote the poem above called. DIVINE PERFUME. I thought it fit the woman's experience perfectly.

Disciples Indeed or Disciples Not

Jesus said in John 8:31 & 32, "If you abide in my word, you are my disciples indeed. And you shall know the truth and the truth shall make you free."

A person recently said to me, "The Bible is flawed and full of errors." He also said of John who wrote down Jesus words, "He is dead and we can't cross examine him to find out if he really wrote this or said it." Finally, he said. "False church scholars threw out the original Bible words and substituted there own flawed version of scripture and that is what we have today."

What about this person who rejects Jesus. Is he a disciple abiding in Jesus' word? Does he know the truth and is he free? it is a lie that someone came along and purposely wiped out original scripture and substituted their own false version which is what we have today.

True disciples or followers of Christ believe Jesus Christ is the way, the truth and the life. They are free! They are not perishing. But to those who refuse to believe, Jesus said, "If you believe not that I am He(the Christ, the Messiah, the Savior), then you will die in your sins and you cannot come where I am."

Lord, please wake people up. "Awake you who are asleep(spiritually) and Christ will give you light." Come to the light. It is shining for you. Don't be like those who love darkness more than light and refuse to come to the light so they can truly see. If Jesus isn't the answer to our greatest needs of forgiveness and eternal life, then there is no answer. But He is the answer. What kind of work do you do, God? "This is the work of God that you believe on His Son!" Are you looking for reasons not to believe and follow Christ or are you a part of God' work, indeed a believing, continuing disciple? You can be a disciple indeed, through the grace of Jesus who said, "Whoever comes to Me I will in no way cast out!' Come to Him and abandon invalid reasons for not believing? Then you will know Amazing Grace! Click below to sing it.

https://www.youtube.com/watch?v=tGlMd53So0A>

Do You Belong to the SSS?

If you look up SSS on Google, you will find it to have many meanings. What I am writing about it means **S**trong **S**upport for **S**aints. To share its meaning we must have a proper understanding of the word Saints. Through the centuries, the word Saints has had a lot of false barnacles attached to its true, original meaning.

So my question is, "What really "ain't" a saint and what is a saint?"

The word saint has been corrupted from its original meaning in the Bible. Some think a saint is someone who has been declared a saint by a hierarchal church of some kind. Such a person must be responsible for two miracles after their death or have died as a martyr for their faith. Some people venerate saints on a level above ordinary Christians based on the idea of the superiority of the "clergy" over the "laity." These are all man made

inventions. They are **not** found in the Bible.

In the Bible all who trust the Lord as their Savior are saints **before** they die. The word saint or saints is found 98 times in the Bible. Saints are people set apart to God by His grace as sacred, holy and clean. The New Testament addresses them in the plural as saints many times before they die. A saint you ain't unless God has made you one by His grace.

So SSS stands for **S**trong **S**upport for **S**aints. When? Right now! The Bible tells all saints to bear others burdens. But it also says they are to bear their own burdens. Sometime we are helped by others who help us bear our burdens. But sometimes we are to bear our own burdens. How do we do that? David Jeremiah in his book, **The Joy of Encouragement**, suggests three Biblical sources for bearing our own burdens. They also consist of three Ss.

First to bear our burdens we must take time to seek God in **Solitude**. Get alone with God as David in the O.T. did of whom it is said, "He encouraged himself in the Lord." 1Sam. 30:6. Then be still as he was and know that He is God, in control, sufficient to strengthen you to bear your burden.

Then mediate on **Scripture**, which is God's word. Alone with God ponder what He says in the Bible. "Blessed is the man or woman who mediates on the word of God night and day. Such a person will be like a tree planted near a river of water whose leaf will not wither who shall be loaded with fruit and prosperous in everything." Psalm 1

Finally, spend time in **Song** praising and worshiping God. David wrote and sang many of His own songs which we have in the Bible. "Bless the Lord O my soul, and all that is within me, bless His holy name." Psalm 103

So the next time you have a burden or even if you don't, take time to practice the three SSS, **Strong Support for the Saints** through encouraging yourself in **Solitude, Scripture and Song.** Here's a song to join in with right now. <https://www.youtube.com/watch?v=IiQzzc41z5Q>

Doors of Acceptance & Transformation

There are many doors mentioned in the Bible but the most wonderful are both mentioned by Jesus. He says of your hearts door, "Behold I stand at the door and knock. If any one hear my voice and open the door I will come in and dine with him and He with me." The other door is the door that represents Jesus Himself. He says, "I am the door, by me if any man enter in He shall be saved and go in and out and find sustenance."

To find acceptance you must open the door of your life and let Christ in. He continues to knock at the door of your life. You must open to Him and let him in to your life. When you do, He will come in to stay. He will bring to your table forgiveness, love, grace, and life eternal. Have you opened the door? If you have you will appreciate him letting you into through door into his life.

Jesus said of himself, 'i am the door. By me if any man enter in he shall be saved and go in and out and find pasture, food for your soul.

Once you open the door of your heart He will be in you. Once you enter Christ as the door you will may go in and out and find food for your soul.

The first door represents Christ in you. The second door represents you in Christ.

<https://www.youtube.com/watch?v=3ssUTrZ9qBc>

Doors of Destiny
by a Disciple Jesus Loves

Throughout our lives we open and enter many doors. They can determine our destiny good of bad. There are two doors which when opened and entered will change our life for good forever!

The first door is a person. Jesus speaks of Himself as a door when He says, " I am the door. If anyone enters by Me, he will be saved..." John 10:9

The second door is also a person. It is you. Jesus speaks of you as a door when he says, "Look! I have been standing at the door, and I am constantly knocking. If anyone hears me calling him and opens the door, I will come in and fellowship with him and he with me." Rev. 3:20

When these two marvelous doors are opened a glorious exchange takes place. You give him your unrest, your sins, your whole life. He gives you His presence, His forgiveness, His love, His purpose for your life.

Right now Jesus door is wide open to receive anyone who comes to Him with a sincere heart. He calls out to everyone, "Come **to** Me all *you* who labor and are heavy laden, and I will give you rest." If you believe Him and tell Him you come He will not reject you. He will give you a new life.

How do you get in His door? Like any door you must enter it, only this door is entered in your mind and heart. Tell Jesus, "Just as I am I come to you, poor, sinful, weak, and hungry, but hopeful and believing." He will receive you. He gave His utmost for you, His life, dying for you and rising again to come to you just as you are to then change you just as you ought to be. Why would He die and rise again for you and then turn you away? No, He won't turn you away **if** you *come* to Him.

As you enter His door you are opening your door, the door to your heart. He will then   enter by His Spirit to live in you, to eat with you when you eat, to listen to you when you talk, to help you know how to live with His perfect plan and purposes for you.

So there they are, the two doors of a desirable destiny and God given purpose for your life. Once you have entered His door and He has entered yours you will have found the true reason why you are alive. His deep desire for you is that you might seek Him with all your heart and find Him. And He tells us how that is done. He is open to you. You must be open to Him. Is your door open to Him? If not, why not choose to open to Him right now? Then after you open to Him spend time getting to know Him every day by talking to Him and letting Him talk to you through His words in the Bible. Here's a good place to start: http://www.whatchristianswanttoknow.com/words-of-jesus-15-amazing-bible-quotes/>

Double Brothers

Jesus' half brothers did not believe in Him at first."(John 7:5) Yet we know clearly that two of his half brothers came to believe in Him for sure, James and Jude and probably all his siblings. (Gal 1:19; I Cor:9:5) So they were related to him two ways, as physical, natural, half brothers and sisters by birth to Mary, and by spiritual rebirth to Him as Savior. It was joyous for them all to know Jesus as a double brother by natural birth and by spiritual rebirth.

The Bible says, ",,,the spiritual is not first, but the natural, and afterward the spiritual. The first man (Adam) *was* of the earth, *made* of dust; the second Man *is* the Lord(Jesus) from heaven. As *was* the *man* of dust, so also *are* those *who are made* of dust; and as *is* the heavenly *Man,* so also *are* those *who are* heavenly. And as we have borne the image of the *man* of dust, we shall also bear the image of the heavenly *Man. (1 Cor. 14:46-49) These verses teach us the fact that we*

are all born naturally and have the possibility of being born again spiritually. The first Adam's trust enabled the last Adam to save him. Thus they became double brothers.

The amazing thing is that everyone, both male and female have the possibility of having Jesus as a brother. "Jesus makes men holy. He takes away their sins. Both Jesus and the ones being made holy have the same Father. That is why **Jesus is not ashamed to call them His brothers.**" *(Heb 2:11)*

I have two brothers whom I love, a natural elder brother named Wayne and a spiritual elder brother named Jesus. It is my desire that my natural brother experience a supernatural rebirth of the Spirit so that we will be double brothers, on two levels, both naturally and spiritually. That is only possible if we have both received Christ and experienced supernatural births as well as natural births.

The first two brothers in history, Cain and Abel were separated by Cain's lack of spiritual trust in God. Cain killed his brother Abel because he rejected God's way. Had he listened to God and his brother who loved him, Cain would have approached God through the offering of a blood sacrifice, which represented forgiveness through the symbolic death of an innocent substitute representing Jesus death. Cain rejected God's way and offered his own way of works. Since Cain did not accept God's way of salvation, love on the highest level, double love, was impossible.

In scripture all believers are called brothers and sisters. The bond between us in Christ is a bond of love. We are to love others who know Christ as Savior as brothers and sisters. This love is on a higher level than just natural blood relatives. It is so strong that it divides natural brothers and sisters from one another so that sometimes those of our own household hate us.

It is the spiritual level which is of highest importance. My continual prayer is for both my eternal spiritual siblings and for those who do not yet know Jesus as savior, to become brothers and sisters on a double, loving basis. If you have a sibling as I do that you think may need to be reborn so you love each other on a double basis **let me know and I will pray for him or her.** *Then the day may come when you both sing with joy this song: < https://www.youtube.com/watch?v=xlT6KoT73O0>*

Any poets out there? If you have ever written any poems about following Christ or about the Bible, I'd be pleased if you shared one with me either by comment, message, or post. Below is one of my poems given as an example. It is called *Dreaming of Days Ahead,* Inspired by Numbers 10:29.

Dreaming of Days Ahead
by DLG

I dreamed a dream of days ahead
When love is pure and never dead
Soon to happen in heaven
To those to whom salvation's given

There's God's Son on His throne
Seated together with all His own
All pure at last in God's sight
Flawless now in heaven's light

Friends are there in glory
Made right by the gospel story
Singing a song of praise by all
Led by the Spirit's choral call

We lift our hands to God in praise
We twirl round Him for endless days
Then fly from the new heaven above
To the new earth, God's land of love

We climb new mountains
Ford sparkling streams
Bask in God fulfilled dreams
Ride high on bright light beams

We hold hands dancing on the new earth
Praising God for His infinite worth
After ten thousands years of joyous days
There are still millions left to give Him praise

We dance in rainbow circle round His throne
He's our treasure in the midst of His own
With hearts full blown
We know we'll never be alone.

These riches are for you my friend
Rainbow love that will never end
So come to the Savior. Join us there
Together in heaven without a care

Numbers 10:29
"We are setting out for the place of which the Lord said, '**I will give** it to you.' Come with us..."

Dual Citizenship?

Most of us born in the U.S. are grateful for being citizens of a great country. We are thankful for our freedom, and its benefits which we celebrate special every Independence Day. Our citizenship which cost others a lot is for free to most of us because we were born here.

While U.S. citizenship is very important to me it doesn't compare to the freedom and benefits I have as a citizen of a Heaven. The Bible says it like this: "...our citizenship is in heaven-and we also await a Savior who is from there, the Lord Jesus Christ who will transform our lowly body that it may be conformed to His glorious body, according to the working by which He is able to subdue all things to Himself." (Phil. 3:20)

My entrance into citizenship in heaven was free to me also just because I was born again from heaven by God's Spirit. But it cost God a great deal. He didn't spare His own Son but delivered Him up to death on a cross so that I might become a member of His family through rebirth.

My great eternal Independence Day happened to me 60 years ago on a Sunday when by God's grace I received His Son by faith. I was set free from the penalty my sins deserved. I was forgiven. The truth set me free!

America's freedoms, benefits and values pale in comparison to heaven's rights to me and to all its citizens. U.S. citizenship is temporary, falling far short of heaven's eternal blessings. It is possible that America may someday lose its freedom and benefits. It may go bankrupt but heaven's freedom and benefits are forever. In fact all believers in Christ are headed for an inheritance incorruptible and undefiled and that does not fade away, reserved in heaven.

Born once to become a U.S. citizen. Born a second time to become a citizen of heaven. I celebrate both citizenships with more than fireworks. I light up for joy in my heart, especially for heaven's citizenship.

So which Independence Day means the most to you? Are you only a citizen of the U.S. but not of heaven? If you want the best, here's how to become a citizen of heaven today. Read and believe these words: "To all who have received Him(Jesus Christ)-those who believe in His name- He has given the right to become God's children who were born...of God. (John 1:12-14)

Happy birthday, citizens of America. Happy birthday to you. Only one birthday will not do. Born again means heavenly citizenship. How many have you?

Eagle's Brain & Wings

Our country needs an eagle's brain and wings. An eagle is smarter than those who run our government because when it flies it relies not just on its left wing but on its right wing as well. If our country ever flies again it will be because both wings, right and left work together!

Eagle's are smarter than most politicians. If the president becomes as smart as one of God's eagles he will work to unite the left and right wings instead of dividing them. And even more he will call on our nation to pray to the God of of our constitution who has endowed us with the rights to life, liberty and the pursuit of happiness.

Then as we wait on the Lord we just might mount up with eagles wings and be endowed with a new vision of government enabled by God, of the people, by the people and for the people's welfare. Our national bird holds a clue to flying high as a nation.

<https://www.youtube.com/watch?v=x5mOq7WgJps>

Earth's Future Clearly Revealed for Stephen Hawking

Stephen Hawking says we only have 1000 years of life to live on earth. Later in his writing he says we have 1000 to 10,000 years left unless we find another planet to live on. Interesting that Hawkins says there is no God but says he likes the King James Version of the Bible. Here is what the King James Bible says about earth's future in Rev. 21:1. "I saw a new heaven and earth for the first heaven and earth had passed away." The apostle Peter inspired by God also tells clearly what will happen to the earth someday. Though the Bible doesn't tell exactly when it will happen, God knows the time, when it will happen. and you can be assured it will happen!

Here is the future of planet earth Mr. Hawking, according to the Bible. the KJ version in 2:Peter 3:**10,13 says,** "But the day of the Lord will come as a thief in the night; in the which the heavens shall pass away with a great noise, and the elements shall melt with fervent heat, the earth also and the works that are therein shall be burned up. **13 Nevertheless we, according to his promise, look for new heavens and a new earth, wherein dwells righteousness."**

It won't be man migrating to another planet that saves our existence. It will be God creating a new heaven and earth for those who believe in Him and believe what He says. Those who don't believe Him will not enjoy the new heavens and earth but will be relegated to the blackness of darkness forever.

Stephen needs to exchange his guessing about earth's future for trust in what God and His Son reveal about its future. God knows the final demise and re-creation of all things. So instead of guessing about earth's future, Stephen and you and I need to trust God's Son who loves us and died and arose again for us. Then we will know for sure what the future holds for mankind. We will also enjoy the new heaven and earth to yet be created by God. Jesus is the way to God, and is the truth of God leading to enjoying the life of God with Him on and in His final heavens and earth.

He tells us to come to Himself and rest in His promise to make a new and final earth which will never pass away. Don't be ignorant. Look to Him who created the present heavens and earth and after it passes away He will create the new heavens and earth wherein is zero evil. It is for all who will believe and trust Him. **Trust Him today before you pass away. Then you will enjoy the final new heaven and earth that will never pass away.**

Stephen ought to be hawking his inadequate brilliance for God's certainty! What we need to know for sure is that this planet earth will be replaced by new heavens and a new earth. Instead of guessing about the planet's future, read what God tells us clearly in Revelation 20 to 22, especially chapter 21. Twenty tells us clearly about what will happen to those on earth and where those who don't believe will go, while 21 tells about the new heavens and where those of us that do believe God will live forever. While some of Revelation is hard to understand, chapter 20-22 is easy! Check it out if you value your future.

https://www.youtube.com/watch?v=4ndMZqT6i4I>

Two Most Profitable Profits

In the times when the nation of Israel was split into two tribes in Judah in the south and ten tribes of Israel in the north, two great prophets of God prophesied and did miracles. There were many unprofitable false prophets during this time. Much idolatry existed mostly in the north but somewhat less in the south. In the midst of much evil going on in the nation two remarkable true prophets of God emerged. The first was named Elijah. His ministry sought to turn people away from false God's to the true God. He not only spoke out against evil seeking to get people to turn to the true God but he ministered to individuals who honored God and him not submitting to the evil that was going on. One account attributes fourteen miracles prophesied by him that came about as he foretold.

He had a protege named Elisha whom he called to join him in ministry. Elisha heard many of Elijah's prophecies and saw many of Elijah's miracles. He walked with and served Elijah for a number of years. Elisha admired Elijah so much that he wanted to be like him. A day came when it was revealed to Elijah, Elisha and fifty other true prophets that Elijah would be taken up to God.

As Elijah and Elisha traveled along together they came to various places including Bethel and Jericho. Elijah encouraged Elisha to stay behind as he went on but Elijah refused. He would not be parted from his beloved mentor on the day God would take him up. He was like a father to Elisha who loved him.

They came in their journey to the Jordan. As fifty prophets stood off in the distance and watched, Elijah took his cloak(mantle) and dipped it in the Jordan river. Immediately the river divided and Elijah and Elisha walked across on the exposed river bed. After their crossing the Jordan flowed once again covering the riverbed.

As they walked along Elijah asked Elisha what he would like him to do for him. Elisha said, " I would like a double portion of your spirit to be on me." He wanted to be doubly like him. Elijah told him that he asked for a hard thing but if he saw him when he was caught up his request would be granted. Elisha not only stuck close to him. He didn't take his eyes off of him. Suddenly a chariot of fire appeared pulled by horses of fire, swung low picking up Elijah and separating him from Elisha. Elijah dropped his mantle and he was caught up in the chariot in a whirlwind into heaven.

Elisha cried out "My father, my father. The chariot of Israel and its horsemen." Elijah watched as he went up till he saw him no more. Out of amazement and grief, Elisha took hold of his clothes and tore them into two pieces. Then he picked up the mantle that had fallen off of Elijah and put it on. He then walked back to the Jordan which was overflowing with water, took off Elijah's mantle and struck the water with it calling out,"Lord God of Elijah, where are you?" Instantly the water was divided this way and that and Elijah walked across on the exposed river bed. This was the first miracle performed by the LORD through Elisha. It showed that Elisha's request for a double portion of Elijah's spirit had been granted him. After that Elisha performed double the amount of prophecies and miracles that Elijah had performed, twenty-eight by Elisha verses fourteen by Elijah.

https://www.youtube.com/watch?v=Q627XeGLeyo>

Encouragers

Friends and those who love and influence you for right are like stars. You can't always see them but they are always there shining on you day and night. They show up best when life gets dark! They help light your way in the dark of God's Heavenly Glory Park. There you can ride with those in charge of the night who silently shout the glory of God.

There you can glide down the milky way of joy, capture the sweet influences of Pleiades, untie the ropes of of Orion, fish in the vault of Pisces, view the star of the Virgin's Child, fly on the wings of the Butterfly Galaxy, dance on the rings of Saturn, watch the true star wars as the stars fight in their courses against Sisera, drink living water from the Big Dipper, gaze upward with a companion of kindness while you laugh together as you watch the Lion of heaven drive the serpent out of the universe. As you learn the lessons of the heavens you will swing on the swings of our Dream Maker's moonlight who lifts you higher and higher to His vantage view of celestial splendor. Thank God then when the night closes in. Look up to the stars and their Maker and you will enjoy God's Starlit Glory Park where you will grin and win!

All God's friends are the true stars.
Dan. 12:3 Those who are wise will shine like the brightness on the heavens. Those who lead many people to righteousness will shine like the stars forever and ever.

What's your favorite star in the verses below?
Gen. 22:7, Numb. 24:17, Judg. 5:20 Job 9:9, Job 38:31,Phil. 2:15, Matt. 2:9

My Books:
Journey Through the Bible: <https://www.ecsministries.org/Page_3.aspx?id=159972>
The Royal Ride: <http://www.authorhouse.com/Bookstore/ItemDetail.aspx?bookid=29837>
Beauty for Ashes: <http://www.authorhouse.com/Bookstore/ItemDetail.aspx?bookid=22613>
The Hair Angel: <http://www.authorhouse.com/Bookstore/ItemDetail.aspx?bookid=40178>

Encouragers versus Discouragers

In this life we meet people who encourage us and those who discourage us. Unfortunately there tend to be more discouragers than encouragers. When Israel was in the wilderness they sent 12 spies into the land of Canaan to check it out. When the spies returned 10 of them gave a report that discouraged the people. Two of them named Joshua and Caleb gave a report that encouraged the people to believe in God's ability to use Israel to win the promised land. The discouragers were filled with fear because they looked at the enemies in the land. The encouragers were filled with courage because they looked to the true God who promised them the land.

It took 40 years to get rid of the discouragers. Then the encouragers, Joshua and Caleb and the people of Israel who had not died during the forty years in the wilderness went in to take the land.

The New Testament teaches Christians to exhort one another to believe God. In choosing out those we need to exhort and those we need to exhort us we need to be careful to choose those who are encouragers and not discouragers. Encouragers point us to believing God. Discouragers point to problems in your life or there own without pointing to God, His word, or the cure for any problems or trials we are going through. Discouragers are driven by fear and faulty comparisons they make between themselves and others. They are quick to point out your shortcomings but fail to see their own failures. They are not gentle in helping you with any faults you have. If you share a problem with them they may throw it back in your face instead of sympathizing and praying for God to give you victory. They may despise and forsake you as a friend if things get tough.

Encouragers find good things in your life to point out to uplift you. They share scripture with you that might be of help. They deal gently with you because they realize their own failures and realize that they may fail

too. If you share a fault, sin, or struggle, they pray with you and for you to have victory. They don't point out wrong in your life without seeking to share God's cure and their loyalty to you.

How can we learn to be encouragers instead of discouragers? Remember the 10 lepers Jesus healed. One returned to give him thanks. If you are a person who is thankful for your brother or sister in Christ and let them know it, they will be uplifted. A word fitly spoken to encourage someone, O how good it is.

God himself is an encourager of his people. He does it in various ways, in dreams, in answered prayer, through angels, through his word and through fellow believers.

Once I prayed to God to help me know if the children I spoke to at camp were really genuinely saved. That night I had a dream. I was in heaven. A line of young people was in front of me that stretched as far as my eyes could see. One by one they came forward and I hugged them. One boy who had been a brat came forward and I said, "You made it." Yes, he said, "I made it Mr. Gossett." I hugged him and then awoke from the dream. That dream encouraged me for many years to come. I kept at it for 30 years before I retired. I get notes from time to time from God's special encouragers telling me that something I shared blessed them. May it be that you will be an encouragers to other believers and not a discourager. Blessed are the encouragers for they are like Jesus who said, "Let not your heart be troubled. You believe in God. Believe also in me. In my Father's house are many mansions. I go to prepare a place for you and if I go away I will come again and receive you to myself that where I am there you may be also. https://www.youtube.com/watch?v=Fd3gVGUMvDU>

Response to Rob Dalrymple's Book
Understanding Eschatology

Rob D in his book makes The Ezekiel Temple and Its Environs to Mean Jesus. But the building of that temple and division of the land to Israel has not yet happened. Rob in his book says the many details of Ezekiel 40-47 is all figurative language that just means Jesus is it all and it just means Jesus is the temple. While all prophecies may not have a literal fulfillment, all the dwelling places of God were and are literal. Eden was real. The Tabernacle in the wilderness was real. The temple of Solomon was real. The rebuilt temple during Nehemiah's time was real. And the temple outlined in Ezekiel will be real. Why would Ezekiel go into such minute detail of the temple and its environs, measurement, people, and ruler if he could have just said, "The final temple will be God himself in the midst." He could have said that in one sentence instead of eight chapters. The problem with Rob's view that Ezekiel's temple just means Jesus, nothing else, is that every temple built or prophesied in the Bible was literally made and fulfilled.

The Ezekiel temple has not been fulfilled but will be some day when the nation of Israel is rescued and redeemed and Christ rules and reigns for a thousand years on the earth while Satan is bound. Then Israel who had been the tail of the nations because of her sin now becomes the head of the nations through her redeemer, King and ruler over all the earth.

To say that none of Ezekiel is going to be literally fulfilled but it just means Jesus is the temple and refers to the new heaven and earth is to deny Christ's 1000 year reign and make the 1000 years mean forever violating the clear meaning of a 1000 years to mean a 1000 years. Since Satan is bound for this 1000 years it can't mean forever since Satan is released after the 1000 years. If the 1000 years means forever then Satan would be released after "forever." Nonsense. After the literal 1000 years Satan is released for short time and deceives the nations. Then he is defeated and thrown into the lake of fire. It is after his defeat that the new heaven and earth begin and last forever.

It is then that the New Jerusalem comes into being which is a city with the Lamb, Jesus being the temple in which the fullness of God is seen and He dwells in His people who are part of that temple dwelling in his many mansions. If the literal sense makes sense don't try to make it out as symbolic sense or it will turn out nonsense. Though he means well, Rob's imaginary interpretations in his book distort the truth about the future.

I would like Rob or someone else to share how many times prophesies turned out to be literally fulfilled and how many did not have literal fulfillment. Over three hundred prophecies have been literally fulfilled about Jesus, 28 literally on the day of his crucifixion. "Approximately 2500 prophecies appear in the pages of the Bible, about 2000 of which already have been fulfilled to the letter."

Rob's understanding of Eschatology really confuses eschatology by making scripture extremely symbolical with highly imaginary interpretations doing disservice to the clear prophetic utterances regarding Israel and the church. His interpretations also rob Israel's remnant of its someday glorious future when it recognizes Jesus as Savior who rescues them and redeems them. Then they enjoy a glorious reign with Christ and the church bringing a thousand years of peace to the earth. During the 1000 years there will be no war, there will be long life with creation renewed and little sin in the world. God keeps all his promises and his promises to Israel and the church will all be fulfilled.

Rob's book though meaning well negates many of the promises of God to those who take part in the first resurrection and to Israel and the church. Not one of God's faithful promises has ever failed. There will be a 1000 year reign of Christ with his people ruling and reigning with him before he creates the new eternal heaven and earth . https://www.youtube.com/watch?v=7BM9E1hEVrg>

Esther Perry
Star In Life & In Eternity
By Gloria Gossett

There are some people you connect with instantly. I felt this way when I met Esther. I had met a kindred spirit. To me she was a perfect example of growing old gracefully. Whining and complaining were not in her vocabulary. Just the opposite! Her spryness, optimism, and zest for life and love for people and the Lord were apparent to all that met her. I remember on more than one occasion teasing her by saying, "When I grow up I want to be just like you!".

When she was about 94 I invited her to a party at our home in Dublin. When I saw she had driven by herself I commented to her on how convenient it was for her to drive the frontage road from Palomares to Dublin. She responded quite indignantly, "Oh no. I took the freeway, of course!!! What a lady! What a role model. Thank you Esther,for being one who finished well. I will miss you.

Tom & Judy & Family
June 30, 2014

Wishing you God's comfort and solace. Your presentation of Esther,your mom's life, was extremely touching. The biography of her life by the family was a wonderful idea, interesting, enlightning, moving and balanced, both serious and funny.

Tom's song was deeply moving. God has certainly blessed him with a heart touching voice.

The slide show was well done. I especially enjoyed the Happy Day song and slides and all the music! **<u>Is it possible to get a copy of the slide show?</u>**

Esther means star. and she was certainly one of God's stars on earth and now in heaven she shines even more brightly.

Elizabeth means "fullness of God or God keeps his oath." She knew some of His fullness on earth. Now she knows it all. He has kept His promise to her. She is like Him for she has seen Him as He fully is.

Perry means pear. She canned them(-:) and was and is fruitful!

Esther's passing on earth has brought us together to see the work of God in her life and the lives of those she loves. Imagine what it will be when we meet again in heaven with our new wardrobe and walk the runway of glory! We will truly be stunned by The Lord and one another. What a day of victory that will be!

Much love to you all!

Dean & Gloria

Heaven's Wardrobe
DLG

Esther's dream has come about,
She's stuningly beautiful inside and out!
No more stains. Nor any wrinkles.
All is neat, glows and twinkles!
Divine botox erased any wrinkles away.
Heaven's runway is her brightest day!
No more washing. No more darning.
All is elegant and charming!
No more does she think, "What shall I wear."
For all are hunks and beauties there!
So says she, The next time you dawn your best attire.
Remember it will be eclipsed when you expire!

Esther was a star in life and is an even greater star in heaven.

Eternity, the Final Frontier
by Dean

The Star Trek movies always say space is the final frontier. It is not! The final frontier is eternity after we leave this life. You will either go to an eternal frontier to a new heaven and earth to experience a place of light, unending peace, companionship, friends and the joy of God's presence OR you will experience a second death which will usher you in to a place of unending darkness, loneliness, and misery called the lake of fire. Which will you choose?

Jesus said to those who come to Him as Savior, "In my father's house are many mansions. If it were not so I would have told you. I go to prepare a place for you and if I go away I will come again and receive you to myself that where I am there you may be also." And what a place it is! Read about it in the last book of the Bible, Revelation chapters 21,22.

Those who refuse to come to Him are excluded from the place He has gone to prepare. He said it this way, "You are from beneath; I am from above. You are of this world; I am not of this world. Therefore I said to you that you will die in your sins; for if you do not believe that I am *He,* you will die in your sins." "and you cannot come where I am." Jesus said to them,"I shall be with you a little while longer, and *then* I go to Him who sent Me. You will seek Me and not find *Me,* and where I am you cannot come." (John 7:33-36; 8:24) So all who do not believe that Jesus is the Christ, the One sent in to the world to reveal God and to save them from their sins- all of them will not enter the final frontier of His presence but will enter the final frontier of eternal destruction.

God who cannot lie promises life eternal to all who will believe and receive His Son, "For God so loved the world that He gave His only begotten Son that whosoever believes in Him should not perish but have eternal life." John 3:16

So how do you choose? The Devil says don't choose Jesus. He says choose religion, choose your own goodness, choose anything but don't choose Jesus. God says to choose His Son. Today make a choice that trashes the Devil's lies.

I believed God and chose Jesus and rest my present and future life wholly on Him. Can't wait for eternity, the final frontier where my tears will be wiped away and I shall enter in to the joy of the Lord's presence forever. How about you? Jesus Loves you! Will you choose to believe him? Listen to this song. Make your choice. Then Let God and others know your choice. "If you confesses me before men I will confess you before my Father," said Jesus.

<https://www.youtube.com/watch?v=LfWSY0XZrp4>

Facing Spiritual Warfare

The Bible clearly teaches in Ephesians 6:12 that there are spiritual forces battling one another influencing nations and people on earth. We don't understand them completely but we can see by what is going on that the evil forces under the Devil's command stir up nations and people to be against the just forces of God.

The Bible says that the world of evil is being controlled by the evil one, Satan. As the time gets shorter he stirs up his followers to resist Jesus' followers and to even kill them. Like Cain who killed his brother, they are murderers inspired by the Wicked One. The shorter his time the more the Devil seeks to wipe out all who follow Jesus. The Devil wants those who follow him to join him in hell. Misery loves company!

The answer for us who follow Jesus Christ is to obey God and to put on the whole armor of God which includes 1. the protective knowledge in our mind that we have salvation; 2. the shield of faith which quenches Satan's fiery darts; 3. the certainty in our hearts that we have God's righteousness; 4. our having the truth of God; 5. our preaching Christ as the true Savior; 6. our sharing the word of God; and 7. our continual prayer against Satan and for his lost followers to be saved. Those are our weapons of warfare against the Wicked One and his evil demons and their false influences. Ephesians 6:10-19

Using our weapons we can defeat the wicked one by winning his followers to Jesus thereby overcoming and putting him to shame. As the day of Satan's final defeat comes closer the Bible tells us we will see his evil influence increase.

Meanwhile our task is to tell everyone the good news about Jesus Christ. He loves them, died for them and will forgive them and save them taking them out of the kingdom of darkness into God's kingdom of light! The main business for all of us who follow Christ, is to see some of the religious or non-religious lost become followers of the Son of God.

To win the battle we must clearly include preaching the good news about Jesus. What are we doing to make Christ known? That is our mission! If we are missing in action the Devil will be more effective in the battle. Who are you and I praying for to come to Christ? Are we praying for our enemies? Who are we telling about Jesus? God, please revive us in our following of Jesus that Satan may lose now as well as in the end when he loses forever in the lake of fire. In Jesus name, Amen!

Whoever reads this if you aren't trusting God's Son, seek Him now! Come to Him for life eternal. He will not reject you if you turn from sin, or false religion and turn to Him for salvation. In Jesus name sing and believe this song and you will be enabled to face the spiritual battles of tomorrow without fear! <https://www.youtube.com/watch?v=4M-zwE33zHA>

Facts or Feelings?

Should facts or feelings govern our lives? It is a fact that driving drunk or under the influence of some drugs may kill someone. So if a person says, "I want to go by my feelings and get drunk," is he wise and just? It is a fact that not telling the truth is wrong. So if a person decides to lie, is he or she wise and just? If a person is factually born biologically a man but feels like a woman is it wise and just for him to act like a woman?

Is it logical that our justice department says it is wrong for a state to pass a law that someone born a man biologically, but feels like a woman, must use a bathroom that fits their biological makeup? Is our justice department logical or illogical? I read today about a man who feels like a dog. You can find this man on the internet under man who feels like he is a dog. He eats dog food and dresses like a dog sometimes. So Attorney General Loretta Lynch, should our U.S. department of justice make a law that says he should be allowed to expose himself and go to the bathroom at a fire hydrant or anywhere else in the outdoors that he wishes? After all, we don't want to hurt his feelings, do we?

Personally, I don't think the U.S. justice department should legislate laws that cater to people's feelings but not to the facts of life. When it comes to making bathroom, shower and locker room laws that permit people to go to bathrooms based on feelings instead of biological scientific facts, is our justice department wise, just or unjust? What do you think?

Here is the answer to have a changed heart that basis actions on truth instead of feelings: https://www.youtube.com/watch?v=DwudqCO7mSQ>

Fear God-Love God

While the Bible clearly teaches that God is to be feared there is a balance between fearing Him and loving Him.

Those who are honest with God when it comes to fearing God admit their sins and failures and find that **"there is forgiveness with Thee(God) that you may be feared."** (Psalm 130:4) Such honest people realize their spiritual poverty when it comes to fearing Him as they should and at that moment find His help and forgiveness and out of gratitude for His love, love Him back. Their fear of Him and obedience to Him is based on the fact that He forgives and loves them. **"We love God because He first loved us!"** (IJohn 4:19)

It is interesting to note that in scripture when sinful men see God they fear him, abhor themselves and repent in dust and ashes. Like Isaiah they say when they truly see God, **"I am an unclean man and I dwell in the midst of an unclean people."** Then God touches them with His cross-pierced-hands of love and redemption and their sin is purged away.

Then it is that His forgiveness lifts them to a level of fear for God filled with a new love of awe and gratitude toward Him that enables them to worship and serve with the love He has shown them. Without His love and forgiveness we can never fear Him with a life of obedience, purity, love, awe, respect and gratitude.

When we really see God in our hearts we fall at His feet in dread and fear. Then He lifts us up, loves us and His perfect love banishes unholy, unhealthy fear. Then we find that God tells us **"Fear not or don't be afraid"** over 300 times in the Bible. If we fear God with a healthy fear based on His forgiveness and love we need fear nothing else for nothing can separate us from the Love of God which we experience in Christ Jesus our Lord! (Romans 8:28-39)

God wants to forgive us in order that we might fear Him in His perfect love which lifts us to obedience expressed in love. "Love lifted me. When nothing else could help love lifted me!" I don't serve and worship Him because I'm scared of Him but I obey Him to return His love. As faith without works is dead, so faith, works and fear without love is dead!(1 Cor. 13) The Devil believes in God and trembles but it does him no good for he doesn't love God. (James 2:19) He knows nothing of faith, hope and love, the greatest being love.(I Cor. 13:13) Let us not boast or glory in our fear of God but only in His cross and love for us! (Gal. 6:14)

Sing About it: <http://www.youtube.com/watch?v=mHQQ7PomyIE>

Feeling Loved or Unloved

The story of Jacob's wives in the Old Testament can be very instructive to us today. One of Jacob's wives, Leah felt unloved by her husband and felt giving him a child would make him love her. What part would feeling unloved do to a marriage? Have you ever felt unloved in your marriage? You don't have to share this out loud but if you have felt that way how have you dealt with it? How did Leah deal with it? Learn from her.

Leah conceived and bore a son, and she called his name **Reuben**; for she said, "The Lord has surely looked on my affliction. Now therefore, my husband will love me." After having her third son she seemed to shift her concern about being loved to God, saying, "Now I will praise God." When we feel unloved by someone does it help to dwell on God's love? Leah had two more sons from Jacob and felt God rewarded her when she had Issachar(rewarded) and she said she was blessed by Zebulun(dwelling) and grateful that Jacob would dwell with her. When Leah's handmaid Zilpah had two sons to Jacob, Gad(fortunate), she felt fortunate and when she had Asher(happy), she said she was happy. She also felt love by other's daughters who called her blessed.

Throughout life I think God is continually seeking to get us to look to Him most and love Him most and to find love in others as well as in our spouse. Jesus said, "He who loves father or mother more than Me is not worthy of Me. And he who loves son or daughter more than Me is not worthy of Me. **38** And he who does not take his cross and follow after Me is not worthy of Me. **39** He who finds his life will lose it, and he who loses his life for My sake will find it." Matt. 10:37,38 Part of taking up our cross is being or feeling rejected sometimes even by members of our own family. According to Jesus, we must put God and his kingdom first and what we truly need will be added to us.

Jacob's wife, Rachel was barren and she felt her husband's love had been stolen by her sister and grieved over it. She blamed her husband, "Give me children or else I die." That angered Jacob because she was putting him in the place of God. Finally she seemed to give in to God in her struggle and her prayers were answered and she had a son whom she called Joseph, meaning "added." She said God will add to her another child which He did but she died giving birth to him. She never got to see in her life time that God blessed her son, Joseph above all of the other sons's of Jacob. Unknown to her, Joseph grew up to be a very righteous, outstanding man who eventually saved his whole family from starving both physically and spiritually. It may be that when we struggle with God and are fruitful that we will never know till we get to heaven how much God has used our struggling times more than our easy times.

Satisfied with You Lord Jesus, I am blest. We are Loved by Christ and loved forever, to the utmost heaven imparts. https://www.youtube.com/watch?v=-gaT4q9eJ1U

Fenced in? Once, Yes. Now, Never!

Before I became a believer in and follower of Christ, the extent of my vision was limited. Now my vision is unlimited. I, as well as all God's redeemed, am told by God, " all things are yours: whether Paul or Apollos or Cephas, or the world or life or death, or things present or things to come—all are yours. And you *are* Christ's, and Christ *is* God's. I Cor:3:21-23

God took Abraham, of Old Testament times, out and had him look over the land and told him as far as he could see it was all his. He was told that his offspring would be as many as there are stars in the sky if he could count them(which he couldn't because no one has counted them yet). We should not limit our selves as if we are fenced in by all that we see now. The song, "Don't Fence Me In" came to my mind in a new, startling and joyous way. Play the song by clicking on the URL after you finish this article and I think you will see the joy of not being fenced in.

Someone has said, "When we get to heaven, what are we going to do forever? Won't it get boring?" That kind of thinking is fenced in. There is no limit to what we will do, what we will enjoy, nor to our relationships with God and His people. We won't just be playing harps. We will enjoy God, each other and the unlimited joys of a new heaven and earth. We will never run of out of unfenced territory!

Now that I am older God's word opens up to me more and more. Once I was fenced in but God's mercy of forgiving me by His Son's death set me free. When we trust God we are given a new heart to experience unfenced panoramas. They can come fresh every morning. His nearness increases. My mind bathes in His continuous revealing of what is and what is to come.

Have no fear all who trust God! We will never run out of time to do and enjoy our future. This world is not our final home. We are not fenced in here. Our treasures continue way beyond the blue. Sing the songs below and let the truth of our endless ride fill your heart! Amen!

https://www.youtube.com/watch?v=lq5vrpwdMGM>

https://www.youtube.com/watch?v=cul1mRlh9Pl

New Version of Don't Fence Me In by DLG

O give me space, lots of space beyond starry
skies above
Don't fence me in.
Let me ride in the wide open heavens that I love.
Don't fence me in.
There I'll ride with my friends in a heavenly
breeze.
I'll hear their soft hoofbeats just as God decrees
We'll ride on forever with heartfelt ease
He won't fence us in.

We'll trot along on a sunbeam steed
Fix our eyes stongly on the horse in the lead.
As we straddle each saddle
The Devil will skidaddle
He won't fence us in!

Our white horses prance along in a mighty show
We watch our Leader as on we go.
With the sword of His Breath
He slices Satan to death!
He can't fence us in!

O give me space, lots of space beyond the starry
skies above
Don't fence me in.
Let me ride in the wide open heavens that I love.
Don't fence me in.
There I'll ride with my friends in a heavenly
breeze.
I'll hear their soft hoofbeats just as God decrees
We'll ride on forever with heartfelt ease
He won't fence us in.

Effective Fervant Prayer

I asked myself the question, "Am I an effective, fervent prayer? According to James 5:16 in order to be an effective fervent prayer I must be righteous. How then do I make sure I am righteous? First, I admit that any righteousness I have is a gift from God. The righteous live by faith. They trust in God's forgiveness through God's Son who died to take away their sins and give them the gift of His righteousness.

The Bible tells us how to be righteous as follows: 1 Peter 2:24 (Jesus) Himself bore our sins in His own body on the tree, that we, having died to sins, might live for **righteous**ness—by whose stripes you were healed. Rom. 3:22 even the **righteous**ness of God (is) through faith in Jesus Christ, to all and on all who believe.

Rom. 4:5 to him who does not work but believes on Him who justifies the ungodly, his faith is accounted for **righteous**ness Rom.5:17...those who receive abundance of grace and of the gift of **righteous**ness will reign in life through the One, Jesus Christ.

Once a person receives Christ and confesses any known sin in his life he is righteous and ready to pray righteously and fervently. (John 1:9)

To be fervent is to be strongly active. I must know God's will in a matter and plead that His will be done. For example, it is God's will that believers in Christ be forgiving toward one another. If two believers are not being forgiving I can pray totally in the will of God that reconciliation take place for that is His will. Then the disputing brothers must get together for forgiveness and restoration. In time as they yield to God the restoration will happen.

Knowing God's will and praying it is the strongest reason we can give to God for answering our prayer. If we ask anything according to His promises He hears us. Not giving up but continually seeking God in prayer is to be fervently effective.

Present your case," says the Lord. "Bring forth your **strong *reasons*,**" says the King of Jacob. Isaiah 41:21. Pray fervently by reminding God of his promises and believing them.

Here find daily promises, 365 in all, to believe and plead to God as strong reasons to be heard. <http://www.365promises.com>

Dear Marsha,

Luke17:3-4 Take heed to yourselves. If your brother sins against you, rebuke him; and if he repents, forgive him. **4** And if he sins against you seven times in a day, and seven times in a day returns to you, saying, 'I repent,' you shall forgive him."

I already responded to your rebuke more than once and repented. If Jesus forgives us does he no longer remain our friend?

Jesus said, "If we don't forgive someone He will not forgive us."
So what must I do to have our friendship and fellowship restored? I've tried more than once. At first I felt hurt, then angry and then I felt forgiveness because of God's forgiveness to me. I forgave you and pray for you and John and your children often. I pray that you and John might be reconciled continually.

You once said I asked for forgiveness too many times. Yet not once did you ever say, "I forgive you." Jesus said if necessary we should forgive someone 70 X 7 equals 490 times. I haven't exceeded more than that toward you have I? In fact I am not completely sure what I said or did to have you not forgive me. The only clear thing I know is I didn't tell you right away when I sent you a classic book on dealing with anger. You never told me clearly what I did that caused you to reject me. Tell me and I will repent. If a person doesn't forgive as he or she is forgiven the Lord says our prayers won't be answered. I don't want that to happen to you.

So please show me some mercy and forgiveness like Jesus has. Please restore fellowship and forgiveness.

Love in our Savior,
Dean

Finished?

Though someone might be finished with you, rejecting you, slandering you, God is never finished with you. If you have trusted Him as your Savior, instead of being finished with you, He will finish perfecting you and using you. He is an all weather friend. He that began a good work in you will complete it as the Bible says, "God began doing a good work in you, and I am confident He will continue it until it is finished on the day when Jesus Christ comes again." Phil.1:6

Cheer up! Out of Christ's rejection came your salvation. Out of your deepest hurts God will bless the world! He finished the sin problem on the cross. He will finish our future because He arose from the dead. He began a new work in us which He will finish come hell or high water! All the forces of evil are no match for our Savior!

https://www.youtube.com/watch?v=pw0FY7ksGHc>

Flying Lessons From Eagle's Wings

God tells us in his word the best place to be.

It is **under his wings** where there is protection, safety, and fruitfulness.

on his wings where there is emancipation, vision and victory.

with his wings where there is healing, power and joy.

The Bible story of Ruth tells of a young lady who leaves her native land with her mother in law, Naomi. She pledges to Naomi, "Where you go, I will go; and where you live, I will live. Your people are my people, your God is my God; where you die, I will die, and that's where I'll be buried, so help me GOD—not even death itself is going to come between us!"

Arriving with Naomi in the land of Israel Ruth meets a godly man named Boaz who expresses his appreciation to her saying, " GOD reward you well for what you've done— and with a generous bonus besides from GOD, to whom you've come seeking protection **under his wings**." She marries Boaz and becomes the mother of Obed who father's Jesse, who father's David the great King of Israel. Through Ruth's offspring a greater David came. He is the Lord Jesus Christ, God's beloved Son, the King of Kings and Savior of all who trust Him.

When we place ourselves under the true God we find not only protection but life and the potential of world wide fruitfulness.

I'm reminded of a true story about a firefighter who came upon a dead bird among the remains of a forest fire. With a stick he turned over the bird and out from under the wings of the charred bird came her babies saved by their mother. She could have flown away but instead she gave her life that they might live.

In order that we might be saved from an eternal death the descendent of Ruth, Jesus, died for our sins. When we place ourselves under his wings by faith we escape death and hell, are forgiven and made fit for heaven.

When we trust in God we also find ourselves **on his wings**. God said to Israel, "'You have seen what I did to Egypt and how I carried you on eagles' wings and brought you to me."Ex. 19:4. He also says to all of us who hope in him, "...the strength of those who wait with hope in the Lord will be renewed.They will soar on wings like eagles. They will run and won't become weary.They will walk and won't grow tired." Is. 40:31

The Israelites were set free from Egypt, metaphorically carried on eagle's wing and given a new vision of God and his purpose for them, to be close to Him, to worship him and to have victory over their enemies. As long as they trusted him their wings of victory were assured.

Finally, we need to not only be under his wings, and on his wings, we need to be **with His wings.** "The Sun of Righteousness will rise with healing in his wings for you people who fear my name. You will go out and leap like calves let out of a stall." Mal. 4:2

When we become one with the Sun of Righteousness, we experience healing of the soul, energy for overcoming the gravity of evil, renewed strength for our way, and renewed, heartfelt joy for each day.

Everyone one of us would like to be able to fly. The good news is that we can fly now in spirit if we place ourselves **under his wings**, **on his wings** and **with his wings.** Then we will be blessed with all spiritual blessings in heavenly places in Christ. Go for it! Fly now on Eagle's wings.

Love to you, Dean
Click below to hear the song, On Eagle's Wings
<http://www.youtube.com/watch?v=MvpjxfWrjzY>

Forgving a Brother Or Sister
Dear Jeff,
You asked me to send you a postcard. Hope you enjoy this one and the little message I have included.

The Lady and Her Gift

A certain woman went to church one day with a large bill in her handbag which she planned on putting in the offering. When the offering plate came around she started to put the bill into it when suddenly she hears the voice of Jesus go through her mind. "If you bring a gift to the altar and you have something against a brother, or they have something against you, go make things right with him. Then come bring your gift to me." Her worship would not be accepted unless she did what Jesus said to do.

She remembered that she did have a brother who had offended her and asked for her forgiveness and the renewal of their friendship. He had been offended by her and told her he forgave her even though she hadn't asked to be forgiven. As of yet she had not forgiven him and become reconciled or on speaking terms with him.

A voice spoke to her inner heart. "Remember all the things I have forgiven and forgot that you did to offend me. I gave my life to lift off your heart and back every sin against me. Now go and be reconciled to your brother. Tell him you forgive him. Lift the load of sins off his heart and back. Then come and bring your gift to me. If you do this your gift will be accepted. If you don't your worship will be rejected."

What do you think she will do? If it was you, what would you do?

When we were at our worst, crucifying Christ, He was at His best, forgiving us. The greatest gift we can give to another is a forgiving heart.

We have been forgiven so much by God it is only right that we forgive a brother or sister for their transgressions against us. If we don't forgive we live with a miserable bitterness that does us no good. Think about anyone with whom you have a problem. Best to go to them and with sincere heart forgive them confronting them and telling them you forgive them and hold no anger toward them anymore. Forgive them and if they have something against you ask them to forgive you. If they won't listen and you have made a sincere attempt then you may want to take along a godly friend that both you and the other party respect. If they still won't listen then take it to the church leaders and finally leave it in God's hands and treat them with love which covers a multitude of offenses and if you have a truly forgiving heart God will take away any anger or bitterness out of your heart. All you will feel is hurt for them instead of anger. If the anger toward them returns attack it with, "Jesus forgave me and forgot my sin. I forgave them and forget it. Get behind me Satan.

Forgiveness Sung by Matthew West<http://www.youtube.com/watch?v=h1Lu5udXEZI>

FORGIVEN! Shout for Joy
How Forgiving Am I? How Forgiving are you?
By DLG

The Apostle Peter asked Jesus how many times he should forgive someone. Then Peter volunteered his own answer, "Seven Times?" Jesus told him that if someone does something wrong toward him and he points out their sin, then if he or she admits it he is to forgive them up to 70 times 7 in one day. Are you that forgiving? Am I? Jesus was and is!

What is Jesus forgiveness like? When He forgives our sin he not only forgives it, he forgets it. To say we forgive someone and then bring it up again proves it was never properly forgiven and forgotten. When my son, Ken did something he shouldn't have as a child I corrected him for it and he admitted it but I made a huge mistake and I brought it up again later which opened an old wound. I learned from that finally to never do it again. If I truly forgive I will be like God who "buries our sins in the deepest sea and removes them as far as the east is from the west and remembers them no more forever."

Lord help us to not have half hearted forgiveness and unwillingness to tell another we forgive them. The Lord says that we must forgive as He has forgiven us or we won't be forgiven. That means our daily fellowship with Him will be cut off until we forgive. Why tell the person we forgive them? Because the words, "I forgive you lift a load off both your back and the back of the one you forgive." We are to not only to forgive but to forget any past grievances as if they never happened.

As we look at our past it is okay to think about what was right, noble and pure but forgiven sins are to purposely be forgotten as if they never existed. At present I can honestly say all sins against me and all sins for which I have been forgiven I relegate to the sea of God's forgetfulness. So I seek to stay close to God and all my brothers and sisters in Christ by forgiving and forgetting all grievances. By God's grace we need to be kind, tender hearted toward all, forgiving one another even as God for Christ's sake has forgiven us.

One man in the Bible committed a very grievous sin then repented for what he did. The Bible told the people to forgive him and make it known to him so strongly that he wouldn't be overpowered by too much grief.

Once I performed a marriage ceremony, came home tired and accidentally put the couple's marriage license away with my marriage notes. Six months later I got a call from the bride that their marriage license had not been filed. I was so humiliated and felt so awful for my oversight. As I apologized to the bride, she assured me all was forgiven and all I needed to do was send it in right away which I did. I was overwhelmed with gratitude by the gracious way she forgave me and assured me it would be okay. And it was! Real forgiveness makes everything okay! Is there anyone you have forgiven or need to forgive today? Share and sing about it: <https://www.youtube.com/watch?v=olbCpy0CQEo>

Job's. He lost all his farm animals, servants and children in one day. His children were all killed in a terrible windstorm. Then his health failed him. Yet Job still trusted God and worshipped him.

Little did he realize that his best days were yet to come when God spoke to him out of a whirlwind which eventually brought him and his wife the greatest blessings of his life. God spoke to him convincing him that He knew what He was doing when he allowed Job's great suffering. Job, though a righteous man who trusted God, abhorred himself for complaining and repented in dust and ashes.

His repentance resulted in blessings beyond his fondest dreams. He prayed for those who had been his miserable comforters, knowing that they too, like him had spoken wrongly and as God forgave him, so he forgave them.

Job and his wife then had seven more sons and three more beautiful daughters and live stock in the multiple thousands. His latter end was exceedingly blessed.

So why do we suffer in life? Because through it all we can learn to trust in God and realize that winds of adversity will finally give way to God's whirlwinds of blessing. Our light afflictions which seem so heavy are slight compared to our final blessings in this life and are nothing compared to our future joy in heaven.

The winds of destruction will be replaced by a whirlwind of blessings as we trust God no matter what. As Job said let us also say and believe, "Though He slay me, yet will I trust Him." God gave His Son, slain by sin, but His love and trust won you, me and millions more to shine like the stars and to be near and with Him forever! His suffering has won us all who have believed and received Him. His whirlwind love revealing Himself to us helps lift us to blessings that will never end. His letter to us in His Word lifts us out of the jail of life revealing His love to us.
https://www.youtube.com/watch?v=vyy9-81g9tl>

Found With The Wind

In the famous movie Gone With The Wind, the civil war caused the south to be blown away, gone with the wind and forever changed.

In the Bible several people found their lives to be renewed in whirlwind experiences which occur many times. One such whirlwind experience was

Friendship in Our Savior
How good to share one's heart with another
A friend who sticks close like a sister or a brother.

A friend who brings to God in prayer and
tears
The hurts and fears of all our years.
A friend who love's God with all their soul.
And encourages me to make that my
goal.
Whose responsive heart lifts me to the
sky.
Where we'll meet our Savior by and by.
On that day and now I thank God for
each dear friend.
How Special our friendship. **It will never
end!**

From Dash - to Infinity

Some day my name and yours will
appear in a newspaper or on a tombstone
like this: Dean Lyle Gossett. May 8, 1935-
May 24, 20??

That dash between birth and death
represents my whole life on earth as your
dash will also represent your whole life.
The dash teaches something about our
lives. First of all, they are very short in
comparison to eternity. One line of a song
speaks of life's brevity like this, "Life at
best is very brief, like the falling of a leaf,
like the binding of a sheaf " All our
experiences here are short in comparison
to infinity which comes next. The question
is "After this short life will we know infinite
life or everlasting death?"

The Bible is clear. It is appointed to
men once to die and after this the
judgement.

The judge will be Jesus. Those who
come to Him now admitting their sin and
need of Him, who believe on His
sacrificial death to put away their sin and
be forgiven, will live in heaven and on a
new earth with Him forever.

Those who reject Him will be lost
forever, experiencing a second death in
what the Bible calls the lake of fire which
is hell, the infinite, eternal place of the
unforgiven. Will your earthly dash be
followed by a joyous or a sorrowful
infinity? It is up to you to choose or reject
Him.

God does not want you to perish. He
wants to forgive and take you to His
infinite home in heaven and on a new
earth. To get there you must choose
God's Son as your Messiah and Savior?
He gave His life for you, died to take
away your sin and arose from the dead
so that you might be with Him forever.
God's desire for you is an infinity of life

and peace. Since misery loves company,
the Devil's desire for you is an infinity of
death & sorrow with him in hell. Chose
today whom you will trust and serve.
Whoever comes to the Lord Jesus Christ,
He will not cast away but will pardon,
cleanse, receive and relieve. That can
mean you!

As for me I have chosen Jesus who is
the way, the truth and the life of all His
children, and I have rejected Satan who
is the wrong way, the Liar and the father
of death to all his followers. Don't be a
fool! Come to Jesus during your dash
through time so you can spend your
eternal infinity with Him. Seek Him while
He can be found. Put your dash into the
Hands of the creator of both the dash and
of infinity!

Click on the song in brackets below and
believe it with all your heart and today will
be your day of salvation and you will have
the assurance of being forgiven and
infinitely with the Lord Jesus Christ.
Just As I Am <https://www.youtube.com/
watch?v=w2VrRk4pZHY>

Dear Pastor David Jeremiah,

I have been listening to your messages for a long time and have been greatly blessed by them. However, Tithing is not taught for the church though people may tithe if so wished. The N.T. teaching is to set aside financial gifts for giving on the first day of the week and promotes giving to be decided before God in response to how He has prospered a person. It does not say 10% is required but says to give cheerfully and not grudgingly or of necessity. Tithing was an Old Testament law that was a necessity. So tithing is not taught in the N.T.

The N.T. teaches giving based on how God has prospered us and it is not under law but giving is according to how we purpose in out heart, not grudgingly or of necessity and scripture emphasizes it to be done secretly and not paraded before the church as many Pharisees did under law which Jesus condemned.

The church I attend, by God's grace and following his teaching on giving, has been amazingly prosperous for many years and the total offerings are made public showing what the whole congregation has given, with no emphasis of what any individual gives. Offerings have been abundant as I have observed them over about 60 years.

Our facilities which are valued at millions of dollars has been paid off for many years and giving is so abundant that we support many missionaries, giving to the poor, and to multitudes of out reaches to the homeless and city missions. No pleading for money ever takes place nor are people told they are to obey the Old Testament law and tithe. They are taught to give as they decide in their heart cheerfully. It sticks to scripture better than churches who continually make a big issue of giving and tithing and announce names of big givers.

I subscribe to George Muller, of Bristol, England's approach to giving, having my own family and ministry needs met telling only God and trusting Him to answer. I have been a pastor and teacher for many years and have never required any money for teaching and ministry and God has always supplied my needs by some who have given to me though not asked for.

I base my giving not on tithing but on praying how much and where and to whom I should give. God has blessed our family so that we have plenty to give now in our old age.

Pledging is not something I practice before men but I pray asking for God to show me and my wife what to give and to whom. I don't pledge something I don't yet have. Nor do I require anyone to pledge to God to meet my needs. Over the years as I have given under grace God has enabled us to give sometimes from less than 10% to 100% I was invited to speak in Georgia with no guarantee of payment for my traveling and living expense. I spoke 16 times and was promised nothing. We went prepared to pay for everything but it turned out that the people where I went to speak were so generous that when we returned to our home in California we had more money than when we left. Everything was taken care of for about two months and we had money left to give as we decided in our hearts..

So teaching people to tithe and pledge under law has never been our pattern since the N.T. doesn't require it. God has always provided our needs and I consider all we have the Lord's not just 10% as required under law.

The woman Jesus praised, for giving more than anyone else, gave everything she had, 100%. not 10%. She didn't broadcast her giving. Jesus did as an example for us.

Jesus condemned those who make a big show in public of their giving, fasting and praying. That should not be the practice of the church.

In England a great example of honoring God was George Mueller who ran an orphanage and asked only God to provide his needs and never told others about those needs. He told only God. When God provided needs as he always did, George told afterword how amazingly God answered prayers and supplied all his needs. He gave God the glory.

Tithing by necessity under law is not the New Testament pattern for giving but deciding to give cheerfully, as one decides in his or her heart, is the pattern we are to follow. My wife and I are both over 80 years old now and plan to give what we have in abundance, with His help, as generously and thoughtfully as we can to our family and to the church and to individuals in need.

As a teacher of God's word and a pastor to His people I hope you will consider what i have shared and if you think anything I said is incorrect, show me from God's word.

Respectfully yours,

Dean L Gossett

We give thanks to God for our daughter from childhood until today. Jan 7,2014

A Birthday Poem for you partly inspired by by Tina M. Marascia's poem, An Angel Left Her Wings

An Angel Gave Her Wings
  by Dad

We had this little angel. An angel gave her wings.
She has no idea how much happiness she brings.
She brightened up our days with her smiles so neat
All the blessings of her childhood remain with us, so sweet.

Her face, it is so perfect, she's sweet and soft and pure.
Sometimes she can be willful and sometimes she is demure.
She tries her very hardest to please and do what's right.
She gives the greatest hugs from morning until night.

Every person that has known her sees a light within her soul
I know that in this whole great world, she has a special role.
She's helpful and considerate to everyone she knows
This light in her shines brighter as our angel grows.

When she sees someone is sad, she opens up her heart.
She wants to do all that she can; she wants to do her part.
She squeezes away our sorrow and makes us forget our pain.
She points us to the Son when we're hiding from the rain.

When very young I read to her as she fuzzed my hairy arm.
Every laugh and giggle were full of youthful charm.

When still young and asked what she wanted to be.
She said,"I just want to be a mother. Thats all I want to be."

Now she's grown. A mother she became
Blessing us with a boy and girl, adding to her fame.
Through joys and trials she raised them til now fully grown.
We're proud God answered her with such gifts from His throne!

I know that God loves us, He showed us with His Grace
We know it completely each time we see her still angelic face.
That very moment when she came into our world,
We knew that she was so much more than just our baby girl.

She has been our sunshine, with a sweetness that won't end.
And now grown up she is a closest friend.
She trusts the Lord in a world oft filled with tests and trials.
It blesses us as we've seen her grow and still share her smiles.

When God entrusted us with you, Glenda, a gift on an angel's wing,
Little did we know what great blessing you would bring.
Through up and downs and roller coasters the best is yet to be
For God saves the best til last in the years we yet shall see.

So on this special day now turned 52.
Don't be blue.
The Lord will be there in your older years
To protect and see you through.

So we thank you Lord for Glenda.
She is still our rage
No matter what her age.
We best finish this cause I've filled up the page.

Global Warming-The Final Big Bang

There is a global warming I believe in, the hottest heat yet to come and there is a lesson for us from it: ..."the day of the Lord will come like a thief, and then the heavens will pass away with a roar, and the heavenly bodies will melt with fervent heat, and the earth will be burned up. Since all these things are thus to be dissolved, what sort of people ought you to be in lives of holiness and godliness...?"

Trust in the warmth of God's love now and honor Him and the final big bang will be a gigantic success as you will experience this promise: "But according to His promise we are waiting for new heavens and a new earth in which righteousness dwells." 2Peter 3:10-13

Only God knows for sure what is happening and He has informed us of this future big bang. Count on it!

For Gloria On our 51st Anniversary

On this our special anniversary you are my Gloria Blanche bride divine. So I lift my voice in thanks that I am yours and you are mine! You are my Gloria, a gift of glory from God to me. You are my Blanche which means pure, untarnished beauty.

On this our 51st anniversary I can truly say that you have been Fully God's gift of glory, purity and beauty to me.

Creative Bible leader for more than 32 years, giver of gifts too each of your many friends, writer of notes with noble ends. Crafty creator of collages for wedded couples, & children's births that adorn the walls of countless homes and nooks.

Master Gardner, consummate home maker, sewer and tailor of clothes for both young and old, I've watched over the years your talents unfold!

My Lover and friend, my back and hair caresser showing me affection That causes my heart to mend. Prayer partner, valued companion daily, as we read, share and discuss God's truth. Helper and comforter in sickness and in health.

I regret that in my older age because of a slight decline at times in my energy I can not show you the manly love that once was ours in fulness. But I still cherish the memories and hope and pray that God in His grace might enable us a final grand and passionate foray! That together we might shout hooray!

We have entered a new golden era, a new time when by God's grace we know a deeper, different loving embrace. So may God grow our love in a new and lasting way until that day when the weakness of earth's short stay will break forth into our final brightest day!

Until then when the shadows flee away I wish you my deepest love on this our special day!

After the poem with tears in my eyes she added to my bliss with a sweet and tender kiss.

Gloria's Teddy Story
Unforgettable Toys by Gloria Gossett

Because I was an only child until I was 14, dolls and stuffed animals became my pretend friends. Of all my little friends, Teddy Bear was my favorite. He arrived in my arms on my first birthday in 1936. For the next 12 years, he was a constant and true friend. In my early years Teddy had to accompany me everywhere...to the store, visits to grandparents, etc. Later, he sat on my bed keeping watch over my room during the day. At night, his fat little tummy became a perfect pillow for my head.

As the years went by, Teddy gradually lost most of his hair. But, loyal friend that I was, I loved him still. Around my 13th birthday I visited my grandmother for a month in another state. Upon my return, Teddy was gone!!!!! My mother sheepishly admitted she had thrown him away! I was devastated. She justified her actions by saying that I was 13 now and almost grown-up, Teddy was old and hairless and....something I hadn't noticed, he smelled!

I turned 80 last month, but I still have lots of fond memories of my best friend, Teddy.

God & Forgiveness

I was asked not long ago by someone why I kept asking for forgiveness. I thought about it and prayed about it and the reason was that I needed assurance. When I asked the person for forgiveness I was never told, "I forgive you." When my granddaughter was caught doing something she shouldn't and admitted it, I told her what scripture told me to do, I said, "I forgive you" and she wept on my shoulder. It was a turning point in her life. Jesus tells us we are to forgive in our hearts anyone who does something wrong toward us and asks for forgiveness.

Peter asked how many times he should forgive someone, "Seven times?" Jesus said, "No, seventy times seven." "Pay attention to yourselves! If your brother sins, rebuke him, and if he repents, forgive him, and if he sins against you seven times in the day, and turns to you seven times, saying, 'I repent,' you must forgive him." So how does one know you forgive him or her? He knows If you mean it and say "I forgive you." You must not say, "That's okay." Nor should you just forgive him or her in your mind. You must forgive from your heart and let him or her know it. It is amazing how many times God forgives us of all our sins and iniquities and tells us so in His Word.

In the light of His love and forgiveness we are to be kind, tenderhearted forgiving as Christ forgave us. To forgive means to lift a load off of someone's heart and soul. If a person asks for forgiveness we are only obedient and Christ-like if we give it. If the person is hurting and asks for forgiveness and we act like it was nothing, or ignore him or her, or tell him or her they shouldn't feel that way, we have stepped on their heart and have been disobedient to the grace of God. How obedient are you and I at forgiving?

God Glad or Sad

In a previous article I shared what eternity will be like for those who believe God and believe in His Son. It showed what the glorious and joyful future in heaven will be for us. The Bible says it like this, "Precious in the sight of the Lord is the death of His Saints(those who trust Him).Why? Obviously God is glad when those who trust Him go to be with Him.

There is another side to eternity that makes God sad. "He takes no pleasure in the death of the wicked(those who reject Him)." Why is He sad? Because when they die, they don't go to be with Him. They don't have their names in the book of life so the wrath of God abides on them. John 3:36 He who believes in the Son has everlasting life; and he who does not believe the Son shall **not** see life, but the wrath of God abides on him."

Jesus did not say people can go to a man-made-up-purgatory where they can pay for their sins and eventually get out and go to be with Him. No, Jesus alone purges us from sin by His one offering on the cross. Heb. 10:14 & Heb.1:3

Some will claim they did great things for God but will be rejected: **Matthew 7:22-24(NKJV)** "Many will say to Me in that day, 'Lord, Lord, have we not prophesied in Your name, cast out demons in Your name, and done many wonders in Your name?' **23** And then I will declare to them, 'I never knew you; depart from Me, you who practice lawlessness!' " They like many religious people think their good works will get the them to heaven but not so because going to heaven is not based upon a person's works but based upon Jesus work, upon God's love and grace. 1 John 4:10 "In this is love, not that we loved God, but that He loved us and sent His Son *to be* the propitiation for our sins." We love Him only because He first loved us.

Jesus doesn't say to those who profess, I knew you and you got away from me. He says, "I never knew you!" 1 John 2:19 reinforces the fact that true believers will continue to trust in Jesus and not leave the faith.They went out from us, but they were not of us; for if they had been of us, they would have continued with us; but *they went out* that they might be made manifest, that none of them were of us."

So what happens to those who reject God and His Son? God is sad because they have to spend eternity apart from Him experiencing the second death. Jesus said, In Matthew 10:28 , "Do not fear those who kill the body but cannot kill the soul. But rather fear Him who is able to destroy both soul and body in hell." Does that mean unbelievers cease to exist? No, because we are told in Revelation 20:10 that "The devil, who deceived them, was cast into the lake of fire and brimstone where the beast and the false prophet *are.* And they will be tormented day and night forever and ever." When the devil is cast into the lake of fire, the beast and prophet were still there after a thousand years.

Jesus told unbelieving Pharisees, priests and officers, in Matthew 7:33,34, "I shall be with you a little while longer, and *then* I go to Him who sent Me. 34 You will seek Me and not find *Me,* and where I am you cannot come."

Notice I used the word hell only once and that refers to geena, the lake of fire. People argue about the meaning of hell in the Bible meaning just the grave but a full study indicates it means more than that. There is no misunderstanding about being apart from God having been thrown into a lake of fire forever and ever. However you interpret the word hell, the meaning is not being with Jesus and instead in a lake of fire. That ought to encourage everyone to come to Him to escape from being apart from Him forever. These verses tell how to come to Christ, to find rest and forgiveness, to be saved, and to escape the second death. John 3:16, Matthew 11:28, Romans 10:9,10 and Eph. 2:8-10. Jesus says that whoever comes to Him, He will in no way cast out." So look up the verses above, believe God and come to Him today.

God is in This Place and I Knew it Not, Until...?

In the Old Testament a man named Jacob was running away from where he lived, fleeing for his life from his brother Esau who he thought wanted to kill him. On the trip he grew tired and laid down, using a rock for a pillow, probably covering it with something soft, and fell asleep.

While he slept he dreamed that God spoke to him and made six promises to him which I will number. In his dream a ladder *was* set up on the earth, and its top reached to heaven; and the angels of God were ascending and descending on it. And behold, the Lord stood above it and said: "I *am* the Lord God of Abraham your father and the God of Isaac; **(1) the land on which you lie I will give to you and your descendants. Also (2) your descendants shall be as the dust of the earth; (3) you shall spread abroad to the west and the east, to the north and the south;** and **(4) in you and in your offspring all the families of the earth shall be blessed.** Behold, **(5) I am with you and will bring you back to this land; for (6) I will not leave you until I have done what I have spoken to you.**"

Then Jacob rose early in the morning, and took the stone that he had put at his head, set it up as a pillar, and poured oil on top of it. And he called the name of that place Bethel, God's house. He said, "God is in this place—truly. And I didn't even know it!" He whispered in awe, "Incredible. Wonderful. Holy. This is God's House. This is the Gate of Heaven."

Then Jacob made three promises to God which I will number. "**(1) If You will be with me, and keep me in this way that I am going, and give me bread to eat and clothing to put on, so that I come back to my father's house in peace, then You Lord shall be my God. And (2) this stone which I have set as a pillar shall be God's house, and (3) of all that You give me I will surely give a tenth to You.**"

How about you? Is God in the place where you are? God had always been where Jacob had been but not until he had an encounter with Him did he realize that God was really there. Is God where you are right now? Yes, He is because we are told regarding God that "in Him we live and move and have our being." However, most people do not realize the presence of God until they have an encounter with Him. How do we have that encounter? It is by hearing God's promises and believing them. The Bible is full of promises, some of which directly relate to you. I will number six of them. John 3:16 promises you that (1) **"God so loved the world that He gave His only begotten Son that whosoever(that's you) believes in Him should not perish but (2) have everlasting life. (3) And this is eternal life, that they may know You, the only true God, and Jesus Christ whom You have sent. John 17:3**

To know Him through believing His promises and coming to Him with all your heart will enable you to know His presence. He will come by His Spirit to live in your heart. Your heart then becomes the home of God. Then you will know every moment of your life **(4) He is with you and will never leave you nor forsake you. (5) He has started a good work in you and will finish it.** You will know for sure that He is present in every place, especially in your heart which will be Christ's home for ever. Matthew 11:28,29 promises that when you come to Him, **(6) He will receive you and will fill you with His rest, His peace and His presence.**

Jacob believed God's promises to him. God keeps every promises He makes. Have you believed His promises to you? Have you come to Him yet? Will you come to Him now? If so sing about it here: <https://www.youtube.com/watch?v=CxA0TFe3-Uo>

God Knows! Grandson Knows!

I woke up this morning thinking about what my grandson said when he was a little boy. I told him that God knows how many hairs he has on his head. A couple of days later he said, "Grandpa, I know God knows how many hairs I have on my head."

"How do you know that," I said.

"I know he counts the hairs on my head because when I wake up my hair is messed up from him counting them."

Funny, yes. But God does know everything about us, doesn't He.

Oh yes! The Bible says "He knows the end from the beginning. He knows everyone of our days before there is one of them." God is omniscient knowing everything. Jesus met a woman at a well who told him she had no husband. He told her "You have said well that you have no husband. For you have had five husbands and the one you have now is not your husband."

She was astonished and said later to people of her home town, "Come see a man which told me all things that I ever did. Is not he the Christ." She then became a follower of Jesus as did many others in her home town.

Jesus knew as did His Father everything about everyone he met.

He knows the reasons for the trial you are going through. He knows that if you are His follower that "all things work together for good to them that love God, to those who are called according to His purpose." That purpose is that you might be conformed to the image of His Son, that you might be like Him in character and actions.

So, the trials you go through, though not all good, are working together <u>for</u> good. If you are not a believer in Christ, your trials are meant to lead you to Him for salvation. If you are a believer in Christ, your trials are meant to lead you to Him for transformation!

What a confidence this should give us in the midst of our trials. God is in control. He knows what is happening. So thank the Lord for sickness, for your long search for a job, for having to move from your large home to a smaller one, for your struggle to love and be loved, for the loss of your loved one, for your spiritual battle against the forces of evil, for your family problems, for those who treat you unfairly, for suffering, and for having to wait so long to get your prayer answered.

I know God that you know the purpose for my life. I thank you for the trials and for the peace you give me when I with child-like-faith give them to You. You are my heavenly Father who gives good things and the Holy Spirit to those who ask.

I rejoice in my weakness and trials because they lead me to strength in You. Now we are in the refining process. The Golden Era is yet to come. "When He has tried me I shall come forth as Gold." Job

Remember, GOD KNOWS and HE CARES!

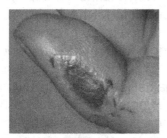

God's Creativity Is Still Going On
by Dean

A couple of days ago I cut my finger which bled a lot. I was grateful that completely without any thought or action on my part my body was taken over by the creative power of blood which stopped the bleeding and has healed it now. That is proof of the continued creative power of God. He has fashioned our bodies so without any thought or conscious mental direction, except for eating and drinking, our body nourishes, heals, and recreates itself continually. This proves that we are not the creation of chance evolution but the creation of a wise and powerful God. He designed us and created us in our mother's womb and we are amazingly and wonderfully made. All things were made by our Lord and for Him and without Him nothing that is made was made.

Someone might say, "Well the body eventually dies or is not always perfect. Why not?" The answer to that is that when God made the first man and woman they were given free will to choose. They chose wrongly which caused a temporary curse of suffering, sin, and evil as well as a blessing of forgiveness, health, right and goodness to take place on earth. Paradise was lost but through God's Son it is and will be regained for all who trust Him.

The creative power of God is also seen in the heavens among the stars and planets. They continue to speed through space upheld by an invisible unseen hand. Century after century the heavens silently shout the glory of God. They speak of His presence upholding all things by the word of His power. The fool says it all happened by chance evolution to which he bows in stupidity. Once I knew an atheist named Worth Ellis who mocked God and said for a time, "He doesn't exist!" If thunder clapped overhead he would call God Pete and shout, "Shoot it again, Pete." Then a marvelous thing happened to Him. He was completely transformed by believing in Jesus Christ as His Savior. Then he glorified God in preaching the God he once denied. He took the step of wisdom from being a fool to having faith in the God who gave him his life and breath.

God continues to be creative in blessing our bodies, in upholding the earth and all the heavenly bodies. He gives us breath and life and countless kinds of delicious food. He determines our place of birth, our number of days, and invites us to come to His Son for eternal life. I came to Him at age 20, 62 years ago, and He gave me eyes to see His glory in His Son who gave Himself for me. He then created in me a new heart. If any person comes to Christ, he become a "new creation, old thing pass away and all things become new." I see Him both in His Son, and in His sun. Both give life, one eternal, the other temporary. I see His handy work in the stars and hear His voice speak with majesty through all HIs creation.

One day He will speak and with the breath of His mouth melt this present earth and universe and speak a new world into existence. All who trust Him will be part of a new creation with a new body to inhabit a new heaven and earth. I appeal to anyone foolish enough to believe in chance evolution to discard it and believe wholeheartedly in the Christ of Creation. Sing about it here: https://www.youtube.com/watch?v=xmBVTlsAWO0> Do I hear an Amen out there?

The Face of God

As you sit where you are now
Thousands and thousands of signals
Traveling through space
Bounce off your head, your body, your face
Carrying messages of knowledge increased
And in our days released.

Why are they there? What is their message?
Is it that it all has happened by chance
To give man glory for his advance?

Or is it because God's face is revealed in man's creativity.
Made in the image of God he unlocks what was there From the beginning, hidden in time and infinity.
Only to reveal a greater view
Of the face of God in what is new.

Man brings out from his mind things both old and new.
Some inspired by an enemy who tells what is untrue.
Others see this increase of knowing power
As prophetic truth unfolded for this very hour.

The internet, knowledge flowing through space
Reveals God's face.
He made this world and all of space unfurled.
It speaks of Him from big to little.
God plays the music. Creative men dance to His fiddle.

History and all its inventions no matter their intentions
Speak loudly to those who have ears.
He is the maker of all the heavenly spheres.

Those who can see beyond their noses
See the face of God in the universes and even in roses.

The Word made flesh gives life that's fresh
That In His Son we might mesh.
Faith in Him opens one's eyes to see God's face
In what is happening in earth's unfolding race.

The days run on like a swift unfolding song
Showing forth His glory all day long.
The blind can't see beyond this mystery.
But those whose eyes are open see in it the trinity.

A three-fold-look at Him that is and was and is to be
Is their's to know and set them free.
They see more than an increase in knowledge
They enroll in God's special college.

They learn of Him in the old and new.
They see the face of God in all that's true.
His glory fills the air as hearts leap up.
They drink each day from heaven's cup.

With eyes of affection on things above
They bask in the forgiveness of God's love.
Each day is fresh with living bread
They see His face who once were dead.

He made everything with potential for today.
The space was there for man to explore
For modern day discoveries galore,
For radio, television, and the internet,
For more to come. You bet!

So what do we do with discoveries call
Boast in a primeval cell that planned it all?
The fool may do that if he chooses.
But in the end He loses.

For God made possible all we see
And soon will make a better heaven and earth
For eternity.
And in that day no one will say.
Evolution did it all-Hip Hip Hooray!

No! God will get the credit for what He has done.
All glory will go to Him and His Son.
Those who believe and give Him space
Will ever, always, look adoringly on His face!
http://www.youtube.com/watch?v=PVCrpGRSlow
Free Bible Course Call 925 828 1623

89

Hi Amit,

We enjoyed our stay at Day's Inn. It was good to talk to you. I hope you have been able to read the booklet LIVING WATER. I underlined parts of the book that totally changed my life for the better 57 years ago. I was in the Air Force, 20 years old and my life was so changed my mother wrote the chaplain at the Air Base and asked him what happened to me. He told her that "He has had a deep religious experience and it will all pass away in a little while." Fifty Seven years have gone by and it has not passed away. Why not? Because it was not getting religion, it was coming to know the God who created me through His Son, Jesus Christ. And the promise of the Bible is that "He who began a good work in me will complete it until the day of Christ, that is the day I go to be with Him forever.

Religion is mostly bad news. Jesus Christ is good news. He gives a person the gift of eternal life. Now isn't that good news. Religion says do this, do that, keep these rules, do these rituals, and so forth. And if you are good enough you will get to go to heaven. That is bad news. The good news is that none of us are good enough but God is good and gives eternal life for free to anyone who will believe and receive His Son. The gift of God is eternal life. Now, that is good news. A gift is for free. Check it out as you read the LIVING WATER booklet.

Thanks for you help and information given us during our stay at Day's Inn.

With best regards, Dean & Gloria Gossett

God's Library-Check it Out

God has a large library of books. In their inspired words are found the reason for our existence. They guide us toward profitable understanding of what is right and what is wrong, of how to be forgiven, and counted righteous. They teach us how to be mature. As well as showing us our purposes for why we exist they also reveal the future of mankind and angelic beings as they unfold the story of the heavens and the earth.

There are lots of books in God's library. Sixty-six of them are ours to read daily, 39 in the Old Testament and 27 in the New. They contain HIs story, the history of man from God's perspective and many of His actual inspired words regarding His plans for you and me and for time and for eternity. Attention to His revealed will means life abundant. Neglect of His library of truth or rejection of It means failure and destruction.

Jesus reveals to us that man must get spiritual food from "every word that proceeds out of the mouth of God."Physical food is temporary. Spiritual food is eternal. If we are wise we will spend much time feeding on the books in God's library.

The books of God are full of daily food which can fulfill all our needs. They are God's blueprints for successful life building. Beyond the 66 books of the Bible are others in HIs library. There is the Book of Life in which are found the names of all whose names are written in heaven. It is a book in which you can know for sure your name is recorded. Knowing your name is in the book of life insures escape from a final death which the Bible calls the second death.

Another of God's books contains a record of all the tears of God's children. Not a tear is shed without Him seeing it and remembering each one. God is afflicted in all our afflictions.

Then there is His book of remembrances in which He keeps a record of all people who trust Him and think about Him. He treasures the thoughts of people who think on His name so much that He calls them "His Jewels." He says, "They shall be mine in the day I make up my jewels."

Then there are His books that keep track of all our thoughts, words and actions. He keeps track of every idle word we speak and we shall give an account for all our thoughts, words and actions. Those who know Him may suffer some loss at judgement time but since all their sins are forgiven, they will receive rewards for all done to honor Him.

Those who do not know and trust Him will be judged out of His books and be cast into an eternity alone and wandering forever. There is no hint in any of these books that a person may spend time in eternity to pay for his sins. To think you can pay for your sins is an insult to God who died to take them away. Jesus said, "If you die in your sins you cannot come where I am."

Then There is God's seven sealed book in Revelation which unveils the future of both earth and heaven. Sealed on both sides, it gives us a split view of things happening or to happen on earth and in heaven. It tells us of a future time of tribulation ending in God's triumph over all evil. It tells of the resurrection of the just who trust Him who will rule and reign with Him for a thousand years on a transformed earth and then rule and reign forever with Him in eternity in a new heaven and earth.

Perhaps eternity will be a time when countless new books are written for of "making many books there is no end." Perhaps we will still read or hear the words of His 66 books in heaven with God Himself unveiling their depths in ways we never dreamed? We can be assured of this- God's Library is the Best! The only library card you will ever need is faith and the will to check out all His books. How are you doing visiting His library of priceless books? By the way-when you check them out they will never be overdue. Just make sure you have sense enough to believe, obey, read and meditate on them continually. If you do, you will be like a tree planted by a river of water that continually bears precious, delicious fruit. Then whatever you do will prosper. "I found Your Words and I ate them and they were to me the joy and rejoicing of my heart(Jer. 15:16)."The B I B L E. That's the book for me. How about you?

Sing about it: <http://www.youtube.com/watch?v=9j9K5m7oP2A>

God's Plans For You & Me

The Bible clearly tells us God's plans for you and me in the Old and New Testaments: **"I know the plans I have for you," declares the Lord, "plans to prosper you and not to harm you, plans to give you hope and a future. Then you will call upon me and come and pray to me and I will listen to you and I will hear you. You will seek me and find me when you seek for me with all your heart." Jeremiah 29:11-13** Finding Him is His first purpose for us as also stated in the N.T. as Acts 17:26,27 says, "...seek the Lord, in the hope that you might reach out for Him and find Him...He is not far from each one of us;"

Jesus tells us clearly, in a story of two men, that finding Him is only a heart felt prayer away. One of the two men found God and the other did not. Jesus' story tells clearly how to seek God and find Him and how not to come to Him: **Jesus spoke this parable to some who trusted in themselves that they were righteous, and despised others: "Two men went up to the temple to pray, one a Pharisee and the other a tax collector. The Pharisee stood and prayed thus with himself, 'God, I thank You that I am not like other men—extortioners, unjust, adulterers, or even as this tax collector. I fast twice a week; I give tithes of all that I possess.' And the tax collector, standing afar off, would not so much as raise *his* eyes to heaven, but beat his chest, saying, 'God, be merciful to me a sinner!' I tell you, this man went down to his house justified *rather* than the other; for everyone who exalts himself will be humbled, and he who humbles himself will be exalted." Luke 18:9-14.**

The story of the Pharisee and the tax collector tell how to, and how not to experience God's plans. The tax collector was forgiven and after praying from his heart was instantly counted right by God. The Pharisee prayed with a wrong view of God and of himself and so didn't find Him and was not counted right by God.

So the first step in knowing His plans is coming to Jesus like the humble, repentant tax collector. Once you admit your total, undeserved need for Him to forgive you and count you right, you will experience the first plan Jesus has for you. That plan is to believe Him, to be forgiven, to be counted right by Him and to have eternal life. Jesus tells us clearly that **"God so loved the world(that's you and me) that He gave His only begotten Son that whosoever(that's you and me) believes in Him shall not perish but instead have eternal life." John 3:16.**

When I was invited to come to Jesus, at age 20, I felt helpless. So I told Him how I felt & asked Him to help me, I said, "I can't come to You unless You help me." And He heard me and helped me come to Him. That was 60 years ago and once I believed that first part of HIs plan for me, I have continued to experience the rest of His plans for my life.

. God'a plans include having **"all things(even failures) work together for good as you love God back for first loving you." Rom 8:28,29** His plans are to prosper you and give you peace. So to find His plans for you come to Him every day, learn and believe His words in the Bible and do what He says. **"Faith (**to experience Gods plans) **comes by hearing and hearing by the Word of God."Rom. 10:17 "He that comes to God must believe that He is and that He is a rewarder of those who diligently seek Him."** Heb.11:6

Sing this song and believe it and for certain you will begin experiencing God's plans for you. https://www.youtube.com/watch?v=866oPHO30m8&noredirect=1

God's Two Books

The prophecy of earth and sky is God's book to you and I
It speaks clearly to all mankind-the hand that made us is divine.
The prophecy of God's Greater Book unfolds a greater look,
A look revealing God's glory and stature
That lifts us higher than His message through nature.
Two books that work together hand in hand
The book of creation and the book of Holy writ
Are the Rock on which I sit.
So I rest in Him without pause.
I joy in Him the uncaused Cause

God's Valentine For You

My Daughter Glenda asked me, "What is the very first Valentine God gave?"

I shared with her both Ezekiel 11:19,26 where it says God takes away a stony heart and gives those who respond a new heart of flesh. And I shared 2 Cor. 5:17,18 where God recreates people who come to His Son for salvation. It says, "If any one be in Christ, he is a new creation. Old things have passed away (an old sinful heart is replaced with a new pure heart) and all things become new.

Glenda's great answer was John 3:16 shared below with you.

John 3:16 For God so loved you that He gave His only begotten Son that if you believe and receive HIM, you will have the greatest gift possible. "Blessed be God our God who gave for us His well beloved Son, the gift of gifts, all other gifts in one."

God's greatest gift Includes truth, a new heart, love, forgiveness, peace, joy, patience, eternal life, goodness, kindness, faith, humility, self control, His purpose, wisdom, removal of the fear of death, heaven, a perfect hope, and certainty.

For a truly Happy Valentine's Day receive God's Valentine, His gift of gifts? if you do then give Him back your heart. By His Spirit Jesus then joins and lives in your heart. Herein is love, not that we loved God but that He first loved us. Then we join with Him and give Him our heart. We return His love because He first loved us! Amen!

We are going to give this Valentine Card from God to a large group of retired people living at Bethesda Retirement Center in Hayward, Calif. Please pray for them and if you have received God's Valentine, you may want to pass it on to someone else. Thank you. Dean

Good & Bad Fear

The Bible mentions fear 501 times in various forms. Healthy fear is to fear God. It is the beginning of wisdom. It means to stand in awesome respect and obedience and even fearful trembling sometimes. Healthy fear puts God first above anyone or anything. Jesus put it this way in **Matthew 10:28,** "And do **not fear** those who kill the body but cannot kill the soul. But rather **fear** Him who is able to destroy both soul and body in hell."

The worst thing you might fear in this life is someone who might and could kill you. But if you fear God rightly by believing Him completely and are counted right before God by faith in His love, forgiveness and promise about His Son who gave His life for you, then you have eternal life and can not perish even if someone kills you. If you fear God in the Biblical sense you need not fear someone killing you because the moment your body is killed your soul lives on forever and cannot perish. If we fear God and obey Him out of fear to displease Him, we need fear nothing else. His perfect love enables healthy fear of Himself and casts out all unhealthy fear.

If it is true that the beginning of wisdom is to fear God, which it is, then the beginning of stupidity is to not fear Him, to not believe in Him or believe Him.

Once we fear Him and believe Him He helps relieve our other fears. We won't have to fear life or death. We know He loves us and we can love Him back. We know He will never leave or forsake us. We know He has gone to prepare a place for us in His beautiful city. We can be sure of that because He is God and He does not lie. It can truly be said, "If we fear God and believe in His Word and Son, and do what He says, we have nothing else to fear!"

Good Birthdays & The Best Birthday

Yesterday I was told by a friend of my wife and I, about her Father who turned 94 today. She told us that happily at 94 he still drives.   I had met him many years before and the minute she told me about his birthday I thought of another older man who was a leader in the land of Israel in the first century AD. His name was Nicodemus. Probably to avoid the crowds who flocked to Jesus, Nicodemus went to talk to Jesus one evening and had a personal interview with him. It turned out to be about two kinds of births, natural and spiritual.

Nic's first words to Jesus were, "Teacher," he said, "we all know that God has sent you to teach us. Your miraculous signs are evidence that God is with you." Jesus replied, "I tell you the truth, unless you are born again, you cannot see the Kingdom of God." John 3

In other words Nicodemus and everyone else needs to have a new birthday in order to see, to comprehend the kingdom of God (God's spiritual rule over all). Our first birthday comes about by the will of our father and mother. Another birthday is needed not by the will of a man and woman but by the will of God. That new spiritual birth enables a person to grasp the things of God.

Nicodemus was confused and asked Jesus, "What do you mean? How can an old man go back into his mother's womb and be born again?"

Jesus explained the need for another birth besides our natural birth,

Jesus replied, "I assure you, no one can enter the Kingdom of God without being born of water and the Spirit. Humans can reproduce only human life, but the Holy Spirit gives the birth of spiritual life. So don't be surprised when I say, 'You must be born again.'   The wind blows wherever it wants. Just as you can hear the wind but can't tell where it comes from or where it is going, so you can't explain how people are born of the Spirit."

"How are these things possible?" Nicodemus asked. Jesus replied, "You are a respected Jewish teacher, and yet you don't understand these things? I assure you, we tell you what we know and have seen, and yet you won't believe our testimony. But if you don't believe me when I tell you about earthly things, how can you possibly believe if I tell you about heavenly things? No one has ever gone to heaven and returned. But the Son of Man, Jesus himself, has come down from heaven"

Jesus has come down from heaven and he explains the difference between natural and supernatural, spiritual birth. We can understand that our natural birth was caused by the conception brought about by our mother and father. We were born of water surrounding us in our mother's womb. We know it has happened. A new spiritual birth is caused by the entrance of God's invisible Spirit which causes us to be born again.

Our friend''s father has had 94 amazing birthdays but the question he and we need to ask is, "Have I had the best birthday of all?" Have I been born from above by God's Spirit? Without that birth I can not see or enter the kingdom of God. So a wise person wants to know how he can experience the best birthday of all, born again by God's Spirit. Natural birthdays are good news. A spiritual birthday is the best news. How does it happen?

Jesus explains how. "And as Moses lifted up the bronze snake on a pole in the wilderness, so the Son of Man must be lifted up, so that everyone who believes in him will have eternal life.? For this is how God loved the world: He gave his one and only Son, so that everyone who believes in him will not perish but have eternal life. Being born again is having life eternal!

The question for our friend's father and all of us is, "Will we do what is right and come to the light and have a second birth or will we reject the light because we have to admit our sins and trust Jesus? My prayer for us all who read this is that we be among all who believe him and accept him, so that he will give you the right to become children of God, born—not with a physical birth resulting from human passion or plan, but a birth that comes from God. If you haven't believed do it today and experience your best birthday ever! John 1:12,13

Good Idea By the Present Pope?

The Pope is advocating marriage for priests.

Roman Catholic Flaws-Will he make more needed changes? Here are some more suggested changes for the pope to bring about.

Only one should be called our true spiritual Father with a capital F, that is God the Father. If RC's are called Father it should be pointed out that scripture tells us to call only God our Father with a capital F. So make sure leaders who lead people to Christ are called fathers with a small f. Actually, being called father by an apostle with a small f is only used once that I can find, by the Apostle Paul. Correct mean if you find more.

Also Peter(Never Called the Pope) was married and Jesus healed his mother in law and she accompanied Peter at least sometimes in his travel. Paul brings this out when he says "Can't we have a wife accompany us as Peter did" though apparently Paul did not have a wife accompany him. Again Paul would have been a better choice for being a pope since he is never spoken of being married and he clearly teaches, while it is good for some to remain single, he never told anyone to vow to be single. That is another example of twisted scripture which has caused much sorrow in the RC church because many so called priests violate their vows committing sexual sin against women and sometimes children.

I read that the present Pope may be advocating marriage by priests. Bravo! Now if he just adds to that all who trust Christ are priests, and that Mary was a sinner saved by grace, and that the wine of communion doesn't change to Jesus' blood when you drink it, and that Mary did die like all of us must and thenwill be caught up to heaven, and that it is not necessary to wear fancy clothes as priests, and that an ordinary believer may partake of both the cup and the bread without a person elevated above the common crowd to do it, and doing away with the hundreds of RC traditions which bring to naught the simplicity that is in Christ. Then if RC leaders don't elevate themselves above the other believers rejecting the doctrine of the **Nicolaitans**, if they preach the clear simple gospel of Christ like Billy Graham and others, IF they do those things contact me and I will support you.

My donations go to people who are in need, to leaders who go into all the world and preach the good news of Christ instead of emphasizing the clergy(not in your Bible) over the laity(also not in your Bible or mine). Beware lest any man lead you astray from the simplicity in Christ through vain deceit and empty repetitions and traditions after the the rudiments of the world and not after Christ.

May God enlighten you by His Word and enlighten me so we stick to the simplicity of Christ instead of the flawed view of Him projected by the world.

He is the Savior and no one comes to the Father except by Him. Amen!

Best Regards,

Dean L Gossett, a sinner saved by grace!

The Good News or Bad News Test

Dennis,

I haven't met you but want you to know that I along with many Americans appreciate the cost you paid fighting for our country. I was in the service from 1954 until 1958 and appreciate every vet like your self who paid a price for defending our country. While in the Air Force I heard good news that totally changed my life. That happened 62 years ago and it is still the most wonderful news I ever heard. It changed my life forever. It is the news in the Bible about Jesus. Some people think it is bad news because they don't really understand it. Is it good or bad news? Check out His words listed below and respond to each by choosing G, That is Good news! or by choosing B, That is Bad news! These are all promises made by God. One thing about promises made by God is that unlike most politicians who fail to keep their promises, He always keeps His promises. Check them out to see what you think.

Here are the promises below made by the Lord Jesus Christ: Mark each one G for good or B for bad.

"I am come that you might have life and that more abundantly." G or B "Whoever comes to me I will in no way cast out." G or B "I am the way, the truth and the life. No man comes to the Father except by me." G or B "Who ever drinks of this water(physical water) shall thirst again but whosoever drinks of the water(spiritual) that I give shall never thirst again but out of his innermost being will flow rivers of living water." G or B "I am the good shepherd. The good shepherd gives His life for the sheep." G or B "Whoever follows me shall not walk in darkness but shall have the light of life." G or B "Let not your heart be troubled. Neither let it be afraid. You believe in God. Believe also in me. In my Father's house are many mansions. If it were not so I would have told you. I go to prepare a place for you and if I go away will come again and receive you to myself that where I am there you may be also." G or B "I am the door. By me if any man enter in, he shall be saved." G or B "I will never leave you nor forsake you." G or B "God so loved the world that He gave His only begotten Son that whosoever believes in Him should not perish but have everlasting life. G or B "He who believes in **the** Son has everlasting life; and he who does not believe **the** Son shall not see life, but **the wrath of God** abides on him." G or B "If you do not believe that I am *He (the Christ, the Savior, the One Sent to fully reveal God the Father)* you will die in your sins and you cannot come where I am." G or B "If you abide in My word, you are My disciples indeed. And you shall know the truth, and the truth shall make you free." G or B

The above quotes are all good news if you believe Jesus Christ's promises in each, but bad news if you don't believe Him. As for me I stand fully on His Word and I am saved and free! How about you? Good news becomes bad news if you reject it. So where do you stand? Believing or unbelieving? Your choice determines your eternal destiny.

Choose the words of this song and jump for joy today for you will have a perfect, not an imperfect hope! https://www.youtube.com/watch?v=QVeHDun_oEQ>

The Bible and the Stars -
VIRGO (A) The prophecy of the promised seed.
- ○ COMA. (= The desired). The woman and child the desired of all nations (in the most ancient Zodiacs).
- **LIBRA** (B) The Redeemer's atoning work.
  - ○ CRUX. The Cross endured.
- **SCORPIO** (B) The Redeemer's conflict.
  - ○ SERPENS. Assaulting the man's heel.
- **SAGITTARIUS** (A) The Redeemer's triumph.
  - ○ LYRA. Praise prepared for the Conqueror.

The Second Book. The Redeemed.
- **CAPRICORNUS** (C) The result of the Redeemer's sufferings.
  - ○ DELPHINUS. The dead One rising again.
- **AQUARIUS** (D) The Blessings assured.
  - ○ CYGNUS. The Blesser surely returning.
- **PISCES** (D) The Blessings in abeyance.
  - ○ THE BAND. The great enemy, "Cetus.".
- **ARIES** (C) The Blessings consummated.
  - ○ CASSIOPEIA. The captive delivered.

The Third Book. The Redeemer. "The glory that should follow."
- **TAURUS** (E) Messiah coming to rule.
  - ○ ORION. The Redeemer breaking forth as Light.
  - AURIGA. Safety for His redeemed in the day of wrath.
- **GEMINI** (F) Messiah as Prince of princes.
  - ○ LEPUS. The enemy trodden under foot.
- **CANCER** (F) Messiah's redeemed possessions.
  - ○ URSA MINOR. The lesser sheepfold.
  - ○ URSA MAJOR. The fold and the flock.
- **LEO** (E) Messiah's consummated triumph.
  - ○ **HYDRA**. The old serpent destroyed.

The Greatest Lesson of My Life

I have learned the greatest lesson of my life in the last few weeks. I had a devastating experience which left me broken at heart as a long time friend forsook me. I called two people and shared it with them. Two leaders in our church, Tim & Gary, both helped bear my burden and counseled and prayed with me. It resulted in my letting go of the problem and giving it to God. They helped bear my burden. The next day I got a telephone call from two people who shared broken heart experiences with me. I was able to bear their burdens and pray for them. The input in my own life of those who shared my burden helped my output to bear the burdens of two others the very next day.

I was able to overcome my lost-friend-heart ache by realizing a little what Jesus felt when all His friends forsook Him and fled. Later they were reconciled. So I was enabled to thank God for my trial and realize that it had a purpose.

All my trials, sufferings, and failures and yours have been allowed in our life that we might relate to the Lord Jesus' sufferings and learn from Him to have patience, to encourage, to comfort and to help strengthen others! Every trial and trouble in our lives has a purpose. It is meant for Jesus' glory and our, and others ultimate encouragement and hope.

God allows suffering for us to identify with Jesus sufferings and victory over them and for us to know the joy that comes after suffering for and with Him. Knowing that there is a purpose for both good and bad experiences will fill your life with not only joy but a heart to encourage others. It was for the joy set before Him that Jesus endured the suffering of the cross.

That joy is His people forgiven, reconciled and with Him forever.

Think about it, Jesus told Paul that he was chosen to show what great things he must suffer for His name's sake! That is true to some degree for everyone who follows Jesus. The trials and sufferings of the present are light in comparison to the joys that are coming to us in the future. Those joys are ours even now as we trust God in the midst of our hurt. I consider the greatest lesson of my life to be learning to trust God in the bad, as well as the easy days,

During the hard days we can suffer and leave Him out and gain nothing or we can suffer and be thankful and triumph in everything we do. Our trials are for our learning that we might grow and glorify God by helping and encouraging others. Bear one another's burdens and so fulfill the law of Christ which is loving others as He did and still does through us. What is your reaction to this? Sing about it here:
https://www.youtube.com/watch?v=X6yDFn3OAFo>

Our Greatest Need Met?

Our greatest need is to be loved, forgiven and accepted by God and to love, accept and make God the center and circumference of our lives. The answer to meeting our greatest need is in the first book of the Bible in Genesis 4. Two brothers approach God. One, Abel, is accepted. The other, Cain. is rejected. Why?

Abel came to God His way. The Lord respected Abel and his offering. God had killed the first sacrifice and made clothing from the skin of the animals to clothe Adam and Eve. His way of acceptance was through offering a sacrifice which Abel did.

Cain refused to come to God His way. Cain had a sinful attitude and a wrong offering. God did not respect Cain or his offering. Cain didn't like it that God rejected him. He became angry and sulked. God gave Cain another chance. He told him that sin was at the door of his life and that he needed to master it.

Cain had a conversation with Abel in a field. It is likely that Abel told his brother the right way to approach God.

Cain inspired by The Wicked One didn't listen to God or his brother. He took out his anger on his brother killing him. Cain was sentenced to a life of misery apart from God in the land of Nod. There he spent his life asleep spiritually

His rejection is a sample of the endless suffering which is the fate of all who reject God's way   Does God want that for anyone? No! No! No!. He is not willing that any should perish but that all should come to Him His way and be forgiven, accepted and fit forever for heaven. Able was accepted because his lamb pointed forward to God's Son who would be the Lamb of God who would sacrifices Himself to take away your sin and mine. All who accept His sacrifice will know His love, forgiveness and acceptance.

To be accepted today, the Lord Jesus Christ stands at the door of your heart. He knocks and says, "If you open the door of your life I will come in..."

If so you will know your reason for being here: From one man God made every nation of men, that they should inhabit the whole earth; and he determined the times set for them and the exact places where they should live." **God did this so that all people would seek him and perhaps reach out for him and find him, though he is not far from each one of us."** Acts 17:26,27

How far away is God?   He is no further away than sincere prayer to let Him in. Then your greatest need will be met.

God bless you,
   Love to you, Dean

Grief Turned Into Joy

I often feel the grief and hurts people sometimes experience, especially those close to me. But I know that God can bring good out of those griefs eventually. **The Devil means our trials and failures to destroy us but God can turn them into good to destroy him.**

I prayed for five years for a failure that caused me grief and God finally turned it into joy. Friendship lost was restored through forgiveness. God is not in a hurry like we are but knows how to eventually bring about good out of our suffering.

Thank you, Lord for being able to bring good out of our bad experiences. May that be true for my friends who read this. In all our afflictions, we know You are afflicted. **Thank You for feeling our hurts which are for a moment and eventually exchanging them for our blessings which are forever!**

Guard the Treasure

Guard the treasure entrusted to you with the help of the Holy Spirit?
2:Tim 1:14
Thank you Lord for the great treasure entrusted to me.
It's a treasure that cost you your Son, but to me it is free!
It is what and who you are.
It shines in my heart
Like a bright star!
It tells me why I am on earth.
It brought me a new and joyous birth,
A new birth of eternal life and peace,""

A joy that will never, never cease
It's a treasure of wisdom & knowledge that will ever only increase.
It's a treasure of golden love
Leading me to a final home a new earth and heaven above!
I treasure it every day and every night.
It gives me wings for daily flight.
It relieves me of sorrow and grief.
It comforts my heart with deep relief.
It clothes me with all that is right and perfect
It dresses me in God's righteousness,
Enfolds me in waves of His graciousness.
O yes I will guard this treasure entrusted to me.
And pass it on to faithful women and men,
Keep it going on always without end.
It's a treasure meant for all.
All who find it stand tall!
Then they share it and pass it on to as many as they can,
For it is treasure enough for every woman and man.
What is this treasure you ask?
It is God's gift to every person with sense enough to believe,
It's God's work for you to receive.
It is the gift of gifts, all other gifts in one.
It is is God's precious treasured Son!
Will you take Him as your own?
If so you'll sit with Him at His eternal throne!

Half-Truths Replaced by Whole Truths

When God put Adam and Eve in the garden he gave them only one command, "Of every tree of the garden you may freely eat: But of the tree of the knowledge of good and evil you shall not eat: for in the day that you eat of it you shall surely die." Gen: 2:16,17 The serpent who is the Devil is evil just like the last four letters of his name. His evil tricked Eve into eating the fruit by telling her a partial truth.

The Devil told her that she would become like God knowing good and evil. That part of what he said was true. But the other parts of what he said were a lie. He emphasized that she **could not** eat of every tree in the garden rather than **she could** eat of every tree but just one. She corrected the Devil's lie telling him they could eat of all the trees in the garden but one and they were not to touch it. If they did she said they would die. Satan then told a boldface lie, "You shall not die."

Eve fell for Satan's lie and Adam followed suit. They did become like God knowing good and evil. God Himself says so, "Behold, the man is become as one of us, to know good and evil:." Gen. 3:22 The problem with them knowing good and evil was that apart from a relationship with God they could do no good and they had already experienced evil's deathly consequences which cut them off from their relationship with Him.

But God who is absolutely good had a solution for Adam and Eve! He in His goodness sought out the sinful pair, killed an innocent animal, and made new animal skin clothing for them. They came out of hiding, took off their fig leaves and put on the new clothes God in love had made for them.

That first sacrifice of an animal was a foreshadowing of God's final sacrifice of His Son. Since we also know good from evil and have failed, so we need God to enable us to be forgiven of sin and to resist evil. We need to put on God's new, totally-good-clothing of righteousness. He accomplished that good for us when His Son met sin and Satan head on at the cross and defeated evil. Jesus is the way to God, **the truth of God**, and the life of God. Trust Him instead of the Devil's evil half truths and He will give you the gift of His own goodness and righteousness.

This Song by F.W. Pitt and sung by Phillip Keaggy sums up the remedy for all that ails us: https://www.youtube.com/watch?v=EISJs-5N3js>

Happy Day Every Day

<u>Psa. 118:24</u> This is the day which the LORD hath made; we will rejoice and be glad in it.<u>Ezek. 39:8</u> Behold, it is come, and it is done, saith the Lord GOD; this is the day whereof I have spoken.

God in grace has made a way
That I can praise Him every day!
He died to put away my sin
And rose to give me life within!
I died with Him upon the cross
And rejoice each day in its loss!
Good riddance to all my faults and sin
Now I can really live and love and win!
For what was bad turned out best
It bought me love and endless rest!
I look anew upon that day
That washed my sins away!
He took upon Himself God's fierce wrath
To put me on His righteos path!
A path that leads through pain
To heaven's glory and endless gain!
So what shall I sing and say
On this happy resurrection day?
I sing happy day! "Happy day!
Jesus washed my sin away!
He taught me how to love and pray
And live rejoicing every day!
"Happy day! Happy day!
Jesus washed my sin away!"
So when they bury me in the ground
Listen carefully- let these words resound.
When you visit my grave's six foot mound
Don't bother to cry as you look around!
Lift your head up high.
Look into the sky
Jesus rose and so have I!
We, His people, are not here. We're living it up
We're drinking from His overflowing cup!
We're in His Mansion in the sky.
Which is more than pie in the sky bye and bye!
Our pain and tears are gone.
We're frolicking and dancing on Heaven's lawn!
We're singing a song of joy untold
While we swirl around on a floor of gold!
Once we were squares on the earth
Now we're square dancing on heaven's turf!
Our enemies are defeated and tossed away
Gone forever On this our Coronation day!
So rejoice in his death and grand resurrection.
Trusting Him was and is our best reflection!

Happy Day! A New First Day

In the first book of the Bible the earth began, dark and void. Then on the first day of the week the light of God burst on the scene. There was evening and there was morning, the first day.

Much later on the third day after Christ's crucifixion a new first day began. The darkness of death was wiped out by the new resurrected life of our Savior. On each of God's creative days, first there was evening and then morning. First the night, then the day. First the physical death of Christ, then supernatural life when the Son rose on that first Easter morning!

So it is with us, if we trust Jesus' finished work on the cross. The darkness of sin came first. It was evening and then the Son rose and His morning of victory became the joy of a new forgiven life for us.

Those who come to Christ are not children of the night but children of the day. We have our dark experiences but they are obliterated. "Tears may endure for a night but joy comes in the morning." Jesus endured the cross because of the joy set before Him. And what is that joy? It is you and I forgiven and set free from our sin and worshipping God as we should. It is you and I being with Jesus, with the Father and with His Spirit forever.

Whatever you or I are going through if we exercise faith in the God who made the day follow the evening, we shall eventually experience the bright joy of victory. Have you lost a friendship, lost a loved one, lost a job, lost your health, lost your joy? Cheer up! No matter how long it lasts, your trust in God will make you more than a conqueror through Him who loves you.

With God commanding the light to shine out of darkness, we will win in the end. Joseph in the Bible rejected by family, thrown into a pit, falsely thrown in prison, was victorious. He went from pit, to prison, to palace, exalted in the end after enduring the night of rejection. Then the sun rose on Joseph.

He lost a coat of many colors. It was replaced by a slaves garb, and then a prison uniform but both were exchanged for a Royal Robe exalting him to second highest leader in all the land of Egypt.

So victory will be with us as we trust! Trust and love are stronger than death! Let's get on board the believing train. Let's march upward to Zion, the beautiful city of God. That is a city with no night! God is it's center and continual light! Because we know Him, soon and very soon we will see the Lord and live with Him and each other in the land of endless day! Amen!

Song, Soon & Very Soon, https://www.youtube.com/watch?v=PkrgFwTXiFc>

Harold Camping's Foolish Predictions

Harold has set a date that the day of Judgement will be today, May 21. Amazingly this same man stated wrongly in his book 1994, that Christ would come on September, 6,1994. Guys like Camping cause some to laugh at Christianity. His dates will live in infamy! At this point date setters for Christ's return have been wrong 242 times.

However, even though Camping and date setters are wrong, we can be assured that Christ IS returning some day. The Bible promises his return over 300 times in the New Testament. Though we do not know the exact date, it is a date everyone will remember.

Because crackpots set dates contrary to what the Bible says doesn't invalidate the truth that Christ will return.

Here is what Jesus says about his return which Camping and other date setters ignore, "But of that day and hour no one knows, not even the angels of heaven, but my Father only." (Matt. 24:36) Again Jesus tells us, "it is not for you to know times or seasons which the Father has put in His own authority." (Acts 1:6)

Christ IS coming back but when? Jesus doesn't give a day or hour but gives us some clues in Matt. 24 ending that passage with these words regarding his return, "Therefore you also be ready. For the Son of man is coming at an hour you do not expect him." (Matt. 24:44)

The important question one must ask himself is, "Will I be ready when Christ returns?" Do you know how to be ready?

Here's how to be ready. Read, heed, and believe in your heart these words:

First, admit that you have sinned by doing wrong and by falling short of doing right. "All have sinned and come short of the glory of God." (Romans 3:23)

Second, admit that you deserve death because of your sin and be ready to receive the gift of God which is eternal life! "The wages of sin is death but the gift of God is eternal life through Jesus Christ our Lord" (Romans 6:23)

Third, realize God's great love for you: "God demonstrates His own love for us in that while we were still sinners, Christ died for us." Rom. 5:8)

Fourth, confess with your lips and believe in your heart that Jesus is your Lord who died for you to take away and forgive your sins, and then he rose from the dead to give you the gift of eternal life. "Say the welcoming word to God —"Jesus is my Master"—embracing, body and soul, God's work of doing in us what he did in raising Jesus from the dead. That's it. You're not "doing" anything; you're simply calling out to God, trusting him to do it for you. That's salvation. With your whole being you embrace God setting things right, and then you say it, right out loud: "God has set everything right between him and me!" (Rom. 10:9,10)

Finally, Receive Jesus Christ right now and experience a spiritual rebirth making you ready for Christ's return. God says, "At the right time I heard you. On the day of salvation I helped you." Listen, now is God's acceptable time! Now is the day of salvation! . "Yet to all who received him, to those who believed in his name, he gave the right to become children of God— children born not of natural descent, nor of human decision or a husband's will, but born of God.

If you really do receive Jesus Christ with all your heart, your faith will be seen by the new life he gives you. Then you will be ready whenever He returns. God never lies so you can really count on his promise when you come to him to give you the "gift of God which is eternal life." (Rom. 6:23) Then you will be ready whenever He comes back!

Love to you,
Dean

He Saves the Best Until Last

All through the Bible God saves the best until last. The apostle Paul says it like this, "Howbeit **that** was not first **which is spiritual**, but **that which is** natural; and afterward **that which is spiritual**. First the natural then the spiritual which exceeds and enhances the natural. 1Cor:15:46

For example the first man Adam failed and was driven from the garden of Eden. About 4000 years later God sent His Son in keeping with His promise that Adam's wife Eve would have a descendent that would crush the serpent who deceived her. The first Adam brought sin into the world. The last Adam, Jesus took sin out of the world for all who believe. First the natural Adam. Then the supernatural last Adam. Jesus. The first man Adam is of the earth, earthy. The last Adam, the Lord Jesus Christ was of heaven, heavenly.

For the one who follows Christ that which is spiritual and best is last. First, we are born of our natural parents with natures that go astray. Then when we hear of Christ and believe and come to Him we are born again, not of natural parents but of our supernatural Father, God. The second birth is absolutely better than our first because the Spirit washes away our sin and gives us a new spiritual, supernatural birth. By that birth we see, comprehend and enter the kingdom of God. First the natural birth which fits us for earth. Then the spiritual birth which fits us for heaven. Have you had that birth?   If not, read John 3 and especially verse 16 and John 1:12-14 which show you clearly how to experience the best last, which is a new life in Christ.

Then the best being last is illustrated in marriage. First Adam married Eve. When they failed by sinning they were ashamed. God came to them in the garden and found them hiding. They were hiding behind fig leaf clothes and hiding among the trees of the garden. He asked them the first questions in the Bible, "Where are you? Have you eaten of the tree which I forbid you?"   They admitted they had disobeyed Him. God was gracious to them. He took an animal, the first sacrifice, which pictured the last, best sacrifice, the sacrifice of Christ. From the animal skin he made clothing to cover them. They got rid of their own fig-leaf clothing effort and hiding behind the trees and came out. Then he clothed them in acceptable clothes of His design. First their failure. Then God's success in clothing them. First, came the natural, then the supernatural which was better.

First, throughout the Bible were the offering of animal sacrifices which cover but can't take away sin. Then the offering of God's Son 4000 years later did more then cover sin. His sacrifice is best because it takes away sin and perfects forever those who trust Him as Savior. First the inferior sacrifices of animals which can't take away sin. Then the superior sacrifice of Christ which washes away our sin completely and gives us the very righteousness of God.

The last marriage mentioned in the Bible also illustrates the best being last principle. It is called the Marriage Supper of the Lamb. The first marriage in Eden and later marriages were good but not the   best because they were   accompanied by failure as well as success. The last marriage will be best because it will be perfect. It is called the Marriage Supper of the Lamb between Christ and His bride the church. It takes place after this life when those of His church are married to Christ. First we die. Then we experience the best as we are raised from death to the final marriage, the joining together of Jesus with us His people. it will not be a marriage as we know it now between one man and one woman but a uniting of all believers intimately close to God and to one another. It will be a marriage feast of joy unmatched. No separation! No death! No fear! No failure! It will be the last and best.   First, the natural marriage.   Then the supernatural, spiritual marriage. Check this out throughout scripture and see over and over again that God saves the best until last. Sing one of these songs, and believe it and you will be present at the last and perfect marriage. https://www.youtube.com/watch?v=3Spl1jCczao>

Headed For the River

I received a note today from my cousin Marsha in Wyoming telling me she was headed for the river in the rain to work the horses. It brought back to mind a miracle that happened on their ranch.

She and her husband, John own a large horse ranch. Once her husband John went out on his horse to work and didn't return. She prayed for the Lord's help. Then ran to the barn and got a horse. She rode off to search for him.

In answer to her prayer she saw John's hat waving above the brush. But before you hear the rest of the story you need to know this.

Earlier in the day Marsha was asked by John to take with him two new books she had just gotten. Their titles were Surrender and Brokenness. Both were by Nancy Leigh DeMoss. Her husband asked if he could take them with him.   He put them in a bag and placed them in the front of his closed coat. Then got on his horse and left.

My cousin Marsha became concerned because John didn't return when he was suppose to. She prayed, then ran to get on her horse. Looking for him, she saw his riderless horse by Crazy Woman Creek on their property. Then she looked around and saw John waving his hat above the brush. She dismounted, got on their four wheeler and went to help him. She found him lying on the ground. His horse had reared up and came over backwards on him. The saddle horn hit

ground. His horse had reared up and came over backwards on him. The saddle horn hit him right in the stomach rupturing his intestines. She drove him to the doctor in Buffalo,Wyoming. The doctor said that the two books Surrender and Brokenness broke the impact of the saddle horn and helped save his life.

As I recalled that story I thought of a song called "Shall We Gather at the River." Here is the first line of the song:

Shall we gather at the river,
    where bright angel feet have trod,
    with its crystal tide forever
    flowing by the throne of God?

This song is referring to the river in heaven to which all of us who know Christ are headed. But right now we experience the creeks and rivers of earth which I believe are meant to reflect the heavenly river in some ways.

Certainly bright angel feet trod at the creek that day when Marsha prayed to find her husband. And the angel touched John at just the right time as Marsha saw his hat waving above the brush.

God acted that day near Crazy Woman Creek where John had fell. How often in the Bible God illustrates his great love and power at a creek or river. During a famine, Elijah was led miraculously to a creek called Cherith where ravens brought him food and he drank from the creek for a long time.

My father told me of Crazy Woman Creek when i was a child. I use to wonder if there really was such a creek. When my father died, he left us a little money which my wife and I used to visit Israel. On the plane from San Francisco to New York our plane was sidetracked due to bad weather. Suddenly the Captain spoke up and said,"Due to bad weather we are diverted around it. Right now we are over Crazy Woman Creek in Wyoming." It was like my dad spoke from heaven. A little thrill went up and down my spine.

My cousin's note, "Headed for the River" meant the Powder River on another part of their property where she and her husband were rounding up horses. It made me think of the great round up in the sky some day when we get to heaven's River of Life. I thought, "Wouldn't it be wonderful if I and all of her friends could be with her and John and sing the song, 'Shall we Gather at the River?'"

How gracious of God that he spared John and Marsha and really all of us through Surrender and Brokenness. Because of Christ's surrender and brokenness we are all headed for the river that flows by the throne of God. We are headed to the place the Lord said, "I will give it to you." Come go with us. We will all sing with joy as we gather together at the great miracle River of Life.

God bless you as you as you listen and sing the illustrated song on You Tube. Dean <http://www.youtube.com/watch?v=F8EIjGXtCLk>

Healing For Broken Hearts

The Bible says "God does not despise a broken and contrite heart." Have you ever had a broken heart? Here are some reasons our hearts are broken: Death of Loved One(s). Loss of a Cherished Pet, Forsaken by a Friend. Unreturned Love. Failed Marriage. Suicide of Family Member. Sinful Failure. Condemned Unfairly. A Situation Beyond One's Understanding. Suffering for Right. Being Misunderstood. Great Economic Loss.

At one time or another I have experienced some of those types of broken hearts. Why does God allow them? Though they hurt terribly God allows them to draw us to Himself desiring that at some point we will come through them victoriously. How? By taking them to Him. I went to Him with a broken heart over sinful failure confessing il and my heart was healed. I lifted my friend who forsook me to God in forgiving prayer. I found my ultimate friend in God who will never leave or forsake me. I have prayed and grieved for family members recovering from a suicide. I have grieved but forgave and prayed for someone who condemned me unjustly. I have left in God's hands mistreatment to me by another that I don't understand. I have given to God my great grief over the loss of loved ones.

In each case my heart has been healed as I believed and claimed God's word. I found that "the Lord *is* near to those who have a **broken heart**, And saves such as have a contrite spirit." Psalm 34:18

no good. Instead giving my heart to God in prayer and thanksgiving worked.. Please join me and others who have gone through a heartache and found healing. Tell Him with thanksgiving all of your concerns. Keep telling Him and thanking Him for what He will do and in time you will know a sense of God's presence and peace. You will realize that everything is working together for good as God heals your broken heart! Phil 4:6-7

One of the greatest helps for a broken heart is to see it as a sacrifice because the sacrifices of God *are* a **broken** spirit, A **broken** and a contrite **heart**— These, O God, You will not despise. **Psalm 51:17** Remember that Christ endured a sacrificial broken heart which was healed at His resurrection. He endured suffering for the joy that was set before Him. That joy is your and my forgiveness and salvation that believed and received heals our broken hearts! At the cross and the empty tomb, our hearts find healing and joy! Then no matter what, if your heart is healed you will find that whatever your circumstances, all is well with your soul. Click here and find an astonishing song showing how Horatio Spafford found healing for his overwhelming heartbreak. https://www.youtube.com/watch?v=X6yDFn3OAFo>

KEEP ME TRUE

Oh for a heart kept true to God
Oh to bless both His staff and His Rod.
Oh for a mind that mediates on His word both day and night.
Oh to hear God say, "I'll keep you on the paths in which I delight!"
Oh for me and those for whom I pray
To walk with God and never stray!
Lead me in paths of right for your name's sake.

Grant this Lord! Keep my heart awake!

Heaven's Itinerary A Time To Serve

Among the many things we do in heaven will be serving God and the Lamb(Rev. 22:3). There will be no more curse related to service as there was on the first earth. With the curse gone in the new heaven & earth service will be a complete joy.

What will we be doing ? On the first earth, before God's curse fell upon it, Adam was given the job of naming all the animals and caring for a special garden. Then paradise, the beautiful garden was lost due to sin. Christ restored paradise for us. Will we be given the service of cultivating a restored paradise?

God has named every star. Will we learn about & serve God in the maintenance of the new heavens & the new earth?

Will some of the different forms of service performed in the Bible be retained but on a higher level? Some of the kinds of service mentioned in the Bible are building, caring for the earth, naming animals and plants, governing, singing, dancing, praising God, prophesying, teaching, learning, encouraging others, and instrumental and vocal worship. Will these forms of service be practiced in eternity on a higher and more magnificent level. Perhaps? What do you think?

We do not know the exact nature of what our service is to be. But we can be assured there will be a new joy in service in eternity not known on earth as we know it now. If man was suppose to subdue and rule over the first earth and failed, why would that same task not be restored on a new earth not contaminated by sin? We are told that in heaven we will see the face of Jesus Christ, the Lamb and that His name will be on our forehead. The idea is that we clearly belong to Him. The mark of the beast means those who rejected Christ belong to the beast. In a similar contrast the name of Christ on our forehead means we belong to Him. What might the word be? The mark of the beast was 666. Will the mark on our forehead be 777 which is a trinity of complete perfection? Or will it say "My Beloved" on our heads. Surely it will not say "Lamb of God" or God on our foreheads for we are not the Lamb or God. It might say, "God's or The Lamb's"? What ever it is it means we are His and He is ours. And it means we will serve and worship Him forever.

We are designed to serve God with delight. Such service will be filled with overwhelming satisfaction as we will be God's people & He will be our God.

Meanwhile now while living on a cursed earth we are to serve Him and gain a partial degree of the joy yet to come.

Serving Him now can be sweet. Imagine the sweetness of sinless, pure service. Looking forward to serve Him with you in eternity, the final frontier.

In His service now, Dean

Sing about it here:: https://www.youtube.com/watch?v=lhTNYAnfutQ>

Rhonda Bigby <rejbigby@comcast.net>
Subject: Heaven At Last

On earth we often like people that we meet immediately based on the fact that we knew someone else that we liked who looked like them. It makes me think that when we get to heaven we will be like Jesus and since everyone of us will be like Him we will immediately like and love everyone in heaven that we meet. What a great day that will be. When we all see Jesus "as He really is, we will be like Him" That will be the moment of a transforming vision beyond our highest dreams!

Heaven at Last
by Dean L Gossett

**Earth is fading
Heaven waits.
The outer man is perishing.
I glimpse the final gates.**

**Earth's vision weakens
My inner longings grow
I long to be strong
To release my grasp below.**

**To grasp and be grasped
By heaven's promises
To lay hold of them and see
That for which God laid hold of me.**

**To rise above
My tossing, restless body
To soar to the Spirit's best
To the vision of His loveliness!**

**At last I shall be fully free
Released from sin and iniquity.
Transformed, fully like God's Son.
'The victory is won!"
Heaven in Your Home**
by Dean

If you want heaven in Your home
Look to the Lord upon His throne.
Be filled with His Spirit and not wine.
He will fill your home with love Divine.

If you want heaven in Your home
Look to the Lord upon His throne.
Be filled with His Spirit and not wine.
He will fill your home with love Divine.

With Heaven in Your home
Husbands and wives won't roam.
Their hearts will be full of song and melody.
Enriched by love, respect and harmony.

.
If you want heaven at your side.
Look to the Lord's love for His bride..
He' gave Himself for her with dying arms spread
wide.
He bled and died to present her spotless and
sanctified.

If you want heaven magnified,
Call to Him who lives in His bride.
He nourishes her, sings over her, cherishes her.
He is one with her in love sacred and ever sure.

If you want harmony that lasts in your home life.
Trust the Lord, ready to live and die for your wife.
Nourish her, Cherish her. Be one in Heaven's
love-.
Bound by His marriage-binding Spirit from
above.

If you want heaven in your family
Apply the scripture's guiding remedy
Children, always do what your parents say.
As they uplift and care for you each day

Then God will fill your cup till it overflows
Watching your family as it grow and grows.
He'll fill your home from His glorious everlasting
throne.
Pouring down harmony to fit you for your final
Home!

Sing About It: http://www.youtube.com/watch?
v=pXa7CSsrUus>

Heaven is for Real & So Is Hell

The book story of the little boy, Colton Burpo, who had an out of body experience and relates what he saw in heaven is very touching and may be a boost to someone's faith in the Lord Jesus Christ. The story is interesting as Colton emphasizes that a person must believe in Jesus as Savior or he or she won't be able to go to heaven. He gives glimpses of heaven, none of which clearly violate what scripture says about heaven. He also speaks of Satan as real and that he will lose in a battle with the Lord and His followers. He mentions hell(the lake of fire) where Satan and all his followers will perish someday. He reveals that unborn babies will be in heaven as well as many little children. These observations by Colton are mostly backed by and not clearly forbidden by the Bible.

In contrast to the book, the movie unfortunately leaves out some of Colton's most important words about the need to believe in Jesus to be able to go to heaven. The movie is not super clear about the need to trust Jesus as Savior in order to go to heaven while the book is clearer. My question to those who made the movie is why did you leave out the parts Colton mentions about the necessity to believe in Jesus in order to go to heaven? Why leave out his mentioning of Satan and his final end? Why leave out Colton's concern about a dying man who he strongly says must believe in Jesus or he can't go to heaven.? Why leave out Colton's mentioning the final battle in history when Satan is defeated and cast into the lake of fire? Why leave out Colton's reaction to Satan? Why picture a woman in the movie who lost a son given comfort as if anyone that lost a son would go to heaven? In the book but not the movie it is clearly shown that her son died before birth insuring heaven for him.

One critic argues against the book because Colton says believers have wings and they argue that no one has a body in heaven until the resurrection, yet what Colton sees is not all present tense but future as well and people and angels in the book of Revelation do have bodies. There is a natural body and a spiritual body of which we have some but not all understanding. Why argue that one is dead when the spirit leaves the body and Colton is never pronounced dead so this shows the story is not true? That makes no sense since in the Bible others were raised him from the dead and the Bible doesn't explain about all the hidden details involving death and life. Why say that the painting Colton saw of Jesus by Akiane Kramatik can not be genuine because she made an image of someone in heaven which the ten commandments forbid? Actually they don't forbid making an image of something in heaven but do forbid bowing down to an image and worshipping it. Many images of things in heaven were created by Old Testament true Israelite

106

because she clearly says Jesus is God. She also believes God is love. Jesus deity becomes meaningful to us when we are born of the Spirit of God as is true of both Akiane's parents if their conversions are true being converted to Christ from being atheists.

A couple of things are absolutely sure, regardless of your response to the book and movie.That sure truth is that heaven is for real and so Is hell. Those who reject Jesus as Savior and Lord will not be in heaven but will find themselves in the lake of fire perishing. That is the real hell! Jesus speaks clearly of, two gates, two roads and two ends for all people. Everyone is either on a broad road that ends with destruction or on a narrow road which ends with life eternal.

The question boils down to this, have you trusted Jesus as your Lord? Have you believed in your heart he died to take away your sins? Have you truly believed that Jesus arose from the dead? Have you been born again? Are you on the narrow road? If so you are saved and will go to heaven.

If you have not trusted Jesus as your Lord, If you have not believed in your heart he died to take away your sins and if you do not believe He rose from the dead to save you, then you are on the broad road, lost and on your way to hell unless you have a change of heart and believe the record of good news that God has given us about His Son.

So heaven is for real. Will you be there? Hell is for real, too! Will you be there? It all depends on whether or not you believe in Jesus as the Bible says and Colton affirms. If you don't believe you can't go to heaven. Heaven will not be real for you but hell will be for real. I pray you will believe the message of God's good news about His Son loving and dying and rising again for you so that heaven will someday truly be real for you.

Heaven is Not Mentioned in the Old Testament. True or False?

Recently I heard a number of people say that heaven is not mentioned in the Old Testament. Look at the verses below from the Old Testament and decide for yourself if heaven is or is not mentioned in the Old Testament.

Heaven is a place from which God speaks: Genesis 22:11,15. The LORD, the only true God, is the God of heaven(Genesis 24:3,7).

Jacob in a dream saw God at the top of a ladder which reached to heaven from whence angels ascended and descended. Jacob called it the gate of heaven. Angels are active there and on earth (Genesis 28:12-17). There are so many of them they can not be numbered (Jeremiah 33:22). In Isaiah 6 God is seen in heaven on a throne filling a temple, clothed in a glorious robe with a gigantic train, with seraphim creatures worshiping Him.

Moses received answered prayer from heaven(Exodus 9 and 10).God talked to Moses and the people of Israel from heaven (Exodus 20:22). Moses, Aaron, Nadab, Abihu and seventy of the elders of Israel saw the God of Israel and under His feet they saw a paved work of a sapphire stone pure, holy and bright which corresponds to Rev.4:6 "a sea of glass" in heaven. (Exodus 24:9,10; Psalm 20:6".

The LORD alone is God of heaven (Deuteronomy 4:39). The heaven of heavens is the furthermost heaven. The heaven of heavens is mentioned many times in the Old Testament and seems to correspond to the "third heaven" mentioned in the New Testament (Deut.10:14 and 2 Corinthians 12:2).

God's peoples' prayers are heard in heaven (1 Samuel 5:12). It is a main dwelling place of God but only one of His dwelling places (! Kings 8:30). While the heaven of heavens is one of His dwelling places it cannot contain Him: 2 Chronicles 2:6

God hears and forgives from there (1 Kings 34. God sits on a throne there in heaven and the holy host of heaven are on each side of Him (1Kings 22:19; Psalm 11:4). The host of heaven don't argue about God's truth. Forever God's word is settled in heaven (Psalm 119:89).

Elijah was taken up into heaven in a chariot of fire and horses of fire. Where he went was obviously not just the atmospheric heavens but the place where God is (2 Kings 2:11). There is the heaven of the earthly atmosphere, the heaven of the starry sky, and then the heaven of heavens which is a main sphere of God's dwelling and spiritual activity

An <u>angel from heaven seeks to punish Israel because of David's sin of numbering the people</u> (I Chronicles 21:16). Angels, from and in heaven, are active in correcting and helping God's people in both the Old & New Testament (Psalm 91:11 and Hebrews 1:14).

God in heaven <u>mercifully reveals secrets to His own like Daniel</u> (Dan 2:18,28; Luke 8:10). God's <u>kingdom is an everlasting kingdom</u>, given from and in heaven, inhabited by His people-the saints (Dan 7:27; Hebrews 4:16;).

Some say the resurrection is not mentioned in the O.T. Nonsense! In Daniel we read of the <u>resurrection to everlasting life</u>. It also tells of <u>the resurrection to shame and everlasting contempt</u> to those who don't know Him. Everlasting life is what heaven is all about and everlasting contempt is what hell is all about (Daniel 12:1-3 & Revelation 20:1-15).

The details about heaven are more explicit in the New Testament than in the O.T., however they clearly agree and expand on what the Old Testament says about heaven. There are many other O.T. scriptures which mention heaven. These few shared here make clear that it is completely false to say heaven is not mentioned in the Old Testament. Heaven is for real in the whole Bible! Hear about God's home: <http://www.youtube.com/watch?v=4ndMZqT6i4I> Unfortunately there is an add before the music which you can click off to hear the music right away.

Heaven's Itinerary -Getting on Board & Understanding What's Next

Since beginning Heaven's Itinerary I have received some questions regarding death, heaven, and what follows. These may be helpful to you to make sure you understand and are on board Flight F I N A L from earth's death to the New Jerusalem.

What kind of form will we have in heaven?

.

When Jesus rose from the dead he ate, was touchable, was recognizable by his disciples. Scripture says, "When we see Him we shall be like him for we shall see Him as he is." We are told that our mortal body of humiliation will be transformed into His likeness and our mortal body will be exchanged for a new immortal body that will never perish. It will be more tangible and real in the ultimate sense than our present bodies.

Has anyone ever came back from the dead to tell us about what it is like or has anyone who has died shown us what it is like?

Two men died in scripture. One who was a beggar trusted God and was carried by the angels into Abraham's bosom, the place where those with faith go and a place of comfort, joy, peace and contentment. The man could see, feel, eat and enjoy refreshing water.

The other man that died was rich but bankrupt spiritually and wound up in a different place than the beggar. He could feel, talk, see and was in torment. He also recognized the beggar that had sat his gate on earth.

Jesus came back from the dead and is alive and we have lots of his descriptions of heaven. There is no night there. We won't need to sleep because we are like God and Jesus "who neither slumbers nor sleeps in heaven." There is no crime, no death, no tears, and plenty of room for each of us to enjoy the city God has prepared for all who trust Him. He said, "In my Father's house there are many dwelling places. If it were not so I would have told you. I go to prepare a place for you and if I go away, I will come again and take you where I am.

Does a Believer in Christ have to worry about what happens after he or she dies?

Jesus told us if we believed in Him as the Christ, our Savior, we not to be troubled in our heart as we face death because it is but a step into a new and glorious eternal city and life. Also there is enough room in that city to accommodate every person who ever lived. Do the math 15,000 miles times 15,000 miles times 15000 miles. They say about 6 billion people have live up to now. Just an educated guess but if you do the math you will find there is enough room in the city to give every person about 5 square miles of space and we are told the measurements are by the calculation of men. Of course not every one will be in the city because 1/3 of the angels won't be there and many people of the human race won''t be there. We will have plenty of room plus we will have a new earth to explore and enjoy as well as a new heaven.

Again, regarding recognizing one another, we read of Moses and Elijah who died many years ago appearing with Jesus on the mount of transfiguration talking about Jesus coming death in Jerusalem. They recognized Jesus. He recognized them and Petter, James and John also recognized them. So we will recognize people in heaven that we have known.

For the believer in Christ the best is yet to come. God always saves the best until last for His people. Will you and I be there? We can know for sure if we believe John 3:16 and Romans 10:9 and John 14. Read them and any weeping you do will be flooded with joy.

What about after we die? Is their an intermediary place we go to.

If someone says, yes, to purgatory there is not one shred of evidence for this in the Bible. In fact Jesus said if we die in our sins we can't go where he is. He didn't say we can go to purgatory and pay for our sins and then join Him. No, because no one can pay for their own sins. Jesus paid for our sins by dying for us. If we could pay for our own, He should have stayed in heaven.

If by intermediary one means where does the body go after death and what happens to our spirit and soul, there is an answer. Now that Christ has died for our sins we are "immediately absent from the body and present with the Lord. But it is our Spirit and soul that go to be with Him Immediately, not our body. The Bible speaks of those who have died in Christ as being made perfect in their spirit and being present in the New Jerusalem which is where Christ is. But the body stays in the grave until it is reunited with the Spirit and Soul and transformed into a body like Christ's. There is some debate about this but this explanation makes the most sense. Absent from the body, present with the Lord today. No waiting around.

Heaven-A Time to Sing!

Some people picture all Christians in heaven only sitting on a cloud playing a harp. There will be a lot more than harp music in heaven. The Bible mentions stringed instruments, harps, trumpets, cymbals, timbrels, tambourines, psaltries, tabrets, pipes, male and female vocal music, angelic music, as well as the singing of God Himself.

There is no doubt that musical instruments and vocal music will be in heaven. In the story NINETY MINUTES IN HEAVEN a man was pronounced dead twice, He tells us he was out of body, went to heaven and came back to life after 90 minutes. He describes music he heard in heaven. He tells how he nears the gate of the heavenly city and hears singing coming from all directions. Even though the songs are different he describes them as perfect in harmony. He felt the music fill his emotions.

Think about singing now. There are a lot of differences in taste and style of music. Sometimes people argue about what is best. Someone once said, "When the Devil fell out of heaven he fell into the choir," meaning that he stirs up dissension among Christians regarding music. That will be gone in heaven.

The Bible is full of singing and heaven will be filled with the singing of angels, God's people and the singing of God Himself.

I've noticed that now on earth people write almost no songs about God singing. Yet the Bible clearly teaches that God sings over His people. We have all thrilled to outstanding singers. Imagine what it twill be like to hear God sing. We will experience that in heaven. The LORD your God is with you, the Mighty Warrior who saves. He will take great delight in you; in his love he will no longer rebuke you, but will rejoice over you with singing." Zephaniah 3:17

Will God the Father, the Spirit and the Son sing as a trio with perfect voices that combine in perfect harmony. His song over us will be filled with emotional joy and love.. Because His emotions are the highest possible, He will enjoy His love for us in song even more than we will.

We will sing to Him as well and perhaps sing together with the Father, Son and Holy Spirit. We are told that a great multitude will stand on a sea of glass, playing harps and singing the song of Moses and the song of the Lamb which is "Great and marvelous are your deeds, Lord God Almighty. Just and true are your ways, King of the ages. Who will not fear you, O Lord, and bring glory to your name? For you alone are holy. All nations will come and worship before you, for your righteous acts have been revealed."

We won't be inhibited. when we sing in heaven. Our vocal abilities will be raised to a higher level. To bless someone with a solo song is a wonderful blessing. I've experienced that only a few times in my life. Once at a kid's camp I sang a song I wrote. Once I included myself singing a song on one of my internet e-mails. To my amazement a bunch of people told me I had a nice voice. Today my 20 year old granddaughter, after Bible study together, asked me to sing to God in worship and she would listen and worship. She went to sleep after I sang for awhile. She woke up and said, "Sing me another song grandpa." So I did. She is a great joy to me. I think in heaven we will all have nice voices but God's will be the best as he sings to us who are the joy of His life.

Looking forward to singing with you, the angels, the Trinity and the music of the spheres.

Heaven -No Cancellations

When we make an itinerary for a visit on earth we are not always sure how it will turn out. My wife and I had a Mediterranean cruise planned just before the 9/11 attack occurred. The cruise line went bankrupt after 9/11 because of cancellations. So our cruise never happened.

Every believer has a Heavenly Itinerary planned out by God for him or her. The things that won't be on that itinerary make it nearly as joyous as what will be on it. If we know Christ our heavenly itinerary is sure. There will be no cancellations because of war, weather, or waning wealth. We are also told that God will wipe all tears from our eyes which means no suffering, no tragedies, no death, no crime, no curse, no sin, and no end to our joys. Heaven will be heaven as much because of what isn't there as because of what is there. Satan won't be there. No one who practices immorality will be there. No phony leaders vying for power will be there. There will be no lying, cheating, pride or jealousy there.

The Bible shows us that God always saves the best until last. Abraham looked for "a city whose builder & maker is God." He was promised to inherit all the land from the river of Egypt to the river Euphrates. Yet he died owning none of it save a cave where he was buried. That's all any of us own on this present earth, a grave. But God saved the best to last for Abraham. Now Abe has gone home and is enjoying part of the best that God saved until last- the heavenly city that he was looking for whose builder and maker is God. Abraham is in the New Jerusalem along with all just people who trusted God. Scripture says such just people have been made perfect in spirit and are now part of the city called the New Jerusalem.

We will see more about that city as we learn about its foundations, gates, streets and inhabitants in Part 2 of our Heavenly Itinerary. Then later we will see how God keeps his promise to Abraham and all who trust God as the meek inherit and enjoy the New Earth. Some day Abraham will inherit all the land promised him because unlike politicians God always keeps his promises.

To be a part of God's itinerary make sure you know your name is in the book of life. God will qualify you for all that He has planned for you if you trust Him & His Son as Savior.

Be ready to trade a temporary grave for an eternal New Heaven and Earth. The best is yet to come Looking forward to going home and seeing you there! https://www.youtube.com/watch?v=TvThHk-wMRk>

Love, Dean

Beggar & Paradise

Has anyone ever died or spoke after they died to tell us about what it is like after death? Yes! Two men died in scripture. One who was a beggar trusted God and was carried by the angels into Abraham's bosom, the place where those went who died before Christ died and rose again. For the beggar it was a place of comfort, joy, peace and contentment. The man could see, feel, eat and enjoy refreshing water.

The other man that died was rich but bankrupt spiritually and wound up in a different place than the beggar. He could feel, talk, see and was in torment. He also recognized the beggar that had sat at his gate on earth. (Luke 16)

Jesus came back from the dead and is alive and we learn Him and His apostles lots of information about heaven and hell. Jesus tells us that "In my Father's house there are many dwelling places. If it were not so I would have told you. I go to prepare a place for you that where I am you may be also." Through the apostle John Jesus tells us there is no night in heaven. We won't need to sleep because we are like God and Jesus "who neither slumber nor sleep in heaven." There is no crime, no death, no tears, and plenty of room for each of us to enjoy the city God has prepared for all who trust Him.(John 14 & Rev. 20,21)

A man named Don Piper was pronounced dead twice by medics. Ninety minutes later he came back to life. He said he saw heaven during those ninety minutes. You can read about it in the amazing book called **90 Minutes in Heaven.** He describes what he saw and heard while there and it corresponds to parts of Revelation chapters 20, 21 which was written by the Apostle John to whom Jesus revealed the future.

A boy four years old in the throes of death, had an out of body experience. He describes what he saw and heard in heaven and it confirms the Apostle John's vision of heaven. The book about this little boy is called **Heaven is For Real.**
What kind of form will we have in heaven?

.   When Jesus rose from the dead he ate, was touchable, was recognized by his disciples. Scripture says, "When we see Him we shall be like him for we shall see Him as he is." We are told that our mortal body of humiliation will be transformed into His likeness and be exchanged for a new immortal body that will never perish.

Does a follower of Christ have to worry about what happens after he or she dies?

Jesus told us not to be troubled in our heart as we face death because it is but a step into a new and glorious eternal city and   life. Also there is enough room in that city to accommodate every person who ever lived. Not everyone will be there so we will have plenty of room plus we will have a new earth to explore and enjoy as well as a new heaven.

Will you and I be there in heaven?

We can know we will be with Christ for sure if we believe   John 3:16; Romans 10:9 and John 1:12,13 & John 14. Read and heed these verses, then believe this song and come to Christ and you will go to heaven <http://www.youtube.com/watch?v=ovYPQl93zro>

What about after we die? Is their an intermediary place we go to?

Some teach we may go to purgatory but there is no evidence for that in the Bible. In fact Jesus said if we die in our sins we can't go where he is. He didn't say we can go to purgatory and pay for our sins and then join Him. No, because no one can pay for their own sins. Jesus alone paid for our sins by dying for us.

If by intermediary one means where does the body go after death and what happens to our spirit and body, there is an answer. At death we are absent from the body and present with the Lord. But it is our Spirit that goes to be with Him, not our body. The Bible speaks of those who have died in Christ as being made perfect in their spirit and being present in the New Jerusalem which is where Christ is. The body stays in the grave until it is reunited with one's spirit and transformed into a body like Christ's.

If you have any more questions, feel free to e-mail me and we can discuss them. God grant you assurance of heaven to come. Love to you, Dean

Heaven's Itinerary - A Settled Destiny

There is a statement in the last chapter of Revelation which   seems to contradict the heart of God as stated in 2 Pet.3:9. We are told that "The Lord is not slow in keeping his promise, as some understand slowness. He is patient with you, not wanting anyone to perish, but everyone to come to repentance.' His heart's desire is to save all who will come to Him. 2 Pet. 3:9

That desire seems to be contradicted in Rev. 22:11 "Let him who does wrong continue to do wrong; let him who is vile continue to be vile;..."   How do we understand these two seemingly opposing ideas? It is God's desire that no one perish yet we read that He says "let him who does wrong continue to do wrong and him who is vile continue to be vile." Doesn't He want them to repent and not perish?

In order to understand this seeming contradiction we need to know when it is said. It is said in eternity after there is a new heaven and earth, and a new Jerusalem.   The first earth and heaven have been replaced and are now new in a settled condition. On earth they who chose wrong and vileness rejected God's love and forgiveness. So they will remain in that condition.

In contrast those who do right and are Holy, made that way through receiving God's Son as Savior, will remain doing right and being Holy continually.   Of those people we read "he that is righteous, let him be righteous still: and he that is holy, let him be holy still." Rev. 22:11

We are told that those people who trust Christ on earth have been made clean, their robes washed by the blood of the Lamb. After death they have the right to partake of the tree of life and may enter through the the gates into the city of God. <u>Rev. 22:15</u>

Outside the city are the dogs(meaning unbelievers), those who practice magic arts, the sexually immoral, the murderers, the idolaters and everyone who loves and practices falsehood. They remain after death in the condition of their choice. They cannot enter the city of God but remain outside.

God's word is forever settled in heaven. The destiny of those who enter eternity having accepted or rejected God's Son is also forever settled.

If you have not yet admitted your sinfulness, changed your heart and mind toward God and believed in His Son as your Savior, don't wait until it is to late. Now is the day of salvation. If you wait until it is to late you will seal to yourself a horrible fate.

It is my prayer that you will make the right choice now and that we may meet in the heavenly city. Love to you, Dean

Here's a song which if you sing and believe with all your heart, you will have settled joy and life eternal.

<u><http://www.youtube.com/watch?v=ovYPQI93zro></u>

Love to you, Dean

Heaven's Itinerary -Part 1

When we plan a trip to a special place we make an itinerary listing when and where we expect to go. My wife and I spent one of our anniversaries in April in Paris; Before we went we prepared for our trip. We knew where we would be staying in Paris, places we would visit like the Louvre, the original opera house, the Seine river, various art museums, a 17th century farmhouse, my ancestors' Gosset Winery in Aye, oldest makers of wine and champagne in all of France dating to the 1500s and homes of my ancestors in Normandy and on Jersey Island. I studied French for 6 months and could read just about anything but couldn't speak it that well. Our itinerary enhanced our trip immensely.

All believers in Christ are going on a final trip from the present earth and heavens to a New Heaven and a New Earth. It is wise that we study and understand what that trip will entail. Much is said about the New Heaven but not much about the New Earth. So lets begin our itinerary with what is ahead for us in the New Heaven.

We have as our guide a most revealing and true document called the Bible. Jesus tells us not to be troubled about our future trip saying, "I go away to prepare a place for you, and if I go away I will come again to receive you to myself that where I am there you may be also." If we are going to be with him we definitely need not fear our trip into death which lifts us out of this world to be with Him forever. Most trips here are temporary. Our going home will be eternal.

We can be sure we are going to be with Christ if we believe who He is. He said, "If you don't believe that I am He(the Christ, the Savior of the world), you will die in your sins and you cannot come where I am." However we do believe, don't we? Don't you? If not, today is the day to trust Jesus Christ as God's Son who died for your sins, who paid the debt of death so you could be forgiven and have life. Before we go any further make sure you have put your full faith in God's Son who is the way to God, the truth of God and the life of God. When you really do that your heart will not be troubled about your future trip from earth into eternity.

Well, what is our first stop in our itinerary? Most likely it is the New Heaven. And what is it like? Before that happens many of us will have ruled with Christ on the millennial transformed earth for 1000 years at the end of which we will enter a totally New Heaven and New Earth. We will not discuss that 1000 years here but restrict our thoughts to the eternal city and everlasting New Heaven and New Earth.

First of all we can expect among other things to see the New Jerusalem descending down out of heaven prepared as a bride adorned for her husband. That means it will be an exciting event viewing the marvelous city that God has prepared for us. It will make

be an exciting event viewing the marvelous city that God has prepared for us. It will make the cities of our present earth seem like zero next to infinity. The city will be dazzling with beauty and light. Its foundations are made of 12 kinds of beautiful jewels. Here on earth our cities foundations are made out of cement, stone, wood in contrast to the beautiful foundations of the heavenly city. Here we walk on pavement of cement, dirt or asphalt.. There we will walk on gold. The most valuable things on earth, gold and jewels will be for walking on and for foundations.. The best is yet to come for all of us who go to our final home. We have just touched on a tiny bit of what is to come.. More in our next Part 2 of our itinerary of the new Heaven and earth. Meanwhile listen to this beautiful song anticipating the glory of going home.
<http://www.youtube.com/watch?v=o2aLSat3h0w>

Heaven's Itinerary, Part 2 -The Heavenly City

Many of us have enjoyed breathtaking views on this earth, the Grand Canyon, Yosemite's waterfalls, grand vista of Half Dome, the grandeur of the alps. the sights of the city of Paris. Our coming itinerary in heaven will eclipse these sights beyond our fondest imaginations.

We have already spoken of the New Jerusalem with its jasper wall, its golden streets, its pearl gates, its jeweled foundations. Now we will think of the size of the city in more depth and ponder the joys of the city for all of God's people.

The city is four square, 12,000, by 12,000 by 12,000 furlongs wide, long and high. Every person who ever lived could possibly have five square miles of space. Jesus said that in the place he would prepare would be many mansions or dwelling places. Doing the math that could mean we would each have a 147 billion square foot mansion to enjoy and share.

We are told that the New Jerusalem which contains all this space comes down out of heaven. Some believe it will hover over the New Earth, however it is my belief that the city may actually sit upon the earth. Why do I say this? Well, Abraham was promised in the O.T. that all the land from the river of Egypt to the Euphrates would be his and his descendants. As far as he could see North, South, Each and West would be his. Yet Abraham never owned any of the land promised him except for a plot of ground he bought in which he was buried. That's all any of us will ever own for a long time, a grave.

God always keeps his promises. So we can conclude that the land would become Abraham's someday. We are told that Abraham went out not knowing where he was going but he knew what he was looking for, a "city that has foundations whose builder and maker is God." Abraham died and his spirit made perfect is in the that city, the New Jerusalem We can be sure that God will keep his promise to Abraham and his descendants. How?

The new earth will have some resemblance to the old but transformed. Some of the new earth may still be similar to the old earth making it possible that he New Jerusalem could sit on the land promised to Abraham. if we take its size long and wide, 12,000 miles square, it would cover all the land promised Abraham and his descendants. So the land promised him would be his as promised as well as the city and heaven blessings. in fact all who trust God for salvation and know him by faith will inherit both the New Jerusalem, the New Earth and the New Heaven. All things are ours and we are Christ's and Christ is God's.

So we will meet Abraham and his descendants in the New Jerusalem and participate in the inheritance of Abraham which includes the land he was promised and the city he looked for and found.

The great lesson we all need to learn is that God keeps his promises. He is not like the Republicans, Democrats and the rest of us who don't always keep our promises. When God says He is going to do something for us, we can count on it. Not one of His good promises has ever failed yet.

That should encourage us to believe His promises that ""whosoever will let him come and take the water of life freely." If should give us assurance that His promise, "whoever comes to me I will in no way cast out." It should help us rest in His words that He has gone to "prepare a place for us and He will come again" and take us to be with Him there.

We are going to the place of which the Lord has said, "I will give it to you." Come and join us. if you haven't come to Christ, do so today and join us as we go to the heavenly city and the new heaven and earth.

We are going to the land of fairest, everlasting day. Sing about it here: <http://www.youtube.com/watch?v=gxJyXLWOkmg>

Forever is Your word settled in heaven and in my heart.

Love to you, Dean

Heaven's Itinerary Part 3

In part 1 of Heaven's Itinerary it was made clear that having an itinerary in advance brings about a greater preparation and appreciation for what is ahead. This is true of heaven. . Part 2 Included our first sight of the heavenly city with its beautiful foundations and streets. Part 3 takes us to the angel attended gates of the heavenly city.

In heaven we will see the 12 gates of the city, each one made from a single pearl and each attended by an angel. We are also told that the gates are named after the twelve tribes of Israel and that the gates are never shut..

So our itinerary includes viewing angels who attend the gates of the New Jerusalem. In the O.T. and new some folks actually saw angels. Most of us do not have that privilege but we will when we leave here to enter our final home. Angels are beautiful, powerful and swift.They are pictured as having wings and continually glorifying and serving God and His people. Scripture seems to teach that every believer has a guardian angel who ministers to him or her. They protect us now, and carry us into eternity when we die. Could it be that we may question our guardian angel and find out what he was doing at various times during our stay on earth?.

The week before my father in law, Carl Kent died, I was talking to him about angels, wondering what they looked like. He died a few days later of a heart attack at age 38 in the arms of his wife, Frannie. The last things he said was, "The Lord is with us always.." And what we had been talking about he experienced being absent from the body and carried spirit and soul by the angels into God's presence. Today we are told not to seek to get inordinately involved with angels, not to worship them, not to seek them out as spiritual guides as some do. But the moment when we arrive at the pearly gates we will see an angel at each gate. I imagine we will be quite surprised by their beauty and presence. So our heavenly itinerary includes our marvelous encounter with God's angels. Will we talk to them? Why not? In the Bible they talk and communicate God's message at various times.

The twelve pearl gates have inscribed upon them the names of the Old Testament names of the 12 tribes of Israel and the foundations of the city are jewels which are inscribed with the names of the 12 apostles of the New Testament. Perhaps the gates represent the entrance of God's plan beginning in the O.T. while the true stability and final revelation of God's plan is based upon the foundation of the apostles with Jesus Christ being the chief corner stone. This is mysterious as on earth we don't start with the gates but the foundations. Can you think of why this might be?

Jesus is the gate or door into salvation. His arms are always stretched forth to receive all who will come to Him. The Door to heaven is not shut but open always to all who will come to Him. Those of us who trust Him are door keepers whose job is to continually point to Him as the door to salvation, to truth and to life. Better to be a door keeper now in the house of God than dwell in the houses of the wicked. We plead with people to come to Him. He forces no one to come but is always ready to receive those who do come to Him in sincerity.

The twelve gates into the city are never shut. What does that mean? When I was a child growing up in a small town called Ukiah, some people never locked their doors. There was little crime in the city then. In heaven there will be zero crime so the gates will be open all the time. Also, it means continual freedom of access into and out of the heavenly city. We will be looking at a later part of our itinerary where we go out of the gates to visit the New Earth. Meanwhile our freedom to behold the beauty of the Lord in the New Jerusalem and to behold the beauty of His dwelling places, and the beauty of fellow believers will be eternally ours.

How great is the itinerary of our coming entrance into the New Heaven. Our trips on earth have often been filled with excitement and enjoyment. God always saves the best until last when we shall enter the New Heaven excelling in excellence all that is past. Setting our affections now on things above enables us to be of the most earthly good! Go for it! Looking forward to being with you enjoying the best which is yet to come.

Love, Dean

It is said of Abraham that he went out from the city he lived in not knowing where he was going but he knew what he was looking for, "A city that had lasting foundations whose builder and maker is God." "One thing have I desired that I may dwell in the house of the Lord forever to behold His beauty and to inquire in His presence..

Will we have a time when we can inquire of the Lord regarding the things we can not know now but will fully understand then? There is nothing the Lord can not answer for in Him are hidden all the treasures of wisdom and knowledge. The things that are secrets to God alone now will be fully known then. Do you not look forward to inquiring of God about everything?

Out of the city of Ur he went
Not knowing where but fully heaven bent.
He knew what he was looking for.beyond this sod,
A city that has foundations whose builder and maker is
God.

Dear Judy,

Yes I was the man who came up to you at the end of the service. After I wrote the poem below that your words inspired. I thought, "I wish I could send it to you but I really didn't know your name or address." But God is good and you knew our address and sent us your sweet and caring card. I thank God that He heard my hearts desire to send you Heaven's Wardrobe.

Below are some thoughts followed by a short poem I wrote in honor of a friend named June who recently went home to be with the Lord at age 93. She was a meticulous dresser. Her memorial service inspired me to write some thoughts about dressing up and a poem below called Heaven's Wardrobe. The poem is in her honor fulfilling all believer's desire at death "not to be unclothed but clothed."

Our Earthly wardrobe will give place to Heaven's Wardrobe. Only Eve could say she had nothing to wear on her first date. Then she wore her first outfit, fig leaves. Bad choice. Her next outfit was leathers provided by God through the first sacrifice of an animal. Good choice! Finally Eve graduated to God's Wardrobe available in eternity. Best Outfit! While the Best Clothing is ours now because we are clothed in His righteousness we have yet to see it fully. But we will see it since Christ is our ultimate designer in eternity. We will all, women and men, walk the runway in the finest of attire. Chester & Mary are already enjoying the best attire because they have graduated to heaven. They are stunning in their new Heavenly Clothing!

Heaven's Looks & Wardrobe
Dean L Gossett

Every believer's dream will come about
We'll all be beautiful inside and out!
No more stains. Not even a wrinkle.
All will be neat, glow and twinkle!
Divine botox erased our wrinkles away.
Heaven's runway will be our brightest day!
No more washing. No more darning.
All will be elegant and charming!
No more thinking, "What shall I wear."
We'll all be hunks and beauties there!
So the next time you put on your best attire.
Remember it will be eclipsed when you expire!

HELLO!

Years ago I heard a message by a speaker named Kent Bolter using the letters in HELLO. It was at a single's snow trip where I met my wonderful wife, Gloria. She happily snowed me and we have been married ever since. The message using HELLO has stuck with me now for 59 years as has our marriage. I want to share the gist or essence of that HELLO message with you.

The first letter H in HELLO, stands for your **H**eart and for **H**eaven! Jesus comes in to every Heart that humbly trusts Him filling it with the certainty of going to heaven.

That brings us to the E in HELLO. I wish you Eternal life. That IS the life of God. Our home here is temporary but you can be sure that you will live Eternally,. The gift of God is Eternal life. God so loved the world that He gave His only begotten Son that whosoever(that's you) believes in Him   should not perish but have eternal life.

That brings us to the first L in HELLO. It stands for Love. God is love. That love was displayed most eloquently when Jesus allowed Himself to be put to death for you and me. He assures us of His Love when we believe His words on the cross,"Father forgive them, for they know not what they do." Part of His Love is forgiveness. One thief on the cross next to Him mocked Jesus. The other thief asked to be remembered. Jesus in Love took him to paradise that day. The apostle John at the foot of His cross grasped His Love so deeply that from then on he called himself "the disciple Jesus loves"

The next L in HELLO is a prayer for you to Learn more and more about   Jesus. Knowing Him as your Savior makes you His disciple, that is His Learner.   Hidden in Him to Learn are all the treasures of wisdom and knowledge. Learn His words and grow in wisdom. He said, "The words that I speak, they are spirit and they are life."

Finally there is the O in HELLO. That means to Obey what He says assuring you of great rewards someday. Even a cup of cold water given in the name of one of His disciples will not lose its reward.

If you don't obey His offer by opening your heart, by believing Him, by accepting His love, by learning of Him

then you take away the O in HELLO and what is left of HELLO will be your destiny. Hopefully and prayerfully you aren't or won't be one who leaves out the O.

v=VLmI99Pqz10&index=4&list=RDXqyNe J6BUXo>

Help for Marriages

Marriage ideas that have helped my wife and I during 59 years of marriage. What has helped?

1. Both of trust Jesus Christ as Savior and learned to not be among those who are inconsistent in attendance to church. The Bible says it like this, "Don't forsake the assembling together of yourselves as is the manner of some but meet together more and more" as you see the day of Christ's return approaching. Heb. 10:25

2.   Pray together daily for others and each other. Share God's word daily. 3. There are two kinds of make up, the kind you wear, the kind you do. Use the second often. Forgive one another and never bring it up again. 4. Don't go to sleep angry. Ask God to help you to forget what made you mad or confront and forgive one another in love which covers a multitude of sin. 5. Encourage one another often. Say please and thank you often and complement each other's work, looks, demeanor. 7. Hug, touch and   kiss each other often. 8. Share the workload in and around the home. 9. Agree in advance on ways and means to encourage and discipline your children. 10. Do things with each other as much or more than with friends. 11. Realize that your body belongs to your spouse as well as to yourself.   1Cor 7: 2-512. Serve one another in love as Christ served. Look not just on yourself but also on

117

each and others needs.13 Study the Bible with each other and your children.14. Make your home a place of hospitality15. Don't let your feelings dictate your behavior. Do what is God's will and right regardless of your feelings.

Satisfaction for the Disappointed

If you are sometimes disappointed in yourself or in others you are among the normal. But who wants to be just normal? I know that I find if I look at myself I often get disappointed. If I look at others they often disappoint me too. Do you ever find yourself going over some past hurt with resentment in your heart? Do you find yourself not living up to what you think your life should be? I suppose everyone is disappointed at some time with themselves and others, especially if you seek to live up to the highest standards in the world as a Christian. We are to be perfect as our heavenly Father is perfect. How can we accomplish such a high standard?

it helps me to think about who I am looking at. If I point my heart toward people expecting perfection I won't find it. If I point my thoughts and heart towards God, I find my disappointments are solved. When someone wrongs me and I look at Jesus Christ I find it in my heart to forgive them as He forgave me. I also find it in my heart to forgive myself because He has forgiven me. Part of being mature is looking away from self to the Savior and forgiving others and yourself because He has forgiven you.

Someone has said that the most toxic thing in life is to believe that someone you love, including yourself, can not change. Yet the Bible teaches that as we see Jesus for who He really is we are changed to be like Him. It all depends on focus. Focus on self with the desire to be admired and liked is a dead end street because the human heart can never get enough admiration. It always wants more. Focusing on Christ instead of self brings ultimate satisfaction. He loves me as I am which satisfies my heart.

The old hymn below sums up proper focus perfectly. Satisfied with Thee Lord Jesus I am blest!

< http://cyberhymnal.org/htm/s/a/t/ satwtlj.htm>

Hopefully, Some Short Messages of Truth That Transforms

We all want to pray effectively for those that need salvation and for those who have it.

God tell us in Isaiah 41:21 that when we pray we should produce our cause and bring forth our strong reasons.

Today I'm sharing just one strong reason to pray for the lost. God tells us that He is not willing that any should perish but that all should come to repentance.

So Lord we agree with you for the salvation of a dying man named Kent, 82 years old who at this point does not believe in a life here after. We pray that Satan' and his blinders may be forcibly removed from Kent's life that He might see clearly His need of you and be enlightened and saved. That is your desire. It is ours, too.

So accept our strong reason which is that you do not wish him to perish and grant him salvation in Jesus name. Will you who have heard this message join in this prayer for Kent today? Sent.

Hello, This is Dean Gossett. The last time I sent you a message of truth that transforms I mentioned God telling us to bring before Him our cause and strong reasons for prayer. I shared that a very strong reason to pray for the lost is because God tells us He is not willing that any should perish but that all should come to repentance. Then we prayed for Kent, the 82 old man whose days are short, that God would force Satan our of his mind so he would no longer be blinded to the truth.

i would like to add another strong reason to pray for Kent and another person named Jac. God says all things are possible to those who believe. A man named George Mueller saw thousands come to Christ because he believed that all things are possible to him who believes. Hr prayed for five men to come to Christ for years. One by one they did come until only one was left. Muller believed with all his heart the man would be saved. And he was, on the day of Mueller's funeral the man received Christ. So let us believe God for the salvation of Kent, and of a new person, to pray for, Jac Christian, who is my cousin's son. Jac was a ski instructor in France, was buried along with a friend in a snow slide. He survived but his friend has been in a coma for a number of years. One Christian had a dream that Jac's friend would come out of the coma when Jac excepted the Lord. That should give us even more motive to pray for Jac. And continue to pray for Kent. I'll update you when the supernatural starts popping!

Hello Again, This is Dean Gossett with more truth that transforms. God wants to know our causes and strong reasons for His answering prayer. Here is a strong reason.: There is more joy in the presence of the angels over over one sinner who repents that over 99 who need no repentance.. Lord we pray for Kent, for Jac, and for my son Ken. You know their spiritual condition and what they need most. Take away Satan's blinders from their eyes and open their minds to the truth about your love and the gift of your Son. What joy it will be when you answer our prayers. Joy will be multiplied in heaven in your presence among the angels. Joy will be multiplied among Kent, Jac and Ken as they receive the joy of sins forgiven and a new life in Christ. And what joy will be ours, all of us who are praying and trusting you to hear and fill heaven and earth with joy.. In Jesus name Amen.

Life's Highest Relationships
DLG, May 19, 2014

What kinship is more than blood related,
A kinship that can't be overated?.
Jesus:said, "Who is my mother, my brother, my sister?
He that does the will of God is my brother, sister and mother."

So our relationship, I think you see it
Is a kinship of both blood and Spirit.
Of all the billions in the world today
We are related by God in this way..

The highest relationship we can voice
Is To do the will of God as our choice.
Aren't we with Joshua in one accord?-
To choose this day to serve the Lord!.

To do His will toward one another.
Caring always as sister and brother,
As mother, son and daughter,
In the high family of our Savior.

Will you agree that it is central
To help each other on God's level?-
To asist each other in our mutual struggle
Against the world, the flesh and the devil.

So let us pray long and hard for each other
That no sister, daughter, son or brother
Lose heart in our common warfare,
That our eyes be open and aware.

Pour upon us your Sprit fresh,
Lord, Crush the world and the flesh.
Keep us always in your care.
Deliver us from the Devil's wicked snare!

Homeless Man Inherits Mansions
DLG

When Jesus was a boy he had a temporary home but when He grew up and began His ministry He had no home in this world. He said of Himself, "Foxes have holes and birds of the air have nests but the Son of Man has no where to lay His head."(Luke 9:58) In other words, "This world was not His ultimate home. He was just passing through." He stayed where He was invited perhaps at his friend Lazarus' place, or He slept in the back of a disciple's boat, or He slept in the outdoors on a mountain side or by a lake.

He was a homeless man, sometimes despised and rejected. He also became poor. Why? "He owned the cattle on a thousand hills, the wealth in every mine" yet choose as a man to be poor so we through His poverty might be made spiritually rich. (2Cor.8:9)

Even the clothes he slept in were stripped off Him at the cross. He died naked and alone, forsaken for a short but agonizing time, yet anticipating with joy His future when He would rise from the dead and go to His true home, to His inherited mansions in the sky. Those many mansions which are in His Father's house cause him great joy for they are also the inherited home of all who trust Him as Savior.(Acts 20:32 & 1Peter 1:3,4)

So his homelessness, rejection, death and resurrection make it possible to go to our own permanent home in His mansions and be with Him forever.

Our present home here on earth is like our lives here, only temporary. So in a sense we are homeless as well. "This world is not my home. I'm just passing through. My treasures are laid up way beyond the blue."

Jesus promised to come back and get us someday so we can go to our true home far away. (John 14:3) He said that His Father's house already had many mansions but He was going to prepare a place for us. Maybe that means, like my wife who is always seasonly redoing our home, He's going to do some redecorating? (-: And what a home it will be. It is in a city that has lasting foundations whose builder and maker is God. It has streets of gold, gates of pearl, foundations of precious jewels. It has Angelic guests, all the saints (those who have faith in God and His Son), loved ones who have gone on before, and most glorious of all Jesus Himself who will be the light of the city and of our home. One great joy will be to hear God sing. Scripture says He will sing over us. Can you imagine God singing? What will it be like? Maybe it will be in three parts with the Father, Son and Spirit singing in perfect harmony?

It will be the place where we hang our hats forever where we never know sin, tears, pain or death ever again. It is a city of pure love, light and life.

I admire people today who give their lives to work with the homeless. They will not lose their reward. Having been homeless Himself, Jesus must have a special place in His heart for those who care for the homeless, the hurting and those often despised. Thank God for our God who became a homeless man for a while that we might have a home with Him forever in the mansions of His Father's house.

This song sums it up for me."I'm waiting for His coming from His mansions in the sky. I'm waiting for Jesus, for He's coming by and by. He promised to take me to dwell with Him in glory fair. He promised to give me a crown of victory to wear. So I'm watching and I'm waiting for the sound of HIs glorious cry. I'm waiting for Jesus for He's coming by and by." What manner of people should we be in view of that coming day? Help us show our thanksgiving Lord by our "thanksliving." Amen! Even so come, Lord Jesus.

<http://www.youtube.com/watch?
v=gxJyXLWOkmg>

Hotline to Heaven
Imaginary Talk with Enoch

Dialing fastest wireless system in existence.
Heaven 777
Hello, whose speaking.
My name is MIchael. What can I do for you?
Please put Enoch on the line will you.
Of course. He is on our Prophet line, as the first prophet, dial 1.
Okay.
Hello, is this Enoch.
Yes.
How are things going up there?
Very good thank you. Just picked Rapture berry Fruit off the tree of life. MMM delicious!
I know things are going well for you now up there but please tell me a about your life on earth.
Well I was born when My dad Jared was 162 years old. He lived until he was 962 years old. Then he died.
Wow he was really old!
Yes but I had a child when I was 65 years old who lived longer. I named him Methuselah. He lived

longer than anyone who lived before the world wide flood.

How old was he?

He died at age 969 just before the great flood came.

How do you know all this?

Because here in heaven God's word is settled and known by His people.

Okay, tell me, how long did you live?

I never died!

You never died?

No, after I had my son Methuselah at 65, I walked with God for 300 more years.

What do you mean you walked with God?

I talked to him continually in prayer and I sought to please Him. Many people had many wives during that time. I pleased God because I had only one wife like Adam.

What was her name? I called her beautiful a lot of the time. We had lots of children besides Methuselah.

My name means initiator and I was an initiator. I initiated my children by teaching them to believe God and to honor HIm. I taught them how to approach God the right way like Abel did and not to be like Cain who wanted to come to God his way instead of God's way. You know that guy Frank Sinatra?

Yes.

Well he got it all wrong. He even sang a song about it called "I did it my way."

He should have done it God's way!

Where is Frank now,

I know but can't tell you now. But you probably already have some idea about that don't you?

Yes.

Let me tell you about one day when something quite wonderful happened to me when I was on earth walking with God.

What was that, Enoch?.

Well I was walking along talking to God and he said, "instead of going to your home come with me to my home." So He took took me out of this life.

Did you die?

No, I didn't. I was removed from earth and did not experience death.

But. The Bible says it is appointed to man once to die.

So How do you explain that you didn't have to die? Is the Bible wrong?

No, up here it I settled that everything God says is true.

A time is coming when I will have to die. Also my friend Elijah didn't have to die either but one day we both will have to die? Right Elijah.

Right!

How will it happen?

Well, when I was on earth before the great flood I prophesied that the Lord was coming to earth at a future time to punish those who we're ungodly. God revealed to me that the Lord would come with ten thousands of His saints & punish those who refused His mercy and walked in their own perverted religion and ungodly ways.

What is this ungodliness like, Enoch?

Well, in my day the ungodly conduct was seen in violence, killing, multiple marriages, Satanic motivation, people being led against God by the Serpent who deceived both Eve and Cain. God revealed to me that way in the future things would get worse.

In what ways?

Well, after His Son came to earth some believed in Him and honored Him but most did not. So gradually the world will get worse and worse. Some will say they believe but use God's grace as a license to live immorally practicing the sins of Sodom & Gomorrah perverting sex and calling it right, calling evil good and good evil, calling black white and white black. Because sinful behavior shall increase the love of many shall grow cold with even righteous men like Lot vexed by the evil in the world. Men will be greedy. Nations will war with one another. The authority of God will be rejected and mocked. False prophets will rise whose motive will be personal gain and fame. Religious rulers will struggle against one another for preeminence. There will be grumblers and fault finders, and boasters who will flatter others to advance themselves in fulfilling their evil desires.

Well, what has all this to do with you and Elijah having to die someday?

It has this to do with it. During the last years of earth there will be a period of tribulation. A beastly ruler will come on the scene who will promise the world peace. All the world who do not know God will be deceived into believing He has the answers for peace. Jerusalem will be the center of world attention because He makes a peace treaty with Israel. For 3 1/2 years there will be a peaceful lull before a final storm of judgement will come on the world.

It will be during those final years that Elijah and I come back to appear in the city of Jerusalem. We will preach the truth in the streets of Jerusalem about Christ and about the evil beastly ruler. We will expose him as a false god motivated by the old serpent.

Some will believe us but most will not. In fact some will try to kill us. At first their attacks on us will fail because Elijah and I have power to call down fire upon our enemies & kill them. Most of the people in the world will hate us.

After a time of preaching God will remove our protective power and we will be attacked and killed. The whole world will see our bodies lying dead in the street.

How can the whole world see you then, Enoch?

You've heard of Television haven't you?

Yes.

Well. there's your answer.

People all over the world will rejoice because we are dead. They will give gifts to one another. But then their joy will turn to shocked horror.

Why?

Because Elijah and I will suddenly rise from the dead and be caught up to heaven.So as it was appointed for man once to die so we died but it is also appointed for all who believe in Christ to die and then rise again. So will we.

What will happen after you die and have been caught up?

I'll tell you about that later. Right now Elijah and I are going for a swim in the river of life. Okay. I'll call you back later.

Sounds good! Bye!

Bye!

Hotline to Heaven
by Dean L Gossett

Dialing 777 on Hotline to Heaven

Hello, whose speaking?

It's me, Michael the Archangel.

Michael, will you put Adam on the line.

Of course.

Hello, Adam.

Yes.

This is me down here on earth.

How are things up there?

Just wonderful. Eve is here with me.

We just finished eating passion fruit off of the tree of life.

Where are you right now.

We are in a beautiful garden. It is called Paradise.

I thought you got kicked out of the garden for eating fruit from the wrong tree.

Yes, we did.

You know you have caused us all down here on earth a lot of trouble.

I know that. I made a huge mistake.

When Eve offered me the fruit I just had to take it.

Why?

Because if you could see how beautiful Eve was, you'd know I couldn't have resisted her.

What do you mean, "Was beautiful." Isn't she beautiful now.

Of course. Even more beautiful than when we were in the Garden of Eden.

After you ate the fruit of the forbidden tree, why did you hide?

Well, we were ashamed. Not just because we were naked but because we knew God saw what we did. Our disobedience was naked and open to Him.

So, did you think you could get away with what you did?

Foolishly, we thought that. We figured we could cover up what we did by making some fig leaf clothes. But we knew deep inside our way wouldn't work.

What did God say when you were hiding behind the trees in your fig leaf clothes?

He asked us a question, He said, "Where are you?"

Didn't He know where you were?

O yes, but he asked it so we would know he knew where we were..

Did God ask you anything else?

Yes, he asked us if we ate of the tree of the knowledge of good and evil.

What did you say?

Eve said she ate of it because the serpent deceived her.

I said I ate it because she gave it to me.

What did God then say to you?

He told us we would have to leave the garden.

Why did he say that?

Because if we ate of the tree of life in the middle of the garden we would live forever ashamed and away from Him.

Were you naked when you left the garden?

No. God had us take off our fig leaves. He killed some of the innocent animals in the garden. I think they were lambs.

Why did He do that?

He took the skin of the animals and made clothing to cover up our nakedness. We felt bad about those animals having to die so we could be clothed.

When you left the garden did you look back?

Yes, we saw angels guarding the tree of life to keep anyone from eating from it.

Why were they guarding it?

We didn't fully understand then but we do now.

No one could eat from the tree of life unless their sin was removed.

Didn't the animal skin clothes take away your sin?

No. They just covered us up until the time God would really take away our sin.

How did He do that?

Well, he told us that because of our sin of taking from the tree of the knowledge of good and evil that we would be cursed until the day He would send a child of Eve's descendants that would take care of our sin by crushing the Serpent's power by dying for us. He also cursed the Serpent and made him crawl on the ground and eat dust suffering the consequences of his deceiving Eve. We didn't know then but now we do, that one of Eve's descendants would take our death on Himself and crush the power of the Serpent.

Did He tell you anything else about what would happen because you disobeyed Him?

Yes, He cursed the ground for my and mankind's sake. It started growing weeds and thistles and it was harder to grow crops after that. So I often asked Him for help as I worked hard by the sweat of my brow. If things had been easy I don't think I would have called out to Him as much as I did.

What else did He tell you?

He told Eve that she would have children in pain.

Was Eve pregnant when you left the garden?

I'm not sure but we had obeyed God and sought to be fruitful having children. But our first child was born after we left the garden.

What did you name him. We called Him Cain.

Why did you name him Cain?

Well, God promised that a seed or child that would come from me would defeat Satan. His name means to procure so we thought maybe he would be the one to redeem us from the power of the Serpent.

Did he do what you thought he would do?

No. He was a terrible tragedy to our family. He was very rebellious.

How is that?

Well, we told him that he should kill an animal and offer it to God as a sign of God's providing us the cover of animals skins, We told him the right way to approach God.

Did he listen to what you said?

No, instead he offered God fruits and vegetable he had grown. It was sort of like our doing it our way by putting on fig leaves. Only we learned from it to obey God His way instead of our own.

Then, what happened?

Well, we had another son. His name was Abel. He was a shepard. We thought our first son Cain might be the one who would crush Satan. When we had Abel we thought he might not be the one since he was not our firstborn son. Boy were we wrong.

Why?

Well, we taught them both how to approach God bringing Him a sacrifice of an animal. When it came time to offer the sacrifice, Cain refused to do it God's way. He thought his own works were good enough and offered God fruit and vegetables instead of an animal sacrifice.

So what happened?

He was rejected by God. But God gave him another chance. He told him to bring the right offering and he would be accepted.

Did he do it?

No, he talked to his brother out in the field. Abel offered him a lamb but Cain got angry. We learned later that the Serpent deceived Cain, inspired him to hate his brother. His brother had offered the right sacrifice and was accepted. Instead of changing his attitude, Cain killed his brother.

Eve and I grieved terribly over what he did.

What happened to Cain?

Well, at that time there were no laws about what to do if one person killed another. So God took care of it. He drove Cain away from us to a land called Nod. We hoped perhaps he would some day repent and regret what he did to his brother. But he never did. It was like he fell asleep spiritually in the land of Nod and never woke up.

Where is Cain now?

Since the wages of sin are death, he is not here with us. It is a great sorrow to us.

How about Abel?

You tell him Eve. Where is Abel now?

O he is here. Not long after we died, we found ourselves here in heaven with our Lord. We later learned that God sent His Son into the world who was a distant "seed" or child of mine through my descendants. And He died to take away our sin and death.

So what kind of clothes are you wearing now in heaven?

O we are clothed in white robes given us after we died. We realize now that the first offering God ever made in killing an animal was pointing to the day His Son would die and take away our sins. So we are no longer clothed in animal skins but our clothing is white. We are clothed in God's righteousness.

Do you have anything to say to folks down here on earth now.

O yes we do. Come to God His way. Believe in His Son. Accept His sacrifice for you. If you do He will receive you and like us you will be forgiven and here in heaven someday.

Thank you Adam and Eve. I've enjoyed talking to you. To say the least, it has been an eye opener.

Before I go tell me, is Enoch there with you?

Yes, he is here as well as everyone on earth who came to God His way before they died.

Well, I'm going to hang up now. Tell Michael thanks for getting us in touch with you both and I'll call back later and hope to talk to Enoch.

Ok, it was nice talking to you. What is your name?

It is Dean. I'm glad I have this Hotline to Heaven. I expect to learn a lot talking to everyone there.

"Wonderful" exclaimed Adam and Eve with one voice. God bless you and goodbye.

I'll see you again in person before Long. Then we'll talk some more. Goodbye and God bless!

How It All Began, God's Plan for Man

Before the creation of the heavens and the earth, from His home in the third heaven surrounded by angels without number God looked on all He had made. He looked at his Archangels, Michael, Gabriel, Lucifer They were beautiful and pure!

He listened as Lucifer called to the angels: "Come bow down to me. I'll give you more than God and set you free. Am I not more beautiful and powerful than Michael, more pure than Gabriel. When it comes to glory, am I not more charming than God and more able! Follow me and we will rule over Jehovah himself. Leave your first estate for a greater and higher fate! Bow your knee to me! Am I not the the son of the morning, creator of melody and harmony? Worship me and rise to the highest heights above our creator. Set your feet above him and reign with me on a higher throne!"

One third of the angels cheered the son of the morning, "Yes! Yes! Hail the magnificence of him who is mighty in his cunning. Let us turn from our creator and ruler. None are more glorious than Lucifer?

"No!"" shouted Michael! "Don't be fools!" cried Gabriel. Lucifer and his followers wouldn't listen. Two thirds of the angels did listen and worshiped and stayed true to their Creator.

Then God himself spoke from the throne to Lucifer, "You were beautiful and pure until this day!"

Yes, you were," said the Father of Eternity. "Yes," joined in the Father's Son. "Yes' said the Spirit of power. Kiss, the Son, bow down to Him who created you before His wrath is kindled against you!"

Lucifer would not bow nor would the angels who took his side. They wouldn't bow. They wouldn't bend. So they would burn.

The voice of Jehovah set his fate, "Go! Your beauty is gone! No longer are you son of the dawn! I have prepared a final place for you. You have sought to exalt yourself above me. You shall descend to crawl like a serpent. You shall fall further into a bottomless pit. Instead of a throne above me, you shall be thrown into an eternal lake of fire where you and your fallen comrades shall burn forever."

So Lucifer, once pure until iniquity was found in him, turned from the glory of his position forced by the superior power of the Father, Son and the all seeing Spirit. He and his followers were ousted with indignant shame to leave the gates of glory. Little did he and his fallen demon angels realize the rest of the story.

Then God stepped out into a new and seemingly endless space and said to the faithful angels, "I'm happy that you have not fallen from your place by my side. I'll create a heaven and earth where the angels that have fallen and you that have not, will see my wisdom and be taught an everlasting lesson."

"I'll make a new creature who will be weaker than you angels. I'll make these new beings in in my image but lower than you. I will exalt those who bow to me to a throne above Lucifer! Instead of "sun of the morning" he will be the father of lies and darkness!

Thus began God's divine plan to make a world for man!

How Many Questions in the Bible?

There are 2540 questions in the Bible. Properly answered they can change your life forever.

The first question in the Bible was asked by God to the first two people who ever lived, Adam and Eve. God placed them in a beautiful garden and had told them they could eat from every tree in the garden accept one. He told them if they ate of it they would die. That death was spiritual in their relation to Him and eventually physical as well. Most of us know the rest of the story. They were deceived by the Serpent(Satan) who lied to them twice. First, he told them a half truth saying God had told them they couldn't eat of every tree in the garden. Actually God had said, "You may eat of every tree in the garden accept for one, the tree of the knowledge of good and evil." When Eve told the Serpent that God had said not to eat of it for it would cause them to die, then Satan told her a blatant lie saying, "You shall not die." Eve listened to Satan and both she and Adam ate of the tree. Thus the process of death for them and all mankind began. The first step in dying was shame which they tried to hide by making clothes of fig leaves and hiding. Then God in love sought them out. He came to them and asked the first question in the Bible. He said, "Where are you?"

That is a question God still asks each of us today. Are you covering up your shame with fig leaves, that is trying to hide your failure by covering it up with your own works. Of course God knew where Adam and Eve were hiding but he wanted them to know what he knew by asking them, "Where are you?" He knows where we are as well. Adam and Eve admitted they were ashamed and hiding. Since we have all sinned and come short of what God wants from us, we also need to admit where we are in relation to God. We need to quit trying to cover our wrong but admit it.

When Adam and Even admitted their sin against God He pronounced the results, the consequences of their sin. Then He provided a covering that represented His solving the problem of their disobedience. He killed an innocent animal from which he made new clothing for them. In symbol He gave them a new covering representing His own perfect righteousness. That animal sacrifice was a picture or symbol of His Son, the Lamb of God who would one day come into the world, take away their sin's curse, which was death, by dying for them and rising from the dead to defeat the Devil who had deceived them. His Son would remove their sin replacing it with His own righteous perfection. Adam and Eve's new suit of clothes replaced the fig leaves and need to hide. Their new clothing was a free gift given them by God. They did not reject God's gift of adornment but accepted it.

You, like I have done, must admit your disobedience to God and believe the good news that His Son, the Lamb of God died to take away your sin, then rose from the dead to give you a new eternal life. The wages or results of sin is death but the gift of God is eternal life through Jesus Christ, His Son. Have you received that gift? Will you receive Him today? Sing this song and believe it with all your heart and God will clothe you in His forgiveness and love: <https://www.youtube.com/watch?v=w2VrRk4pZHY >

More answers to come to some others of the 2540 questions in the Bible. God bless you. Dean

I asked one of our pastor's, Gary Darnell, at our church if he had a favorite question from the 2540 in the Bible? He immediately answered quoting Jesus question to His disciple, "Who do you say I am?" Then I asked my wife for a favorite question. She quoted the jail keeper who was astonished when the jail doors all opened when Paul and Silas were singing in the jail. He asked, "What must I do to be saved?" Do you have a favorite question

How Many Times Have You Been Born?

Not long ago I was asked to speak to a group of young people at an AWANAS meeting.I asked the young people if they had been born only once, or if they had been born a second time. I explained what was necessary to have a second birth. First, you must realize your need to be born again. Our first birth includes a nature that goes astray and is prone to sin. As the Bible says, "All we like sheep have gone astray. We have turned everyone to his own way." Our own way is a sinful way. The Bible tells us many ways, that we go astray, lying, cheating, empty talk, dishonoring God, sexual sin, coveting what doesn't belong to us.

I learned about a year later that one young girl was deeply touched by knowing she was going astray. She went home and confessed to her mom what she called a lot of "rotten things" she had done. Her mom was amazed because up to that point in her life she would never admit anything wrong that she had done. Her mom told her the same remedy I had shared that Christ died for her sins and took upon Himself all her sins. Though she had gone astray the Lord had laid on Jesus the iniquities, sins of us all which meant her. Then she led her in a prayer to accept Christ. A long time after that her daughter asked her mom if she had a second birthday . Then she told her mom she was born again when she prayed with her to accept Christ as her Savior. Her mom assured her that she too had been born again though she didn't know the exact date.

How about you? Have you had a second birth? Jesus said that each of us must be born again. "Unless you are born again, you cannot enter the kingdom of God. It is an absolute must. It happened to me at age 20 when with God's help I went forward at a meeting and received Christ. John 1:12 describes what happened to me, to the young lady from the AWANA club and to her mom. It says, " Yet to all who received Him(Jesus Christ), to those who believe in His name he gave the right to become children of God-children born not of natural, nor of human action, or a husbands will, but **born of God.**"

Have you received Him as your Savior? Have you believed in Him with all your heart? If not, why not do so right now. The benefits are incalculable. They include your name written in the book of life which makes impossible your experiencing the second death. You are forgiven. Your final home will be heaven. You will be able to share with others the wonderful news that they too can have a second spiritual birth. Old things pass away. All things become new. God is your Father. His Son is your Savior. His Spirit is your everlasting companion.

If you are born only once you will die twice, first, physically, then eternally in the lake of fire which is the second death. If you are born twice you will die once, only physically but triumph over your physical death to live forever in a new, eternal risen body. It's your choice. Jesus came to give us a second birth. He said, "All that the Father gives me will come to me, and whoever comes to me I will never cast out." John 6:37 Have you come? Will you come? If so let others know. "Jesus said, "Whoever acknowledges me me before men I will also acknowledge before my Father in heaven. Whoever disowns me before men, I will disown him before my Father in heaven." Matt. 10:32,33.

What are you waiting for? Today is the day of salvation! If you are already born again you may want to pass this on to someone who needs a second birth.

https://www.hymnal.net/en/hymn/h/1046>

How Valuable Are You?
By Dean for You

While walking around my block praying for you and others I thought on this verse spoken by Jesus in Matthew 10:29-32 "Are not two sparrows sold for a copper coin? And not one of them falls to the ground apart from your Father's will. **30** But the very hairs of your head are all numbered. **31** Do not fear therefore; **you are of more value than many sparrows."**

Once I attended a funeral at a grave side. As I sat there the message came through loud and clear about the value of the person who died. Beside the grave a sparrow had died. He lay on his back with his feet pointed up to heaven. I wondered for a moment, "Did the preacher put the sparrow there?" I knew for sure God put him there because not one sparrows falls to the ground apart from His will.

Today, I don't know how you are feeling, but I want you to think about the fact that God loves sparrows but **He loves you more**. He knows what is on your agenda and mine. And he cares. In fact he cares so much he keeps track of how many hairs are on your head at any given moment.

When my grandson, Tyler was little, he once said, "I know God counts my hairs grandpa." I said, "How do you know that." He said, "Because every morning when I wake up my hair is messed up from Him counting them."

up my hair is messed up from Him counting them."

Well, I am writing this because I know God cares about you. He values you so much He gave His only unique Son, Jesus to die for you so you can know you have eternal life and will never perish. All you have to do is admit your need and truly believe Him.

He cares about your day today. Whether you are going through blessings or trials, God values you. In all your affliction, the Bible says, He is afflicted. So I pray you will thank Him for both your blessings and your trials. I ask Him to help you right now and know He will. He said, "Whatever you ask believing you shall receive." So enjoy your day as you think about how valuable you are. Also pray for me and my grandson, Tyler. I am working on getting more exercise and ask that you pray that I'll get at least four hours a week walking and stretching and praising God. Please pray for Tyler, in rehab and needs the Lord's help. Let me know if you have something specific to pray for and I will do it.

Thank you. May the Lord today be your shield and exceeding great reward. His eye is on the sparrow and I know He cares for you. Sing about it here: <https://www.youtube.com/watch?v=zpUslbCal34>

I Am Addicted

I am addicted to two kinds of food, physical food & spiritual food. There are such things as good addictions. All kinds of physical food are to be received with thanksgiving of them who love and know the truth. We all need and enjoy food. Don't ever eat and you will die.

But physical food is not enough according to what Jesus said, "Man shall not live on bread alone but on every word that comes out of the mouth of God."

Many a person is addicted in a good way to food but has no addiction to his greatest need to eat of the Spiritual food of which Jesus spoke when His disciples encouraged him to eat. He said, "I have meat to eat that you know not of."

They couldn't figure out what he meant and speaking of physical food said,"Has anyone brought Him meat?"

Yes, someone had brought Him meat but not the kind they were thinking of as Jesus clarified saying, "My meat is to do the will of Him who sent me and to finish His work."

And what is God the Father's will and work, Jesus? "This is the work of God that you believe on Him whom He has sent."

And how do we become a part of that work? By feasting on what God says. "I found your word and I ate it and it was the joy & rejoicing of my heart."

I am joyously addicted to God's library of truth! It has become the joyous food of my life. If God says it I believe it. I take it in daily & often hourly. It is the meditation of my mind and the Royal food of my soul.

Have you yet become an addict to the truth of God's word? Morning, noon & night do you meditate on God's word?

There is no enduring life apart from it. Blessed is the man who refrains from evil and instead delights in every word that comes out of the mouth of God meditating on it day and night?

Do you spend as much time eating spiritual food as you do physical food? I challenge you and myself, seek out the book of the Lord and read, heed and digest it! Be joyfully addicted to God's word. Open His library of truth. Eat at least three square meals a day from God's truth in order to be a well rounded person. Without His food you are dead. With it you renew your strength. You get a second wind. You get wings to fly above and feast on the God of love. You get peace like a river attending your soul. Climb truth mountain and get joy like a fountain. What are you waiting for? Do it and enjoy life now and eternally. Share it with your kids, too!

My Way Or His Way?

Here is a rendering in new form, elevating
the mundane words of Frank Sinatra's song,
" I Did It <u>My</u> Way" to the Eternal Words, "I Did It
<u>His</u> Way!"
It contains words of final-graduate-resolution for
all years to
be happy ones!

I Did It His Way
by DLG

My life it was a mess
I knew nothing of peace I must confess
My friend, I'll make it plain
I'll state it as it was, filled with pain
I lived an empty life
I traveled a road once filled with strife
Until I met my Lord and did it His way.

Regrets, I've had a lot
Because of sinful things I sought.
I did what I sought to do and saw it
through with deception
I planned each sinful course, each
wrongful step along the byway
Then one day I heard God say, "Do it My
Way!"

Yes, there were times, I'm sure its true
When I tried to do more than I could do,
But through it all, when there was doubt
I confessed it and spit it out
I faced it all and knew His help and did it
His way.

I've loved, I've laughed and cried
I've had my fill, my share of losing
And now, as tears subside, I find it all so
transforming
To think I knew His love
And may I say, not in a shy way,
"Oh, no, oh, no, not me, I did it His way"

For what is a man, what has he got?
If not his God, then he has naught
To lean on God he truly must and live a life
of love and trust.
May the record show I loved & kissed His
Son and did it His way!

Stand Amazed
Romans 8:33-39

Do you long to be pure in the depths of your
heart?
Do you hate the sins of your past?
God's precious forgiveness amazes me
Our sins need not hold us fast.
Cleansed by His precious blood
I rest in the price He paid.
My sins are gone, on Him laid.
No thought against me stands
For He has cleansed my heart and hands.
As at His feet let us bow
There is no condemnation now!
Your thoughts and accusers can't condemn you.
No charges of man or Satan will ever stand.
His gift of righteousness has freed and made you
grand.
Be gone all who accuse and condemn.
His death and risen life banish you to oblivion.
I stand holy and pure in God's grace.
And in that certainty I see His loving face.
Pure at last, held secure in His loving grasp.
No foe above or here below
Can wrench me from his hand.
I live and die in trusting Him
Pure in God alone I stand.
Embraced by His gift of perfection
Secure in His selection-
Chosen in Him before the foundation of the earth.
Rest purely then in His gift to you of faultless
worth.
You can say, "I am His and He is mine.
In Him I am immaculate and fine."
Be gone thoughts of worthlessness
For you are made pure by God's gift of holiness.
Of this be sure Jesus blood has made you pure.
So you shall to the end endure.
His Spirit makes your triumph sure.
His grace and love are your healing cure .
When this life has come and gone
You'll awake in heaven's dawn
You'll see Him as He is for sure
And be like Him,
Amazed forever more!

Make it Yours-Sing About It:<http://
www.youtube.com/watch?v=xo5rEYaRNiM>

I Will Praise God

I will praise God when I'm up.
I will praise him when I'm down.

I'll praise him on the mountain top.
And I'll praise him in the town.

I'll praise him when I''m sick
And praise him when I'm well.

I'll praise him till
He wipes out the gates of hell.

I'll praise Him when he binds up the devil.
I'll praise him till crooked is made level.

I'll praise him while I'm living
I'll praise when I'm dying

I'll praise hiim when I'm happy
And praise Hm when I'm crying.

I'll praise him when I'm sighing
And praise him when I'm flying.

No matter the lot in life I'm given
I'll praise him when I fly away to heaven

I'll praise him on his throne
I'll praise him in my final home.

I'll praise him when life on earth is gone
I'll. praise him with an endless song

My praise will go on and on and on
In tune with heaven's blood bought
throng!

<https://www.youtube.com/watch?
v=64tgkqaNX1I>

To My Son & Grandson, Feb 12, 2014
Rudyard Kipling
If

If you can keep your head when all about you
Are losing theirs and blaming it on you;
If you can trust yourself when all men doubt you,
But make allowance for their doubting too;
If you can wait and not be tired by waiting,
Or, being lied about, don't deal in lies,
Or, being hated, don't give way to hating,
And yet don't look too good, nor talk too wise;
If you can dream - and not make dreams your master;
If you can think - and not make thoughts your aim;
If you can meet with triumph and disaster
And treat those two imposters just the same;
If you can bear to hear the truth you've spoken
Twisted by knaves to make a trap for fools,
Or watch the things you gave your life to broken,
And stoop and build 'em up with wornout tools;
If you can make one heap of all your winnings
And risk it on one turn of pitch-and-toss,
And lose, and start again at your beginnings
And never breathe a word about your loss;
If you can force your heart and nerve and sinew
To serve your turn long after they are gone,
And so hold on when there is nothing in you
Except the Will which says to them: "Hold on";
If you can talk with crowds and keep your virtue,
Or walk with kings - nor lose the common touch;
If neither foes nor loving friends can hurt you;
If all men count with you, but none too much;
If you can fill the unforgiving minute
With sixty seconds' worth of distance run -
Yours is the Earth and everything that's in it,
And - which is more - you'll be a Man my son!

Dean L Gossett
If

If you can admit each sin and fall,
And trust in God's Son who forgives them all.
If you can put your faith in God
And look to Him beyond this barren sod.
Then you will be a new Man son
And in the game of life you will have won!

If I Were the Devil

Instead of my weekly illustrated news letter I'm passing on to you this famous broadcast on ABC radio given 47 years ago, April 3, 1965 by Paul Harvey, famous news caster. It was broadcast over 1,200 radio stations nationwide and **we have seen some of the**

rest of the story unfold since then.   It is only 3 minutes long, less than Lincoln's Gettysburg Address and more insightful. Dean
<http://www.youtube.com/watch?v=LJc8MzgOC-c&feature=player_embedded>

If You Walk With God

If your prayer is empirical, you are bound to see a miracle.
If your trust is always strong, you are sure to be blessed all day long.
If you look to Jesus every day, you will surely find your way.
If you ask and listen prayerfully, then you'll choose carefully.
If you confess your sin, Jesus will forgive and cleanse your heart within.
If you obey God every day you'll surely be happy on your way.
If you look up, then God will fill your cup.
If you look to the Rock from which you are hewn, you'll sing a lofty tune!
If you enter the narrow gate, a joyous end will be your fate.
If you look to God above, your heart will fill with love.
If you are poor in spirit, God's kingdom you will inherit.
If you believe Jesus died for you, old things will pass away and you'll rejoice in Him every day.
If you die in grace, a smile will adorn your face.
If your always on the level with the Lord, He will guide you with His Word.
If you look above to heaven's vision, It will guide your every decision!
If you do everything you read before, you will have good success for sure!

If you listen to this below, your heart will be touched, your tears of unity will flow and the unity of all God's children, you will know!
Click below:

https://www.facebook.com/bryant.seabrooks/videos/10208641612752284/>

Impossible Dreams Realized

I dreamed some impossible dreams.
Is anything to hard for God?
No! With God's help & power
My dreams have or will come true:

I'll Love an unloveable world
Win unwinable souls
Reconcile unreconcilable enemies
Forgive unforgiven wrong
Destroy undestroyable death
Empty my unemptyable grave
Defeat my undefeatable enemy
Fly an unflyable flight
Soar to Jesus in the light

Write an unending song
Live an unlivable life
Win an unendable crown
Sing a victorious song
See Jesus fulfill in reams
My impossible dreams:

No longer a dream afar
I'll sit beside my Shining Star.
I'll Meet Him face to face
Live joyfully in His embrace

All that seemed impossible
He made possible for me
He saved my soul
He made me whole

He fulfilled each impossible goal
Made every dream come true.
So Lord Jesus, My Alpha & Omega
I worship You!

"I worship you O Glorious Lord
Forever be Your Name adored!"
<https://www.youtube.com/watch?v=EfPJ4j5P5X8>

The Never Ending Song

Sung to the Tune of Doe a Deer
by Dean L Gossett

C for Christ, the Christ I love
D He Died upon a tree
E Eternal life is mine
F By Faith I have been saved
G My God is on my side
A Assurance now is mine.
B Be sure you know my Lord
That will bring you back to C

When you know my Lord and King
How can you do less than sing:
Back to C. Then Repeat it Forever!

An Indestructible Foundation?

"In the beginning God created the heavens and the earth." Gen.1:1

This first verse in the Bible is a rock-solid foundation upon which all that is to come is built: It assures us of the existence of God and of His creative power. Upon it all the rest of the Bible depends. If God did not create the heavens and the earth, then the rest of the Bible can not be trusted. But He did create them. No scientist has ever disproved that fact. And He did it through His Son, the ever existing Christ. In the beginning was the Word, the complete expression of all that God is. And His complete expression was with Him and His complete expression was Him. All things were made by Him and for Him and without Him nothing was made that was made. He spoke the world into existence. Then the complete expression of all He is became human in the flesh and lived a miracle life among us for a little over 30 years At the end of that earthly life He died for our sins and rose again to prepare a place for all of us who will come to Him.

Before He came to earth He spoke the world into existence. He has made us and we are not an accident. We did not make ourselves. He gives life and breath and light to every living person. His purpose for us is to seek Him and find Him and He is not far from any one of us-only a prayer of faith away. Because He lives we can believe He exists and will reward us when we diligently seek Him.

He is that Rock upon which we need to build our life, a Rock that withstands the "foolosophy" of man that says there is no God. On the contrary, He is the Rock upon which we need to build our lives and in so doing we will be able to stand the storms of evil, the ridicule of thinkers who build upon the sand of pseudo science and the taunt of Satanic deception.

God is a builder. As the carpenter's Son He can tear down and rebuild a life. He rebuilds by forgiving one's sins and fitting him or her for a new life and a new kingdom whose foundations are unshakable.

Someday God will release a heaven quake and an earthquake with a big bang that will melt the present heavens and earth. Then He will make a new heaven and new earth that cannot pass away. Those who come to Him in trust admitting their sin and receiving forgiveness will be a part of that new kingdom forever. They will withstand the fiery furnace that will destroy what can be burned and shaken. Like Daniel's friends, they will emerge untouched by the final fire that removes of the temporary things of this earth.

The Bible tells us that when the foundations are destroyed there can be no certainty or stability. That is true of earthly foundations. But there are foundations which can and will survive the greatest catastrophes of all time. God has prepared for us who trust Him a city which He has made. He laid its foundations and they can never be destroyed. Through His Son he is building a church made up of living people who trust Him. "The churches one foundation is Jesus Christ her Lord. She is His new creation through water and the word. From heaven He came and sought her to be His Holy Bride. With His blood he bought her and for her sake he died."

All who build their life upon the Rock, Jesus Christ , are resting upon a sure foundation, indestructible, immovable, and incorruptible. Are you building your life on Him? If so your foundation is sure. Nothing can destroy those who come to Him upon whom His church is being built.

The gates of hell can not prevail against you. Nothing can separate you from the love of God which is in Christ Jesus our Lord. Though some foundations can be destroyed, His cannot. Those who trust God's Son have won! Their life is built upon upon the only reliable, indestructible foundation. If you are still building only on earthly foundations which can be removed, why not shift allegiance and trust in the impregnable foundation provided by God's Son? "On Christ the solid Rock I stand. All other ground is sinking sand."
<https://www.youtube.com/watch?v=ndBh1ltWYfc

A Perfect Peaceful Remedy for Failures & Grief

by Dean L Gossett

Have you like me felt shame for failures in your life? Have you felt sorrows and grief for things you have done or what others have done? While writing this I recalled things I or others have done in life that have been failures and caused me grief! Sometimes they come back to bother me and make me feel terrible. So what is the remedy?

First of all we need to realize that most of our failures are due to what the Bible calls sin. All sin or wrong is failure to be all that we should be. It is not only doing wrong but failing to do right. If we are honest we have all failed in a variety of ways to live up to our own standards. And more seriously we have failed to live up to God's standards. Only one person, Jesus Christ never sinned. The rest of us have sinned and come short of what God wishes.

Different kinds of failures are spelled out in the Bible showing our transgressions, sins and iniquities as well as those by others that affect us. Isaiah says in the Bible " All we like sheep have gone astray; we have turned every one to his own way." Going astray our own way rather than God's way is shown approximately 765 ways in the Bible,

Below are just 25 of those ways. I found that I have gone astray clearly from this list at least 17 times. How many of them have you committed? It is obvious that I need a solution for my failures and that which will relieve me of griefs and sorrows. How about you? As you look over the list below how many failures have you committed, or someone has committed against you?

1. Murdering (Hating) 2. Stealing 3.Bitterness 4.Bearing False Witness 5. Adultery

6.Falsely Accusing Others 7. Being Lazy 8.Proud 9. Not Obeying God 10.Not Doing Right 11. Not Worshipping God 12. Worshipping an Idol 13. Using God's Name in Vain 14. Sins of Ignorance 15, Denying the Lord and Others 16. Being Unforgiving 17.Drunkenness 18. Greed 19. Breaking Government Laws 20.Planning Evil 21. Pornography 22. Using Filthy Language 23.Dressing Indecently 24. Sexual Sin with & Animal or Person 25.Complaining

So what is the solution to get rid of our sins and griefs? Here is wonderful good news for all who will believe and receive it: God' has brought about a perfect solution for the removal of our sinful failures and sorrows which is found in the Bible in Isaiah 53:6. "The LORD had laid on him, His Son, the iniquity of us all." He has borne our griefs and carried our sorrows. So we do not have to be punished for all we have done wrong and for all that we have not done right. Jesus was punished for us.

God says through Jeremiah the prophet· "I will cleanse them from all the guilt of their sin against me, and I will forgive all the guilt of their sin and rebellion against me."

How does He cleanse and forgive us? He sent His Son who takes away the sin of the world. John saw Jesus coming toward him, and said, "Behold, the Lamb of God, who takes away the sin of the world!"

The Bible says what causes our sin and grief and how God has dealt with it. By Christ's one offering of himself for sin He perfects forever those being set apart as pure. (Heb. 10:14)

So What do we have to do to be set apart as pure? We have to admit our sins. Psalm 32:5 tells us, "I acknowledged my sin to you, and I did not cover my iniquity;I said, "I will confess my transgressions to the Lord,"and you forgave the iniquity of my sin." *Selah(Pause and think about it.)*

You have to believe the good news of what Jesus did for you to eradicate your sins. Then he will remove your failures as far as the east is from the west and they will be buried in the sea of God's forgetfulness. Jesus tells us "whoever confesses him before men he will confess before his father in heaven" I have received Jesus and confessed Him. My sins are gone! Have you received and confessed Him? Will you do it now? Fail to believe and do it and you will perish. Sing this song and believe it and your failures and burdens will be lifted through Calvary where Jesus died for you. <https://www.youtube.com/watch?v=QgkZznGP3dY>

Is The Worst & Best Yet To Come?

After the mass shooting in Nevada we need to ask ourselves what events on earth are yet to unfold? The Bible describes the last days leading up to the return of Christ as the worst but after His return earth will know its best time ever for 1,000 years. Stay tuned.

First, the worst times as outlined in **2 Timothy 3:1-4**. " But know this, that in the last days perilous times will come: For men will be lovers of themselves, lovers of money, boasters, proud, blasphemers, disobedient to parents, unthankful, unholy, unloving, unforgiving, slanderers, without self-control, brutal, despisers of good, traitors, headstrong, haughty, lovers of pleasure rather than lovers of God,"

Jesus tells us of this time in Matthew 24:6-7, " And you will hear of wars and rumors of wars. See that you are not troubled; for all *these things* must come to pass, but the end is not yet. For nation will rise against nation, and kingdom against kingdom. And there will be famines, pestilences, and earthquakes in various places."

Revelation teaches us that there will come a terrible time called the tribulation which will last for 7 years. During this time on earth. we are clearly told that there will arise a man called "The Beast." He will come to power world wide and make a treaty of peace with Israel which he will keep for 3 1/2 years. He will require everyone to have a mark, called the mark of the Beast, in order to buy or sell. Then he will break the peace and seek to wipe Israel off the face of the earth. At some point the Lord Jesus Christ will return (the exact time is not given). Jesus will defeat the Beast and the evil on earth.

The good news for earth is that finally a perfect man, God's Son, will bind Satan for 1000 years and reign on earth during that thousand years. Imagine what it will be like. No war for a thousand years. Wrong will be swiftly dealt with. The life span of people will increase to the point that someone dying at a hundred will be thought of as a child. People throughout the world will worship the true and Living God. All false religions will be exposed.

Israel who had rejected Christ as Messiah will accept Him when He rescues them from destruction. Then Israel who had been the tail of the nations will become the head of the nations, not because they are in themselves better than other nations but because God through rescuing them has given them a new heart to honor Him.

During Christ's Thousand year reign on earth people from the nations will go to Israel to worship God. Israel and the nations will turn their weapons into agricultural implements to feed the world.

So the worst is yet to come but be cheered. It will be followed by the best! If you believe God you will be part of those resurrected to rule with Him and enjoy the greatest blessing ever known on planet earth. Why should you believe this? Because about 2000 prophecies have already been fulfilled to the letter, 100% right. That means that of the near 500 yet to be fulfilled, they will absolutely happen. Critics have said that the prophecies were made after they happened. But that criticism has been silenced for all time by the discovery of the Dead Sea scrolls which prove the prophecies were made many years before they came to pass.

No religious writings come anywhere near the revealed truth in the Old and New Testament. One of the greatest truthful promises in the Bible was made by the Lord Jesus. He said, "If I go away, I will come again and receive you to myself that where I am you may be also." Be wise! When Jesus returns the best is yet to come. If you believe God who never lies you will be a part of it.

After the thousand years of Christ's reign on earth Satan will be loosed from being bound. He goes out and deceives the nations again. God has had enough. He defeats Satan and casts him into the lake of fire along with all his followers. Then God destroys the earth as we know it now with a violent explosion and creates a new heaven and earth in which only right exists forever. So, be wise. God wants to give you eternal life through His kiss of love demonstrated by His Son upon the cross. Return His kiss of love and thrive or reject him and perish.

Sing About it! <https://www.youtube.com/watch?v=Q00TXBPl9i4>

Is Your Name in The Book of Life? 1 Great Thing God Has Done For My Wife and Me.

How important is it that your name be in the Book of Life? It is an absolute must according to the Bible which says, "...And I saw the dead, small and great, standing before God, and books were opened. And another book was opened, which is *the Book* of Life.... Then Death and Hades were cast into the lake of fire. This is the second death. **And anyone not found written in the Book of Life was cast into the lake of fire.** (Rev. 20:11-14) To know that your name is in the Book of Life means you will go to heaven instead of the lake of fire which is called the second death.

Well then how do you and I make sure our names are in the Book of Life? Jesus sent his apostles out to preach. When they returned and told Jesus how joyous it was that they healed folks and cast out demons his reply to them shows what is most important. He said **"Notwithstanding, in this rejoice not that the spirits are subject to you; but rather rejoice because your names are written in Heaven."**

The apostles knew their names were written in heaven because Jesus told them so. At this point in their lives one could argue that Judas had his name in The Book of Life because Jesus told all the apostles their names were written in heaven. But when Judas failed to ever believe in Jesus, it is certain that his name was blotted out of the Book of Life. If you fail to ever trust Jesus as your Savior, your name will be blotted out also. Some think his name was never there. That is one view. My view is next.

For many years I thought a person's name was put in the Book of Life when he believed in Christ as Savior. After studying all the related passages I came to believe every one's name is in the Book of Life at first, which supports the fact that Jesus doesn't want anyone to perish. What is important is that one's name stays there. It doesn't stay there because you do good things but it stays there because God did a wonderful good thing for you. He died to put away your sin and rose to give you eternal life and assure you that your name will stay in the Book of Life.

The Spirit tells us that those who overcome will not have their name blotted out of The Book of Life. Some think a person overcomes by doing good works beyond salvation. Others believe as I do that one overcomes by faith not works as John says, " For whatever is born of God overcomes the world. And this is the victory that has overcome the world—our faith. Who is he who overcomes the world, but he who believes that Jesus is the Son of God? (1John 5:4-6) So one overcomes by faith that produces good

works enabled by God.(Eph.2:8-10) So It is not good works but faith in the Son of God that overcomes by which we know our names are in the Book of Life .

Some believe there are two books of life, one called the Book of Life and one called the Lamb's Book of Life. Such belief in two Books of Life is questionable. Regardless of who is right about how many books of Life there are or when one's name is put in the Book of Life, it is an absolute must if you want to go to heaven that you make sure that your name is there.

Scripture teaches that all who who know Christ as Savior have their names in the Book of Life. (Phil.4:3) A person who takes away from the meaning of prophecy as given in Revelation is not a believer and shall have his or her name taken out of the Book or tree of Life.(Rev. 22:19) So it must be there to begin with if it can be taken out. An unbeliever's name does not remain in the Book of Life.

How about me, my wife and you? Do my wife and I have our names in the Book of Life? Yes, because through Christ we are over comers. (1John 5:4-6) **A Great Thing God Has Done For Us Is to Assure Us Our Names Are In The Book of Life?** And God promises us that our names will never be blotted out. What about you? Look these verses up and believe them: John 3:16, Romans 10:9,10 and Ephesians 2:8-10. Then you will know for sure your name is in The Book of Life. Once you trust Him as Savior he promises to "never, never leave you or forsake you." If you do receive Christ as Savior please share that with me and others. If you are not willing to confess Christ before others then your faith is empty and continue to reject Him and he will reject you forever! If you know your name is in the Book of Life please pray for anyone reading this to know it as you do. Sing about it here: <https://www.youtube.com/watch?v=Wlrnr7c35gA>

Is Your Name in The Book Of Life 2 ?

I have a birth certificate as normally all do. It puts my name in the county-court-house book of temporary life on earth. There is another greater book in which my name was put before the foundation of the world. It is called The Book of Life. It is very important that my name stay in the Book of Life. Here is why:

The Bible teaches that God has books and that one book is called The Book Of Life. To go to heaven to be with Him your name must be in it and stay in that Book of Life. Everyone's name is written originally in the book of the living or book of life but those who reject God and do not believe will have there names blotted out of the book. Psalm 69:28 says, "Let them be blotted out of the book of the living,And not be written with the righteous." Anyone who is not counted righteous by faith in God and His Son will be blotted out of the Book of Life.

Since everyone must die that does not mean your name is not in the Book of Life. A person can die and be righteous. Psalm 69:28 is talking about people who die and are not counted righteous because they reject God and His love and grace. The book of the living in the Old Testament is another name for the Book of Life as it is called in the New Testament.

. To be blotted out of the Book of Life means a person will be lost forever, thrown into the lake of fire and tormented day and night forever. The fact that your name is in the Book of Life from the foundation of the world shows God's desire that everyone be saved. All names are in the book of life at first but those who are not righteous because they do not believe God are blotted out.

Acts 3:19 tells us that those who repent and are converted have their **sins** blotted out and their names **will not be blotted out** of the Book of Life. Those who overcome by believing that Jesus is the Christ will not have their names blotted out of the book of life. 1 John 5:5 tells us how to overcome, "Who is he who overcomes the world, but he who believes that Jesus is the Son of God? Revelation 3:5 tells us that "he who overcomes shall be clothed in white garments, and I will not blot out his name from the Book of Life; but I will confess his name before My Father and before His angels."

During the great tribulation those who have rejected Christ as savior will not have their names written in the Book of Life and so will worship an evil ruler called the beast. Rev. 13:8 The beast will take part in a phony resurrection which the lost will be duped into believing which shows clearly that they are not in the Book of life. Rev.17:8

To sum up, I think everyone's names are in the book of life but it does not stay there if a person rejects God and His Son. Those whose name does not remain in the Book of life are in the end cast into the lake of fire forever. Make sure your name is in the book of life by believing God and His Son .

We can know our names are still in the book of life by what the Apostle Paul, the apostle John and Jesus say. Paul says in Philippians 4:3, "And I urge you also, true companion, help these women who labored with me in the gospel, with Clement also, and the rest **of** my fellow workers, whose names *are* in the Book of Life. John says in Revelation 3:5, "He who overcomes shall be clothed in white garments, and I will not blot out his name from the Book of Life;(If a person is told his/her name won't be blotted out doesn't that imply it can be blotted out for those who don't believe?) but I will confess his name before My Father and before His angels." and in 1 John 5:5 who overcomes, "Who is he who overcomes the world, but he who believes that Jesus is the Son of God? And Jesus says in Luke 10:20 Nevertheless do not rejoice **in** this, that the spirits are subject to you, but rather rejoice because your names are written in heaven." Is Your name written there? https://www.youtube.com/watch?v=saunAY6_jDk>

Is Israel's Blessing As A Nation Forever Finished?

Some believe God has finished dealing with Israel and that the Christian church has replaced Israel. They say it is true because the nation rejected Jesus as their King and Savior and He has no more plans for Israel.

Yet we are not told that God is finished with Israel but that believers are grafted into Israel as a remnant. In the church there is neither Jew, nor Greek, slave or free, male nor female but that we are all one in Christ. That does not do away with the fact that each of us is in this world also as either a Jew, a Gentile, a servant, a free person, a male or a female. Our spiritual standing is the highest but that doesn't do away with our natural positions in this life.

It also does not do away with Israel's natural position as a nation. In the O.T. the nation Israel had many ups and down, failures and successes. When she obeyed God the nation was blessed. When she didn't obey spiritual decay and suffering followed. Though Israel was stiff necked, God chose them to show the world His will and ways. Israel grumbled, complained, sinned, and displeased God too many times but there was always a small revived remnant through whom He worked.

Satan sought to wipe out the ancestors of Jesus on numerous occasions. Israel was attacked through war, through famine, through compromise, through idolatry, through mixed marriages and through doing what was right in their own eyes instead of God's. Finally, due to their sin they were scattered throughout the nations. But God promised to bring them back someday. For a while they would be the "tail of the nations" and then a "cup of trembling in the hands of the nations" but when they finally repent as a nation upon Jesus Christ's return, they will be spared and become "the head of the nations." Their blindness so very great will only be outweighed by their final day of enlightened redemption.

Their return to become a nation on May 14, 1948 was the beginning of a new day for Israel. She came back in disbelief of her Messiah Jesus but her new existence is preparing her for the day of belief and national salvation. Attacked on five fronts she miraculously survived.

Paul says clearly that Israel has fallen but not beyond recovery. He tells of a coming time of their full inclusion, of their acceptance from the dead, of their being grafted back into their own olive tree, of their partial hardening until the full number of Gentiles are come in to salvation. All Israel will be saved when the deliverer turns godlessness away from Jacob(Israel). That is his covenant with them when He takes away their sin. They may be enemies of the gospel for the sake of those being saved now but they are loved on account of the patriarchs. God's promise to bring them back to Israel from the four corners of the earth happened. Jesus return to rescue, to redeem and to restore them, is certain. Even though they may not realize it yet, the final future of Israel is as bright as His promises to them. The redeemer will come out of Zion and all Israel will be saved. Count on it!

Jerusalem City of God's Choice, City of Light & Evil

During the second world war many sang a song,'When the lights come on again all over the world." That song predicted the partial end of the darkness of war and evil. When it ended people danced in the streets. People's lives lit up all over the world for a while.

A greater light is prophesied in 1 Kings 11:36, " And unto his Son will I give one tribe, that David my servant may have a light always before me in Jerusalem, the city which I have chosen to put my name there." David was promised that one tribe, that of Judah would have a son of David to be a light before Him in Jerusalem. A Son that would come would be a true light. But before He came Judah in the south of Israel had 20 rulers, only 8 of which were good Kings who were lights to Jerusalem and the world. The other rulers were bad and spread evil instead of light throughout the kingdom. Jerusalem became so bad that in Rev. 11:8, it is called 'Sodom and Egypt where our Lord was crucified" . But it won't stay that way!

Jesus Christ the true King defeated death outside the city walls of Jerusalem. Then He arose and will someday ascend the throne of Israel to be a perfect light to the world. His greatest moment of light was when He died upon the cross for the sin of mankind and rose to forgive all who would believe in Him. He brought life, and light, truth, forgiveness and immortality to light through the good news of His resurrection. He arose to build a New Jerusalem in which all of His followers will rule with Him someday. He is the King descended from David of the Old Testament upon whose shoulders the government shall remain forever! He is the wonderful counselor, the everlasting Father, the mighty God, the prince of peace.

His kingdom is not of this present world. It is yet to be fully made known. Every knee will bow and every tongue confess that He is Lord to the glory of God the Father.

When Jesus walked the earth He was the light of the world. Whoever followed Him then and whoever follows Him now will not walk in darkness but have the light of life. In the New Jerusalem, the city of true peace, there will be no evil. There will be no need for the light of the sun or the moon for God and the Lamb are its light and shall be forever!

Will you be in that city of peace and light? You can be for sure by believing in God's son as the way, the truth and the life, by believing in Him who died and rose for you.

Paris is now called the city of lights, but its lights will go out when the first heaven and earth pass away. But the lights of the city of Jerusalem shall be forever lit up never to be extinguished. Those lights are Jesus and those who followed Him on this earth. They shall shine as the brightness of the stars forever. It is my prayer that all who read this will be a part of the glorious city lit up by God and His people forever.

Today Jerusalem and the world is experiencing spiritual warfare. Someday the evil of darkness will be put away and the lights will come on again all over the New World and the New Jerusalem Believers in Christ will enjoy forever the New Jerusalem, city of lights and peace!

Hope to see you there! Love to you, Dean

I Need Never Doubt His Love
May 21, 2014

I have a friend in Jesus.
He is more than life to me.
He lifts me up when I am down
And sets my sad heart free.

He does not despise my broken heart
As others who seem not to care.
He sees my struggle & looks not down on
me
Nor treats me with words unfair.

He does not call me a baby when I shed
a tear.
Instead he loves me still
And takes away my fear.

He does not deal with me as my sin
demands
But forgives me & tells me so
And holds me with His hands.

So I seek him when I am low.
Because his compassion knows no
bounds
I'm lifted up and made to grow.

Some people are like Him when I share a
fault,
They show compassion
And restore me without assault.

Others attack me and seek to bring me
low.
Their compassion falls short of real care
Even though God and I have born the
hurts they share.

So I'll spread my heart before the Lord.
I need never doubt His love.
He stoops and lifts my heart to heaven up
above.

Jesus Miracle Builder

It is interesting that Jesus was a carpenter, a builder, because He was building things before He was born. Before Jesus became a human in flesh, He was God, the Christ, and the Son according to Psalm 2. He said of Himself, "Before Abraham I AM (I

existed)." The name he claimed, "I AM " is the name for God the Creator.

So what had Christ already built before He was born? When Genesis 1:1 says, "In the beginning God created the heaven and earth, it was the pre-incarnate, coequal Son who did it. Jesus, the Word, made all things.

When He finished it He said, "It is very good." It was very good until Adam and Eve exercised their free will and plunged the world into a flawed state. Death and a curse came upon the world. While it is still a magnificent creation it is now flawed as death and suffering entered the world. Jesus the master carpenter's plan had been flawed but being the expert carpenter He is, He knew how to take up His tools and redeem his fallen creation.

He symbolized His plan for restoring what was lost in the designated manner in which He had people approach Him who trusted Him. He had them come to Him based upon a sacrifice offered on an altar which they were to build. Able found acceptance in the fallen world through offering a right offering on an altar of God's bidding. Cain refused God's plan and was rejected.

All through the Old Testament we see God giving plans which reflect His redemptive plan. He gave Noah the plans for the ark which saved him and his family. He gave Israel the plans for a tabernacle dwelling which was built based upon blueprints in heaven. He gave Solomon the wisdom to build a more permanent temple which again reflects God's provision through sacrifice to allow man acceptance with Himself.

All of His buildings were meant to point forward to something more wonderful that He would build, His church. When Peter acknowledged Jesus as the Christ, the Son of the living God, Jesus announced that upon Peter's revelation and confession of faith that He would build His church and the gates of hell would not be able to prevail against it. So today He is building His church, not a denomination or a building but a group of people who trust Him as Lord and Savior. The wonderful thing for us who believe is that death and the grave will not win out against us. Jesus conquered death and the grave for us who believe by dying and rising.

That bring us to another most wonderful place God is building. It is called the New Jerusalem. Centuries before when Abraham left his home it says, "He did not know where he was going but he knew what he was looking for, "a city that has foundations whose builder and maker is God." Jesus is the builder of that city for he said, "I go to prepare a place for you." Its foundations are made of twelve kinds of precious stones. It gates are made of twelve giant pearls with angelic doorkeepers. Its streets are made of gold. Earth's most precious metal is made to walk on in heaven. It's gates are never closed because their will be no crime there, no death, no tears, no suffering, no sin, no pain. All who enter its gates will know unending gain. Read more about it in Revelation 21,22. Will you be there?

Let all who love our God the marvelous builder fall down before Him and adore Him. Who is like our great Savior, builder of the universe, of the church, of the New Jerusalem, and creator and builder of a final new heaven and earth for His people to enjoy in His presence forever! Let every knee bow and every tongue confess that Jesus Christ is Lord creator of all that is wonderful and everlasting. Amen! http://www.youtube.com/watch?v=Xn2A0cZLcFc

Jesus Most Painful and Most Blessed Moment

It hurt when Judas betrayed Jesus. It hurt more when Peter denied him. It hurt even more when all his disciples forsook him and fled. But it hurt the most when he was made sin and during those moments his Father turned his back on him and as a man he was forsaken by his Father and he cried out, "My God, My God, why have you forsaken me?" Why was he forsaken? So that you and I might be forgiven, reconciled to God and never forsaken.

In my life so far I have only had one close friend in Christ forsake me and it is a devastating feeling. But It does not compare with the grief Christ felt when he was forsaken. However, it helps me understand a little what he went through.

Thankfully, the Lord Jesus Christ's being forsaken was not forever for we read his Father's response to those abandoned,"For a brief moment I abandoned you, but with deep compassion I will bring you back. Isa. 54:7

So with great joy Jesus conquered sin and was restored and elevated above his sorrow as he was reunited with his Father and all his true followers whom he loves. That includes me and you too if you have trusted him as your Savior.

There is yet hope that the one friend who has forsaken and abandoned me may yet be reconciled with me, hopefully someday on earth but for sure in heaven.

While being forsaken hurts deeply restoration makes it worthwhile. It was for "the joy that was set before him that Jesus endured the cross despising the shame, and is set down now at the throne of God." Heb. 12:4 Restoration Is the joyful message of the cross and the perfect hope of all who trust Jesus Christ as Savior.

Being forsaken was Christ's worst moment. Being raised to be reunited with his father and his own, his most joyous moment. I am convinced that the light sufferings of this life are nothing compared to the weight of glory that is to come!

Forsaken and alone
For our sins to atone.
The weight of sin fell on his soul.
That we might be whole.
Forsaken there for me
That I might never forsaken be.
Risen now his joy known
By Him and all his own.
Exalted to his throne
Never again forsaken or ever alone.
<http://www.youtube.com/watch?v=BjKTUCUWvFw>

Card my son Ken sent me for my
80th Birthday. Sweet!
How many millions are His
followers today?
I'm one. How about you?
Yes? No?

Muslim Religion & Jimmy Carter's
Remarks

Does the bible speak of terrorist Muslim actions?
Rev. 17:13,14 These are of one mind, and they will give their power and authority to the beast. **14 These will make war with the Lamb, and the Lamb will overcome them,** for He is Lord of lords and King of kings; and those *who are* with Him *are* called, chosen, and faithful." John 16:2 They shall put **you** out of the synagogues: yea, t**he time will come, that whosoever kills**

you will think that he does God service.

Ex President Jimmy Carter,
You spoke of Islam and called it a "great religion." There are approximately 1.6 billion Muslims in the world and 2.2 Billion Christians in the world. So is it great or just big? Look at its roots in Mohammed. Was he a true or false prophet?

Many who who have studied Mohammad in depth conclude as follows:

"Satan used Muhammad as a pawn and Islam as a tool to attack the people of God. As Muhammad grew in power, he used violence to subdue those that disagreed with him. He denied the Sonship of Jesus, making him an anti-Christ, and denied other key doctrines of Christianity. Muhammad eventually urged his followers to oppress Christians and instituted laws that deny people basic human rights. Today in Muslim countries, Christians are victimized by those laws. Many of them have been murdered, executed, and or oppressed for their faith. If a Muslim converts to Christianity, he is under a death sentence for apostatizing. In his last few hours of life, Muhammad asked Allah to curse the Christians. Real Islam is a weapon Satan uses to make war upon God and His people."

All of the above is explained at this site:
http://www.answering-islam.org/Silas/demons.htm

March 19,2014

Hi John,
God confirmed something to me today. I have been writing special notes to folks to encourage them in their Christian life. Both you and Marsha came to mind. I

kind of wondered if I should write to you. Then two things happened within a few minutes apart. First, Gloria and I got the special 51st anniversary card from Marsha and you. I was reminded of our time in Hawaii celebrating our anniversaries. It was a great time getting to know you and Marsha. Then a minute later Gloria was going through an old annual and there was an article my mom sent me in 1980 called <u>For This Cowboy-Better Than a Rodeo</u> by John Christian.

I read it through and it confirmed in my heart that I should write to you. I was quite moved by the experiences that led up to your conversion and the change in both you and Marsha's life. I read about how you responded to Paul Decker's message and "asked Jesus to come in to your heart" "Then you went forward for prayer and after that your life was never the same." Because I know you, it brought tears to my eyes. The salvation of a soul, especially when it's one"s own, is the most wonderful new beginning in the world.

I read about your struggle with cleaning up your language, how God gave you victory. You said He also helped you get your priorities straight, "The Lord first, your family second, ranching third and roping fourth.".

You also said, "Even when I am not too keen about what he wants me to do, I have joy and peace when I say,"Yes, Lord."

That was 30 years ago, John. And I know that you like me have had many struggles over the years in our walk with God. We've found that God has a rope in his hand and has to rope us in some times. Our struggles may be different but we all have them including your wonderful wife Marsha who is learning to control anger and rage and when she does God uses her sweet way of praying

for people to bring them into the corral of obedience.

I know that you have been dealing with some depression but since your name John means "God Is Gracious," I know God is going to be gracious to you and help you with those struggles. Our wives love for us to share our feelings and be thoughtful with them. It isn't easy but it is possible and it is an area of life I know God is going to help you with. Marsha helped me a lot to do better in sharing my feelings and love with Gloria.

Since your name means God is gracious I pray this prayer for you. Fill John with your grace that he may be a man of godly taste. Grant him to be an example to his Son Jac whose name also means "God is gracious." Help him to be gracious in his heart to everyone he knows that people will see that through him Your Spirit flows.

What Could Be Worse Than Noah's Flood?

Most of us know the story of Noah's Ark and how it ended. After the flood God promised to never wipe out all people by a world wide flood again and gave us the sign of the rainbow to remind us of His promise. But He never promised to not wipe out the world of unbelievers by an explosive fire judgement that would someday destroy both the earth and the heavens.

Jesus and the Apostle Peter and people who believe God know the flood really happened and warn us of a greater judgement to occur when Jesus returns. Listen to Jesus validation of the reality of the days of Noah and the certainty of His return to judge the world. "**And as it was in the days of Noah, so shall it be also in the days of the Son of man. 27 They did eat, they drank, they married wives, they were given in** marriage, until the day that Noah entered into the ark, and the flood came, and destroyed them all...so it will be in the day when the Son of Man(Jesus) is revealed (to judge the world) (Luke 17:26,27)."

The Apostle Peter's words in his two New Testament letters validate the time of Noah's ark when the world that then existed was deluged with water and perished. Then he clearly tells of a worse judgement to come.**The apostle Peter tell us "The heavens and earth that now exist are stored up for fire, being kept until the day of judgment and   destruction of the ungodly. 8.But do not overlook this one fact, beloved, that with the Lord one day is as a thousand years, and   a thousand years as one day. 9 The Lord is not slow to fulfill his promise   as some count slowness, but   is patient toward you,   not wishing that any should perish, but that all should reach repentance. (2Peter 3:7-9) (3:19-22 and 2Peter 3:7-9.)**

God does not want you to perish when the world is melted by fire but wants you survive in an ark of safety. Jesus tells us He is the door of the final ark of salvation, "I am the door. By me if any man enter in he will be saved..." If you trust Jesus Christ you will never perish. Knowing Him as Savior, you will come through the fire even as Noah came through the flood. And then you will set foot unsinged on to new heavens and a new earth in which only right will exist. By believing in Him as your Savior you will find shelter and peace in him and be counted without spot and blameless. The eternal God will be your refuge and hold you safe in His everlasting arms.

A greater than Noah, **Jesus** preaches to you today saying, **"Come to me all you who labor and are heavy laden and I will give you rest. He also says, "Whoever comes to me I will in no way cast out."**   Peter clarifies the need to come to Christ because   **"the day of the Lord will come like a thief.   The heavens will disappear with a roar;   the elements will be destroyed by fire,   and the earth and everything done in it will be laid bare.   11 Since everything will be destroyed in this way, what kind of people ought you to be? You ought to live holy and godly lives 12 as you look forward to the day of God and speed its coming.   That day will bring about the destruction of the heavens by fire, and the elements will melt in the heat.   13 But in keeping with his promise we are looking forward to a new heaven and a new earth,**

where righteousness dwells. 14 So then, dear friends, since you are looking forward to this, make every effort to be found spotless, blameless   and at peace with him.   (2Peter 3:10-14).

_ Will you be like the unbelieving, ungodly fools who rejected Noah's message or will you be like Noah and his family who believed God? Will you reject Jesus' message or will you come to Him and become a born again child of God which fits you to overcome the final destruction of the present earth and heavens? John 1:12-14 tells you how to overcome by being born again of God. If you come to Him and enter into faith in Jesus Christ, then the coming heaven-and-earth-fire-melting judgement will usher you into new heavens and a new earth far greater and exceedingly more glorious than the day Noah stepped out of the ark. You will see a rainbow encircling the Lord upon His throne and be saved and safe forever.

<https://www.youtube.com/watch?v=0kvQB8hWVQw>

Keep Yourself in the Love of God

Keep yourself in the love of God who is able to keep you from falling and to build you up in your vital, true, and pure faith.

By night on my bed I sought Love. I searched the romances of the ages but they came up lacking. Then I found love on a cross outside a city wall. There all my sins and failures died. There I found forgiveness. There I left my sorrows, my hurts and my pain. I left them there on the Son of God who came to mend my broken life. I found dying love not in religion but in a Person. I believed in Him who took my sins upon Himself and set me free from them all. I went with Him to a tomb where all my failures were buried, banished forever in a grave of love.

But true love could not be kept in a grave. Like a new born baby it must rise from death's womb. So It rose beyond Calvary's hill, beyond the tomb to a higher room. Yes, I found love risen, carrying me into the room of grace and peace and never-ending joy. The love I found in Jesus Christ my Savior lifted me from death into life, clothed me in the character of God and elevated me into the pure love of God's presence.

I sought love and at last I found it in a person crucified, died,risen and glorified. I am His and He is mine. I rest in His love Divine. The Spirit says, "Keep yourself in the love of God." So I say, "Yes, it is His will so I must obey. I will keep my mind and heart in that love."

I will keep myself in His love which is higher than the highest heaven, deeper than the deepest sea, wider than the universe, broader than my transgressions and enduring beyond time. I will bask in it, bathe in it, soak it up and give it away. It can never run dry. It can alleviate each sigh. It is for now, not just for pie in the sky by and by. I will make my home in the heart of God's love. I will keep my affections on Christ above. Then the arithmetic of grace, mercy and peace will be added, multiplied and divided with others, while sin is subtracted from my life. That is my aim, to keep myself in the love of God.

Giving a gift to someone you love is a great delight. God gave to you the gift of gifts, all other gifts in one, His Son. He loves you and delights in you. Keep yourself in that love always! The love that lifted me is too big for just one person.. That love is for you as well. I want to pas it on. Have you or will you join me in receiving and keeping yourself in that love?

Love to you, Dean Let Love Lift You with this song:
<http://www.youtube.com/watch?v=mHQQ7PomyIE>

A Prayer for Our Granddaughter
Upon Her Graduation
May Our God be Your Foundation
and Utmost Admiration!

Lord, we look beyond this earth to
You upon your throne.
Let your River of life fill Kirsten with
a life sweeter than cologne.

Fill her heart to over flow to future
sisters and brothers.
Let the water of Your Word spring
up through her to others.
For whoever believes in Me,
said Jesus, "Out of her innermost
being shall flow rivers of living
water."
Amen! Let it be!

Help her come boldly to Your
throne of grace to find help and
mercy in time of needs.
Let her pluck 12 kinds of fruit
continually from the tree of life upon
which she feeds.

Let the river of Your Spirit's grace,
love, joy, peace, patience,
gentleness,
goodness, kindness, faith, hope,
healing, and truth
be always in her embrace.

Help her find health and pass on
healing from the leaves of
heaven's tree.
Grace her with the fruit of the Spirit
to set others fully free.

Unlike the Garden of Eden's
restricted tree, forbidden!-
Let her partake of the tree of life as
she reaches up to heaven.

Give her grace to drink from the
river of God.

Grace to pour out living water on earth's barren sod.
Grace to quench her thirst and the thirst of Your own.
Grace to nourish Your sheep as she waits before Your Throne!

Replace her suffering with your joy and gladness
Let our dear granddaughter rise above her past sadness.
May Kirsten Victoria Kline be Victorious as she walks Your line.
Fill her life with everything wonderful, beautiful and fine.

Grandpa Dean and Grandma Gloria, June 7, 2009

Special Prose, Poem and Prayer for Kirsten Victoria Kline from

From Her
Grandpa Dean

I want to love God with all my heart and love all His people too. That's why I'm writing this poem and prayer specially for you.

Did you know that your name Kirsten means a follower of Christ and that Victoria means victorious. Others comment on your quality of boldness and with His help fearless care, compassion and encouraging heart. Your last name Kline means small of stature. You enjoy a name related to Paul whose name was altered from that of an Old Testament character named Saul who was extremely big and tall yet he failed in his relationship with God. Saul in the new testament thought to highly of himself until he met Christ. From then on Saul saw himself as small and seems to have abandon his name Saul being known mainly as Paul, small from then on. So God was able to use him in big ways. This fits you Kirsten because you became small in your sight and God became big. As God used Paul so He has been using you.

Kirsten follower of Christ in whom you delight, though you are small in your sight, through you will be displayed His victorious might. Full of bold and fearless love, compassion for the needy and poor, God will light on you as the Spirit Dove! He will enable you in power to set prisoners free and then be saved to dance with glee. You are a partner in prayer, who as I, have felt joy and despair whose aching and caring heart has lifted others on prayer filled wings of healing into heaven's fragrant air. You long as I with zealous heart to lift all God's people to His grace and mercy laden chair, there to receive marvelous answers to prayer.

May your words through the Spirit's care, carry His people beyond their despair where giving Him their ashes they will in exchange be clothed in His beauty that awaits them there. If our simple words can do this for His own then our hearts would dwell in awe at His merciful, gracious throne! Oh let it be for you, for me and all His own!

Let our little hearts lift all God's blood bought people into heaven where together we gaze upon Your beauty to be raptured in Your goodness, to be filled with Your purity, for it is in Your purity that we are pure. It is in Your love that we can truly love. It is in your presence we shed tears which Your tender hand wipes away. It is there that we set our affections on things above where from glory to glory we bathe in Your everlasting love!

Lead Me to the Rock

One of the first verses I ever learned in the Bible, when I was 20 years old, has been a continual blessing to me. It is **Psalm 61:2,** "From **the** end of **the** earth I will cry **to** You, When my heart is overwhelmed; **Lead me to the rock** that is higher than I."

When I am low the Lord lifts me to the Rock that is higher than I. The view from the Rock is magnificent. I'm able to see how the Rock has blessed others and blesses me. In the Rock is shelter. In the Rock is protection. In the Rock is victory. In the Rock there is refreshment. On the Rock there is stability. In the Rock there is sweetness! In the Rock there is revelation and salvation. From the Rock there is also a marvelous unfolding of God's purpose for our lives.

So what and who is the Rock? Moses tell us who the Rock is in a song in Deut. 32:**4,** "He is the Rock, his work is perfect: for all his ways are judgment: a God of truth and without iniquity, just and right is he." Hannah, an Old Testament lady also tells us the answer to who the Rock is. God miraculously answered her prayer and gave her a child. Her heart had been overwhelmed with sorrow so she sought her Rock, her Lord, for a child. He answered her and led her to the Rock that was higher than her. He lifted her out of depression to the heights of joy by giving her Samuel who turned out to be a great man of God. She tells us in her joyful prayer,"No one is holy like the Lord, For *there is* none besides You, Nor *is there* any rock like our God."

In the Old Testament days of Israel's trek in the wilderness we are told how God caused water to flow out of a rock and quench the thirst of the whole nation of Israel. In the New Testament we are told who the Rock of the nation really was, "**1 Corinthians 10:4** and all drank the same spiritual drink. For they drank of that spiritual **Rock** that followed them, and that **Rock** was Christ." So from the Rock, Christ, flow all the great blessings of God. Christ told a woman at a well that if she drank of the water he would give her, she would never suffer spiritual thirst. He would quench her thirst forever. i have drank the water he gives. As my Rock, he satisfies my eternal thirst. How about you?

He also is the Rock on which a wise man builds his life. "On Christ the solid Rock I stand. All other ground is sinking sand," He is the Rock who was rejected by many but became the eternal foundation of his church. He is the Rock out of which honey flows sweetening my life daily. He is the Rock in which a cleft exists from where I see the goodness and glory of God. He hides my soul in the cleft of a Rock and covers me there with his hand. in the Old Testament Moses in the cleft of a rock, got to see God's "back parts" which displayed all his goodness. In the New Testament believers who are in the Rock get to see his front parts. All we 'beholding as in a glass the glory of the Lord are changed into his image from glory to glory." Seeing him we see God. In heaven we shall see him totally in high definition in all his dimensions and be like him forever!

So Jesus Christ is my Rock. Is he yours? If so sing about it. This song will lead you in your experiences to the Rock: https://vimeo.com/30653908>

Leadership from On HIgh
Jan 2,2013

The USA needs some Esthers and Mordecais.
O Lord raise some up before our nation dies.
Rid us of any Hamans in power in congress.
Hang them out to dry to clean up the mess.
O for a government that solves the deficit dent,
That won't bankrupt us with OUR money spent,
Give us leaders to help our need to be freed
From corporate, national & personal greed.
Most leaders in Washington D.C. are very rich.
They seldom cut spending in THEIR own wealthy nitch.
We need more leaders like Lincoln who tell the truth,
But keep them from being shot down by a William Booth.
Help eliminate the current tax system with its loopholes.

Replace it with a new one fair to all our nation's souls.
Our country is still a wonderful place to be alive.
But adding some wise fixes would make it thrive!
So may we add some Esthers and a head Mordecai
To guide us from on high, lest our nation die!

Less is More

When Jesus was given 7 loaves of bread he fed 4 thousand people and 7 baskets full of bread were left over. When he fed 5 thousand people with 5 loaves and two fish, 12 baskets full were left over. He fed more with the little boys lunch of five loaves and two fish than he fed with seven loaves. Less was more in the end. Often we think of God working in big ways but don't think as much about how he works in small ways. A cup of cold water given to a disciple will not lose its reward. The woman who gave the Lord a couple of copper coins worth less than a penny was declared by Jesus to be the greatest giver though others put in much large amounts. Why? When we have little to give and we give it to God, it becomes gigantic. His strength is made perfect in weakness. I've got lots of weakness to give Him. Perhaps He will use me in greater ways because of that. We are not to despise the day of small beginnings. The first stone laid in the temple is significant as is the last. They who endure to the end must at least get started. The first shall be last and the last first. So when you do anything with a right attitude, no matter how small it is, you will be rewarded. Less is more if God is in it!

Dear Barbara,

I"m typing this out rather than sending a hand written note because my handwriting is a little shaky these days.

Thank you so much for your nice card. Every time Don and I talked each week in his last days we would pray for others. We always prayed for you and together prayed the verse in the Bible which Mark explained in his talk about Don's faithfulness. I still pray it. It is John 1:12 in the New Testament. I will continue to pray for you. Don always prayed for my son Ken and grandson Tyler. If you are so inclined you might pray for them. They both need to come to the Lord for transforming salvation as did my granddaughter this year. She is a new person in her heart. Old things passed away for her and all things became new. She was delivered from addiction, self centeredness and cares deeply for the homeless and addicted and the up an outers too.

God bless you and keep you and make His face shine on you,

I'll miss Don but even though he has died, his life still speaks doesn't it.

Love,
Dean

Dear Devin,

Thanks for writing back. The book I ordered for you should come to you in about a week. Regarding why you are in jail for a crime you did not commit. Perhaps it is to help you identify with Jesus who was put to death and was totally innocent. Only, He did it for us all who have sinned and come short of what God wants. Out of Jesus suffering came the greatest blessings the world has ever known. People by the millions have come to Him in faith and found forgiveness. His act of undeserved suffering was turned around to bless the whole world. God can use your experience that way as well.

Of course while you and I are not guilty of certain crimes we are guilty of sinning against Him. All you have to do is look at His commandments to see that we have broken them. You might read them below and see which ones you have broken so that you will come to Christ to have them forgiven. The Bible says the law is not meant to save us but to drive us to the Lord for forgiveness. Here they are: In my life I have broken for sure before I became a Christian the ones mentioned in verses 7, 8, 12, 14, 15, 17,

1 And God spoke all these words: 2 "I am the Lord your God, who brought you out of Egypt, out of the land of slavery. 3 "You shall have no other gods before me.
4 "You shall not make for yourself an idol in the form of anything in heaven above or on the earth beneath or in the waters below. 5 You shall not bow down to them or worship them; for I, the Lord your God, am a jealous God, punishing the children for the sin of the fathers to the third and fourth generation of those who hate me, 6 but showing love to a thousand generations of those who love me and keep my commandments. 7 "You shall not misuse the name of the Lord your God, for the Lord will not hold anyone guiltless who misuses his name. 8 "Remember the Sabbath day by keeping it holy.
9 Six days you shall labor and do all your work, 10 but the seventh day is a Sabbath to the Lord your God. On it you shall not do any work, neither you, nor your son or daughter, nor your manservant or maidservant, nor your animals, nor the alien within your gates. 11 For in six days the Lord made the heavens and the earth, the sea, and all that is in them, but he rested on the seventh day. Therefore the Lord blessed the Sabbath day and made it holy.
12 "Honor your father and your mother, so that you may live long in the land the Lord your God is giving you.13 "You shall not murder. 14 "You shall not commit adultery. 15 "You shall not steal. 16 "You shall not give false testimony against your neighbor. 17 "You shall not covet your neighbor's house. You shall not covet your neighbor's wife, or his manservant or

maidservant, his ox or donkey, or anything that belongs to your neighbor." 18 When the people saw the thunder and lightning and heard the trumpet and saw the mountain in smoke, they trembled with fear.

What if a person only broke one of them. The Bible says if we break one we are guilty as if we broke them all. Why? Because one sin deserves death. The wages of our sin is death. It is like a ten link chain that holds your watch to your belt. Break one link and your watch is detached and no longer works. Break one commandment and be detached from God BUT God still loves us so He let His Son who never broke any of the commandments die for us. (He is the only person who ever lived that was sinless).

Once we trust Christ we are no longer under the law or 10 commandments. Why? Because once we believe God we seek to please Him and all He requires is that we love Him above all and we love others as we do ourselves. Will we ever fail to love God and others after we believe Him. Yes, but He is faithful and fair to forgives us our sins and cleanse us from all that is wrong. It's like your mom who most likely punished you a few times for things you did wrong but forgave you and does not reject you. That is love.
Perhaps that is why God is allowing this in your life that you might come out a new and dedicated person both to God and others. Think about it. Praying for you ever day as I have for years.

Dean & Gloria

Dear Devin,

I had them send my book to you. Maybe you will be able to do it while your are there.If you would like Gloria and I to come by and visit you, we'd be glad to. You don't have to be embarrassed because of what is happening as far as we are concerned.

I correct correspondence courses from guys in jail every week. I've found that many of them are freer in jail than most on the outside. Why? Because as Jesus said, "You shall know the truth and the truth shall make you free."

.

God bless you. I pray for you daily and have for years. I believe God will use this for your best interests and that some day you will find that out.

An Open Letter to Dr. Jeffery Long Regarding Your Book, Evidence of the After Life

My experience was both an in-and-out-of-body spiritual experience. I came to understand it in depth later as I read the Bible explanation of my death to self and life through my new birth. "If any man be in Christ, he is a new creation, old things have passed away and all things become new." After i experienced my new birth I immediately asked the question in my mind, "How do I live this new life?" A man came up to me an answered my question that I was thinking but didn't say out loud. He said, "If you want to know how yo live as a follower of Christ you need to study this book. He held up the Bible and said, "Faith comes by hearing and hearing by the Word of God." He suggested I start with the book of Romans which clearly explains how and why a person needs God's good news and word to have power to live and understand one's purpose for life. I have studied Romans and all the Bible for many years. Once while reading about Billy Graham who practiced preaching alone, I read that something inside him said, "Someday there will be thousands" of people, not trees, who come to Christ. I wept and felt God was saying that to me. Though I am not worthy to untie his shoes God has enabled me to share the good news of dying with Christ and rising with him both now and in the future. Many have come to Christ by God's grace through my preaching, teaching and writing.

When I heard your book about Near Death Experiences It strengthened my faith BUT one part of what you shared, Dr. Long, bothered me. You said that everyone after death will have it wonderful. While many will, the Bible is clear that many won't find it wonderful. Jesus said," The gate is broad and the road broad that a leads to destruction and many are on that road, but the gate is narrow and the road narrow that leads to life and few there be that find it." FEW!

Your research covering thousands included those who had a hellish experience. You must realize that you did not research the millions and even billions who may have had an out of body experience that was not wonderful. I read of one experience a man had while dying. He said, "Cast me into help but deliver me from frown on Jesus face." Not everyone who says Lord, Lord will enter into Jesus presence at death. Read Revelation 20. While I regret that anyone perish in hell, Jesus does too. He takes no pleasure in the death of the wicked. Jesus tells of two men who died, one being in inescapable torment while the other was in paradise in great joy. No one that I saw questions you or asked about your Biblical beliefs. I can assure you that the Devil is in the deception business. He appears to be an angel of light to deceive people. Your saying everything will be wonderful for everyone after death is deceptive. Do you really believe that? What are your beliefs regarding Jesus Christ? Is he the answer for ending wonderfully? Is HE the narrow door through which we must go to be on the road to life? He says, "No one comes to the Father but by me." Do you believe that or do you believe the lie that all religions lead to heaven?

I wanted to ask questions regarding your beliefs as I listened to others questions you were asked, but none that I heard asked you what you believe about Jesus Christ and whether or not you believe that knowing Him assures heaven and eternal life, but rejecting Him means you will perish and not know God's eternal life. I wanted to ask you questions via email but couldn't find how to email you except through this form you have provided.

I hope I might hear from you clearly stating your belief in how one ends up with a wonderful life in heaven or if you really think everyone does?? Please let me know.

Thank you,
Dean L Gossett

Emmaus Bible College

Dear Sirs:

I am happy that my my book A *Journey Through the Bible,* which I did for free, was first printed in 1973. It has been revised many times which is fine but I regret that on no revision was I ever consulted. Originally in the first printings from 1973 to 1978 the amazing thing that helped inspire my book

was printed on page 1. It told about a miracle answer to prayer that happened in a philosophy class which related to the first chapter of the book about God's plan for Creation, and it led to the instructor asking me to speak to his class. That invitation was a miracle answer to prayer. In all my years in college it was the only class except for a speech class that I was asked to speak.

Once at a family reunion I prayed that I would be able to share the gospel with all my family on my mom's side. On Sunday, my aunt whose husband was a dying believer, asked all the family who were not all believers to go to Minnie Ha Ha Covenant church. As I walked in the church door I was handed a bulletin with the text on it I had chosen to share with my family which no one but God and I knew. Also a photo of a Monarch butterfly was on the bulletin, which I planned to use as an illustration of the resurrection. Then the pastor, whom I never knew and had never met approached me and asked if I would take the message. Would I? Oh Yes! It was just one of over 76 miracles I have experienced so I am strong on believing modern day miracles should not be left out of books. Have you ever heard of a pastor,on the spur of the moment ask someone else he never knew to speak instead of himself?

The first miracle experience in A *Journey Through the Bible that happened in* the philosophy class was after a number of years left out. I don't know why ? Can you explain why?

Also in the last revision in chapter 9 the printed out questions given to students to complete, question 9 says Nahum and Obadiah are each only one chapter. Wrong. Obadiah is one chapter but Nahum is not. Are you going to fix this error in the questions given out to students?

I appreciate being a part of over 1,000,000 people who have completed my book. I have been having a Bible study one on one with a Mike Teague who told me my book is the first one to be done on the internet. Is that true?

Thank you for your ministry and outreach to people all over the world, especially those in jail. I have corrected A *Journey Through the Bible* answers by three people in jail every week for many years. Many share how they came to Christ and how God is using them in jail.

One person at ECE told me no one ever contacted me about my book because they thought I was dead. No, I am still alive at age 82 and busy writing, doing one on ones with three guys, speaking at Bethesda Retirement Center, and teaching small groups. I have completed three other books outside ECE and have written many hundred articles sent out regularly to about a thousand people. One book, **The Royal Ride; Esther in Seven Acts,** I offered to ECE years ago but it has at this point never been done as a correspondence course though it has been taught at VBC at the Crossing in Pleasanton, Calif. and in small groups on more than one occasion. Esther is the most ironic book in the Bible!

Thank you for sending my book out to over 1,000.000 people who have compleed it.

Sincerely yours,

Dean L Gossett

Mar.10/2014

Dear Glow!

Thank you for the belt. It is a gift that really lifts me up where it counts!
Also, looking forward to reading the 365 day Chronological Bible. I will especially cherish the verse in the Middle of the Bible, Psalm 118:8 It tells what is better there!

Loved your card which says all the 23 things I like to hear from you. I'll put it by my bed and you can read one to me every night.

Megga Exclmation
Marks
!!
!!!!!!!!!!!!!!!!!!!

Love from your favorite Husband of All!

To be with you, to listen to you, to love you, to talk with you,
to walk with you, to spend time with you, to listen to music with you,
to read with you, to hold you, to cry with you,to think with you, to do things with you,
to have dinner with you, to touch you, to dream with you, to explore with you,
to drive with you, to play with you, to dance with you, to run with you, to snuggle with you,

to   hug you, to tell you again I love you, I love you.

Thank you for those "to's" Favorite Wife of All!

Love, Dean
One of the above a day keeps the blah's away.
Two a day make the blessings stay.
Three a day drive the night away.
Four a day, well what can I say!
Hip Hip Hurray!

Go for it!

Hi Gary,
I don't know about you but I feel you and i clicked as brothers and friends. I alway like someone with whom I can confide and trust to share thoughts and conversation about our Lord and His work. I feel that way about you.

Regarding your new series on heaven and hell. Here are A few thoughts about them with emphasis now on heaven. i feel that we must take all the "symbols" about heaven and hell and realize that the sum total of them all is a greater reality than each symbol by itself. All words of course are symbols. That does not mean they don't represent reality. In fact reality is greater than any symbol. The American Flag, symbol of the U.S. certainly falls far short of the reality of all that the U.S. is, has been and shell be. For example, the church is pictured as a bride, building, body, pearl of great price, set of living stones, and as a city in which God dwells forever. The bride and bridegroom symbol of course shows the intimacy that God wishes to have and will have with the church. The pearl of great price symbolizes the great value He places on the church. The building and the city with its golden streets and pearl gates symbolizes the eternal wealth that we have in Christ forever and the unending access to His glory. The City comes down out of heaven prepared as a bride adorned for her husband.

I tried to capture that beauty in a poem I wrote for June Rice's daughter Judy after the death of her mom. June was a meticulous dresser and a writer and lover of poetry as is her daughter. This poem captures something of the beauty ahead for us all. We will "not be unclothed but clothed upon" in a heavenly wardrobe beyond our fondest dreams.

Heaven's Wardrobe

Every believer's dream will come about
We'll all be beautiful inside and out!
No more stains. Not even a wrinkle.
All will be neat, glow and twinkle!
Divine botox cleansed our wrinkles away.
Heaven's runway will be our brightest day!
No more washing. No more darning.
All will be elegant and charming!
No more thinking, "What shall I wear."
We'll all be hunks and beauties there!
So the next time you put on your best attire.
Remember it will be eclipsed when you expire.

Life's Worst & Greatest Exchange

To gain the whole world and lose one's soul is the worst exchange anyone can ever make. To exchange ashes for beauty is the best exchange.

I aw a photo of a picture of a glass egg. It is made from the ashes of Mt. St. Helens. The ashes were transformed by a heat process. That which was once not considered of much worth and useless was changed into an object of beauty by the talent of a master glass maker's hand.

There is a hand that is Divine that can take our ashes and exchange them for God's Beauty. That is one of the reasons Jesus came- to give us "beauty for our ashes."(1)

If we come to Jesus Christ and receive Him as our Lord and Savior he replaces our sins with the gift to us of His righteousness. Abraham of old found that out. He said to God, "I who am but dust and ashes have taken upon me to speak unto the Lord." (2) And God heard Abraham and gave Him a gracious answer to his prayer. By faith in God's word Abraham was counted righteous.

When I was about 20 years old I called out to God to make me clean inside. He heard my prayer, forgave my sins and created a new heart in me. He gave me beauty for my ashes and the oil of joy in exchange for my mourning over my own sinfulness.

Jacob called out to God and He changed Jacob from a trickster to a Prince of God. Both Abraham and Jacob made marvelous exchanges with God. Both had their name changed. Abraham was first called Abram which means father. God changed His name to Abraham which means high father or father of many nations. Jacob which means suplanter(offender, wrong doer) had his name changed to Israel(Strong Prince of God).

The Bible actually tells us that all who know Him through faith receive a new name given by God. (3) We don't all know what it is yet but in eternity we will know it.

So if we are wise we will admit our need and smallness and reach out to the God who alone can meet our greatest need, to be changed from glory to glory as we behold our God in the face of Jesus Christ. Scripture sums it up neatly. "If any man be in Christ, he is a new creation. Old things have passed away. All things have become new." (4)

Austin Miles came to Christ and found he had a new name and wrote this song:
https://www.youtube.com/watch?v=wC5qZscVMLw>(1) Isaiah 61:3 (2) Genesis 18:27 (3)Revelation 2:17

Longing For Jesus
Mar. 19, 2014

How I long to see you Jesus.
Risen, shining your face on me.
How I long to live purely for You,
With Your Spirit setting me free.

My heart aches to know You.
My mind grasps for Your thoughts
My feet seek Your path of grace
My eyes fix on your unseen face.

Why do you seem so close yet far away.
I long to see more answers to prayer
As I ask great things of you and dare
To expect daily answers that show you
care.

If my heart longs daily for you,
Ought I not see you work wonders
Bringing tears of gratitude to my eyes,
Causing continual thanks to you to rise!

So hear me then my dear Lord Jesus
Be all you can be to me.
Crucify my sinful nature
With your fulness fully fill me.
And I shall joy always, only, in Thee

I found life in a look at my Savior
Life overflowing with God's favor.
Life abundant and free for you and for me!
So look to Jesus to forgive. Look and live!

When the serpent's poison bite turns your
day to night
Look to Jesus on the cross. He'll Turn your
dark to light!
The Devil has bitten us for sure.
We must Look to Jesus for its cure.

When sin in you shows it's ugly face
Filling you with shame and disgrace
Turn to look on Jesus dying face.
Taste in full His loving grace.

Be gone then shame and guilt!
Jesus took my sins' sword to the hilt.
Leap up O feeble heart! Upon His face fix
your gaze.
Jump for joy! Sing His praise!

When Satan accuses me in life or death,
I'll look on Christ till my final breath!
Then I'll rise to meet Him at heaven's door
To look on Him forever more.

I'll see Him as He fully is,
Know Him as I'm known.
Sit by Him upon His throne
Worship Him and Him alone.

I looked to Him on earth.
I lived- Set free!
I'll look on Him in heaven
Perfect for all eternity!
<http://www.youtube.com/watch?
v=vFCUTPB_Vm0> >

Look & Live

I looked at my sins and I was frightened.
I looked to Jesus and my heart brightened.
I saw Him dying for me on a tree.
My sins were gone and I was free!

Sometimes It is Good Just to Go Outside
& Look Up and Listen to the Stars

Twinkle, twinkle little star,
I understand now what you are,
Up above the world so high,
You're God's spokesman in the sky.

Twinkle, twinkle, now I see,
You unveil God's mystery,
You're a light to guide my eyes
To the Maker of the skies.

You're a voice that speaks to me
About our God of Majesty.
You're a wonder rare
Of the God who placed you there.

You're a voice to all mankind,
Stirring thoughts in every mind,
To each mind below a sign
Of the heavenly and divine.

You're a language from afar
Pointing to the greatest Star,
A voice lofty and high,
Announcing Jesus who would die.

Beyond the twinkle in my eye
I see the God of earth and sky.
He, through you, does proclaim
Signs and seasons in His name.

You are fulfilled, pointing us to the King,
Inspiring hearts and lips to sing!
Silently I hear you shout,
"God is what I'm all about!"

Losing a Friend
Feb 22, 2014

How hard it is to lose a friend
When hope was it would not end.

To pray & wish your friend well every day
With little or no response coming your way.

I'm so glad Jesus is different than that.
His mercy, forgiveness & love is a constant
fact.

He forgives seventy times seven when I
confess.
His love is sweet, tender and gives me rest.

He is a Friend who never forsakes my face
But stays close and makes me feel His
grace.

So I will pray for my friend as Jesus did upon
the cross.
Forgive O Lord & let my friend suffer no loss.

For I know all will be right when life on earth
is complete
And we meet in heaven at Your feet.

But Lord it would be nice if that friendship
renewed on earth.
Such a reality would be of double worth-

Both here at present to reflect Your grace
As well as in heaven when we see Your
Face.

The story behind the hymn, What a Friend
We Have in Jesus
<http://www.youtube.com/watch?
v=tKjUoE2fack>
The Whole Song: <http://www.youtube.com/
watch?v=4XRmGEbH0qs>
Note especially the last line of this song:
Do your friends despise, forsake you.
Take it to the Lord in prayer.
He will never leave you.
You will find a solace there.

Anne Rice who use to write Vampire books got converted and says now she will "only write for the Lord."
We corresponded via email and she asked special prayer.
She Lost her daughter on August 5th.1972. She told me she
felt tormented by the devil sometimes thinking she will never see her little
child again who died of Leukemia at the age of six.
I wrote her the following to comfort and encourage her.

Dear Anne,
When I got your message about your dear daughter,
my heart went out to you in prayer. I am reminded of
David who lost his child. He said, "My child won't come to me but I will go to him." And the words of this poem seemed to come to me unsummoned
as I sat on a rock and first wrote them on my iPhone.
May they comfort and encourage your heart.
Dean

God's Encouragement Regarding Your Child
by Dean L Gossett

The loss of a child is a grievous thing
But God gives new hope with the arrival of spring!

That which was barren and appears as death
Revives as God renews **all** with His life giving breath!

The seeds in their graves die, yet rise again
As they reach to the sun and new life enters in!

So those little children who have passed away
Will rise like a flower to a glorious day!

Look up oh heart filled with grief
Don't listen to the devil, that blasphemous thief!

You shall see your child, a tender and magnificent sight
And you will embrace her again with endless delight!

You can know this for sure. God has promised it to His own
And His word is as pure and sure as His heavenly throne!

So take heart oh you of strong hope
He is to be trusted so you can cope!

You shall see your dear child on a glorious day
When all tears and sadness are wiped away!

In view of eternity it will only be a little while
Till you walk the streets of gold with your little child!

That day will banish your sorrow and grief
Uniting your hearts with joy beyond belief!

Lost in the Crowd?
by DLG

On this earth it is possible to be lost in the crowd feeling alone, unloved and unnoticed.

Thinking about that I wondered for a moment,"Will it be possible to be lost in the crowd of heaven?" The answer came flooding into my mind sent from my final home.

No, in spite of the enormous crowd in heaven I will never feel alone, unloved or unnoticed.

Everyone in that crowd will love me and I will love everyone of them. Everyone in the crowd will care about me and I will care about everyone of them. None of them will feel alone nor will I.

Most important the Savior who loves everyone in that great cloud of witnesses loves me personally. Because He and all in heaven know His presence forever, we'll never feel alone.

In heaven in contrast to earth we'll never be lost in the crowd, we'll be found in the crowd.

Since we will be found among such a great a crowd of caring witnesses should we not run with patience the race set before us looking to Jesus the great shepherd of the sheep to help to win others now lost in the crowds of earth? Lord help us to point others to You so they though lost in the crowd of earth may be found in the crowd of heaven. Help them and each of us to know that we need never walk alone.

Songs- I'll Never Walk Alone. Take your pick.
By a Guy: <http://www.youtube.com/watch?v=pklsCwbj_QM

Jesus Risen Restores Peter

Because He lives and loves we can live and love, too.

When failure and love meet, love wins! As your brother I will pray for God's best for you. Jesus is our biggest brother who sticks close to us, never forsakes us, says, "Come near." And when we do, we know tears of love, tears of joy, tears of peace, tears of patience, tears of goodness, tears of kindness, tears of faith, tears of humility, tears of change that control us from that time on.

His love is stronger than failure, stronger than hate, stronger than bitterness, so strong we can never be the same again. We love Him because He first loved us. And in that love we are set free.

This Easter I wish His risen love to be your love and love that He has created in us to be each others. Love and forgiveness are stronger than death and Jesus proved it!

May God's grace rest upon your heart,

Dean

Love Displayed in a Sermon & In a Father's Arms

Sunday, May 15th my wife Gloria and I were sitting in church behind Jason and Natalie Moog and their little girl Autumn wanted to be held by her dad who picked her up. She snuggled up against him and he held her in his arms. She was perfectly content. I smiled at her and she smiled back.

After the service I said to Jason, "I think your little girl really likes you." He agreed and it was obvious that he had loved her back as he held her in his arms. It reminded me of God's love as a Father to all of us who are his children. He, like Jason and Natalie, had a great part in bringing us into the world. Born once through our parents, when we came to our Father's Son we found pure love and were born a second time.

God's love as a Father to us is genuine. There is no one else like him. The Bible says it like this, ""*There is* no one like the God of Jeshurun, *Who* rides the heavens to help you, And in His excellency on the clouds. The eternal God *is your* refuge, And underneath *are* the **everlasting arms**;" Deuteronomy 33:26-27 Jeshurun is another name for Israel to whom God chose to be a Father and whom he created and counted to be right even though she went astray. He disciplined Israel's people, helped them, rescued them and held them in his everlasting arms many times.

So like Israel, Jason is his daughter's refuge. She finds help and love in his arms which are underneath her upholding her and always will be. God loves us, his children, too. He loved us first and we love Him back. The Bible says it like this, "Herein is love, not that we loved God but that He loved us and sent his Son to be the propitiation(merciful sacrifice, forgiver & payer) for our sins. 1 John 4:10 The Bible says, " We love him, because he first loved us." 1John 4:19 How did he love us? He died for us to forgive us and arose from the dead to give us eternal life.

Will Autumn always do everything that pleases her dad and mom? No, but they will always love her no matter what. Will we always do everything that pleases our heavenly Father? No, but his love for his us, his chosen, who chose him back, will never fail. One born into God's family by faith in Jesus will always be loved and return his love.

The message given by Gary Darnel during the service which told of God's great love for us was illustrated before my eyes also in the tender, caring love Jason and Autumn clearly displayed in their love for one another. Don't let anyone corrupt you from the simplicity in Christ and depth of God's love that will not let you go. 11Cor. 11:3 Click on the song about God's unfailing love below. Will it bring tears to your eyes as it did mine?
https://www.youtube.com/watch?v=nt69WDtYNLo>

Love His Appearing

In life there are people who appear to us that we love to be around. We like to see them and hear them. Why?

It is usually because they are encouragers who say and do things that brighten our day. We know they care about us because they are interested in our lives. They are forgiving, they help us and listen to us and so we look for ways to love them back. This last week I spoke to friends on the phone about the Lord and their lives. I couldn't see them but had immense joy just talking to them.

My wife and I were looking at photos of our wedding taken 57 years ago on July 25th.
I loved her appearing that day and walking down the isle with me. "She came down the isle wearing a smile, a vision of loveliness." When I was told I could kiss her she put her veil back. After we kissed, I thought, "What do I do with the veil?" I thought, "Put it back, she's mine now." We struggled between me trying to put it down and her not letting me.The audience laughed and the veil was kept back as it should have been. I loved her appearance that day. I had a crew cut so my appearance didn't look all that great to me but she sure looked wonderful. Later after our marriage I went away to speak at camps in Alaska and various places. I always

thought of her and my children and looked forward to her and their appearance when I returned.

The Bible speaks of those who love Jesus' appearing in 2 Timothy 4:8. "Henceforth there is laid up for me a crown of righteousness, which the Lord, the righteous judge, shall give me at that day: and not to me only, but unto all them also that **love his appearing.**"Actually Jesus already appeared once to put away our sin, to forgive us, to live inside us by His Spirit. But he left earth and even though we haven't yet literally seen Him we still rejoice in who He is and what He has done. Jesus said to his disciple Thomas, " Jesus said to him, "Thomas, because you have seen Me, you have believed. Blessed *are* those who have not seen and *yet* have believed."John 20:29 We see Him by faith now but someday He will return and we will see Him fully as faith gives way to sight. We will see Him as He is and be transformed to be like Him forever!

His appearing will be glorious! The Bible says that everyone who loves His appearing will be given a crown of righteousness. What a day of rejoicing that will be. When we all see Jesus, we'll sing and shout the victory.

A proof that we know God is that we believe in His first appearance and that we look forward to His glorious return appearance when He takes us to be with Him where He is, to behold His beauty, and to glory in His presence. We often love the appearance of our spouses, friends, family and cherished acquaintances. How much more will we love the glorious appearance of Jesus. Having loved and believed in His first appearance on earth though we didn't see Him, we will love His next appearance way more because we **will** see Him! Now we see Him as in a mirror not fully but when He returns we will see Him face to face

Do you love His appearing? Sing about it. Face to Face with Christ My Savior:
https://www.youtube.com/watch?v=ElewCUR57dw>

Full & Lasting Love Realized at Last

The Search for love is life's greatest mystery.
It's there in the very beginning of history.

The first couple had it in paradise
With God as their companion everything seemed so nice.

They walked hand in hand among the fruitful trees.
More in love than the birds and bees.

Then the knowledge of good and evil beset the pair.
The Devil interrupted their perfect love, his plan,
Impair God's plan without a shred of care,

Shame entered their relationship.
So they hid in fig leaves from God's fellowship.

But a greater love than theirs was at play.
The love of God. through the first sacrifice covered their sin
And removed them from the garden to start again.

Now love was tarnished mixed with pain and strife.
Yet God loved and provided for them all their life.

He promised a child to Eve who would elevate love to a new height,
Who would take away the curse and restore and elevate them to higher, unfailing delight.

Many loves have come and gone since the beginning of time.
Some quite grievous while others touched the sublime.

Puppy love, real to the puppy.

Family love, real to most.
Father and Motherly love.
Sister and Brotherly love.
Friendship love
Romantic love
Married love
Broken Love
All will soon be past.
For love on this earth will never last.

For in every love a flaw is found-
On earth each lover must die and return to the ground.

Even our loving pets we cherish so well.
End in tragedy with death's knell.

So love seems doomed through our decease
But God had a better idea to give us lasting life and peace.

He sent His Son, delight of His heart,
To bring salvation from which love could never part.

He promised those who would come to Him
Everlasting life and love that would never dim.

He proved His love by giving His life
By taking our sin and banishing death's knife.

It pierced through Mary's heart as she saw her son hanging upon the cross,
Later she realized His death redeemed her from endless loss.

He died for us out of pure love,
A love that can raise us to heaven above.

Romance as we know it today will vanish from God's plan.
In heaven there will be no marriage between a woman and a man.

Everyone will love God and one another
without the terrible sins of earth.
That is everyone who has received Christ
and has had a second birth.

Contrary to some false religion
No marriage between man and woman
exists in heaven.

So pure love will exist between God's
own.
Earth's curse,sins and jealousies all
gone, banished by His throne.

Instead all will love God and one another
without earth's stain.
Love will rise to its highest heights as we
sing love's refrain:

"Loved with everlasting love, Led by
grace that love to know;
Gracious Spirit from above, You have
taught me it is so!

O, this full and perfect peace! O, this
transport all divine!
In a love which can not cease, I am His
and He is mine!"
*George Robinson

In eternity all will love each other purely
and freely,
Hugging and Holy kissing with no hint of
earthly lust or jealousy.

No longer will loved ones depart to break
our heart
We shall be forever won, restored by
God's Son.

Perhaps we will be reunited forever with
those of our "puppy love."
Hopefully our family members will be
above.
And our friends we have lost.
And our romantic loves risen beyond
earths flaws replaced with heavens laws,

Laws of love, all broken friendships
restored- All divorce gone forever more.
Perhaps even our lost loved pets we'll see
again removing all our past regrets.
There will be surprises that have not
entered our thought.
Lifting us into new love and joys that
God has wrought.

We'll live in God's eternal love that holds
us fast,
Imbued with Perfect, Full and Endless
love at last!
https://www.youtube.com/watch?v=l-tXgsBq418>

Love, Strong, Stable, Simple & Sublime!

How can you tell if you really love someone? If they hurt, you hurt. If you can help in anyway you do it. You take time to pray for them. If you are aware that anything they are saying or doing is harmful to them you tell them. You don't encourage them to do anything wrong. You forgive them for failing and don't bring it up again. You help lift their spirits by praying for them. If they fall you help lift them up. You ask them to forgive you if you do anything wrong toward them. You don't hold a grudge against them. You like their company and friendship. You are happy when they succeed at something. You like to help feed them and provide for their needs. Your love is stable through tough times lasting until death and beyond.

How can you tell that God loves you? When you hurt He hurts. He tells you clearly what will harm you or what is harming you. He sees the hurt of your sin & wrong which earns death. He took your death upon Himself so that if you believe and receive Him you have eternal life and escape forever a second death in the lake of fire. He wants to be close to you so much that He comes by His Spirit to live inside you.

He wants to be near you always, so much so that He says, "I will never leave you or forsake you." He loves it when you succeed honorably. He loves to be around you to feed you earthly and heavenly food. He even creates and sings songs about you. He will never condemn you!

He has gone away to prepare an everlasting home for you. When you die He will strip away that part of you that caused you to sin and give you a new sinless body. If you have trusted Him as your Savior you will be with Him forever to be loved and to love Him back forever.

That is how we know we love someone and how God loves us and how we love Him back. Such love is stable always, stronger than death, and both simple & sublime. So rejoice in His love all the time. It will not let you go ever. Sing about it.

<https://www.youtube.com/watch?v=nt69WDtYNLo>

Love the Atheist. Hate His Sin.

Some atheists have put up a sign that says Jesus is a myth while elsewherethey say Santa is okay. Seems to me they"mythed" the mark getting it backwards.

Since I am a Christian I must love my enemies. Love points out error that will hurt someone. So Mr. Atheist, take a look around. God sends his rain to make crops to feed you. He gives you breath which you can use to denounce Him. Right now your blood is flowing through your veins at His command and you don't even realize it.

The psalmist got you right when he said,"The fool has said in his heart there is no God."I would appeal to you to turn from being a fool to being wise like the wise men of Christmas who worshiped Jesus as Savior. The wiseman says in his heart, "There is a God and I trust Him."

I once knew a man long ago, now dead and in heaven who was an atheist. When he was an atheist and lightning would flash overhead he would reach up to heaven and mock God saying, "Shoot her again, Pete." Interesting how many atheists talk to God. HIs name was Worth Ellis.

Well anyhow He read about Jesus in the Bible and realized His sinfulness and accepted Christ. After that he preached the Jesus who he once saw as a myth realizing instead that He is the way, the truth and the life through whom we know and find God.

So in love, please quit being a fool. Turn your foolishness over and become a wise man. Seek God and live. If you don't you will "myth" the mark!!

Making America Great Now

America will only be great if we put God first. If we seek first the kingdom of God and His righteousness then what we really need will follow. Our freedom of religion, which originally meant trust in the true God and His Son Jesus Christ, is what our country was founded upon. It is not freedom FROM Religion but freedom OF religion which is what our constitution says.

Athieists are violating the constitution and God's word which teaches that respect and fear of God should be first for everyone because it is the beginning of wisdom. Some Atheists attack freedom of religion. Not putting God first will destroy America and not make it great.

Happy is any nation whose God is the Lord and who seek to honor Him first. It is not exalting man but exalting God who makes any nation great and who makes any person great. Right is an honor to any person or nation, and sin and wrong is a reproach to any person or nation. If we don't seek first the guidance and rule of God then America will never be great nor have its true needs met. God is true and every person a liar who rejects His love, forgiveness, will and guidance!

Sing about it here with Kate Smith <https://m.youtube.com/watch?v=rEJo7x9y3D4>

Making Smart Phones Smart

Smart phones in the hands of kids & teens sometimes turn into dumb phones. I speak at a retirement center and notice, and I am happy, that none of them act dumb by looking at a smart phone when I speak. Perhaps it is because they were taught to listen to others when they speak.

My son, who is a high school teacher, says that when school starts this year a new rule kicks in, so smart phones have to be turned in so they can't use them during class. What will happen? Withdrawal symptoms? They are more lonely, isolated, depressed, suicidal now using their phones. What will happen without them?

I recently gave a helpful comic book to a friend to share with her grandchildren. Only one was interested in it? Why? We concluded that it might be because they are devoted to their smart, or should we say dumb phone video games.

Now in reality the smart phones in themselves are neither good or bad. What we do with our phone determines whether it is good or bad. That is true of all things. Use a shovel to plant a garden, good. Use it to hit someone over the head, bad.

Use a phone to watch pornography, to bully, to hate, to lie, to hide from life, bad. Use it to learn, study, , share truth, to build friendships, and to encourage others, good.

For example, I look for ways to encourage and pray for others on Facebook, and for stories to share and write articles meant to build others up. On the internet I look for things to learn about history and deepen my knowledge of the Bible.

One person told me he was going to quit Facebook. I encouraged him to share prayers and what God is doing in his life. Since then he has blessed a lot of people.

Parents and teachers ought to be teaching their children good things to do with their phones making them truly smart phones. How? By teaching them to look on FB for ways to encourage their friends, by sharing written prayers for them, by looking up information related to what they are studying in school or the Bible and by playing games that are not only fun but teach them something, and courteously to put their phones down when talking to someone. That will help make smart phones truly smart.

The Man Who Wouldn't Let Go

Did you hear about the man who on a pitch black dark night fell off a cliff. He reached out desperately and grabbed hold of a limb which to his relief stepped his fall. He prayed as he hung there in the dark. Something inside said, "Let go of the limb." He looked down into the total dark and was afraid to let go.

He held on for dear life and when the sun rose and the light came he saw that he was only one foot from the ground.

So he let go in the light of what he was afraid to do in the dark.

When Jesus was before Pilate, he toldl Pllot that he had come to "bear witness to the truth." He told him that "everyone who is of the truth hears My voice. " Pilate responded by saying, "What is truth?"

Jesus had just told Pilate what the truth was, "hearing His voice." But Pilate didn't get it. The truth was standing in front of him, close enough to touch, but he didn't get it. When it came to truth, Pilate was in the dark. grasping the limb of unbelief. In his case the "light was shining in the dark but the darkness could not comprehend it." Did he ever really hear the voice of Jesus and come to Him. I hope so. We are not told.

Jesus came to bear witness to the truth. He spoke of Himself as being "the way, the truth, and the life." He said no one could come to the Father except by Him." Many have heard the voice of Jesus and know the truth, that He is their Savior because they came to Him. He promised that anyone who comes to Him would not be cast out. He is truth so you can count on His promise.

If you are In the dark clinging to a limb of unbelief, there is hope for you. Look to Jesus and the light can rise and shine through driving away the darkness. Let go of what is false and rest on Jesus, the Rock of truth.

How sad that Pilate, standing so close to truth, at that moment didn't get it. Later one of the thieves got it as he hung dying. At the last moment he let go of everything else and cried out to Jesus for salvation and in that moment passed from death to life, from the darkness to the light, from the potential of hell to the paradise of heaven.

Do you get it? Have you heard the voice of Jesus? Do you believe that He is the way to God, the truth of God, and the life of God? I pray that is so for you. If not, why not let go of darkness and come to the Light today. He is as close to you today as He was to Pilate, only a prayer away. Will you let go of the limb of unbelief and trust Him?

May God's grace be real to you, Dean

Amazing grace! How sweet the sound--
that saved a wretch like me.!
I once was lost but now am found, Was
blind but now I see.

Click below to enjoy God's grace in song and sight:
<http://www.youtube.com/watch?v=cyFxArMeRDI>

Special Prose, Poetry & Prayer for Marsha Helen Christian

I want to love God with all my heart and love all His people too That's why I'm writing this specially for you.

Your name Helen means beautiful woman of light and Marsha means Warrior so you are God's Beautiful Warrior of Light? No wonder you are a spiritually outgoing shining light into people's lives. Jesus said of you, "You are the light of the world. Let your light so shine before men that they may see your good works and glorify your Father in Heaven." I have Experienced the power of your good works, Your prayers, hospitality, insight and care giving gifts which have changed my life and many others for God and good. I'm glad that your war like faith is controlled. And to great delight you have given up child like anger and brought it into captivity to Christ as a woman of warlike faith exchanging it for gracious love which never fails.

You Marsha, with war like faith, are God's Helen of light, cousin of kindness, friend of sweetness, partner in prayer, who as I, have felt joy and despair whose aching and caring heart has lifted me on prayer filled wings of healing into heaven's fragrant air. I long as you with zealous heart to lift all God's people to His grace and mercy laden Chair! There to receive miracle answers to prayer. May your words through the Spirit's care carry His people beyond their despair. May they give Him their ashes and in exchange take His beauty waiting for them there. If our simple words could do this for His own then our hearts would dwell in awe at His merciful, gracious throne! Oh let it be for you, for me and all His own!

Let our little hearts lift all God's blood bought people into heaven where together we gaze upon His beauty to be raptured in His goodness, to be filled with His purity, for it is in His purity that we are pure. It is in His love that we can truly love. It is in His presence we shed tears which His tender hand wipes away. It is there that we set our affections on things above where from glory to glory we bathe in His pure unfailing love!

Shine on, shine on Helen, continue Marsha in winning the good fight of faith. The crown of light and glory await you as He says, "Well done Marsha Helen Christian. Enter into the light of My Rainbow encircled, treasure filled Home!!"

Mary's Children

One huge thing is assumed by the Roman Catholic teaching that Mary never had any more children. They say Joseph died and had no children by Mary. Actually NO ONE KNOWS WHEN JOSEPH actually died but we do know he was still alive when Jesus was twelve and most likely alive when Jesus began his ministry. Scripture says Joseph didn't know Mary until after the birth of Jesus. Scripture was obviously not talking about knowing her as a person but knowing her as a wife. To "know" between a man and wife was to have sexual relations which in marriage is NOT sinful. So it is pretty obvious that Joseph "knew her" after Jesus was born.

Joseph and Mary had been married 12 years when they went to Jerusalem when Jesus was 12. You can have a lot of children in 12 years. The false idea implying that Mary would have had to remarry to have half brothers is utter nonsense. She could have had at least 6 or more children by the time Jesus started His ministry. Scripture clearly indicates in John 6:42 that the people at the time Jesus was teaching knew Jesus father, Joseph and mother, Mary. So in all probability Joseph may have died not long after Jesus was aged 31. So being married to Mary for many, many years enabled Jesus, as scripture says, to have brothers and even sisters. Luke 8:20 speaks of Jesus' mother and brethren seeking to see him and in Matthew 13:55 his brethren are identified as brothers James, Joses, Simon and Judas and his sisters are mentioned so it is pretty clear that Jesus had at least 6 if not more half brothers and sisters. Also in Matthew 13:56 it indicates that the carpenter's son, Mary, James, Joses, Simon, Judas, and Jesus sisters "are they not all with us." Still alive.

The RC twisted doctrine of Mary's eternal virginity is based on false piety, an invented religious superiority based on the false notion that Mary had a sacred womb only for the virgin birth of Jesus. They also believe that sacred womb would be defiled by the birth of another child or by intercourse. Total Nonsense! It is about as truthful as the other RC false doctrine of Mary being sinless when she herself said, "My spirit has rejoiced in God my savior." Only a sinner needs a savior + scripture clearly teaches that all of us are sinners "all have sinned and come short of the glory of God" except for Jesus who knew no sin, did no sin and no sin was in Him. Because RCs put tradition and their own declaration above the pure word of God they have come up with all kinds of things that are not scriptural.

Going through all the names of the various apostles as RC's do to try and show Mary had no more children is superfluous. What has just been shared above in paragraph two shows God's great blessing on Mary having many children besides the Savior of the world. It gives more glory to God that she was a mother of many rather than just one child whose Father was God. The idea that those who protest RC teaching think she remarried is held by no one that I know about. That is an RC imagination put on to others without analyzing what scripture really says about Mary's other children.

Mending a Broken Heart

Psa. 34:18 The LORD is close to the brokenhearted and saves those who are crushed in spirit. The more broken the soil the more fruit it bears. Perhaps that is why as believers we are crushed into tiny bits. When he has tried me I shall come forth as gold and produce 30, 60 and a 100 fold!

God's Starlit Sky Park

Friends and those who love and influence you for right are like stars. You can't always see them but they are always there shining on you day and night. They show up best when life gets dark! They help light your way in the dark pointing you to God's Sky Park. There you can glide down the milky way of joy, capture the sweet influences of Pleiades, untie the ropes of Orion, fish in the vault of Pisces, view the star of the Virgin's Child, fly on the wings of the Butterfly Galaxy, dance on the rings of Saturn, watch the true star wars as the stars fight in their courses against Sisera, drink living water from the Big Dipper, gaze upward with a companion of kindness while you laugh together as you watch the Lion of heaven drive the serpent out of the universe. As you learn the lessons of the heavens you will swing on the swings of our Dream Maker's moonlight who lifts you higher and higher to His vantage view of celestial splendor. Thank God then when the night closes in. Look up to the stars and their Maker and you will enjoy God's Starlit Sky Park where you will grin and win!

All God's friends are the true stars.

Dan. 12:3 Those who are wise will shine like the brightness of the heavens. Those who lead many people to righteousness will shine like the stars forever and ever.

What's your favorite star in the verses below?

Gen. 22:7, Numb. 24:17, Judg. 5:20 Job 9:9, Job 38:31,Phil. 2:15, Matt. 2:9

A couple other of **My Books:Journey Through the Bible:** <https://www.ecsministries.org/Page_3.aspx?id=159972>

The Royal Ride: <http://www.authorhouse.com/Bookstore/ItemDetail.aspx?bookid=29837>

May God Light Up Your Marriage

This is the essence of a letter I sent to a married couple struggling and estranged.

God's heart breaks for husbands and wives who are estranged. You both once loved each other very much. You both have put up a wall of rejection between you. It's a wall that can be torn down. It seems impossible but with God nothing is impossible. I realize how deeply couples hurts over their estrangement. I plead earnestly for God to break down the wall between you. I am aware of how much more God weeps for you both. How much more The Lord would use and bless you if you loved each other as a husband and wife should.

Here are some necessary steps for those who are trusting Jesus as Savior that will transform your marriage. The husband should take the initiative & ask his wife to pray together sharing prayer needs aloud with each other and praying aloud each for the other. Then read 1Corinthians 13 together every day for a month asking God to make real His love in your lives. God will begin to renew real love in your lives and join you back together if as a husband you love your wife as Christ loved the church and gave Himself for it. Then you as a wife must in turn respect and love him back.

Over time as you practice love toward one another God will tear down the wall between you. Love in I Cor. 13 involves right actions, not feelings. Love suffers long and is kind. if you forgive each other from the heart as Christ has forgiven you, the bad feelings of distance will gradually but surely begin to disappear. As you toss away all records in your heart of any wrongs shown each other you will be like the Lord Jesus Christ who forgives and forgets the confessed sin of His people.

One man told me he was tired of seeking to love his wife because she always emotionally slapped him in the face. So what does Jesus tell us to do if someone slaps us on one cheek? He says to turn the other one and let him or her slap us on the other cheek. Jesus did what He counsels us to do. That is supernatural so you must pray together for God's kind of love. The actions of love will eventually over time heal your marriage.

That love is my fervent prayer for you both. Reconciliation is the power of the cross. Remember his mercy and forgiveness for you both. Apply that mercy and forgiveness to your relationship and God will lift you up together to begin restoring first love. **While we are powerless to help the Lord Jesus is powerful to heal and change our lives and character.**

That is my prayer for you both. God has given me a love for you both that will not give up in prayer, hope and faith that my tears and the Lord's will rescue and restore your first love for Him and each other. What I have just shared is 100% God's will and needs to become 100% your will. Of course both partners must do His will. You must agree together to apply God's will to your lives. I plead with you in Jesus name. Be reconciled to God and each other.

When you are reconciled God will use you both in immeasurable Godly success. God will open the gates of heaven and pour out a blessing so great that you will be astonished.

Your marriage is to be a picture of Christ's love for the church and the church's respect and love for Christ. While you remain estranged God can not use your gifts and service as he wishes.

I beg you with tears. Be reconciled to one another through The Lord Jesus. Practice the love of God as told you in 1Cor.13 and it will work. If you don't do it nothing will happen. Believe God and then do His will. That is a sure way to success in marriage. Also, you may want to involve someone who is in tune with God to counsel you together, someone who puts God's word and wisdom as preeminent in their counsel.

My heart and God's will continue to break for you both until you allow God to love one another through forgiving and giving hearts. Lord Jesus Christ grant that these words be accepted for your glory and that this couple will have a renewed and restored relationship. In the powerful name of Jesus, Lord light up their lives together. I love you both in Christ, Dean

Miracle Relief in the Midst of Your Pain

Recently I sat in the dentists chair being prepared for a tooth implant. Usually dental pain was not so bad but this time it was excruciating for a while. It felt like a jack hammer shaking my jaw. I found relief by thinking of our Savior's pain. His was so much worse than mine.

I thought of The prophetic words regarding His suffering, "Behold all you that pass by and see if there has been any sorrow like My sorrow?" The answer came, 'No there has been no sorrow like Yours, no greater pain." The sting of the whip lashes; the hurtful curses of the mockers; the shame of the piercing crown of thorns; the spit in Your face by those You loved; the intense pain of the nails piercing Your feet and hands; the nails suspending Your weight, every movement intensifying the agony; Your cry, "I thirst" met with the revolting offer to You of bitter vinegar and gall that you tasted and then refused.

But these agonies paled in comparison to the inner spiritual horror You felt. You, who had did no sin, thought no sin and in whom there was no sin became sin for us, for me, tasting all the sins I did, and that I thought. Then in those moments of physical and spiritual distress You felt the worst agony of all, forsaken by Your Father. Then You asked why Him why He had forsaken You? The answer fills my heart with joy-Forsaken that I might never be forsaken! The pain of the drill is almost forgotten and becomes bearable as I sit there pondering in the midst of it all Your forgiving love to me, Your consoling words to Your mother and friend John, and for Your comforting words to the thief to whom You promised paradise.

A miracle occurred in my soul- Your dying loved eclipsed my pain as I beheld Your finished sorrow & in relief began to pray for others in the midst of my now tiny dental pain. I found relief because of your sorrow, remembering that it was over now. You overcame the rigors and terrors of the cross and rose in triumph over them.

The dentist was finally finished. Along with my new implant was implanted the insight of how to be relieved from temporary pain and sorrow. Pain may endure for a while but joy will follow surer than the rising Sun.

May these thoughts help you when pain and sorrow are your temporary grief. All pain and sorrow for the believer is temporary when compared to eternity. Our light affliction are small compared to the eternal weight of heavens joy and glory. Remember as well that in all our afflictions He is afflicted. Pain need not reign over you while the King enlightens you!!

Love to you,
Dean

Mother Nature & Father God Warnings

Today I heard Al Gore say that mother nature is giving us a warning through climate change and we need to listen. Is he right? Perhaps, but Father God gives us a deeper warning. He warns us that if we do not believe in His Son we will perish without having eternal life. Global warming may cause natural death but refusing to believe God's warning means having a second painful eternal death. (John 3:30)

Who will you listen to most, Al Gore's mother nature warning or Father God's eternal warning?

Death will gore us all whether by climate change, old age or some other calamity. So God warns us to believe in his Son so that in spite of natural death we may enjoy eternal life with Him forever.

Some mother nature weather predictions are right. Some are not. Jesus warned us about being able to tell signs that indicate some understanding about natural weather signs but missing the signs of the times that indicate spiritual realities. (Matt 16:3)

What God says is totally sure. We may argue about climate change but it is stupid for anyone to to disagree with what God clearly says. He says plainly that if we trust his Son we will spend forever with him. He also says if anyone rejects his Son that person will die forever apart from him.

It is foolish to accept climate change based on possible scientific evidence and reject eternal truth clearly told us by God. If you do reject God's sure truth you will wind up gored on the horns of everlasting death. But that is not what God wants for you. Instead of eternal death, He wants you to have eternal life. Believe Him and enjoy double security. You will be rescued by both God's hands and the pierced hands of His Son. You will know you are forgiven and counted righteous, Then you can rest safe in Christ's love, held close in the everlasting arms of both the Father and the Son. Amen! Sing about about it here: <https://m.youtube.com/watch?v=caUOl-URnNM>

Reminder for Sunday Byron, Sharon, Turhan & Melanie + some thoughts about Mother's day.

Hope you had a great Mother's Day Sharon & Melanie!

On Sunday quite a few folks shared about their moms. Gloria shared how her and her mom were born on the same day. How could that be? They both went forward at a Billy Graham crusade on Mother's Day in 1958, both born again on the same day.

I could have shared a few things Sunday about my mom but just listened. My mom encouraged me once a lot. Believe it or not I was very shy as a teen. Once in a car everyone was talking and I wasn't. One of the kids said about me. You are sure quiet. How come? My mom stuck up for me and said, "Still water runs deep!" I never forgot that. Now I probably talk too much. Two things we all remember best: encouraging words which help and poorly spoken words which hinder.

I prayed for my mom after I accepted Christ at age 20, for about 16 years and she came to Christ at age 59 on the beach in Hawaii. Sometimes I ask Jesus to tell her I love her. I look forward to seeing her soon. We are not suppose to pray to the dead but I see no harm in praying to Jesus to deliver a message of our love to anyone in heaven we love. Try it. I think you will be blessed by it.

What about your moms? What do you remember about them!?

Please continue to pray for my energy. I'm reminded of God's promise to Asher, " Your shoes will be iron and brass and **as your days so shall your strength be**. "God rides upon the heaven to help you and in his excellency in the sky. The eternal God is your refuge and underneath are his everlasting arms." He helps us. He hides us. And He holds us! Deut 33:25-27. Once I got to share those verses about Asher with a Jewish Doctor named Asher. He had a long line waiting to see him. He shut the door and talked to me for a long time about the Lord. I believe Asher's shoes were metaphorical, made of iron and brass because they never wore out. You remember the scripture says the Israelites shoes never wore out during the whole time they were in the wilderness. What we need he provides! I pray that for you Byron and Turhan and for strength for all four of you this Sunday. Praying for your mom and dad, Melanie, as you asked me to do and for your tooth pain to be relieved, Sharon. We have a dentist named Dr. Chew who is really good and might help you if you wish.

Please don't hesitate to share any prayer requests with me. **I'm not very good with physical tasks anymore but prayer enables me to aim for availing much on behalf of others.** Some time when you have a few hours I'll share a few dozen of the many miraculous great things God has answered in prayer. (-:)

Fellowship with you all is upbeat,neat and sweet!

Dean & Gloria

PS If you have a few moments here is a song that may bring tears to your eyes about your mother: <https://www.youtube.com/watch?v=1LFbaD5n2pl>

Music In My Mind
Jan.19,2013

In the music of my mind
There lives a song of longing

A song of love and care
That shimmers like sunshine in my hair.

It is a song that lingers
In the touch of its fingers,

Fingers that caress my heart
A song that shall never depart,

It abides deep within my soul
Lingering silently like a partly reached
goal,

Sometimes I forget it days at a time.
Then it breaks forth like veiled sunshine.

The song though hidden is real to me
It sings again and won't let me free!

But some day in eternity the song shall
be known
Released in worship to God upon His
Throne.

The mystery of the song
Will be known to a heavenly throng.

For life gives us songs of love that are
deep.
Songs that give joy yet make us weep!

Their meanings-felt by us, but understood
by God alone,
Only in eternity will all be known.

My & Your Patmos

The apostle John was on the isle of Patmos in about 95 A.D.for the Word of God and the Testimony of Jesus. Alone on that sterile island He was given a message from God unveiling the Lord Jesus Christ. He was to pass on things that are and things to come which must shortly come to pass.

If you are one of Christ's servants you also have a "Patmos". You are where you are because of God's plan for you. The Bible teaches clearly that where we are is determined by God as well as the number of our days. And we are where we are to seek God and find Him and He is not far from any of us. (Rev. 1:1-3 & Acts 17:26,27)

Once we find Him we are to be a witness to Him and His word where ever we are. It may be in a lonely sterile place like Patmos or in your house and city where you live.

What God has revealed to you about Jesus is to be shared with others.The Bible says, "Let the redeemed of the Lord say so whom he has redeemed from the hands of the enemy." We are to tell how we were once going astray driven by Satan and our old nature which was contrary to God's wishes. Then God in grace revealed salvation to us in His Son and in His Word. The Word became human and dwelt among us and we beheld His glory, the glory of the only begotten of the Father full of grace and truth.

We came to know Him through faith and became a child of God born again of God's Spirit. Then by God's grace we began to serve Him in newness of the Spirit. If any man be in Christ, he is a new creation. Old things are passed away and all things become new." That newness experience of salvation is available to all who hear and come to the Lord Jesus. He then washes us in His own blood cleansing us from all sin and makes us kings and priests to God.

That is a great privilege because in the Old Testament a person could be a king or a priest but he could not be both. New Testament believers are both kings reigning in life by Jesus Christ and priests enabled to go to God in prayer on behalf of themselves and others.

On our "Patmos" where ever it be are opportunities to preach in writing or by word the good news of Christ.

We are on the narrow road that leads to life and our message to others is "We are setting out for the place of which the Lord said, '**I will give i**t to you.' Come with us, and we **will** treat you well;...Numbers 10:29   In the O.T. the place was the land of promise. In the New Testament the place is heaven. Jesus said, "I go to prepare a place for you and if I go away I will come again that where I am you may be also." How are you doing on your "Patmos"? How am I doing on mine? Our privilege and duty is to share the good news of Christ and invite others to join us where ever we are. Tour of the Island of Patmos: <https://www.youtube.com/watch?v=-54UiPIWb20>

Where ever we are His people are marching to Zion, beautiful, beautiful Zion. We're marching upward to Zion the beautiful city of God. Any who hear this who wish, come join us in our upward march to Zion.

Share it and sing about it: https://www.youtube.com/watch?v=mzmYuOFsYtU>

My Cousin Marsha
March24, 2014
I have a cousin who some would call a cow girl.
But I think of her as God's special shining pearl!

She lights up others lives with light Divine.
When it comes to cousins I praise God that she is mine!
Sometimes we pray together and share our trials.
And I am filled with heaven's smiles!
Sometimes we pray together and share our success
As heaven comes down to straighten out an earthly mess!
Sometimes like a tea kettle she lets off steam
And it hurts my heart and self esteem!
But I have learned to listen to her feelings & show forgiveness
And when she does the same it builds togetherness!
The world that is wrong side up is turned upside down
Filling a moment with God's love in which I happily drown!

My Creed - My Beliefs
(Share Yours if You Like)

I have been reading a book that shares a creed created centuries ago by a group of men. While I agree mostly with it, I feel it is far to short to really sum up a truly fitting creed to express a person"s belief. So here we go. My Creed.

While I think this line is nice in a song, "I believe for every drop of rain that falls, a flower blooms," I believe more strongly that for every drop of truth that falls and is believed, new freedom and life bloom." My experience with truth began at age 20 when I was in the Air Force. I won't go into all the details of how truth totally changed my life except to say I trusted Christ with God's help, with tears in my eyes, my sins were forgiven and I obeyed Christ and was baptized. So my creed, my belief   includes the absolute necessity of receiving Christ as Savior. I also believe salvation is to be followed by baptism, studying and praying through the Bible and by remembering the Lord's victorious death in communion.

I have studied the Bible and prayed about it for over 62 years. I believe it from Genesis to Revelation. All of it is inspired by God and divinely transforming. It teaches me what is right and reproves and corrects me when I am wrong. It teaches me fully how to experience true life, divine love from and for God and others, and has imparted to me forgiveness, freedom and the experience of success, happiness and joy.

But there is much more. I believe the hundreds of prophecies in the O.T. are fulfilled in the N.T. The prophecy in Isaiah of a virgin conceiving and having a child, was fulfilled in Mary who brought forth our Lord Jesus Christ before she later had children with Joseph including at least two daughters and four sons. I believe that teaching it was not possible for Mary to have sons and daughters with Joseph because her womb was Holy violates the beauty, procreation, protection and joy of married life.

I believe that Jesus began His ministry of teaching and numerous miracles of all kinds of healing after he was baptized by John in the river Jordan. I believe completely that He loved and showed compassion through many kinds of healing, including giving sight to the blind and even raising the dead.

I believe that after Jesus died He arose three days later and stayed around for another forty days talking to and instructing His apostles and disciples both men and women. He taught them to go into all the world to preach the good news of His love for mankind and His victorious death and resurrection for them.

I believe He started His church built upon Himself as the Rock, the chief cornerstone and upon His people who are lesser foundational rocks upon which His church is built. For over 62 years I have been going regularly to meet with His church and to share that good news either verbally or in written form and He in grace has blessed it.

I also believe that Jesus Christ will return to earth someday and rule and reign for a thousand years during which time Satan will be bound unable to deceive the world The world will know peace for that 1,000 years. No war. Animal life will be changed. The lion will lie down with the lamb and eat straw like an ox. People will live long lives. A person dying at age 100 will be thought of as a child.

During that 1000 years I believe Satan will be literally bound as the Bible says. Then when the thousand years are up, he will be set free for a little while. Then he will once again deceive the nations gathering them to war against God and His people. The Lord will have had enough. He will destroy Satan with the breath of His mouth wiping him and his followers out in an instant.

Then I believe the Lord Jesus will cause a giant explosion, a true big bang, and melt the present heaven and earth. He will then create a new heaven and earth in which He is glorified as creator and sustainer of everlasting life and right. I believe that those who don't believe God but reject Him will not be part of the new heaven and earth, sad to me and God, because He takes no pleasure in the death of the lost. But in contrast all who know Him as Savior will inhabit and enjoy that new heaven and earth forever. There is much more I believe but won't share it here. Where do I get all this? Study the Bible yourself.

What do you believe? What is your creed? I hope you will join me and be among those enjoying eternal life and the joy of God's presence on the new heaven and earth. Let me know if you have believed or will believe now. Sing about it: <https://www.youtube.com/watch?v=5KMWd8nEQ2s> Share your creed.

My Creed #2

I believe that chance evolution did not cause animals and plants to come into existence. Brian Thomas of Creation Science institute gives evidence that dinosaurs are not millions of years old but are less than 100,000 years old. Twenty five dinosaur fossils have been tested and have carbon 14 in them and carbon 14 is never over 100,000 years old and therefore dinosaurs are not more than 100,000 years old and could be even 4 to 10 thousand years old. So Evolution that teaches dinosaur fossils are millions of years by his calculation is false. Hey, that would back up the facts of Genesis that God created creatures after their kind and banish the falsehood that some species while showing change over time never evolved into another species. There is not one missing link in chance evolution but thousands. Chance evolution forced into our schools is one of the biggest unproven theories ever designed.

If we look around at animals and plants today do we see any that don't produce after their kind as the Bible says? No. Dogs still have dog babies. Squirrels have squirrel babies. Tomatoes produce tomatoes on and on ad infinitum.

Speaking of procreating after one's kind, that fits us humans also. God created the first two humans in His likeness and they reproduced after their kind, They had children who had children. They are our ancestors. Today we have a world filled with all kinds of people and none of them have evolved from a cell in the ocean, or a species not their own. So I believe you were born with the image of God, not the image of a creature from the ocean or from an ape. There is zero proof that we evolved from another species.

Think about that. You are three in one, body, soul and spirit. You have free will as God does. You have the ability to think, create, and love like God. Think of your amazing body. How many times have you bled from a cut or wound without having to go to a doctor. Count your scars which are left from your body healing itself. Blood flowing through our bodies constantly nourishes us, fights off disease, heals our wounds, and cleanses us.

Some people call Christianity a bloody religion. Well, it is in a good sense. Think of this, the Creator of the universe came to earth, became flesh, grew up and shed His blood out of love for you and me. If our blood can cleanse us, heal us, nourish us and we are in the image of God, how much more can Jesus blood shed for us cleanse us from all sin as we believe in Him? His blood shed nourishes us, heals our hearts, makes it possible to have all evil washed away when we trust Him. The blood in our bodies which heals and nourishes us testifies to the greater blood of Jesus Christ that does the same thing on a higher eternal, spiritual level. Every day our body made in God's image shouts out silently for us to believe in His Son. So if we are smart we will rejoice in the blood of Jesus shed for us. If you haven't trusted in Him and His blood shed for you, will you do it today? Why not? Sing this song and believe it and be cleansed now in body, soul and spirit. <https://www.youtube.com/watch?v=pZhAWErbbwUhttps://www.youtube.com/watch?v=pZhAWErbbwU

My Creed #3 Beliefs-Share Yours If You Wish

I believe that when we study the Bible we need to approach it rightly. If I read a passage I need to ask myself if the literal sense makes sense and if so, I should not try to make it into metaphorical, or mystical sense or it will all come out nonsense. An example of this is Revelation 20 which says that Christ and His people reign with Him a thousand years and Satan is bound for the thousand years. One church group falsely says Christ is reigning only through them and they are binding Satan. The problem is that church has been around for well over a thousand years and it is obvious that Satan is not bound now. Take the thousand years literally and Christ is to yet return and reign for a thousand years exactly as it says.

Another proper way to approach Bible analysis is that if the literal sense does not make sense you must understand it in a metaphorical or figurative sense or it will also come out nonsense. Examples: Jesus is called the lion of the tribe of Judah in Revelation. Is he a literal lion? No! Figuratively He is strong and powerful like a lion. He is a King. Jesus is also called a lamb in the Bible. Is He a literal lamb? No, but He is meek and sacrificial like a Lamb. Jesus says, "I am the vine. You are the branches." Is Jesus a literal vine and are Christians literal branches. No. But as branches depend upon the main vine, so we depend on Christ to be fruitful.

Jesus said of the bread and cup of wine he passed to the apostles, "This is my body which is broken for you. Then he said that the cup of wine was his blood.' Was the bread his actual body? If so, then his body was in two places at once standing there in front of them and again in the bread. If the cup of wine was his literal blood then his blood was in two places at once also, in the cup and in His body as He stood before them. He was speaking truthfully but figuratively.. He would give up His body in death and shed His blood upon the cross and then believers, in his death and shed blood, would remember that His death once for all is represented by the bread and cup. This is made clear in scripture when it says we do it "In remembrance of Him" until He comes again.

Believers throughout their lives then take the bread and cup representing His victorious death for them. The bread and cup do not turn into His body and blood every time they are taken or He would be dying and suffering again and He only was offered once to procure our forgiveness and salvation.. Jesus authenticated this when He said, "Unless you eat my body and drink my blood, you have no part with me." Many reacted strongly against what He said and quit following Him, not realizing He was speaking truly but figuratively as He explained, "The flesh profits nothing. The words I speak to you are Spirit and they are life." In other words we take all He is into our life spiritually which is beyond just his flesh. We take his body and blood spiritually not literally. No one ever cut up His body and ate it but as His followers we do see His body offered for us literally and spiritually and say, "All Jesus is, body, soul, spirit, words, God, resurrection and life, I fully believe and take into my heart.' Such is my creed which I stake not on the bread and cup but upon the one they represent. I worship not the bread and cup of wine but the one they point to spiritually. I stake my whole life and future upon Jesus Christ to which the elements point spiritually. How about you? Sing About it here: <https://www.youtube.com/watch?v=mPGiVA731lM>

Happy New Year
Jan. 1,2013
We Share Our Dreams with Special People

In the Bible we read of people actually hearing the voice of God speak to them. I've been praying that if it is God's will I might have that happen. Then I think it partly happened in a dream.

In my dream I was in a room with an old friend who had died some time back. His daughter that I taught in Sunday School over fifty years ago was there. We hugged each other and wept on each others shoulders for a long time.

Then a song came to me in the dream. I started looking for paper to write it down and had a hard time finding someone to give me paper.

Finally someone gave me some large pieces of paper partly written on.

Then as I walked along I felt the presence of someone beside me. I'm not sure who it was but felt like it was the Lord or a friend or all my friends beside me as one.

I said, "Will you listen to my song." Then I sang it and it came out in a melodious tune and words I still remembered when I awoke.

The first part of it are words I clearly remember from the dream. Some later parts I made up when I woke up and wrote them down on my iPhone "paper". After all, life is about dreaming and sharing our dreams that come true when we awake. Here is the song I felt God spoke to me:

My Heart His Home
Complete & Never Alone

I felt the Son shine down on me.
In my heart I felt such mystery.
At His feet my soul broke free
I felt my life complete.

I saw my Savior face to face
I knew the rapture of His grace.
He said to me,"Fully at My feet

Your Life will be complete."

I'll Know Him as I'm known
My heart IS His home.
He is the answer to life's mystery
I'll never be alone!

Face to Face <thttp://www.youtube.com/
watch?v=hH5mHXvEawQ>

Jason, Natalie & The Quest Gang

How blessed It was to listen to folks at the VBC Quest share last night how God answered their prayers and to share two of my Ebenezer stones with them.

I shared the story of Samuel's carving EBENEZER on a rock as a memory of God's helping Israel. Samuel had led Israel in a 20 year old revival of prayer. At the end of that time their enemies, the Philistine army marched on them to attack them. At that moment God caused a gigantic thunder clap to scare the Philistines out of their wits. In confusion they ran helter-skelter from them and Israel defeated them.. Answered prayer gave them victory and peace for many years. Samuel made a memorial of their victory by writing EBENEZER on a large rock which means "Hitherto God Has Helped Us!" It was a perpetual reminder of God's help.

So I brought a container of numbered rocks to Quest representing my Ebenezers. Each rock represents a prayer God has answered to help me. The first rock #1 reminds me of the night I heard the good news of Christ at Bethany Bible Chapel in Augusta Georgia 60 years ago. I was standing in church with a hymn book in my hand as everyone sang. Then the preacher invited anyone who wanted to come forward to receive Christ as Savior.

I was deeply moved and wanted to walk forward. In my heart I prayed, "God I cant do this unless you help me," and He did. With tears flowing down my cheeks I stepped out and walked foreword alone with my hymn book open. When I got to the front the preacher guided me in to a small room where I prayed to receive Jesus. As I walked out of the room I thought in my mind, "My life has been so messed up. How an I going to live this life?"A man approached me and answered the question I was thinking in my mind but hadn't asked aloud. He said,"To live the Christian life you must study this book." He held up a Bible and suggested I read Romans which says,"Faith comes by hearing and hearing by the word of God." So I read it which made clear to me my salvation and how to live inspired by God's Spirit.

Many years later I gathered unique rocks on Gold Beach in California and started my collection of Ebenezer rocks as reminders of God's help through answered prayer. Rock number #1 reminds me of God answering my prayer that evening when I asked help to come forward and confess Him as my Savior. He heard and helped me.

My #2 stone represents an answer to prayer to share the good news of Christ with all the men at the Air Force base where I was stationed after my conversion. One day I was reading in a break room next door to the radar room where I worked. I got carried away and failed to repot to duty on time. A sergeant came into the room and said "You are late, Gossett." Oh no, not reporting for duty on time was serious. I went in with him to the officer in charge who looked at me and said,"What shall I do to you Gossett? I know, next time the chaplain speaks you have to speak too." I looked sad on the outside but was rejoicing on the inside. My punishment was getting my prayer answered.

I spoke and shared the good news of Christ with the men. I told the men that they would only be right and live right if they came to Christ.. I didn't know a lot but shared what God gave me. So Ebenezer # 2 is the rock that reminds me of the great and mighty thing He did in answering my prayer, helping me share Christ with all those men.

If you know Him He will help you, too. His help is for all His people who take time to call upon Him. If you would like, email me a prayer request and we will pray together. God hears and will say yes, no or wait. God bless you! Dean

Sing about it: https://www.youtube.com/watch?v=xg282my5QyU>

My Happy Life Dream

Last night I had a dream. In it I was talking with a group of mostly young people, Someone asked, "What's the secret of a happy life?"

One said, "Make lots of money so you are financially secure."

Another said, "Eat good food, drink good drinks and party while you can because life is short so live it up."

Another said, "Have lots of sexual conquests before you marry and settle down."

Another said, "Gain power over people through wealth, stardom or political office. Make a name for yourself. Become famous."

Still another said. "Get religion. Any kind will do because all roads lead to heaven."

It was my turn, I said, "The secret of a happy life is death to self for the benefit of others." One responded to my statement with a scornful look.

When I awoke I realized that my statement was mine but I had learned it from Jesus who said to his followers, "Whoever wants to be my disciple must deny themselves and take up their cross and follow me. For whoever wants to save their life will lose it, but whoever loses their life for me will find it. What good will it be for someone to gain the whole world, yet forfeit their soul?"(Matt. 16:24-26)

Then I asked myself, "How well am I doing in denying myself for the benefit of others? How about you? Jesus denying Himself to the point of dying on a cross has won forgiveness of sin and salvation to millions who have come to Him. His denial of himself, followed by defeating death and rising from the dead has brought great joy to himself as well as all who trust him as their Savior. He is the way to God, the truth of God and the life of God. He is the only door and road to heaven. " He said of himself,"No one comes to the Father except by me." (John 14:6)

So Jesus purposely gave up his life to gain an eternal kingdom of blessing, forgiveness and salvation for millions. He said, "I lay down my life-only to take it up again. I lay it down of my own accord." (John 10:18) His denial of himself and triumph over death has brought ultimate joy and peace to both himself and all who know and follow him.

So Lord help me to follow in your footsteps by denying myself, taking up the cross of suffering for the benefit of yourself and others. Out of the denial of self for the benefit of others comes the true meaning of abundant life. You have proved it Lord Jesus. I come now to you. Help me and all who know you to learn and practice your life giving will of self denial for your benefit and the benefit of others.

Jesus I Come to You- <http://www.youtube.com/watch?v=zja-Nx9Kb80>

My Happy Life Dream

Last night I had a dream. In it I was talking with a group of mostly young people, Someone asked, "What's the secret of a happy life?"

One said, "Make lots of money so you are financially secure."

Another said, "Eat good food, drink good drinks and party while you can because life is short so live it up."

Another said, "Have lots of sexual conquests before you marry and settle down."

Another said, "Gain power over people through wealth, stardom or political office. Make a name for yourself. Become famous."

Still another said. "Get religion. Any kind will do because all roads lead to heaven."

It was my turn, I said, "The secret of a happy life is death to self for the benefit of others." One responded to my statement with a scornful look.

When I awoke I realized that my statement was mine but I had learned it from Jesus who said to his followers, "Whoever wants to be my disciple must deny themselves and take up their cross and follow me. For whoever wants to save their life will lose it, but whoever loses their life for me will find it. What good will it be for someone to gain the whole world, yet forfeit their soul?"(Matt. 16:24-26)

Then I asked myself, "How well am I doing in denying myself for the benefit of others? How about you? Jesus denying Himself to the point of dying on a cross has won forgiveness of sin and salvation to millions who have come to Him. His denial of himself, followed by defeating death and rising from the dead has brought great joy to himself as well as all who trust him as their Savior. He is the way to God, the truth of God and the life of God. He is the only door and road to heaven. " He said of himself,"No one comes to the Father except by me." (John 14:6)

So Jesus purposely gave up his life to gain an eternal kingdom of blessing, forgiveness and salvation for millions. He said, "I lay down my life-only to take it up again. I lay it down of my own accord." (John 10:18) His denial of himself and triumph over death has brought ultimate joy and peace to both himself and all who know and follow him.

So Lord help me to follow in your footsteps by denying myself, taking up the cross of suffering for the benefit of yourself and others. Out of the denial of self for the benefit of others comes the true meaning of abundant life. You have proved it Lord Jesus. I come now to you. Help me and all who know you to learn and practice your life giving will of self denial for your benefit and the benefit of others.

Jesus I Come to You- <http://www.youtube.com/watch?v=zja-Nx9Kb80>

My Love for You
God's Love For You

How deep is the ocean?
God's love for you is deeper!
How wide is the universe?
God's love for you is wider!
How long is infinity?
God's love for you is longer!
How high is the sky?
God's love for you is higher!
How sweet is a pumpkin pie?
God's love for you is sweeter!
And Why?
Because the ocean, universe,
infinity, sky and pumpkin pie
Will cease!
But God's love will forever increase!

O Love that will not let go of me
I give back my love to Thee,
That in its endless depths our love shall richer,
fuller be!

God Sings Over Us

Zeph. 3:17 The LORD your God is with you,
He is mighty to save.
He will take great delight in you,
He will quiet you with His love,
He will rejoice over you with singing."

My Never Ending Ecstacy

I love you child with tenderness.
I love all you are to Me
I sing my love that set you free.
You are My eternal ecstasy.

I touch you now with gentleness
Love of My heartfelt tenderness
You are My trophy for eternity
My never ending ecstasy.

I love you child with joyfulness
I joy in all you are to Me
You are the life of My love
My ever lasting ecstasy!

I touch you now with gentleness
Love of My heartfelt tenderness
You are My trophy for eternity
My never ending ecstasy

You are My blood bought child
My love for you is gentle and wild.
You are Mine and I am yours
My ever lasting ecstasy.

I touch you now with gentleness
Love of my heartfelt tenderness
You are my trophy for eternity
My never ending ecstasy

Rest now My tender love
Quiet yourself my gentle dove
We are one for eternity.
In ever lasting ecstasy

I touch you now with gentleness
Love of my heartfelt tenderness
You are my trophy for eternity
My never ending ecstasy

My Prostate Story

Hi John,

I've been praying for God's guidance in your prostate treatment. I sent you a text message about this but guess you don't get text messages or usage of your phone is restricted? So I'm sending you this snail mail.

I had aggressive prostate cancer in 2003 and was told I would have only three years to live if I didn't do something about it. The doctor told me to get radiation right away, not to think about it, nor study it but just go do it. That's not the kind of person I am so I prayed about it, and went to the elders and was anointed with oil and prayed for twice.

Then I studied it. A friend of mine called me and told me about a treatment he had done called triple block hormone treatment which he said worked very well. I later learned it was effective 95% of the time. So I asked my doctor at Kaiser about it. He said that they didn't do that kind of treatment. So I decided to become a vegetarian which I was for over 8 months. I also went to a special cleanse for 10 days put on by Christians. I lost about 20 pounds. But it didn't stop the cancer.

I finally decided to travel to Southern Calif where the triple block treatment was done. It was going to cost me a lot of money but I thought it was better than any thing else I had studied. I was going to fly down their and called the doctor their at Mt. Sinai Medical center. I told him the story about Kaiser not being willing to do the treatment in Pleasanton because the doctor and Kaiser hadn't done it before.

He told me a doctor from Kaiser in Southern Calif did the treatment and he would get him to call my doctor at Kaiser in Pleasanton. He did call my doctor and told him how to do the treatment and the Kaiser doctor agreed to it.

So I got the treatment which does not involve surgery where you have to wear diapers afterword and may become impotent. I also didn't have to use chemo or radiation which can also cause lasting after effects. I just got a Lupron shot once a month for 12 months and took some pills. It worked. My PSA went to zero BUT that doesn't mean the cancer is totally gone but just in remission. So every time my PSA goes above 4 I have to have a new shot of Lupron. That brings it way down to about 2 and it takes about 8 months to go back up beyond 4. The last four months before I get a shot my energy level goes up. If it ever stayed below 4 I would never need another shot. This year I haven't yet had to have the shot going on one year now.

I get a little tired when I take the shot but other than that everything is normal. So thats the story and I'm grateful for near 10 years I have had since my diagnosis when i was told I had three years left if nothing was done. I'm still able to do what I want to do though I get tired more easily but that may also be because i'm almost 79 years old.

If a miracle ever did occur beyond the miracle of the past 10 years I've had, I believe I would feel it in my body and sleep like a log all night instead of a log cut in four parts which means I have to get up three or four times a night to natures extended call.

That's the story. I hope your prostate cancer is being controlled. How are you doing? Anything I can pray for you? I'll continue by God's grace to pray for you and Marsha, your mom, Jake, Sarah. Melisa, Zach and Kinsey and all your family. God bless you. Say hi to Marsha for Gloria and I.

In Christ's love,
Dean

My Son Ken & Fulfilled Bible Prophecy

When my son was a young boy I heard him crying in his room in bed. I didn't know what was causing his tears but tried to make him feel better. I shared God's love for Him by telling Him about Jesus dying for him and rising from the dead to forgive him and give him eternal life. It didn't seem to help.

Then he asked me a question which revealed his problem. He asked, "Dad, has anything the Bible said would happen, happened in your lifetime? He needed to know something that God did while I was alive and not miracles that happened thousands of years ago.

So I shared a miracle that had happened in my lifetime. In 1948 Israel became a nation again after not being a nation for many years. I told him how the Bible foretold how the people of Israel, due to their sin against God, would be scattered all over the world but God would restore a remnant of them to their land after many years and the Bible said their nation would be born in a day. It happened when I was thirteen years old on May 14, 1948, 2500 years after they had ceased to be a nation. Hearing that seemed to satisfy him. He quit crying and rolled over and fell asleep.

It has been many years since that happened. My son, now a very successful teacher for 18 years, is in his fifties. I was rethinking about that time when as a young boy I shared the fulfillment of prophecy with him.

I actually could then have shared many other fulfilled Bible events besides the rebirth of Israel in 1948, events that happened in my lifetime. Here are seven of them: 1. At age 20 God fulfilled His promise that if I came to Him He would give me rest and His purpose for my life to know Him and make Him known. 2. He kept His promise that if I believed in His Son who gave Himself for me, that He would give me eternal life, and I would be born again and would never perish. 3. Then he promised me in His word, the Bible, that if I did wrong after trusting Him as Savior He would still love me and would forgive and cleanse me as I admitted and confessed my sin to Him. That promise has been fulfilled many times. 4. He told me that if I stayed close to him I would have joy and have a fruitful life which has happened. 5. He told me not to worry about anything but to tell Him about it and trust Him to help me and He would replace my worry with peace. He has fulfilled that wonderful promise! 6. He has also kept His promise to never leave or forsake me. 7. He has also fulfilled His promise to answer yes to my every prayer that was His will. So far He has said yes more than 76 amazing times.

So I have believed His prophetic promises and they have been fulfilled and still are being fulfilled every day of my life. As I share this with tears of gratitude, I pray that my son and you will know the same seven wonderful prophetic promises fulfilled in your life as they have been fulfilled in mine. Everyone who truly believes God is satisfied and becomes a part of the fulfillment of prophecy! It is worth singing about. Click below.

Songs, I'm satisfied: <https://www.youtube.com/watch?v=E1bhFdLHReg>

Standing on the Promises: <https://www.youtube.com/watch?v=S1tH6h2v_0c>

God's Vineyard
Inspired by Isaiah 5

She looked on Me like a cooing dove
I asked her what I could do to show my love.
I know, she'll be My vineyard. I'll watch her grow.
I'll circle her around with romantic care.
Ti'll tender buds turn heavenly blue.

I'll taste her love sweet & true.
She brought a cluster from the vine to our bed.
To my dismay our love was dead.
To my shock & horror the moment turned sour.
The grapes were bitter spoiling love's power.
I spit them out & stormed off to the vineyard's tower.
I thought she'd be My pleasant vine.
And we could share heaven's wine.
But I would not tolerate a vineyard with grapes that are sour.
So our courtship turned bitter that very hour.
I tore out its hedge and broke down it's tower.
So have I given up on love & wine?
No a day is coming when I'll have a wife divine.
I'll make her anew into a beautiful bride.
Together we'll have a royal ride.
I'll plant her afresh in fertile soil.
She'll produce grapes royal.
My beloved will be to me
All ripe, sweet and loyal!

Mystery In The Bible

Have you met anyone who doesn't like to see a mystery solved? The Bible has quite a few mysteries in it. Sixteen mysteries, some which overlap, are listed below. Many people think of the mysteries of the Bible as not being solved. Yet, the opposite is true. A mystery in the Bible is something that may not have been understood but is now made known. In other words the mysteries of the Bible are solved as they have been revealed through His inspired prophets. Only two of those mysteries will be explained here.

The **mystery of the gospel** is that God announces through his servants the good news that His Son has died for our sins and rose again for our justification. It includes the mystery that Christ lives in all those who now trust Him as Savior, both Jew and Gentile.

The other mystery covered here is the **mystery of the last trump and shout of Christ** which reveals that the Lord Jesus Christ is returning at the sounding of the last trump by an angel and the shout of our Savior at which time those who have died will rise to meet Him in the air. Those who are alive at His coming will be raised and transformed receiving new, incorruptible, glorious bodies. What will He say when he shouts? When Jesus raised one man from the dead, he said, "Lazarus, Come forth!" Perhaps He may just shout, "Come forth!" and all who know Him will rise to meet Him. These two mysteries revealed insure the reality of a victorious present and glorious future for all of us who know Christ!

Which of these mysteries do you think is the most exciting?
The Mystery of

1. the kingdom of God Mark 4:11) 2. partial blindness. Rom 11:25) 3. God's wisdom. 1Cor.2:7) 4. the last trump & transforming shout. 1Cor.15:51) 5. His will. 6. Christ.Eph 1:9 7). marriage & the church. Eph 5:32) 8. the gospel. Eph 6:19) 9 the indwelling Christ, Col. 1:27) 10. God, and the Father and of Christ, Col. 2:2) 11. iniquity. 2Th. 2:7) 12. faith. 1Tim 3:9 13). godliness, 1Tim. 3:16 14) the seven stars. Rev.1:20) 15. of God. Rev.10:7) 16. Babylon the Great. Rev. 17:5)

Mystery of Gospel & Last Trump

Often in the Bible mysteries are spoken of in the singular as is **the mystery of the gospel,** but in Mark 4:11 Jesus speaks of **the mysteries of God in the plural** which were often revealed by parables and his teaching which his disciples sometimes understood while others did not. Why? Because Jesus and the Holy Spirit revealed and explained the mysteries to His followers.

This article will share just two mysteries taken from about 57 parables Jesus told. He told the **mystery of a planter of seed** whose efforts in sowing seed produced four kinds of results, only one of which produced really good crops. Only good soil produced those bumper crops. This mystery reveals our need to be ready to receive God's Word. If our lives are not good ground we need to pray that God would break up the soil of our hearts that we might have a deep realization of our need to be made ready to receive His Word. Only then can we have truly fruitful lives.

Everyone of Jesus parables and all His teaching reveal truths to transform our lives. Jesus also reveals **the mystery of two gates, two roads, and two endings at the end of the roads.** There is a wide gate, and a wide road that ends in destruction. Many people are on that road. Then there is a narrow gate, a narrow road and that road leads to life. Few people are on that road. Jesus is the narrow gate or door through whom

we are saved from destruction and given life. All who come to God through Christ become fruitful ground and are on the narrow road that ends in life eternal.

These two mysteries revealed by Jesus assure true believers of a fruitful life and a glorious end.

For those of you who want to learn more of his transforming mysteries revealed through Jesus' parables and teaching click on the following which will take you to about 57 parables in all: <http://www.lifeofchrist.com/teachings/parables/default.asp> Many people do not believe the story of the rich man and Lazarus is a parable because it names names which parables do not, however it clearly teaches us about life after death.

Which of these mysteries do you think is the most exciting?
The Mystery of

1. the mysteries of the kingdom of God Mark 4:11) 2. partial blindness. Rom 11:25) 3. God's wisdom. 1Cor.2:7) 4. the last trump & transforming shout. 1Cor.15:51) 5. His will. 6. Christ.Eph 1:9 7). marriage & the church. Eph 5:32) 8. the gospel. Eph 6:19) 9 the indwelling Christ, Col. 1:27) 10. God, and the Father and of Christ, Col. 2:2) 11. iniquity. 2Th. 2:7) 12. faith. 1Tim 3:9 13). godliness, 1Tim. 3:16 14) the seven stars. Rev.1:20) 15. of God. Rev.10:7) 16. Babylon the Great. Rev. 17:5)

Mystery of Iniquity & Godliness

Two of the most interesting and revealing mysteries in the Bible are the **mystery of iniquity** and the contrasting **mystery of godliness.** We are told that the mystery of iniquity is already at work. When did it begin? Iniquity was born When Satan decided he wanted to exalt himself above God. He then lost his position and caused one third of the angels to fall with Him. Since then his wickedness has caused a lot more than a third of mankind to join him in His rebellion. Most of mankind are on the broad road that leads to destruction.

Iniquity's greatest manifestation will occur when God stops hindering wickedness and allows it to have free

course. At that time a man of sin will come on the scene of world history, exalt himself, take control of much of the world, do miracles and proclaim himself to be God.   When the man of sin arrives his basic wickedness is the same as his inspirer, Satan. He exalts himself as God. He enslaves much of mankind by not allowing them to buy or sell without the mark of the beast, #666.
(2 Timothy 2:5-9)(Rev. 13:16-18)

Enter **the mystery of godliness**: God came to earth in a body as a baby who grew into manhood. Though He was of equal standing with God He did not think of clinging to that standing. He humbled Himself as a man, was declared to be the Son of God, gave His life to save all who would trust him. He was proven God's Son by the Father who spoke from heaven about Him on three occasions. He was also proven to be the Son of God through His miracles, teaching, by the Holy Spirit, and by His resurrection from the dead.   He was seen by angels and ministered to by them. He was preached to the world some of which believed in Him. He ascended into glory where He sits today at the right hand of God the Father. His was a godly life In contrast to Satan who is wickedness personified. Phil. 2:5-10 & I Tim. 3:16)

Satan, the perpetrator of iniquity and its chief proponent is filled with sin, is a liar in whom no truth exists, and many of his acts throughout history were to promote his desire to be worshipped as God, to destroy Israel, and to keep the Son of God from being born. Unable to accomplish his purpose he makes one final attempt by taking over the life of a man who is called 'the man of sin." That man inspired by Satan fulfills a final act of iniquity and infamy claiming to be God. In response the Lord Jesus Christ returns to banish Satan, the man of sin and all his followers forever to a second death in the lake of fire.

Those who are wise have faith in the mystery of godliness which includes sacrifice, forgiveness, love and eternal life personified in the Lord Jesus Christ. Christ will crush Satan under the feet of all who trust Him. Then they will be among the wise who will enjoy the glories of heaven forever!

<https://www.youtube.com/watch?v=192WObhJNEg>

Mystery of Israel's Partial Blindness

We read of Israel's partial blindness as a nation in Paul's letter to the Romans   as follows: "For I would not, brothers, that you should be ignorant of this mystery, lest you should be wise in your own conceits; that blindness in part is happened to Israel, until the fulness of the Gentiles be come in."

Who causes this blindness of Israel and what is the extent of that blindness? We are told that "the god of this world(Satan) has blinded the minds of those who don't believe lest the glorious light of the good news of Christ shine into them and they be saved."   Note that this is partial blindness caused by Satan to some Israelites but not to all of them. A remnant of believing Messianic Jews still exist whose minds are not blinded to the truth. Israel is blinded in part, but not all Israel.   We are told that

God has left a remnant of believing Jews which persists until today.

It is estimated that there are 15,000,000 Jews in the world today. World wide there are still some millions of Jews who trust Jesus as Savior. According to what is revealed Israel's partial blindness will someday come to an end.

Romans 26 tells us that all Israel will be saved, as it is written: "The deliverer(Jesus Christ) will come from Zion; he will turn godlessness away from Jacob." Through Christ's return the nation Israel will be spiritually born in a day, will mourn because of what they finally realize they did to their Messiah and receive Jesus as their Savior. When will this happen? It will happen when the fulness of the Gentiles is complete, that is the last Gentiles to believe in Christ are converted. Then the nation Israel who only had a remnant of believers will become a whole nation of believers. Israel who had been the tail of the nations for so many years will become the head of the nations with Christ as their King. Israel who had been a cup of trembling in the hands of the nations will become a cup of blessing. In that day the blindness in part of Israel shall cease and the glory of the good news of Christ shall shine forth to the whole nation.

Rejoice Israel for the mystery of your partial blindness is solved. Once you were blind in part but your blindness will be removed forever by Jesus who is able to give sight to both the physically blind and the spiritually blind!

Listen for the line in this song that shows God healing blind eyes. https://www.youtube.com/watch?v=tGlMd53SoOA>

Mystery of the Seven Stars

Revelation 1 speaks of the mystery of the seven stars in Christ's right hand and seven lamp stands by which He is surrounded. Christ Himself reveals their meaning saying "The seven stars are the angels of the seven churches. That they are in his right hand shows He has complete control over their messages and activity. Each angel delivers a message from God Himself to each one of the seven golden lamp stand churches mentioned in Revelation 1,2,& 3, to Ephesus, Smyrna, Pergamum, Thyatira, Sardis, Philadelphia and Laodicea. The seven churches are called "the seven golden lamp stands." This obviously means that the seven churches are to be a light of truth to the world. An interesting verse in Amos tells us to "seek Him that makes the seven stars..." God asks Job if he can " bind the sweet influences of Pleiades?" Pleiades is a constellation made up of seven bright stars called seven sisters. They are represented as women. What are the sweet influences of Pleiades? Not certain about that except that God asked Job if he could bind or control them. Of course he couldn't. Only God can control the stars and they do have a sweet influence upon those who have eyes to see beyond them to their Creator!

Let's take a closer look at the seven stars and seven churches. Are they not meant to be a sweet influence upon the world? Is not the light of the golden lamp stands meant to be a blessing to the world? Is not the church spoken of as a woman, a bride of Christ. Is not each of the seven churches seen in a feminine sense as meant to be a blessing? Are not all the churches bound together in the hands of Christ?In order to be a blessing, there are certain things the churches need to be told by Christ through the angels or messengers He has at His command.

If you read the messages to each of the seven churches you will find a pattern. First they are commended for anything right that they are doing. Then they are exposed to anything wrong that they need to correct. Finally they are admonished to overcome something and promised a special blessing if they do. Even the church of Laodicea which is often strongly criticized is promised the blessing of Christ's dining with anyone who opens the door of their life to Him and He promises that they will sit upon His throne if they repent and overcome.

We can learn from God's dealings with the churches in Revelation how we should deal with people who are Christians. First we should look for that which is right in their lives and encourage them. Then in as gentle a way as possible we should seek to restore them from any wrong in their life. Finally, we should remind them of the great blessing God promises to them for any proper response they make to His will for them. Many people are not Godlike in their approach to believers but critical, condemning and judgmental without reaching forth with a promise of forgiveness, change, hope and peace. Christians are told to forgive others as He forgives them. But in the real world to often Christians say they forgive then relegate the forgiven person to shunning and disregard. Thank God Jesus is not that way. When He forgives He restores fully! If you read Paul's letters to the churches and John's and Peter's you will find that almost if not all of them start off by a promised blessing, by commending what is right, and by giving instruction for walking in a path that pleases God. Their letters are full of encouragement, blessing and love as well as instruction in right living. Sin must be dealt with but it Is best dealt with by an attitude like Christ's, "Father forgive them, for they know not what they do." "Their sins and iniquities I will remember no more forever! Is that the kind of person you are toward those who sin against you? Is it true that an ounce of encouragement is worth a ton of criticism? In my life people who corrected me in love have been the most influential. How about you? https://www.youtube.com/watch?v=FvgspvBVEUo>

Mystery of the Sunflower

Examine a sunflower seed. What are God's two great books? Nature and the Bible. What is the first time seeds are mentioned in the Bible?Gen 1:11,12 Third day. Second Time Gen 4:1

The Bible and the Sunflower Seed Reveal All the Mysteries of Death & Life

Examine the Seed. What do you see? In this simple small sunflower seed God has revealed the mystery of death and life. It is both dark and light. You and I are like this sunflower seed. It is both dark and light. So are we. We have a mixture of good and evil. Jesus said, "If you being evil know how to give good gifts to your children, how much more will your heavenly Father give good things and the Holy Spirit to them that ask."

One part of the seed reminds us that we are capable of good but the other part reminds us that we have an evil sinful nature. All of us have sinned and come short of the glory of God. The result of that sinful nature is that we all have to die. But that death can be glorious if we wake to the sunshine of God's love and forgiveness. It can be wonderful if we listen to the voice of the raindrop bright, the Word of God which is like water to our thirsty souls.

Do you see anything else beyond the shell of the seed? In it is hidden the potential for a beautiful flower. But something must happen first. What must happen to this seed for it to fulfill its potential? In order for the beautiful flower to come out? Jesus tells us in John 12:23-26 Jesus replied, "The hour has come for the Son of Man to be glorified. 24 I tell you the truth, unless a kernel of wheat falls to the ground and dies, it remains only a single seed. But if it dies, it produces much fruit with many seeds.. 25 The man who loves his life will lose it, while the man who hates his life in this world will keep it for eternal life. 26 Whoever serves me must follow me; and where I am, my servant also will be. My Father will honor the one who serves me.

SAY WITH ME this poem: "In the heart of a seed buried deep so deep a little plant lays fast asleep. Wake says the sunshine and creep to the light. Wake says the voice of the raindrop bright. The little plant heard and arose to see what the outside world might be."

God sees beautiful potential in you but it requires death to bring it about. The sunflower seed must die to germinate and bring forth the beauty hidden within it. it must let the water of life resurrect its inner being and come forth to meet its new and glorious potential.

Jesus had to die and rise again to produce fruit, to be all that God wanted him to be. That is true of you too. You must die to the dark side of your nature and be reborn. How can that be? God calls you to two things, death and life. Death to your sin. Jesus took that death. When you believe in Him as your Savior God counts it as if you died with Christ on the cross and Christ pays the debt of all your sin. Then you believe in His defeating death and rising from the dead. When you confess with your mouth Jesus as Lord and believe in your heart that He has risen from the dead, God counts his risen life to you. He gives you HIs Spirit which regenerates you like a seed is germinated and has new life, you are born again and that new birth is beautiful. With that new birth you begin to produce all the fruits of the Spirit which are love, joy, peace, gentleness, goodness, meekness, faith and self control.

I invite you to plant a sunflower seed. I invite you to plant yourself in Christ, to die to yourself and live to God.

Jesus in the Bible is called God's seed. He died once and for all, the perfect seed for the imperfect seeds that we are. His death offering and risen life if received can regenerate new life in our sinful selves.

That Jesus died and rose again has been verified by over 500 witnesses as they saw him at various times over a period of 40 days. Since then countless people have believed in His death, burial and resurrection for their sin and have experienced the germination of new life in their souls.

In order to experience that germination or regeneration of life you must obey the gospel, believe the good news about Christ loving you, dying and rising again for you.If you have done that something wonderful is at work right now inside the shell of your life.

There is a new beautiful you living inside you. You are a new creation. Old things have passed away.

Christ lives in you. All things have become new. How many know for sure that you have been born again? How many not sure?

The apostle Paul experienced this new life and speaks of it this way. " I am Crucified with Christ, nevertheless I live, yet not I but Christ lives in me and the life I now live I live by faith in the Son of God who loves me and gave Himself for me."

He says he was crucified with Christ. That is true of every believer.

This next poem song has to do with you when your body dies. It is appointed to each of us to die physically. It is appointed to all who trust Jesus as Savior to rise from the dead, get a new, beautiful body and be with Him forever in the garden of God.

In the heart of the earth buried deep so deep a lifeless body lays fast asleep. Wake said the voice of God's Spirit bright. Wake said the voice of the Son of light. The little soul heard and rose to see what the world would be like in eternity!

Lord, help us lose our life to you that we might gain it. Help us realize that the bitterness of death to self now and actual physical death lead us to the sweetness and bliss of eternal life in your presence forever. So come death. Take away our shell that we may bloom for you.

In closing let's remember that we all have a cross to take up and bear. Let us take Jesus' cross for its life giving grace. Let us be content to endure suffering that we might know gain through our loss. Let us cast our longing hearts upon Thee Lord and glory in Thy cross! A poetic song follows which tells us who believe that we have a beautiful Christ who lives in us. It is called **Christ Liveth in Me**.

1. Once far from God and dead in sin,
    No light my heart could see;
    But in God's Word the light I found,
    Now Christ liveth in me.
    ◦   *Refrain:*
        Christ liveth in me,
        Christ liveth in me,
        Oh! what a salvation this,
        That Christ liveth in me.
2. As rays of light from yonder sun,
    The flow'rs of earth set free,
    So life and light and love came forth
    From Christ living in me.
3. **As lives the flow'r within the seed,**
    As in the cone the tree,
    So, praise the God of truth and grace,
    His Spirit dwelleth in me.
4. With longing all my heart is filled,
    That like Him I may be,
    As on the wondrous thought I dwell
    That Christ liveth in me.

Mystery- Babylon The Great

Babylon the Great is the final out growth of Babel(Babylon) "the small" mentioned in the O.T. It is believed that Nimrod a mighty hunter and leader motivated the people who lived on the plain of Shinar(near modern Baghdad) to build a tower before 3500 B.C. to reach into the heavens. They wanted to make a name for themselves while revolting against God. So God came down and confused their language(Babel means confusion). So they quit building the tower and migrated in clans based on the language each group spoke. One estimate says they were broken into 72 basic language roots from which the rest of the languages morphed into all the languages of today. The important thing to remember is Babel means confusion. When people rebel against the true God the result is confusion about all of life.(Genesis 11)

After Babylon "the small" came the larger nation of Babylon. This city is named some 257 times in the O.T. from From 2nd Kings 17:24 through Zechariah 6:10. We might call it Babylon the bigger. Babylon the bigger was like Babel the small for much of its history-in rebellion against the true God except for some years when Daniel and his three friends had a true Godly influence on it. But their influence did not last. Babylon the bigger was known for being a city devoted through false gods to materialism and the pursuit of sensual pleasure. Confusion ruled and it was destroyed in the sixth century B.C. as Isaiah prophesied in the 13th chapter of his book.

In the 17th chapter of Revelation we read these final words about Babylon: MYSTERY, BABYLON THE GREAT, THE MOTHER OF HARLOTS AND ABOMINATIONS OF THE EARTH. Babylon the great is pictured as a woman riding on the back of a 7 headed, 10 horned beast. The woman represents Satan's counterfeit religion and a city in power over most people of the earth. The woman representing false religion is supported by the rulers of an economic, materialistic world system. They support her for awhile. Then turn on her and destroy her. It is the ultimate example of mankind using false religion to support their materialistic and sensual desires. Once the harlot is destroyed they usurp power over most of mankind seeking to exalt themselves above God. In the end they too are destroyed by the Lamb of God, the meek and mild Jesus showing His complete power to destroy evil religion and evil materialism.

Babylon the small, Babylon the bigger, and Babylon the Great are all energized by Satan and in the end are defeated by the power of God. **Babylon the Great, though a mystery, is revealed as the ultimate evil system.** In each case throughout history Babylon represents confusion because God is left out and false religion, Satan and materialism replaces Him. In the end the whole system reaches its peak of evil. Then in one hour Christ wipes it out. Then those who have trusted the true God become rulers with Him over His new heaven and new earth. Babylon the Great and its followers will be banished forever while those who trust the Lamb will rule with Him forever.

The message to us is " Come out of her(Babylon the great), my people, so that you will not share in her sins, so that you will not receive any of her plagues;" We come out by coming to God's Son who said,"Come to me all you who labor and are heavy laden." Whoever comes to HIm shall be saved from being a part of the confusion of Babylon the Great and shall instead be a part of Christ's Greater New Heaven and Earth where confusion is replaced forever with understanding. freedom and peace.
https://www.youtube.com/watch?v=eW2mOBZ3rTs>

Need a Helping Hand?

When my daughter Glenda was a little girl, about five, she accompanied me to our church where I went to open the door for a man who was delivering a heavy load. As he went in the door he said to her, "I have to be strong to carry this." My daughter said immediately, loudly, and with perfect confidence, *"Strong is the Lord God!"* Rev 18:8 The delivery man looked at her with amazement. She had just quoted her Bible memory verse.

Did you hear about the little boy who was trying to move a large rock in his back yard. He couldn't lift it. His father saw him and asked, "Want me to help you?" The little boy nodded his head. "Put your hand under the rock son." When he did his dad put his right hand under his son's right hand and together they lifted the rock. He needed a helping hand from his father and he got it. He needed and got the helping hand of his father.

God who is the Father of all who believe Him and trust His Son today wants to give us a helping hand which we often need no matter how old we are because we are often unable to lift every load in our life. Isaiah 41:13 says, *"For I, the Lord your God, will hold your right hand, Saying to you, 'Fear not, I will help you."* If He is the Lord your God He promises to give you a hand. In Isaiah 41:10 the Lord says, *"Fear not, for I am with you; Be not dismayed, for I am your God. I will strengthen you, Yes, I will help you, I will uphold you with My righteous right hand."*

Notice our Father in heaven promises to help us with His *righteous right hand.* That means if what we need help in is right or righteous He will help but don't expect Him to help if what you need help with is unrighteous. When my son Ken was a boy he saw me about to throw some tree limbs into my neighbors backyard. They were cut from our neighbor's tree that had grown on our side of the fence. He said, "Do you think Jesus would do that, Dad?" I didn't throw them over the fence but kept them on my side and threw them into the disposal can. I did right because of what he said and I think God helped me through my son.

Often God will help us when we seek His help from those who are in His forever family because they will do what our Lord says in Gal. 6:2, *"Bear one another's burdens, and so fulfill the law of Christ."* So when we need a valued, loving, helping hand, let's ask our Father and His people for it with gratitude. Sing about it here: Love Lifted Me!

<https://video.search.yahoo.com/yhs/search?hsimp=yhs-att_001&hspart=att&p=song%2C+lovelifted+me#id=3&vid=19e0661e469a0c3eba33cab334e645d6&action=click>

New Creation
Jesus Cries from the Cross- Carving Out a New Creation-

In six days God finished the the heaven and the earth and rested on the seventh day. In six utterances from the cross Jesus carved out a new creation and after his seventh cry, He rested.

The first three things Jesus uttered while hanging on the cross show His and His Father's love for all mankind. "Father forgive them for they know not what they are doing." These words characterize His new creation as one characterized by love and forgiveness.

Jesus shows his love for both His mother and his disciple John as he speaks for the second time from the cross.When Jesus saw his mother there, and the disciple whom he loved standing nearby, he said to his mother, "Dear woman, here is your son," and to the disciple, "Here is your mother." From that time on, this disciple took her into his home. These words characterize His new creation as one of care for His people. Those who are related to Him by faith are cared for by Him and by those who follow Him.

Jesus third cry from the cross shows his concern for each individual to come to Him that he might rescue them from sin and fit them for paradise and heaven. While being mocked by one thief, the other thief calls on Jesus for help. The thief said, "Lord, remember me when you come into your kingdom." Jesus answered him, "I tell you the truth, today you will be with me in paradise." Those in His new kingdom creation may call on and believe in Him as they are dying. He will not cast out anyone who comes to Him in faith. Then they will be with Him in paradise forever.

Jesus fourth and fifth cry from the cross reveal his concern for Himself as related to His desires for closeness to His Father. His fourth cry involved thirst both physical and spiritual. After this, Jesus knowing that all things were now accomplished, that the scripture might be fulfilled, said, "I thirst." He thirsted for spiritual as well as physical water that those in His new creation would never have to thirst. Whoever receives Him has an endless supply of spiritual water to continually quench his or her thirst.

Christs fifth cry from the cross spoken in a loud was "My God, my God, why hast thou forsaken me? He was forsaken so that no one in His new creation would ever be forsaken. He says to those who truly know Him, "I will never leave you nor forsake you."

His sixth cry indicated His finishing the work of carving out a new creation for His Father. As God finished his first work of creation so Christ has finished all that is necessary for His followers to be forgiven and made into new creations. They knew that His work for them on the cross perfected them forever so that they would be a part of His new creation composed of people who would be like His Son.

Finally, Jesus last cry on the cross was "Father, into your hands I commend my Spirit. Then He gave up His life and found rest and resurrection in His new risen life. That God had accepted His finished work is seen in His triumph over death and the grave. Now He is risen and waits for you to come to Him and be a part of His new creation. His new creation will also someday bring all who believe in Him a new risen body, a new heaven and earth, and a new and everlasting joy where they dwell in the House of the Lord forever. Are you a part of His new creation? If so then you will rejoice with Him forever!
https://www.youtube.com/watch?v=gxJyXLWOkmg>

Luke 23:34; John 19:26,27;Luke 23:42 ,43; John 19:28 ;John 19:30; Matthew 27:46; Luke 23:46

No Choice or Choice? Ultimate

Satisfaction!

In this life there are things most of us are forced to do having no choice in the matter.. Here are some things we have no choice over:

1. Being Born, who our parents will be and when & where we are born.

2. Being totally dependent as Babies, weening, teething, learning to talk.

3. Going through childhood, youth, puberty, school, and adult hood.

4. Working, eating & drinking, feeling, tasting, smelling, seeing & hearing

5. Sickness, suffering, length of physical life and death.

Then there are things we go through based on our choice. Some examples:

1. Doing well or poorly in school and choosing life vocations

3. Selecting a wife or husband.

4. Choosing a new home or locating in a new spot on earth.

5. Choosing acceptable or non acceptable behavior.

6. Deciding what we believe about our reason for existence

7. Choosing to believe or not believe in God and to seek or not seek Him.

8. Choosing to find or refusing to find God & to honor & to serve Him or to reject Him.

9. Believing God's word as found in the Bible or refusing to believe it.

10. Choosing things that give some temporary satisfaction

11. Choosing something that gives ultimate, supreme, eternal satisfaction.

12. Choosing to accept God's gift of forgiveness & eternal life.

Since we cannot change things forced upon us we need to seriously seek to choose rightly among things not forced upon us. If we are wise we will seek things that satisfy us legitimately both temporarily & eternally.

One who lives only for temporary satisfaction is a fool! One who lives for eternal satisfaction is wise. Unfortunately most people live for temporary satisfaction often being based on self gratification.

What have you chosen to make your main pursuit in life? The Lord Jesus Christ gives us the greatest wise direction for how to choose rightly. He tells us to seek not for that which perishes but for that which lasts forever which He, the Son of God will give us. He tells all who come to Him that they will find rest and eternal life. He tells all who seek Him whole heartedly that He will not turn them away. He promises all who come to Him that they will find the way to God, the truth of God and the life of God. He warns those who refuse Him that they will not have eternal life but everlasting death.

In the end one who comes to the the true God through His Son finds ultimate, supreme satisfaction for he or she knows God and says with confidence, "I will be satisfied when I awake in Your likeness. I know that when I see you I will be with you and like you forever!

So what are you choosing from the things you are not forced to do? As for me and my house, we choose to believe and trust in God's Son and to seek to know, love and serve Him forever. Have you made that choice? It will never be forced upon you. Will you make that choice today? He is no fool who chooses ultimate, supreme satisfaction above temporary satisfaction!

Sing About It: <http://www.touchjesussongs.net/lyricspage48.html>

No Longer Alone
Valued Like a Precious Stone
by Dean

Alone in the night in a cave
A single diamond lay alone.
Century after century without value it lay.
Then one day a Miner's hand plucked it from its tomb.
Now it is no longer alone or without value.
It shines brightly in a crown upon a throne.
In life we are alone until God touches us and values us as His own.

Then they that feared the LORD spake often one to another:
and the LORD hearkened, and heard it,
and a book of remembrance was written before him

for them that feared the LORD,
and that thought upon his name.
And t**hey shall be mine, says the LORD of hosts,
in that day when I make up my jewels;** (Mal. 3:16,17)

No Such Thing As Absolute Truth? by DLG

I was recently told by someone that there is "nothing we can know that is absolutely true." That statement can be disproven three different ways.

First, the statement that there is no absolute truth is declaring itself as absolute.

Second, people often say things that **are not** absolutely true, but some people say things **that are** absolutely true. For example, when I was about 10 years old I was riding in a car with my mom at the wheel on a rainy day. Suddenly going around a turn the car spun around in the road and slowed near the edge of the road. My mom's high heel on the brake broke and the car backed over the edge of a cliff that led to the Eel river below. Suddenly the back end of the car hit a tree which stopped us from falling into the Eel river. Her heel broke. We backed over the cliff. That tree saved my life.. I can say absolutely that our lives were saved by that tree. When I grew up at age 20 I heard the good news about Christ dying on a tree, a cross made from a tree. I was told he died for me and if I would believe I would be given the gift of forgiveness and eternal life. I believed and was saved a second time by a tree that represented His death for me. I have eternal life now, absolutely!

Third, Jesus said of himself, "I am the way, the truth and the life. No one comes to the Father but by me." What Jesus said is absolutely true. How do I know? Because God, who cannot lie, says so. Men may lie and not be absolutely true but God is not a person that could ever lie. God is absolutely good and true. A person may not believe in absolute truth but that does not do away with its reality. When I was a child I had a neighbor who said often when something bad happened, "It just didn't happen!" She had a religious belief that sin did not exist so denied the reality of the existences of anything bad. Of course she was 100% wrong. Also 100% wrong are those who say there is no absolute truth. Jesus is truth, absolute truth. When we know Him that truth sets us free, <u>absolutely</u>! Put your hand in the hand of truth. Sing about it by clicking below.

https://www.youtube.com/watch?v=ZNrVed6dP6s&spfreload=10>

Leper, Leprosy, Leprous, Lepers

Leprosy is a picture of sin. We are all spiritual lepers in need of cleansing. It started with the sin of Adam and Eve which has spread to all mankind. Some people have leprosy not because of their sin but because of communicable disease allowed into the world. We are conceived and sin is spread to us.

Not everyone has natural leprosy but everyone had spiritual leprosy. Moses sign of putting his hand in his bosom, bringing it out, putting it back and bringing it out again healed, pictures Israeli's and all mankind's need to have sin purged away. It can only happen by the power of God. Leviticus' offering of turtle doves pictures removal of leprosy both natural and spiritual. One bird dies. The other flies away picturing resurrection. Blood and oil applied to ear, thumb, toe and head pictures cleansing of hearing, doing, walking and thinking by the blood and change to listen, act, walk and think to please God. Some became lepers for a while but were healed like Miriam, Naaman, and the lepers Jesus healed.

We are born spiritual lepers so the glory of God may heal and cleanse us and transform us. The reality in full of the cleansing and filling of God's Spirit will be seen fully when we rise from the dead and fly away to be with Him forever. Below are passage about leprosy.

Some Important Times Leprosy is Mentioned in the Bible

Exodus 4:5-7New King James Version (NKJV)
5 "that they may believe that the Lord God of their fathers, the God of Abraham, the God of Isaac, and the God of Jacob, has appeared to you."**6** Furthermore the Lord said to him, "Now put your hand in your bosom." And he put his hand in his bosom, and when he took it out, behold, his hand *was* leprous, like snow. **7** And He said, "Put your hand in your bosom again." So he put his hand in his bosom again, and drew it out of his bosom, and behold, it was restored like his *other* flesh.

Leviticus 13, 14   Diagnosing and Healing Leprosy

Numbers 12:1-15 Miriam Becomes Leper & Healed

2 Kings 5 Naaman the Syrian healed from leprosy. Gehazi 's greed and lying end in his leprosy. Luke 4:27 Many lepers in Israel in time of Elisha but none cleansed except Naaman the Syrian. Those in synagogue filled with wrath and tried to kill Jesus. Why?

2 Kings 7:3 Leprous men blessed with Syrian treasures left behind when they fled.

2 Chronicles 2:26 Uzziah's pride ends in leprosy on his head

Matthew 8:3 Jesus touches and heals leper who cried out,"If you will you can make me clean.   My healing from spiritual leprosy. Move your hand and I'll be clean. The book of the generation of Jesus Christ answer to cleansing there but took over 60 years to realize it.
Mark 1:42 Leper cleansed told not to tell. Tells everybody.
Luke 5:12 Same man?
Matthew 10::8 Apostles were given power to cleanse lepers, heal sick and raise the dead.

Luke 7:22 John the Baptist convinced Jesus was Messiah by his miracles.

Luke 17:12-19 Ten lepers cleansed. One returns to give thanks, a Samaritan.

From Deeply Sad to Glad
by Dean L.G.

Oh broken heart so deeply sad
A word from God **will** make it glad.

Someone I cared for has gone away.
Will we be united again one day?

Your answer "Yes!" fills me with delight.
It comforts me in my night.
The one I loved though gone
Will be restored in heaven's dawn!

Thank you Lord,
Your word brought me rest.
You moved the hurt off my chest.

Your word is far better than all,
It seasons my heart through winter and fall.
It floods me with the joys of summers and springs,
It lifts me up to heavenly things
Where I fly with joy on the Spirit's Wings,
While all within me shouts and sings!

Oh broken heart so deeply sad,
A word from God **has** made it glad!

Isaiah 40:8 (NKJV)
The grass withers, the flower fades,
But the word of our God stands forever.

O Great I Am
by Dean L Gossett

(To be Sung to the tune, Jesus the Very Thought of Thee)

O Great I AM I sing to Thee, Thou self-existent One.
Your bread feeds my hungry sold, Your Light illumines me.

Your life gives me strength to pray. Eternal joy is mine.
I gaze anew on Your dear face. I see your Glory shine.

O Christ of God You know all things, You dove anointed King.   You are a King, a
Prophet, Priest. This all your loved ones sing.

You are our Father's unique son. You God and man are one.   We rapture in You O
loving One, Your work that saves is done!

You are the Door of Noah's ark, the Door of Israel's Boy.
Our Door in Christ swings open wide. Our hearts all burst with joy.

O Great I AM I love Your name. I love to sing its worth.
It is music in my ears, the Greatest name on earth.

O soon coming One, I wait for You. You are my all in all.
Soon I will hear Your loving shout, respond to Your dear call.

And so O Lord, O living Vine, I would abide in Thee.
That what You are, O I may be, through out eternity.

I would be fruitful in every way, in thought and word and deed.   So let Your living sap,
O Vine, my empty heart feed.

O Great I AM, I am Your child. I search for all Thou art.
My being melts, it groans to find the greatness of Your Heart.

On Her Birthday Serving at Camp-"29 Again
Aug. 13, 2014

Up to the mountain top she goes
Blossoming like a fragrant rose.
On the way she enjoys a prayerful homily.
Then she arrives at camp to happy friends and family.

At that mountain camp she enjoys food, fun and respites
Her heart is elevated to pleasant heights
Uplifted by A "Happy Birthday" wished by all
But then, "What's that?..handwriting on the wall:

Time is swiftly passing by
Year by year O me O my.
The candles increase each year.

But don't count them and you need not fear.

She has turned "29" again to inner cheers
For she counts not youth by outer years
In her mind and heart she still is young.
Her outward visage changes a little with time.
But her inner woman is still sublime.

Charm is deceitful and beauty is passing
But a woman who loves God is always
dashing!
The fruit of her heart overflows with
inspiration.
Her gorgeous acts are crowned with
admiration.

Poems like this are written by amateurs like
me.
But only God can help us really see
That true beauty is on the inside
Though our aging outer self comes along for
the ride.

Soon we'll have a final birth in heaven above
Leave behind the old self,
Bury him or her on an earthly shelf.
We'll never ever have to pout,
We'll be forever young both inside and out.

One In Tune With God Beats the Devil

Once when King David ruled over Israel he had a bad idea. Incited by the Devil He decided that numbering Israel's army was a good idea. He thought there would be power in knowing the size of his army. 1 Chron. 21

That seemed to him to be true but it shifted trust in God to human power based on size. Seventy thousand men lost their lives because of David's sin in relying on numbers instead of relying on God. God illustrated many years before the fact that having God on your side is the source of power, not numbers!

That fact was brought out in the life of a man named Gideon. Judges 6-8 In the Old Testament Gideon was told to go and fight against the Midianites. Gideon had a large army of 22,000 men. God told him to thin it down by having all the troops who were hesitant to return home. Twelve thousand departed and 10,000 were left. God still saw that amount as large. So He told Gideon to have all of the 10,000 drink water from a river. Those that put their face in the water to drink were told to go home discharged. Those that lifted the water to their mouths and lapped it were to remain part of the army.

Nine thousand seven hundred didn't lap the water so were sent home. That left 300 men who lapped the water and became the small band of men who were led by Gideon. Then God defeated Midian by Gideon's hand in a unique way. They didn't have to lift a sword to win. **God's word became their spiritual sword.**

Instead of an actual sword Gideon had his men put a trumpet in each right hand and torch-filled-pitchers in each of their left hands. Then that night they stood on the hills above the Midianite army. Gideon broke his pitcher and blew his trumpet, Each of the 300 men also broke their torch-filled-pitchers. Then they sounded their trumpets and shouted, **"the sword of the Lord and of Gideon**." The giant enemy army of Midianites in the dark below were so frightened by the lights and trumpet sound that they started fighting and killing each other and were totally defeated. Gideon, in tune with God with his small army, was a winning majority.

That is true today! It is not the size of the army but the size of one's faith in God that wins! Even today one person in tune with God is a winning majority. While Gideon trusted God, David the king lost his battle because he trusted numbers.

Two Examples of the truth that one in tune with God beats the Devil.

SGT Alvan York First World War. Greatest hero of World War 1 conscientious objector convince from scripture to go to war. Did so with idea of trying to save lives. He killed 25 fGermans. Ran out of bullets with his rifle. Then drew his pistol. German leader surrendered. Almost single hand eded he led ad way 132d surrendered German. Medal of honor. After war.

Second example. Desmond Demos. Conceits objector. Medic carried no weapon. Saved the lived of 76 men on Hacksaw Ridge. Men who made fun of him so cared for him that when he lost his Bible risked lives to get it back to him.Wounded, recovered.Given Congressional Medal of Honor

Christians usually fight spiritual battles, not against flesh and blood but spiritual forces. When we are in tune with God one person, man or woman is a majority.

Lord help me, and those who read this, to be like Gideon, weak people in whom your strength is made perfect.

Invitation. Prayer. Help us defeat Satan by trust instead of troops! Help us become spiritual winners on your side against the Devil and all his evil. Help us know that our spiritual victory in battle is today dependent on You and your strength made perfect in our weakness. 2Cor.12:9

Help me, in my weakened 82 yer old age, to be strong in faith trusting you for victory over evil no matter the odds. Defeat Satan and his spiritual demons because Christ lives in me and I am in tune with You! Please grant that same spiritual strength to all who believe You.

Sing about it. Christ Lives in Me: <https://www.youtube.com/watch?v=LdjcuHb7J7U>

The First & Last Adam

. Some people call Christ the second Adam. Better to call Him the last Adam. There won't be a third Adam.The first Adam was the head of the first creation who bequeathed to us sin, death and the curse. The last Adam, Christ, is the head of a new creation which gives us the gift of forgiveness, righteousness, everlasting life and will finally remove the curse. Give me the last Adam! I'm fed up with the first.

The First & Last Adam

One pair, Adam and his wife caused earth's fall!
Together they caused sin's stall and pall!
The first Adam brought our demise.
The last Adam will cause our rise!
Adam the first brought our curse.
Adam the last lifts us from its morass!
Once slaves to Adam's sin,
Now kings and queens when Christ lives within!
Lifted from deaths' dark graves

We rise in newness through Him who saves!
The past is over and gone.
The time of singing spurs us on!
What the first Adam lost
The Last Adam regained by paying the cost!
Through death He defeated death,
That we might joy in Him with every breath!
The curse of the first Adam will be totally gone some day
When the last Adam returns in battle array!
With the breath of His mouth sin will end its day
The last Adam will blow it all away!
His new heaven and earth
Will be here to stay!

Opened Ended Stories

There are a number of stories in the Bible left open ended. One is the story of Jonah after his finally obeying God and preaching to the Ninivites & winning the whole city to the Lord. Jonah went to rest afterward unhappy that God had spared the city. So God caused a fast growing plant to shelter Jonah from the heat. However, it was eaten up quickly and gave Jonah no more shade. So Jonah complained. God told him he was concerned about his comfort and admonished him to have some compassion for the repentant Ninivites and the children there. Jonah's response to God's rebuke is not given. Did he have a change of heart?. We don't know the rest of the story. It is left open ended.

Another open ended story about a the prodigal son's brother who was unhappy that his brother had returned home and was given a grand party. He complained to his father, " I never wasted your money or ran away and you never ever had a grand party for me." And he refused to join in the joyous return of his brother. His father reasoned with him. "All I have is yours. It is fitting that we have a party for your brother who was lost but now is found." Did the prodigal's brother respond in response to his dad's encouragement? Did he join the party? We don't know the rest of the story.

In all these cases we hope the rest of the story was good for those who were left with a choice, Did Jonah admit his self centeredness and learn to have a heart of compassion.Did the the prodigal son's brother quit sulking and join in welcoming back his brother? How would you have each of these stories end?

These stories apply to you, too. Like the prodigal son, God invites you to receive His Son as your savior. What will you do about it? Will you accept God's love as shown by His Son dying for you? If so you will find yourself on the way to a place God has for you to a great celebration.

If you receive God's Son you will gain a compassionate heart to share the good news with others and see them forgiven and on their way to heaven to join the great celebration prepared by our heavenly Father for you. If you trust Him you will find your heart rejoices when the lost are found. If not you will find no joy in seeing other prodigals found who have been lost. If not you will know the sorrow of those who have no compassion. The rest of the story depends in your decision whether or not to receive God's wonderful invitation. How will the rest of this story end for you? It's your choice! Choose wisely for your whole future good or bad depends on the rest of your story. Amen!

Summing Up On Our 50th Anniversary

It all started in my 1938 Dodge as Gloria laid her head on my shoulder.

Naturally I returned the move and got bolder.

Then Fifty years of wedded bliss
All started with a well placed kiss!

We started out with a coffee can filled with forty bucks
In spite of that our Yosemite honeymoon was deluxe.

We held hands and hiked the trail to the bridal falls
Enjoying first love with all its thralls!

I rejoiced then with the wife of my youth.
Her love satisfied me and that's the truth!

I fished for hours in Yosemite river
While Gloria waited on a rock with restrained ardor.

We never saw a soul at the river all that time
If we had I couldn't have made up this rhyme.

We watched the fire-fall from up above
It's falling embers as hot as our glowing love!

The fire-fall at Yosemite has long been canceled.
But our love goes on still unbridled!

After that life then took on a great deal more formality.
We returned home to work, school and family reality.

Then 1+1 before long brought us to four
Caused by the fruitfulness of me and Glor

First there was Glenda with her golden hair
With Her sweet smile and her face so fair!

Then their was Ken who couldn't sit still.
Now he's as calm as a sleeping pill!

Then those four turned to six
It's all part of the matrimony fix.

There's Kirsten who never does slow.
And Tyler sensitive and caring, daring to
grow!

Today Gloria and I are back to 1+1 and that's
no pun
I can say with joy, the empty nest syndrome
is lots of fun!

We were married you know in July the month
of fireworks.
And believe me it has had its perks as well as
quirks!

After fifty years we still send up skyrockets to
high places.
And to our joy and amazement they burst
into smily faces!

Thanks to God's grace after all these years
Our love for each other still adheres! (sticks)

Gloria was the wife of my youth whom I
pursued.
Now she is the wife of my decrepitude.

As the wife of my youth and old age
Together were still on the same page-

A page of love that lasts till its final perigee
(lowest point, death's short separation)
When divine love lifts us to heavens apogee!
(highest point)

We' ll meet again where we'll never shed a
tear
Together forever in eternity, the final Frontier!

Can we improve as we stay upon our
journey.
You bet, but this I can say clearly-

God , our perfect hope and trusted guide
Has kept us all these years on a Royal Ride-

A Ride that ends in glory
Where if you believe, you'll hear the rest of
this story.

Until that day dawns and shadows flee away.
Thanks for joining us on this our special day!

I gave my wife Gloria a golden coffee
can filled with stimulus bills and other
girts. Here is what was in the golden can.

1. Fifty dollar bills, 8 of them. 8 is the
number of a new beginning in the Bible.
Fifty is the number of a new beginning,
too. Pentecost was on the fiftieth day
after Jesus resurrection when God
started something new, the church which
started out **Glor**iously! In Israel the
Jubilee came every fifty years. All debts
were forgiven, property returned to its
original owners, slaves were set free
and there was a big celebration! Gloria,
my queen, that makes me a king,
hereby forgive all debts and acknowledge
all believers in Christ set free!!

2. Gloria's engagement ring, wedding ring
and ruby ring all soldered together
with gold. Looks like our marriage has
stuck. Though our faith has been tried
as we have grown old, our commitment is
as good as gold!

3. A set of sunflower coasters.
Sunflowers are Gloria's favorite flowers.
She
is my favorite flower! Because we share
mutual faith in God's Son
who created the flowers, we can
say together: The Best is Yet to Come!

4. A fancy flowered wine cork which says,
"Aged to perfection." That's her!

5. A golden book mark with a swan swimming across the top. You can

read into that whatever you wish. Just remember to keep it graceful like

the swan.

On the side of the golden coffee can with the golden ribbon on top it
says: Yuban. Lord may You ban from our life all the displeases you. Ban
the Devil and his schemes. Ban all lack of faith and trust. Replace
them all with a close walk with you and love for reach other until death
do we part.

The gifts in the can replace the caffeine stimulus with 5 other stimulaters already mentioned. Instead of getting on our nerves may those gifts stimulate us to gratitude and relaxation in You.

It also says Organic. Organic means pesticide free life. Stimulates us with Your life more abundantly and keep away the pests and Satanic pesticides!

In order to come out good the coffee has to be ground and to go through fire and heat. Help us as we grow old though tried and tested to come out as gold!

It is premium coffee. We thank you for the premiums of the Christian life.
All blessings are ours in Christ!

The can container is made from recycled materials. How often have
our bodies been recycled and renewed. Someday they will receive a final
recycling to come out transformed, incorruptible, immortal fashioned like
Jesus' risen glorious body. Let it be! Amen

Our Greatest Need

What is our greatest need right now? Hebrews 11:6 answers that question.

"But without faith *it is* impossible to please *Him,* for he who comes to God must believe that He is, and *that* He is a rewarder of those who diligently seek Him."

Our greatest need is to come to God with faith. We must believe He exists and we must diligently believe and seek after who He is, what He says and what He wants. The result will be great rewards, great discoveries, great gifts, great blessings and great cleansing and forgiveness from God Himself.

So what is the first step in pleasing God? It is coming to Him. Jesus said, **27** "All things have been handed over to Me by My Father. No one knows the Son except the Father, and no one knows the Father except the Son and anyone to whom the Son chooses to reveal Him. **28** Come to Me, all who are weary and burdened, and I will give you rest. **29** Take My yoke upon you and learn from Me, for I am gentle and humble in heart, and 'you will find rest for your souls." It is like the little boy trying to move a big rock and it won't budge. His father says, "Let's do this together son and together they push the rock and it moves. Faith enables the Father to lift your burdens.

Little did I realize over 60 years ago that something I memorized held the key to coming to God, knowing Him and becoming clean inside. When I was in the Air Force at age 18 I was on my way to Japan. Secretly I had decided to live a life to fulfill the lies I told my buddies that I was experiencing when in high school. We used to drink illegally, sit around and brag about what great lovers we were and tell each other lies about our female conquests.

On the ship going overseas I planned to live those lies with Japanese ladies when I got to Japan.. On the ship one day I happened upon a group of airmen gathered around a chaplain telling about a man named Jesus Christ. He asked if anyone wanted to receive Jesus Christ as Savior to raise their hand. I raised my hand but no one said any more to me. The crowd dispersed and I walked away.

But something happened inside me. In Japan I did live some of the lies I had told. i felt pleasure inside for a little while but after words I felt miserable. I found out that there is pleasure in sin for a little while but afterwards it makes a person miserable. I began to pray and asked God, "Move your hand and I will be clean inside." To the guys I was just one of the boys living it up off base like most of them were doing. But i didn't let on to them that doing sinful things made me feel miserable afterward.. Unknown to them, I came to God and prayed for Him to make me clean inside. I didn't seem to get an answer so after a while the thought occurred that maybe God would hear my prayer if I memorized the Bible. In those days everyone in the Air Force was given a New Testament so I started memorizing the first chapter in Matthew, " The book of the generation of Jesus Christ, the son of David, the son of Abraham..." I Didn't understand it so I quit. If only I had known what that the family tree of Jesus meant but I didn't then. About two years later I heard Jesus Christ preached in a church, I came forward and accepted Him as Savior. Over sixty years have gone by since Jesus Christ forgave me and made me clean inside.

I now finally realize clearly that the verse I memorized, if I had understood it, would have make me clean inside. Jesus name means "He will cleans his people from their sins." I admitted I was unclean because of my sin and His shed blood cleansed me from my sin. His name Christ meant He was promised to come into the world and save His people from their sin. The solving of my unclean sinfulness was solved by the first person mentioned in Matthew, Jesus Christ. He saved me and cleansed me and will do it for you if you come to Him.

"Pray with me now. Lord Jesus I right now come to you and bring you my need to be cleansed from all my sins, I receive you and accept your saving and cleansing power. In the name of Jesus Christ, my Savior. Amen!

There are over 2500 reasons why you should believe the Bible is true and Jesus is the only Savior who loves you and wants you to look to him and be forgiven and given eternal life.

The Bible has approximately 2500 prophecies of which 2000 have been fulfilled to the letter.

These prophecies were given through men of God who describe a coming event long before it happened. Four hundred of these prophecies point to Jesus Christ, his birth, life, death and resurrection. Jesus fulfilled every one of the prophecies proving he was and is the Messiah, God come in human flesh to save us from our sins.

A few fulfilled prophecies are that he would be born of a virgin in Bethlehem. He would be both the Son of God and the son of man. Some would receive him and some hate and try to kill him as a child. He would be called Immanuel(God With Us). He would be zealous for God. He would do many miracles including healing the sick, praying for his enemies, raising the dead, and forgiving sins. He prophesied his own death, burial and resurrection. He would be betrayed by a friend for 30 pieces of silver. He would be mocked, smitten and spit upon. His hands and feet would be pierced as he was crucified with thieves. He would be buried in a rich man's tomb and rise from the dead three days later. These are just a few of the Messianic prophecies of four hundred that were fulfilled literally exactly as foretold. If you want to know them all search in google under "Messianic Prophecies Fulfilled"

So you have four hundred miracle prophecies fulfilled by Christ, evidence beyond a shadow of a doubt that you should trust him as your Savior. But there is much more. The Bible has 1600 more prophecies made in the Bible about various events which have also been fulfilled. And there are 500 more prophecies which will yet come true. A few examples are the promised return of Christ, an explosion that will melt the heavens and earth, and the creation of a new heaven and earth.

Then there are over 500 more reasons why you should trust Him as your Savior. After he died and rose from the dead over 500 eyewitnesses saw him alive over a period of 40 days. Among those witnesses were those who saw him ascend into heaven after telling his disciples to go into all the world and preach the good news. Whoever believes the good news will be saved. Whoever doesn't believe it will be lost. Since then millions of people have been forgiven, saved and transformed by the Spirit of the risen Christ. These millions give good reasons to everyone to "Believe on the Lord Jesus Christ and you (too) shall be saved." The good news for you has been proven beyond a shadow of a doubt is that Jesus is alive and offers forgiveness to you if you will come to him. (Matt. 11:28) Then like Simeon of in the Bible you will be able to say, "Now I can depart this life in peace for my eyes have seen your salvation."

The fulfilled prophecies and eyewitness accounts of Jesus birth, life, death and resurrection prove the fact that Jesus is the way to God, the truth of God and the life of God. Trust him today. Only a fool would reject over 2500 proofs that Jesus is the only Savior, and Lord of creation, life and death. Don't put off believing in him. Receive him today as your Savior and Lord. No one who ever truly trusted Jesus Christ as Lord and Savior ever regretted it.

Further proof is that all things work together for good to those who know God's love and love him back. Nothing can separate them from his love. No one can condemn them. No one can successfully bring a charge against them. Why not? Because through his death and resurrection he forgave them of all their sins, and justifies them counting them perfect in his sight. That is the good news of God's word. Be wise and believe it. Then you will rejoice! The Bible says it clearly, "As many as received him he gave the right to become children of God, to those who believe in his name, who were born not of blood, nor of the will of the flesh, nor of the will of man, **but of God." John 1:12.** One last proof. I was born of God at age 20 and 58 years later i am still his and he is still mine. Join the wise of earth. Sing and believe this song and have eternal life.<http://www.youtube.com/watch?v=w2VrRk4pZHY>

Password to Peace, Purpose & Power, by a Learner Jesus Loves

We all know the significance of passwords. They allow us admittance to many spots on the internet and else where. The greatest password is one that enables a person to communicate effectively with God. Jesus Himself tells us what it is. It is His name, the Lord Jesus Christ. It is not a magic formula but a name, whose meaning when believed, allows us to pass into the presence and the blessings of God. He clearly tells us to ask in His name. What does that mean?

His name represents who He is. His name is the Lord Jesus Christ. That means we fully recognize that He is **Lord**, the most high God all powerful, all knowing, and open to respond to our access. **Jesus** means we acknowledge that He saves His people from their sin. **Christ** means we know and believe He is the Spirit anointed one sent by His Father to come to earth to totally reveal the true nature of God and to fulfill His promises and purposes.

So to know peace, power and purpose, believe in and call on the name of the Lord Jesus Christ to approach God. It is a name above every name. There is no other name given among men by which we must be saved.

God is open to anyone who believes in and appeals to Him in prayer in the name of His Son. The door of salvation then opens wide. His Spirit wirelessly enables us to know and experience His plans, love, forgiveness, justification, eternal life, Spirit, strength, answer to prayers, intercession, goodness, joy, peace, patience, gentleness, faith, humility, kindness, and self control.

What are you waiting for?(-:) Call upon Him now. "Whosoever shall call on the name of the Lord shall be saved." And that is just the beginning. The rest of your life you will be calling upon Him about all that pertains to this life and the next. You may frustratingly lose or forget your passwords on the internet; however, if you are wise enough to access and experience the peace, purpose and power of His name, you will never forget His password. It enables the fastest wireless communication possible. He is always on line by His Spirit to help us keep our steps in line with His will.

https://www.youtube.com/watch?v=R0S8Z-dMM40&spfreload=10>

Inspired by Gary Darnell's message at Valley Bible Church at the Crossing in Pleasanton, Ca. at 11:00 AM on May 24, 2015..

Patterns

"make it according to the **pattern**" Acts 7:44

I have watched my wife Gloria use a pattern to make a beautiful dress. I have read about God's pattern to make a beautiful life. Which can be more beautiful, a pattern or a completed dress or a pattern for an unfolding life being completed?

The first time we see the word pattern used in the Bible is is when God tells Moses to make a tabernacle, a dwelling place through which God will reveal Himself to His people. . He says in **Exodus 25:9** "According to all that I show you, *that is,* the **pattern** of the tabernacle and the **pattern** of all its furnishings, just so you shall make *it.*"

Moses did what God said. He made a tabernacle patterned after the dwelling of God exactly as he was told. Later Solomon made a more permanent but still temporary temple in Jerusalem patterned after God's dwelling place. Both the temporary tabernacle and more permanent temple are still only patterns of what is God's eternal dwelling place but they are adequate to give us a picture of what is to come. They are like shadows which direct us to the more glorious sunshine.

Both the tabernacle and temple had rules of conduct. Priests chosen by God carrie out the responsibilities of them both. They represented God and brought about the acceptance of the people by offering blood sacrifices from the animals brought to the priests. The blood sacrifices of animals never took away sin but represented the covering of sin until Jesus Christ's blood was shed and paid in full the debt of sin. By the one offering of Jesus shed blood He perfects forever those set apart to Himself.

So the temporary tabernacle, temple and Old Testament priesthood patterns were fulfilled in Christ. The temporary animal sacrifice pattern was forever replaced by the one time eternal sacrifice of the Lord Jesus Christ. The Old Testament priesthood was replaced by the priesthood of all believers, a royal kingdom of priests all enabled to go to God on behalf of others. 1Peter 2:5,9

The New Testament is called new because it fulfills the old and builds on it with wonderful new truth and some new patterns for a follower of Christ. The Apostle Paul indicates that his transformed life and the changed lives of New Testament followers of Christ are patterns for us to follow. Look at their lives and find out how the

Lord wants us to pattern our lives and Christ's life after them. Actually life itself is meant to be a pattern of what God wants our life to be. Enjoy the patterns but be sure to look beyond them to the finished products shown in the poem below, The Weaver.

The Weaver

"My life is but a weaving between my Lord and me,
I cannot choose the colors. He works steadily.
Ofttimes He weaves sorrow, and I in foolish pride
Forget He sees the upper and I, the underside.
Not till the loom in silent and the shuttles cease to fly
Shall God unroll the canvas And explain the reason why.
The dark threads are as needful In the Weaver's skillful hand
As the threads of gold and silver in the pattern He has planned."

Some pattern practices in the Old Testament replaced by the New Testament are sadly still wrongly taught by some. They are: 1.Blood sacrifices. 2. Priesthood of some but not priesthood of all believers in Christ. 3. Restrictions still on eating certain creatures forbidden in the O.T. but not the new. 4. Temporary coming of Spirit on people in O.T. instead of sealing with and indwelling of all true followers of Christ until the day of Christ. 5. Traditions not taught in N.T. like confessing sins to a priest hidden by a chamber when N.T. says we are to confess sins to God and can also confess to other followers of Christ. 6. Restricting giving out wine and bread at communion only to supposed ordained priests. 7. Teaching Jesus' mother Mary was sinless and didn't die but was caught up to heaven like Jesus. 8. Making a pope the head of the church when Christ is clearly the head of the church. 9. Making binding vows to refrain from marriage by both priests and nuns. 10. Teaching that works save instead of teaching that they follow in the life of a truly saved person. 11. Teaching the rule of one pastor over a church instead of a plurality of pastors with equal authority. 12. Teaching that tithing is a New Testament necessary requirement of all members of the church rather than each person "purposing in his or her heart about how much to give, not grudgingly or of necessity but with a cheerful heart."

Perfected Forever?

There have been from the beginning of time those who have offered to God good works, gifts of money, prayers, incense, and personal sacrifice with the belief that such acts and words will make them acceptable to God. But such offerings apart from God's one great offering are worthless to bring about forgiveness of sin or make them right with God. The Bible tells us clearly that "By one single offering Christ has perfected forever those who are set apart as Holy." Heb. 1014

This one offering for sin to perfect us forever is wonderfully good news to all who will cease from their own self efforts to be acceptable to God and instead accept His effort through Christ to make them acceptable and count them perfect. Have you accepted God's way of salvation and rejected any of your own self effort to bring about your salvation?

From the time of Abel until now the world has been divided between those who believe God's way of salvation and those who do not. The first example is seen in Adam and Eve's two sons. One, Cain thought he could offer God his works produced through farming to be accepted by God. He was rejected. The other, Abel offered God a lamb as a blood sacrifice pointing forward to Christ who would be the final and only acceptable means of acceptance with God. Abel's offering cost him his life. His brother killed him because Abel was accepted and Cain was not. God offered Cain another chance. He refused that second chance and was rejected.

All though the Old Testament under God's direction millions of innocent animals were offered which could never take away sin. The New Testament sums it up beautifully, "And every priest stands ministering daily and offering repeatedly the same sacrifices, which can never take away sins. **But this Man(Jesus Christ), after He had offered one sacrifice for sins forever,** sat down at the right hand of God," Heb. 10:12

What then were the reason for the Old Testament animal sacrifices? They were a shadow or symbol of Christ's final sacrifice for sin which makes all who believe both perfected forever and Holy. So no longer must we live in the shadows or symbols of the Old Testament. **Now we may experience the sunshine of complete acceptance, forgiveness, perfection and endless love.**

So God calls us all to come out of the shadows. Come out from religious self effort and offerings offensive to him. He has made the one and only offering through his Son to gain you perfection and count you Holy forever! So listen to his voice, "Today, if you will hear His voice, Do not harden your hearts." Today cease from your self efforts and enter into the rest of receiving God's gift of eternal life.

If you will believe God and receive his son, today will be the day of salvation for you. God will count you perfected forever when you receive the free gift of his salvation. Once you receive his gift then your good works and offerings will be accepted because they will be brought about by his cleansing blood, inspiration and power.

Song: Now is the Day of Salvation. https://www.youtube.com/watch?v=aDiul4lojS0>

A Personal Guard of Peace For You Every Day
Independence Day from Anxieties

I was inspired last Sunday by Jason Moog, one of our young leaders at the church my wife and I attend. He spoke on Phil. 4:4-7 which relates to reconciliation with others through nearness to the Lord, joy in Him and showing gentle reasonableness to everyone. The passage also shows us how to deal with all kinds of anxiety by taking it to the Lord in prayer and believing with gratitude that He takes it for us on Himself. The result is that we have a supernatural guard over our hearts and minds called the peace of God. As long as we do what these verses say we will have our hearts guarded by peace that goes beyond our understanding. Most important in Philippians 4 context we will successfully deal with anxiety sometimes caused by our relationships with others.

As we practice what we are taught in these verses we will learn how to refrain from adding the sin of worry and anxiety to the many troubles of each day and help heal any troubled relationships. Every day can truly be an Independence Day from Anxieties if we practice these verses Jason spoke about:

Rejoice in the Lord always; again I will say, Rejoice. 5 Let your gentle reasonableness be known to everyone. The Lord is near; 6 do not be anxious about anything, but in everything by prayer and supplication with thanksgiving let your requests be made known to God. 7 And the peace of God, which surpasses all understanding, will guard your hearts and your minds in Christ Jesus.

Think about it. Those of us who trust Jesus Christ as Savior can know the joy of having our own personal guard at the door of our hearts and minds. Human guards may fail us but our Divine Savior will never fail us. Every hour as long as we take our anxieties and worries to Him He relieves us of their hurt. Thank you Lord and thank you Jason for reminding us of our Guard of Peace who enables us to banish anxiety from our lives.

I was especially blessed by Jason's message because I once had him in second and third grade many years ago. I taught him and prayed for him. I wrote him after hearing his message and thanked him for his teaching and asked him to pray for my grandson and me. So things have come full circle. I once taught and prayed for him and now to my joy he is teaching and praying for me. As my mother in law Frances Kent said often, "What goes around comes around." May it come around to you today and bless you.

Sing about it here: <http://www.youtube.com/watch?v=_WSAZRggozs>

Physical & Spiritual DNA- His Crime Found Him Out After 30 Years!

I just read about about a cold case murder that was solved after 30 years. DNA tests proved that Kenneth Lee Hicks 49, of St. Helens raped and murdered Lori Billingsly on Oct. 10, 1982. His crime found him out because of modern day technology.

DNA has been in every person since man was created. We all are unique and distinctly marked with deoxyribonucleic acid which sets us apart from every other person under the sun.

As I thought about this into my mind popped an Old Testament verse which says "Be sure your sins will find you out." Numbers 32:23

Billy Graham tells of a time when he was young and experienced the reality of Numbers 32:23. He was told not to pick any of the watermelons growing in the field planted by his father. Billy picked a ripe one, went under a bridge, ate it and then buried the seeds and remains in the dirt. The next season watermelon grew under the bridge. His sin was found out and his dad punished him.

Wrong and right are another kind of DNA, spiritual DNA, which I label Divinely Nominative Attestation. In other words God has a spiritual reality built into our lives. It is that He Divinely Names all we do which Attests as evidence to all our behavior. He sees all we do and knows all we say. Nothing escapes his knowledge either bad or good. We are told by God in scripture that "Every word spoken in secret shall be shouted from the housetops." We will be held accountable for every thought, ever word, ever deed. All things are open before Him to whom we are responsible. All the hairs on our head and all the days of our life are numbered. DNA is based upon numbers, a double helix of acidic elements. Life is truly analyzed by the numbers.

Hicks could have possible covered his DNA tracks had he known how to do it in 1982 but he didn't. Spiritually we can't cover or hide anything we do that is wrong. But there is good news. While we cannot do away with spiritual DNA which reveals the bad we do and say, we can have it removed. How?

Christ who was free from any sin became sin for us taking away the penalty for our sins. He died to remove ALL our guilt and sins. He, the only just man who ever lived, died for all of us unjust folks. Why did He do it? Because He loved us and wants to free us from spiritually immoral DNA. He takes away our sin and give us the gift of His righteousness in exchange. He gives us beauty for our ashes, the oil of joy for our mourning. He is the Lamb of God that takes away the sin of the world. He who created DNA died for all of us who have sinned and come short of what God desires. Our sin caused Jesus death. We are all guilty And Christ says, "Father forgive them for they know not what they do."

So your bad spiritual DNA can be removed by confessing with your mouth Jesus as Lord and believing in your heart that he died for your sins, was buried and rose again. That is the gospel, the best good news ever proclaimed on planet earth; the guilty pardoned, the sinner forgiven and counted perfect before God. "God has perfected forever those set apart to Himself by the one offering of His Son."

It is okay to have your spiritual-DNA-sins found out if they are forgiven and forgotten forever. Have you had that happen to you? These singers have.

<http://www.youtube.com/watch?v=vEckaBT1x6Q>
<http://www.youtube.com/watch?v=UqHixv5zuJs>

Physical & Spiritual Warfare

In 2 Samuel 11:1 we are told that David, King of Israel, after many great successes in warfare, failed to go to war "in the spring of the year when kings go out to battle.." Instead David sent his army to war with the Ammonites. He remained in Jerusalem. Staying behind was a devastating decision for David. It led to an adulterous affair with a beautiful woman named Bathsheba. It also led to David's hypocrisy with Uriah, her husband, and to David's evil plan that led to Uriah's death. Thanks to a tactful rebuke about a year later, by Nathan, a true prophet of God, David repented. He was forgiven but his sin led to to the death of his child and the rebellion of some of his own sons and others who sought to rip the kingdom from his hands.

In the Old Testament there was literal physical warfare between the people of God and idolatry laden enemies. In the New Testament followers of Christ fight a different kind of battle. It is not against flesh and blood but against spiritual wickedness in high places. As followers of Christ we are told to pray for our enemies, even told to lay down our lives for them just like Christ did. To die for Christ, not to kill for Him, is a high honor for true Christians.

New Testament followers of Christ are in a battle but it is a spiritual one. As David failed to go to battle against flesh and blood in his day ending in sin and failure, so also believers in Christ should never fail to fight the good fight against spiritual wickedness. Failure to go forth to spiritual battle can lead to all kinds of sin including adultery, lying, coveting, greed, spiritual defeat of all kinds. True followers of Christ are to never refrain from the spiritual battle in which we are to fight the good fight of faith.

Eph. 6:10-20 tells us how to win our spiritual battles, "10 Finally, my brethren, be strong in the Lord and in the power of His might. 11 Put on the whole armor of God, that you may be able to stand against the wiles of the devil. 12 For we do not wrestle against flesh and blood, but against principalities, against powers, against the rulers of the darkness of this age, against spiritual *hosts* of wickedness in the heavenly *places.* 13 Therefore take up the whole armor of God, that you may be able to withstand in the evil day, and having done all, to stand. 14 Stand therefore, having girded your waist with truth, having put on the breastplate of righteousness, 15 and having shod your feet with the preparation of the gospel of peace; 16 above all, taking the shield of faith with which you will be able to quench all the fiery darts of the wicked one. 17 And take the helmet of salvation, and the sword of the Spirit, which is the word of God; 18 praying always with all prayer and supplication in the Spirit, being watchful to this end with all perseverance and supplication for all the saints—"

David failed because he avoided battle as a King. As believers we are all called kings, priests and saints. We fail as kings when we neglect our battle as spiritual warriors against evil. In my life I have failed when I didn't ask myself, "Is what I am going to do right and based on God's truth? Have I prayed about it?" Had I asked those questions I wouldn't have failed. We must put on the whole armor of God every day and never take it off as we fight the good fight of faith.

This rendition of Onward Christian Soldiers is a Priceless motivator! <https://www.youtube.com/watch?v=YJgt2ktRJME>

Pleasures Forevermore

In life, as we know it now, we find pleasures in the presence of spouses, family, and friends. Some give us pleasure more than others. Sadly we must part from them in this life.

But there is something much more wonderful to come for all who are part of Jesus Christ's forever family. Psalm 16:11 tells us about it, "...in Your presence is fulness of joy; At Your right hand are pleasures forevermore." Imagine that! Many of those we have enjoyed and loved long ago will be there at His right hand. We will see Him as He is and be like Him in character and love forever. We will be with those others who know and love Him and enjoy their presence too.

There will be no jealousy, lust or sin of any kind but only what is right. Old age, wrong and death in life now rob us of our pleasures. But then we will never grow old but enjoy eternal youth and perfect love in His presence forever. Now that I am 82 I know my days are shortened. Now is my final salvation nearer than when I first believed 62 years ago. I look forward more and more to the time when fulness of joy will be mine, not temporarily, but forevermore! How about you? Sing about it here:

<https://video.search.yahoo.com/yhs/search?hsimp=yhs-att_001&hspart=att&p=land+where+we+enver+grow+old+song#id=4&vid=9d186131b1bc86c1b23f0b8bf2176a4a&action=click>

The Pope, Kids & Marriage & What the Bible Really Says

The Pope says folks ought to have kids instead of just pets. How does he apply that to himself and the priests who never marry? Does he take into account that the scriptures encourage marriage and having children and the fact that while a few leaders in scripture did not marry, they were never required to make a vow of celibacy.

That man-made celibacy rule has led to many cases of sexual immorality. Paul said he "had the right like Peter and some other apostles to carry about a wife." Peter(the supposed first Pope) WAS married. Why shouldn't the Popes and priests have that right since "marriage is honorable in all" and it can keep many from immoral sexual behavior outside marriage. " In 1 Timothy 3:1-13 and Titus 1:6-9, the Apostle Paul seems to assume that elders, bishops, overseers, and deacons will be married;

notice the phrase "the husband of one wife" (1 Timothy 3:2,12; Titus 1:6)"

All Christian's are priests and saints. Leaders were called apostles, elders, sheperds, overseers and deacons, not priests. Let's stick to the Bible!
Read more: http://www.gotquestions.org/celibacy-priests.html#ixzz3Nbt8as7l

Praising God
Dec. 1, 2013

I will praise God when I'm up.
I will praise him when I'm down.

I'll praise him on the mountain top.
And I'll praise him in the town.

I'll praise him when I"m sick
And praise him when I'm well.

I'll praise him till
He rips out the gates of hell.

I'll praise Him when he binds up the devil.
I'll praise him till crooked is made level.

I'll praise him while I'm living
I'll praise when I'm dying

I'll praise him when I'm happy
And praise Him when I'm crying.

I'll praise him when I'm sighing
And praise him when I'm flying.

No matter the lot in life I'm given
I'll praise him when I fly away to heaven

I'll praise him on his throne
I'll praise him in my final home.

I'll praise him when life on earth is gone
I'll praise him with an endless song

My praise will go on and on and on
In tune with heaven's eternal throng!

"Praise Him. Praise Him Jesus my blessed redeemer.
Praise Him. Praise Him Ever in Joyful song."

Open Thir Eyes
Feb 24, 2010
Father through the truth Open Ken,Tyler & Jacs eyes.
Deliver them from the father of lies!
Turn them from darkness to light,
From guilt to forgiveness and right!
Tie up the strong man-spoil his goods and glee,
Break his prison chains and set them free!
Tear off the veil that blinds their mind.
Let them see the glory of Christ Divine!
Loose them from seeing the truth of the Spirit as idiocracy.
Help them discern spiritual things as God's truth in symphony!
As God the Father, the Son and I pray for each one,
Save them completely as they come to God through Your risen Son!
And I'll say "Praise you God for what you have done!

Prayer in the Night for Light Answered
Jan 29, 2014

Come Read my prayer though short on style
Still It will engage your heart and faith for a little while!

Tonight, at 3 AM as I lay upon my bed
This is what my longing heart said:

Lord Jesus, I look up to you upon Your Throne
My heart is reaching out and seeking You alone!

Hear my requests which are more than a few
Grant me faith to seek and find You too!

Be not far from my voice and my cry
Fill me with your Spirit or I'll die!

I want to be pure in heart so I can see your face
So I can keep in step with your Spirit"s pace!

Show me tonight your splendid glory
That I might proclaim love's greatest story!

Lead me to the Rock that is higher than I
To see you God now, not just bye and bye!

And what do I see as I look upon your forms?
I see a Father with outstretched arms
I see a Son with heaven's charms.
I see your Spirit strip me of all that harms!

I see love like a giant river of peace
Wash away my sins and cause them to cease!

I hear the voice of God in answer to prayer
"Fear not, I'll give you more than you ask or dare!"

So here now are my I requests-
They will be mine with your bequests!

Release dear Anne from torment in her mind
Help her son find salvation and peace divine!

Grant John and Marsha your first love
That they might know the joy of heaven's Dove!!

Please Join in This Prayer for Yourself & Our Nation

Spirit of the living God fall afresh on me. Spirit of the Living God fall afresh on our nation. As you saved the whole city of Nineveh through the preaching of Jonah, raise up leaders who will not run away from You but run to You. Through Godly people restore us to morality and right in your eyes. Help us overcome hate with love. Mold us. Use us. Revive us. Hear us. Forgive us.. Save us. Create new hearts within us. Uphold us. Free us. Spirit of the Living God as we humble ourselves before You, as we turn from our wicked ways, forgive our sins and heal our land. Banish division. Unite us. Fall afresh on anyone who reads this and calls upon You. In Jesus name let it be for Your glory and for the good of the whole world.
Sing it...
<https://www.youtube.com/watch?v=lhhQACwrEFM>

Prophecy Yet to Be Fulfilled
Jeremiah 23:5-6(NKJV)
5
"Behold, *the* days are coming," says the Lord,
"That I will raise to David a Branch of righteousness;
A King shall reign and prosper,
And execute judgment and righteousness in the earth.
6
In His days Judah will be saved,
And Israel will dwell safely;
Now this *is* His name by which He will be called:THE LORD OUR RIGHTEOUSNESS.
7 "Therefore, behold, *the* days are coming," says the Lord, "that they shall no longer say,
'As the Lord lives who brought up the children of Israel from the land of Egypt,'
8 but, 'As the Lord lives who brought up and led the descendants of the house of Israel from the north country and from all the countries where I had driven them.' And they shall dwell in their own land."

Isaiah 22:22 (NKJV)
22 The key of the house of David
I will lay on his shoulder;
So he shall open, and no one shall shut;
And he shall shut, and no one shall open.

Psalm 2:6 (NKJV)
6 "Yet I have set My King
On My holy hill of Zion."
Ezekiel 37:24-28New King James Version (NKJV)
24 "David My servant *shall be* king over them, and they shall all have one shepherd; they shall also walk in My judgments and observe My statutes, and do them. **25** Then they shall dwell in the land that I have given

to Jacob My servant, where your fathers dwelt; and they shall dwell there, they, their children, and their children's children, forever; and My servant David *shall be* their prince forever. **26** Moreover I will make a covenant of peace with them, and it shall be an everlasting covenant with them; I will establish them and multiply them, and I will set My sanctuary in their midst forevermore. **27** My tabernacle also shall be with them; indeed I will be their God, and they shall be My people. **28** The nations also will know that I, the Lord, sanctify Israel, when My sanctuary is in their midst forevermore."'"

Daniel 7:14 New King James Version (NKJV)
14
Then to Him was given dominion and glory and a kingdom,
That all peoples, nations, and languages should serve Him.
His dominion *is* an everlasting dominion,
Which shall not pass away,
And His kingdom *the one*
Which shall not be destroyed.

Aug. 6, 2010
Psalm 23
The Lord is my Shepherd = That's Relationship!
I shall not want = That's Supply!
He maketh me to lie down in green pastures = That's Rest!
He leadeth me beside the still waters = That's Refreshment!
He restoreth my soul = That's Forgiveness!
He leadeth me in the paths of righteousness = That's Guidance!
For His name sake = That's Purpose!
Yea, though I walk through the valley of the shadow of death= That's Testing!
I will fear no evil = That's Protection!
For Thou art with me = That's Faithfulness!
Thy rod and Thy staff they comfort me = That's Discipline!
Thou preparest a table before me in the presence of mine enemies = That's Hope!
Thou annointest my head with oil = That's Consecration!
My cup runneth over = That's Abundance!
Surely goodness and mercy shall follow me all the days of my life =That's Blessing !

And I will dwell in the house of the Lord = That's Security!
Forever = That's Eternity! Face it, the Lord LOVES US: That's Joy!

Psalm 151?
Why We Exist
By DLG
Hear my cry, O Lord. Show me why I exist.
With all my heart I insist. Answer me out of the midst.
On my bed in the darkest night
I seek You God. I seek your Light.
Grant me the essence to see life's gist.
Show me fully why I exist.

Out of the whirl wind of life
The answer came loud and clear:
"You exist to seek Me(God) and find me.
I'm not far away. So then draw near.
I made you that of your own free will you
Might seek Me and find Me and be set free.
I determined when you would live and where you'll be.
I knew your end from the beginning, that you should know Me.
I know each day that you'll live and how you'll fare.
So , reach out to Me and find me anywhere.
Listen to my words that show that I truly care,
I'm not far away. Reach out to me in prayer.
Seek me with all your heart.
You will find Me, for I'm not hiding in the dark.
In me you live and move and have your being.
Ask, seek and you'll start seeing,
Seeing who I am and who you are. Get to know Me, I'm not far."

I heard Him speak with listening ear
Gone, gone were my doubts and fear.
"I came to earth" said He, "that you might see and be free!
I sent my Son to live and die and live again in thee.
Look on Him lifted up to die upon that cross of wood,
That you might know Me as you should."

Yes, Lord, I look! I come!! I see!!!
Your death and risen life justify me.
In gratitude I shout with joy. At last I'm free!
I exist to know you. That is true! and now I do!!
But you are so vast! So huge! One look is enough
to save.
Sufficient to lift me from my grave,
But I need to know You more, to know You to your
core.

Then I heard Him say, "That's what's In store for
you, to know Me more.
You know me dimly now, but soon you'll see Me
face to face.
Then you'll Know fully My heart and limitless
grace.
You'll know as you are known,
On that day I lift you to My throne!"
**<http://www.youtube.com/watch?
v=XbhplrinxPU>**

Prevailing With Puppies

In the Bible wild dogs are seen as often
negative but there is one tender story of the
beautiful humility and the faithful dependence
of puppy dogs.

It happened when a Canaanite woman
came to Jesus to ask Him to heal her
daughter who was miserably controlled by
demonic behavior. Jesus went out of HIs way
to go to the area where she lived. Canaanites
were despised by many in Israel. Some of
them in derision called them gentile dogs. We
will see from this story how Jesus turned that
saying around for a special blessing for the
Canaanite woman who cried out to Jesus,
"Lord, Son of David, have mercy on me! My
daughter is cruelly afflicted by an evil spirit."

At first Jesus didn't respond to her plea and
his disciples wanted Him to send her away.
Jesus then spoke of His first mission to save
lost Israelites. " I'm busy first dealing with the
lost sheep of Israel."

Then the woman came back to Jesus, went
to her knees, and begged. "Master, help me."

Had Jesus and his disciples been some of
Satan's wild dog, prejudiced, religious haters
their response would have been, "Cut off her

head. She is an infidel." Well, Jesus <u>was not</u>
one of those!

He didn't send her away but stirred her to
faith. He said, "It's not right to take bread
out of children's mouths and throw it to
dogs." She was quick: "You're right, Master,
but puppy dogs do get crumbs from the
master's table." She took a puppy's place in
humility and faith and prevailed as she heard
Jesus say, ""Woman, you have great faith! Your
request is granted." And her daughter was healed
from that very hour."

My granddaughter, made a similar prayer to
God who delivered her from addiction and evil
behavior. Her mother and many of us prayed for
God to have mercy on her and deliver her. He
heard and receiving Jesus as Savior she has been
set free for over four years now. Her new life is
filled with care for both up and outers and down
and outers.

She and her husband recently Got a little puppy
called Nahla. She visits our house some times and
goes throughout the house with her nose down
sniffing for any left behind crumbs. She is a joy
and totally dependent upon her "masters" to take
care of her and feed her. She is full of puppy love
for everyone. That is what Jesus is looking for,
humility and trust. Puppy Faith Prevails with
Jesus and creates returned love because of His
gracious provision of mercy.

Listen to this fun song about a doggy in the
window: https://www.youtube.com/watch?
v=fC5Yf9rmKto>

Reasons for Where You Live, How
Long You Live and Why You Are Alive

Why do you live where you do at this
time? Who determines your life span?
What is the reason for your existence?
The answers are in the Bible. In a New
Testament book called Acts we are told
the answers to all these questions about
your life.

"From one man he made every nation
of men, that they should inhabit the whole
earth; and he determined the times set
for them and the exact places where they

should live. God did this so that men would seek him and perhaps reach out for him and find him, though he is not far from each one of us (Acts !7:26,27).

So we live where we live because God determined it. We die when we do because God knows the number of our days before there is one of them. We are here on planet earth to seek and reach out for Him and find Him. It is not complicated for He is not far from us and He tells us how to find Him in many places in the Bible. If you seek Him with all your heart you will find Him. I found him 57 years ago and He changed my life forever filling me with forgiveness, loving me, answering my prayers, helping me grow through failure and success, enabling me to care about others, lifting me up when I fall down spiritually, assuring me that He will never leave me or forsake me, guaranteeing a meaningful life now and assuring me of eternal life to come with Him forever. The good news of the Bible is that you can know God now through His Son Jesus Christ. It is not getting religions or following a set of rules and rituals made up by men, but it is being regenerated to become His child and walk with Him through life and someday take a small step off of earth and land in God's heavenly city. It is a small step of faith that leads to a giant step of certainty about why you are here and where you are going.

If you desire to seek Him, there are passages in the Bible that tell you how to find Him. Why not begin seeking Him today? How? Get a Bible. Pray to know Him. Then read and ponder these verses. Take hope also in the fact that God is seeking you while you seek Him.

Romans 3:23, 6:23, 5:8 and 10:9,10; Ephesians 2:8,9. Respond to Christ's invitation to believe and receive Him:

Matthew 11:28-30; Revelation 3:20; John 1:12,13; 3:16..

When you find Him, share it with me or someone else. Romans 10:9,10. Matthew 10:32,33. To share it with me call 925 828 1623 or email me at deanlgoss@att.net. I will rejoice with you. God bless you. Dean

Reassurance That God Forgives

I was once told by a fellow Christian that I asked forgiveness of them too many times. The reason was that up to that point that person never ever told me, "I forgive you."

How wonderful is God's reassurance! How many times does He say he forgives us in the Bible? To forgive is mentioned 147 times in the Bible, 77 times in the Old Testament and 59 times in the new. Sometimes the verses tell us of God's forgiveness. Other times they tell of a person forgiving another person. Peter asked,"How many times should I forgive someone, seven times." Jesus said, "Seventy times seven. If someone sins against us and repents asking forgiveness we are to tell them we forgive them 70 times 70 which is 490 times. Matt. 18:22 And we are to forgive them from the heart. If God expects that kind of forgiveness from us, how much more can we depend upon His forgiveness?

God says of those of us who have accepted His Son as Savior. "Their sins and iniquities I will remember no more forever." "As far as the East is from the West so far has he removed our transgressions." If we confess our sins, He is faithful and just to forgive us our sins and cleanse us from all unrighteousness." 1John 1:9

Why does God repeat His forgiveness of our sins so often? Is it because we need reassurance. Do you need reassurance?

In the Old Testament Joseph's brothers treated him horribly, first putting him in a pit, then selling him as a slave. They told their father he was dead, a lie. Actually, Joseph was taken to Egypt, a ten day trip away from where his family lived. Joseph after more undeserved trials was exalted to be head of all the land of Egypt under Pharaoh. After a little over 20 years Joseph's brothers and family came to Egypt for food and he forgave his brothers and was reunited with his father.

Then after 17 years of being forgiven and cared for by Joseph in Egypt, their father Jacob died. They feared Joseph might seek revenge after their father died so they went to him and told Joseph that their father said this, 'This is what you should say to Joseph. "Please, forgive your brothers' sins and misdeeds, for they did terrible things to you. Now, please forgive the sins of the servants of your father's God."'"

Joseph wept when they spoke to him. He had shown them forgiveness for 17 years, cared for and loved them all that time, and now they doubted his love and forgiveness. That is why he wept. He reassured them of his forgiveness saying, "But as for you, you meant evil against me; *but* God meant it for good, in order to bring it about as *it is* this day, to save many people alive. Do not be afraid, for *am* I in the place of God? Now therefore, do not be afraid; I will provide for you and your little ones." And he comforted them and spoke kindly to them." Gen. 50:19-21

Do you ever doubt God's forgiveness and love for you? If you believe God, trust that you ARE forgiven.Your sins were paid for by His Son. Be reassured in the wonderful, matchless, love and forgiveness of God. Also, don't find fault with someone who asks for your forgiveness. Don't rub it in. Instead reassure them, comfort them, and speak kindly to them.

Click here to inspire forgiveness: https://www.youtube.com/watch?v=olbCpy0CQEo>

Reliable Proofs of Jesus Resurrection from the Dead

There are many reliable proofs of the fact that Jesus defeated death and rose from the dead. After he died and arose alive he appeared to many people over a 40 day period many times proving that death did not keep him in a tomb. He arose from the dead as he promised before he died saying in Luke 24:7, "'The Son of Man must be delivered into the hands of sinful men, and be **crucified**, and the third day rise again.'"

Hebrews 12:2 tells us that we should continue "looking unto Jesus, the author and finisher of *our* faith, who for the **joy** that was **set before Him** endured the cross, despising the shame, and has sat down at the right hand of the throne of God." Jesus is the only man in the history of the world whose death and resurrection was foretold in the O.T. and by Jesus himself and **it happened!**

On the internet a Timeline records all his appearances occurring for 40 days after his death and resurrection. They give us many proofs of why we should believe the Bible and put our faith in the risen Son of God. Absolute final proof that he is alive will come when he keeps his promise to all who trust him, **John 14:1-3 (NKJV)** "Let not your heart be troubled; you believe in God, believe also in Me. **2** In My Father's house are many mansions;[a] if *it were* not *so,* I would have told you. I go to prepare a place for you.[b] **3** And if I go and prepare a place for you, I will come again and receive you to Myself; that where I am, *there* you may be also."

Since all scripture is given by the inspiration of God you can count on his appearances over forty days and for his certain, for sure appearance when he returns to take all who trust him to be with him in his Father's house. Will you be one of his own to dwell with him forever in his many mansions of glory? Romans 10:9,10 tells how you can be sure.

Right Focus

When I was in my twenties I once hitchhiked to Maryland to buy a car. A man picked me up and said to me, "You know what the most beautiful sight in the world is?"

"What is it.? I asked?"

"Texas in a rear view mirror," he said. I laughed.

Today I heard someone talking about how a rear view mirror is small and a front view windshield is big and wide. When we drive we look back in the rear view mirror for just a second and then look forward focusing more on what is ahead than what is behind.

Jesus tells us we are not fit for the kingdom of God if we put our hand to the plow and look back. That means we are fit for the kingdom of God if we don't look back.

God values us so much that He wants us to focus on the future and only look back for a moment to learn from the past, then work on forgetting it. Looking back can be devastating as we learn from Lot's wife. Not that we should never look to the past but that we should learn from it then focus on the future.

Where I've been is important but where I'm going is more important. God tells us to look to the rock from which we are hewn & the pit from which we are dug (Isa. 51:1) which keeps us humble. Then we should join the Apostle Paul who tells us to forget the things that are past and reach forth to those thing before us, to press toward the mark of the high calling of God in Christ Jesus. That should be our constant attitude toward life. (Philippians 3:13-16)

Finally, we are told to Look to Jesus who focused on the joy set before Him which enabled Him to endure the cross. Looking to Jesus will enable us to endure all our trials and suffering.

When Peter focused on Jesus he walked on water. When his focus shifted from Jesus to the storm, the winds & the waves, he began to sink; however, Jesus lifted Him up & they both walked on water back to the boat.

Stepping forward by faith focusing on Jesus is worth the risk & the joy of His presence even if we start to sink because He will rescue us! Right focus is the secret of success no matter what happens.

God help you and me to continually look to Jesus who then keeps our minds in perfect peace and enables success even when we may partly fail.

Sing about it with Alan Jackson: <http://www.youtube.com/watch?v=nO4ulyz_d90>

Ezekiel's Temple Real?

Proof that Rob Dalrymple's teaching is incorrect that Jesus is Ezekiel's temple and not a building.

Ezekiel outlines a temple and its environs as well as what is going on there. Rob says we should check with what prophecies meant when first uttered. Well. when first uttered it meant a real temple. People die during the time of the temple. People are married during its time. Israel is restored during its time.

The temple mentioned in Ezekiel 40-47 has never existed yet on earth. The only thing that makes sense is that this is the millennial temple built when Christ restores Israel's remnant, rescuing them from their enemies and setting up his 1000 year reign on the earth. Contrary to his assumption that Ezekiel's temple is the final temple, it is a real temple built after Israel as a remnant nation realizes Jesus truly is their savior and they will weep for what they did to him. He then will restore Israel and rule with his redeemed church and Israel over the earth from an earthly Jerusalem for 1000 years.

As in the days of Adam and Eve who fellowshipped with God before the fall, the inhabitants of earth will have their eyes opened to the spiritual world. That the temple of Ezekiel is not Jesus in the eternal state is seen in that during this time when the glory of God fills the temple there is still death on earth, marriage and some suffering. It can't be the eternal state with a new heaven and earth when Jesus and the people of God are indeed the temple. Why not? Because when there is a new heaven and earth people don't die nor are men and women united in marriage.

So Rob's interpretation of what he calls apocalyptic language while meaning well is definitely wrong when we compare scripture with scripture, when we see the Prophet Ezekiel's original intent to show Israel someday restored and their 1000 years of peace on earth only disrupted at the end by Satan' being loosed for a while to attack the people of God. He is defeated, cast into the lake of fire and Jesus people then live with his presence forever with Jesus as the temple and his people as the temple living in many mansions in the New Jerusalem and on the new earth.

Rob's Putting Jesus at the center of everything is right only he forgets about Israel's restoration, the 1000 years of peace the Ezekiel temple illustrating the work of Christ but the final everlasting temple to happen only after the destruction of the old earth and heavens followed by Jesus being the temple as well as the people of God being the temple. This does not restrict their joy to one place but allows them joy and peace forever with Christ being present everywhere throughout a literal new heaven and earth with the joys of Eden and the fellowship of the saints forever!

Is Romans The Best Book in the Bible to Study?

Cody,

I think this might be helpful to you. When I came to Christ to accept him in church as Savior at age 20, one of the first things I thought was, "How am I going to live this new life?"

A man came up to me and answered my question which I was thinking but didn't ask out loud. He held up a Bible and said, "If you want to have faith to live a right life you need to study this book." He then said, "A good book to start with is the Bible book of Romans. It says that faith comes by hearing and hearing by listening to and learning the word of God. Romans 10:17

I took his advice and began to read Romans over and over. I think it probably is one of the best Bible books to read. Why? Because it explains clearly what the gospel of God is. Gospel means good news. Romans tells what the good news of God is all about. It explains the reason why we need the good news and what the good news clearly is. Unfortunately many people think the Bible is bad news. Is it bad news to save a drowning man? Is it bad news to rescue someone you love? Is it bad news to be forgiven and know you have eternal life? No! No! No!

The book of Romans starts by saying, "Paul, a bondservant of Jesus Christ, called *to be* an apostle, separated to the gospel of God **2** which He promised before through His prophets in the Holy Scriptures, **3** concerning His Son Jesus Christ our Lord, who was born of the seed of David according to the flesh, **4** *and* declared *to be* the Son of God with power according to the Spirit of holiness, by the resurrection from the dead." Romans 1:1-4

Paul calls himself a bondservant of Jesus Christ. Why? Because he came to know and believe that Jesus Christ bought him by dying for him. He had been a slave to sin and when he by faith met and believed in Jesus Christ he gladly gave up his slavery to sin exchanging it for slavery to the only Perfect Master. He realized that Christ died for him and rose again from the dead to give him forgiveness, love, eternal life and his reason for existing. That is not only good news, it is great news.

Everyone is a slave to someone or something. If you call all the shots in your life and leave God out then you are a slave to yourself. If you live for sinful pleasure then you are a slave to sin. If someone bought you as a slave like happened to some in ancient Rome, then you became a slave to an entirely human master. That isn't good either. Paul exchanged his slavery to self, and to sinful pride, to accept the good news that Jesus Christ bought him not with money but with his blood. Greater love has no man than this that he lay down his life for someone. That is what Jesus did for Paul and you and me. Paul believed it and he spent the rest of his life living for him and making him known. That is what the book of Romans is all about, knowing and being right with the true God and sharing the good news with others. That is our main purpose for existing, to seek God and find him, which is the good news of Romans.

Paul clearly tells us that the gospel of God, the good news of God was promised before through the Old Testament prophets. Hundreds of times in the Bible God speaks through prophets who foretell his miracle birth, life, teaching, death and resurrection. Gen. 3:15 is the first verse to promise his coming to defeat Satan through death destroying him through deception brought sin into the world. Isaiah 53 tells about him hundreds of years before he was born, how he would suffer and die to bear our sins and put them away forever. That's good news, the gospel of God. The Old Testament also told that he would be a descendent of David who was a king over Israel. As David was a man after God's own heart so also was Jesus, except David failed and Christ Jesus, the greater David, did not fail in any way. The prophets tell us that someday that Christ, the greater David, would rule and reign over a new people who would hear the good news, realize their need of Him and come to him. For that reason Paul also calls the good news, the gospel of Christ. It is the good news of God. It is equally the good news of Christ. The good news is that Christ is God's Son and that he died for Paul and for you and for me. Once Paul believed the good news, he calls it "my gospel," my good news. So in the first chapter of Romans we have the reason for Paul's writing it. The good news was for all that were in Rome, for Paul and for all who will come to Jesus. it is my gospel, too. I have believe it! How about you?

I suggest you read and absorb the magnificent book of Romans. Roam through it. Take your time. Ponder it. Pray about it. Believe it. Digest it and you will come to know the joy of being a servant and child of the true God. You will like Paul spend the rest of your life sharing the good news with others and rejoicing in its simple but deep meaning.

Love in Christ,
Dean

Invited to a Royal Wedding

Were you invited to the Royal Wedding in England? I suppose like my wife and I, you were not. However, we are looking forward to a much greater Royal Wedding. It is called the Marriage of the Lamb. It will be a wedding unsurpassed in royal glory and grandeur. How Blessed are they who are invited to that marriage followed by the Marriage Supper of the Lamb. It is called the Marriage Super of the Lamb because the Bridegroom, Jesus, laid his life down like a lamb led to the slaughter. He suffered and died for his bride

to be, then rose again to claim her as his own. Never in human history has anyone else truly died to win his bride, then came back to life to marry her.

It is called the marriage of the Lamb because He is both gentle and unsurpassed in His sacrifice and love for His bride. He is the King of Kings, powerful and stronger than steel. He is the Lamb with velvet gentleness and endless love.

"Let us be glad and rejoice, and give honor to him: for the marriage of the Lamb is come, and his wife has made herself ready. She is given a bridal gown of bright and shining linen. The linen is the righteousness of the saints. Rev. 19:7,8

What of the Royal Bridegroom's dress? His Bride, dressed elegantly, fixes her eyes not on her garments but upon her Bridegroom's face and regal appearance. He stands dressed in a robe reaching down to His feet and with a golden sash around his chest. On his head are many diadems. His face shines like the sun. Thousands upon thousands of angel's watch and listen as the music of heaven fills the regal mansion. The Bride joins the Bridegroom and they are pronounced as each others. NOT until death would they part. Their marriage is FOREVER because what God has joined together in heaven can never be torn asunder. Like his word it is forever settled.

The Groom and the Bride join all who were invited and called to the marriage supper of the Lamb. Seated at a table spread out as far as the eye can see are the Groom, His Bride and the guests. The Lamb keeps his promise and drinks the new wine of heaven with his Royal Bride. All the guests make a unanimous responsive toast shouting, "Glory to God in the highest. His new creation is filled with his glory! Let every thing that has eternal breath praise his name." Another mighty shout bursts forth at the marriage feast, "Glory to the Lamb upon His throne and to His Bride."

The angel choir sings a song to the Lamb and his Bride, "Blessed and honorable and glorious is He who sits upon His throne. Let the Bride throw her crown of diadems before His feet." She bows and places her crowns before his feet. He wears them for a moment then with great affection placed the diadems back on her head and kissing her says,

"Mercy and truth are met together; righteousness and peace have kissed *each other.*" Psa.. 85:10

AND THEY REALLY DID LIVE HAPPILY EVER AFTER!

Will you be at that great Royal Wedding? You can be. Jesus invites you to come to him. Let all who are thirsty come and take of the water of life freely. Whosoever will let him come. The voice of the Bridegroom calls somewhat like this to you today. "Come to me all you that labor and are heavy laden. I will give you rest. I will betroth you to me and you will be a part of my Bride. If you come I will never leave you nor forsake you. I will be your beloved and you will be my beloved. I'll bring you into my house of wine. You will stand upon my merit. I love you, you are pure, without spot or wrinkle cleansed by the divine botox of my blood. Together we shall share forever the glories of my kingdom which like our love will never pass away."

So it is written. So it shall be. For God does not lie and in his hands are the keys to eternity. If you haven't come to Jesus and believed in Him as your Savior, won't you come to him today? You will never regret it throughout eternity. Anticipate the wedding by clicking below.

Love to you,
Dean

<http://www.youtube.com/watch?v=1BaOhZrdLVY>

Words for you to Chew!
Salvation takes Two!
By Dean L Gossett

We got into the mess of sin because of a woman and a man, Eve and Adam. We get out of it because of a woman and a man, Mary and Jesus. Jesus is called the last Adam, Why? Because he is head of a new creation. It took two to mess us up. It took two to straiten out the mess.

It takes two to make salvation real to you. It takes Jesus and you cooperating with him. He stands at the door and knocks. If you hear His voice and open the door He comes in and begins a relation ship with you that is the closest possible on earth. He dines with you and you dine with Him. "Oh I am my beloveds and my beloveds mine. He brings a poor vile sinner into a meal divine! It is a one on one relationship which makes two.

Two are better than one for if one falls, he has someone to lift him up but if He is alone he has no one to lift him up. Jesus lifts me up. if I fall seven times He will lift me up. The eternal Jesus is my refuge and underneath me to hold me up are His everlasting arms. If I fall 7 x 70 times He is there to forgive me and cleanse me from all unrighteousness! It takes two to tango and two to triumph in life. The Lord is my leader in the dance of life! He talks to me as we dine. He tells me I am His own and the joy we share at His table rare no one else can ever know! All who dine with Him know a fellowship sweetly unique to the two that share it!

His heart is my home and my heart is His home. He abides in me and I abide in Him. This twosome is true now and shall be forever. It is a mystery but so wonderfully true. As the Sun is one and shines specially on me to enjoy, so it shines on you to enjoy! But our experience is as unique as it is heart warming.

In life it takes at least two to not be alone. So it takes two to know salvation which goes beyond forgiveness to an eternal relationship. As the full reflection of the Sun can be shown in a tiny drop of dew so the full presence of the Son may be reflected by me and you.

The Son of God came not just to save us from our sin but to bind the two of us together in an everlasting relationship of love. There is no greater joy than to sit down with Jesus and love and be loved. That is what we were created for that our two lips might speak to Him, our two eyes see Him, our two arms and hands embrace Him, our two feet walk with Him, our two ears listen to Him, as He in turn speaks,sees,embraces, walks with and listens to us! Salvation takes two, the Savior and you!

Saved Three Times by Trees

When I was about 10 years old I was riding with my mom back from Eureka, Ca. toward my home in Ukiah. We were on a wet road. As we went around a corner the car started to skid. Instead of putting her foot on the gas my mom put it on the brake. The car spun around in the road, hit a tree and almost stopped on the edge of a cliff which led below to the Eel River.

A truck driver saw what was happening. He said it looked like the car was backing over the cliff. What happened was my mom's high heel broke and her foot came off the break. So we went over the edge of the cliff. Thanks to a tree the back of our car crashed against it and stopped us. I bumped my head hard but was not really hurt. In fact no one was hurt. After being pulled back up to the road the car had a big dent in the rear and one head light was out but we were able to drive it home. That tree saved my life.

Ten years later at the age of 20 I was saved by another tree. This time I was in Augusta, Georgia. I was at a church service with a man and wife who invited me. The speaker told about how the Lord Jesus Christ died on a tree which the cross is sometimes called because it was made from a tree. I learned how by partaking of forbidden fruit from a tree that our first ancestors, Adam and Eve, brought sin into the world. Because of their sin they tried to hide from God but it didn't work. God then told them that because of their sin they could not eat of a tree called the Tree of Life, lest they live in a state of sin forever. They were driven out of the garden and the whole world of people from that day forward were born with sinful natures.

God knew how to solve our sinful plight and sent His perfect Son into the world who died upon a "tree" to take away the sin of Adam and Even and all who had faith in God and His Son.

That evening the speaker invited people to come forward and receive God's Son and have their sin forgiven and removed. I was standing in the isle with tears flowing and I prayed, "I can't come to You unless You help me." The next thing I knew I was walking down the isle all by myself with my hymn book in my hand. It was like a magnet drawing me forward. I prayed to receive Christ and my life was saved again by a tree, the cross on which Christ died and took away my sins. That was 55 years ago.

There will be one final tree which I shall be forever saved by and indebted to. It is called the Tree of Life. In the book of Revelation all believers have access to that tree which is eternally healing and nourishing. It bears 12 kinds of fruit and produces a crop every month. The tree that Adam and Eve were forbidden until Christ came and died for their sins is now available for all who trusted Him on earth which includes me.

Thus I was saved physically at age 10 by a tree, spiritually at age 20 by Him who hung upon a tree, and will be saved forever by the Tree of Life in the paradise of God! Thank you God for the magnificent trees that you have made to illustrate your great saving love and purpose for us all!

God's Secret & Revealed Things

There are secret things about us and God that are only known to God.. Then there are other secret things that God reveals which can be understood by all who trust Him as Savior. A wonderful verse from the Bible makes clear that "The **secret** *things belong* to the Lord our God, but those *things which are* revealed and can be understood *belong* to us and to our children forever,..."Deut. 29:29.

One marvelous benefit of knowing what God has revealed is that such knowledge demolishes every thing that exalts itself above the truth of God. The Bible is attacked by people as not being true because of its supposed contradictions or inconsistencies. Upon further sane thinking we find that those contradictions and inconsistencies aren't really so. You may want to click here later and read with an open mind and heart about 10 Bible Contradictions that Aren't: <http://listverse.com/2013/03/20/10-bible-contradictions-that-arent/>

We don't know some secret things known only to God, like exactly when we will die, or what will happen tomorrow to us and to others, but God knows them all. He also tells us not to worry but to trust Him no matter what. While we don't know many secret things, God does. We are clearly told in the Bible many things that He has revealed. He has revealed our main purpose for existing "that we might seek Him and find Him and he is not far from any one of us." Acts 17:26,27. We find Him through believing and receiving His Son as our Savior who died for us and rose again to forgive us for our sin and give us eternal life. I have sought Him and found Him and besides finding Him, He has revealed many other purposes for me revealed in His Word, the Bible. Those purposes include sharing the good news of God's love with you and others, loving all people and doing good to them. Forgiven sinners know they have been forgiven, so they pray and share the good news with the hope that others will have the same joy of finding forgiveness. Have you found Him?

God also reveals that those whose names are in the book of life will enjoy eternal life with the Lord forever, while those who don't know the Lord, those whose names are not written in the book of life, will experience a second death with the devil and his demons forever in a lake of fire.

Jesus, Creator of the present heavens and earth says, "Heaven and earth will pass away but My words will never pass away." God also reveals that our present earth and heavens will explode and melt with fervent heat followed by His creating a brand new heaven and earth absent of any evil or sin.Those are just a small sampling of many marvelous things God has revealed clearly in Revelation 21 to 22 and I Peter 4:6-9.

Some secrets are known only to God but we can rejoice in the fact that secrets that can be understood are supernaturally revealed in scripture. So best to put what can't be understood in file 13, the waste basket. Don't waste your time trying to figure out God's personal secret things but instead study the Bible to find out the secret things He has revealed. What God has revealed in His Word about the future helps us believe them even though we may not understand other secret things known only to Him and not revealed to us.

Click on these great songs below that sum up the secret things known only to God and the secret things He has revealed to us. Listen and believe them and know great joy and satisfaction. https://www.youtube.com/watch?v=eB-8-lyDwhQ> https://www.youtube.com/watch?v=AGsn8ql0mIg>

Secretariat Had a Big Heart
How About You & I?
The movie Secretariat begins and ends quoting God's words to Job. While scrubbing down Secretariat in one scene the music in the background is "Happy day. Happy Day, when Jesus washed my sins away."

The greatest line in the movie is stated by Penny Tweedy before Secretariat's greatest race. The gist of what she says is "We have won no matter what because I didn't quit." What a great appllication to the life of prayer. If we do not give up in our requests to God

based on His will we win no matter what becauise we didn't quit.. That takes a big heart.

Secretariat sired 600 colts & was found at death to have a heart weighing 22 pounds, about 2 1/2 times the size of a normal horse's heart.

If we are big hearted as believers we are more fruitful and apt to be winners in the race of life. Only God can enlarge our hearts through His creative grace. God give me a big heart!

Marriage Riddle
by Dean
Want to read what one husband or wife says about their spouse? As you read what they say, please ask yourself this question, "Is it about a husband or a wife saying this?" Is it you? Listen and decide who it is? A prize to the couple who gives the best answer. So listen to the riddle

My spouse submits to me. My spouse does not give up being kind to me. He or she doesn't get jealous of my accomplishments, doesn't do wrong things to me, thinks of me above self, Is not arrogant, irritable, resentful or rude. Doesn't stay angry with me, does not keep track of any suffering that comes from my being hurt by him or her, puts up with me with loving forgiveness when I fail. My spouse is not happy about sin but is happy about right and truth. He or she never gives up believing in me. He or she is a leader either by being male or by delegation to me as a female to lead in my areas of strength. He or she never looses hope in our relationship & never fails showing me love.

He or she lives for me so I think he/she would die for me. I value her/his leadership or guidance or delegated leadership. He/she looks beyond my wrinkles, flaws and faults seeing the inner me as handsome or beautiful just the way Christ sees me. He she/loves me as much as he/she loves herself or himself. We are so close we are like one flesh. I love and respect him/her just like the Lord loves and respects me. My body belongs to him/her and his/her body belongs to me. As long a we are capable we don't refrain from intimacy unless it is to give ourselves to prayer & fasting for a while.

Then we reunite in intimacy so as not to cause each other to be tempted.

When he/she does all these things it is like Christ lives in our marriage and is guiding our home continually. Who is this person? Is it you?

This is how Christ treats us continually. He through His cross, His forgiveness and cleansing sees and treats us as prefect and beautiful "For by one offering He has perfected forever those who are set apart to Him."Heb.10:14 That is the way we should view and treat our wife or husband. High standards! Yes, the highest!

Seeing Glory Changes Us, So?

Those who know Christ as Savior have been changed by seeing the glory of God. Jesus lived on earth among us and showed the glory of God to us through His birth, through His life, through His resurrection, through His living in us and by His promise to come take us to be with Him forever. As the Bible says, "The Word (or Voice,Jesus Christ) was made flesh and dwelt among us and we beheld His glory full of grace and truth."John 1;14 "God, unseen until now, is revealed in the Voice, God's only Son, *straight from* the Father's heart." John 1:18

So if we accept what God has said and done for us we find God's glory of forgiveness and a changed life. If any person be in Christ and Christ in him or her, old things have passed away and all things become new. We look at life from the splendor of glory heard in the voice of Jesus and seen in his actions. "But we all, with unveiled face, beholding as in a mirror the glory of the Lord, are being transformed into the same image from glory to glory, just as by the Spirit of the Lord." 2Cor. 3:18

So today will you with me take a fresh look at him and be changed to be like Him? No one can truly see Jesus and remain the same. Our first real look at Him as our Savior brings us forgiveness, eternal life, joy, and peace. But our look at Him now is only partial. We see Him reflected as in a mirror. As we go through life continuing to look at Him freshly each day, we see Him more fully and experience deeper change. Our final and total change will only come when we see Him totally face to face.

In the Bible John sums it up like this, "Beloved, now we are children of God; and it has not yet been revealed what we shall be, but we know that when He is revealed, we shall be like Him, for we shall see Him as He is. And everyone who has this hope in Him purifies himself, just as He is pure."

Today I was a little down until I took a fresh look at Jesus and now I am up. The best way to be up is to look up to Jesus through His word and on His throne of mercy and grace.

Lord show us your glory. Enable us to love like you love. Enable us to live as you lived, purely and honorably. Enable us to give as you give without reservation. Enable someone who reads this to seek you, and to hear and see you today and share below what they find with You and others. In Jesus name, Amen!

Sing About it: <https://www.youtube.com/watch?v=c-MWobHX7_w)

Seek the Things that Are Above

by Dean L Gossett

The Bible clearly tells us to "seek the things that are above where Christ sits on the right hand of God." What are the things that are above.?

Foremost we need to seek Christ Himself. He sits upon a throne of grace and bids all who know Him to come boldly to Him to receive mercy and find grace to help in time of need. So His grace and mercy await us from above. His compassions and His mercies are available to us every day.

But there is much more for us where He sits above. There is a place He is preparing for us. It is a glorious city with 12 gates of pearl, streets of gold and foundations of precious jewels. Gold and jewels, most valuable on earth, will be ours to walk on in heaven. Treasures are ours there also. All who know Him will be rewarded for the service done for Him. An inheritance awaits us, reserved for us. It is unending, unfading, and incorruptible. All things are ours and we are Christ's and Christ is God's.

There is music there of the greatest intensity and quality. There are marvelous voices blending in perfect praise and harmony. There is a river of life there from which we may drink and It will never run dry. There is a tree of life from which we may pluck fruit of 12 kinds. There are gifts there because every good and perfect gift comes from above from the Father of lights in whom there is no ambivalence. There is creativity given to those who ask. There is peace, joy, love, gentleness, patience, goodness, power under control, and perfect order. There are angels beyond number. There are innumerable believers whose spirits are made perfect. The Father is there. The Son is there. The Spirit is there. God's word is there. No one argues there about what God says. Forever His word is settled in heaven.

Perhaps just as amazing are the things that are not above. There is no night, no curse, no sorrow, no suffering, no pain, no death, no sin, and no sun or moon. God and the Lamb are the light of the city there. There is no crowding since the city is 1500 miles long, high and wide. There is room for every person who ever lived with space left over since not everyone will be there. Satan, his followers, the world as we know it now, and the old nature of sin will not be there, banished forever

God even says those who know Him are by the Spirit seated now in heavenly places in Christ. God sees it as if it has already happened because He promises it all and He never lies. So no lies but only truth fill heaven.

So take time to seek Christ above and the other things that are there with Him. The more real heaven becomes the more genuine becomes our walk with God on earth now. It is not really possible to be truly heavenly minded without being of earthly good. When we seek the things above, heaven comes down and glory fills our souls. That is what Jesus meant when he told us to pray, "Thy will be done on earth as it is in heaven." When we really focus on the things above, then His will on earth will be known as it is in heaven. Thinking about it make me feel good all over. How about you?

Love to you, Dean

<https://www.youtube.com/watch?v=pXa7CSsrUus>

Why should we seek God?

Seeking God is the reason for our existence according to Acts 17:26-28. If we don't seek Him we will experience spiritual death.

Below are thoughts about why we should seek God and what the results will be. The thoughts I share are below based on 28 passages   about seeking God and the results from scripture.

God continually looks down to us on earth to see if any of us are seeking Him.You must believe that He exists. You must reach out to Him with your whole being. You must be diligent in seeking Him. You must "call upon the Lord by name" and call your self "the Lord's," like the offspring of Seth did in the early days of human history. You must acknowledge you are the Lord's by believing in your heart and even writing "I am the Lord's" on your heart or your hand. Prov. 7:3 MSG

God promises to respond to you with love and to reward you. He promises to be good to you when you seek Him. You must ask Him to know Him, seek to know Him, knock on His door as He knocks on the door of your life. You must seek Him now while He can be found. Today is the day of salvation. Put him off all your life and you will never find Him.

You must admit any sinfulness, wickedness and ungodly ways and God will have compassion on you and forgive you through the offering of His Son's life to forgive and put away your sin. If you draw near to Him with a pure heart and a single mind, He will draw near to you. In fact He seeks after you more than you do after Him. He came to seek and save all who are lost. He knocks at your life's door and asks to come in and dine with you.

You must ask Him to help you not wander from His commands for your life. You must heed Jesus' mother's words, "Whatever He(Jesus) says to do, do it." You must obey his command to obey Him in baptism as an outward symbol of coming to Him. You must in your weakness seek the Lord's strength and presence continually. You must seek first His rule and kingdom believing he will take care of your needs. You must commit any causes you have to God and expect Him to do great and marvelous things in response.

You must believe that seeking God will enable you to lack no good thing. You must rejoice in the Lord and tell Him how great you think He is praising Him for His wonderful salvation.

When in a dry or dangerous situation you must cry out to God to protect and satisfy your thirst for Him. Like David & Jonah when in distress you must admit your need and call out to God. You must trust the Lord's promise that He won't forsake you. What ever you say and whatever you do you must do in the name of Jesus giving thanks to Him in everything. You must keep His word   with all your heart and confess sins for immediate forgiveness and cleansing.

You should continually offer Him the sacrifice of praising lips. You must humble your self, turn from all evil and He will hear and heal your ways and perhaps even your body. When you believe in and seek and find the Lord you will have an endless supply of spiritual water flowing out of your life. Because you seek and find Him, even though persecuted or afflicted, you will be satisfied and have a heart that lives overflowing forever with praise. As you look to Him your fears and your weariness will be alleviated. God will make you radiant and enable you to soar on wings to view life from heavens perspective. You will experience alation(Look it up).

Pick One Passage below a Day Seeking God and See What happens

Acts 17: 26,27 And he made from one man every nation of mankind to live on all the face of the earth, having determined allotted periods and the boundaries of their dwelling place, that they should seek God, in the hope that they might feel their way toward him and find him. Yet he is actually not far from each one of us, **Gen. 4:26** To Seth also a son was born, and he called his name Enosh. At that time people began to call upon the name of the Lord. **Psalm 14:21T**he Lord looks down from heaven on the children of man, to see if there are any who understand, who seek after God. **Deut. 4:29** But from there you will seek the Lord your God and you will find him, if you search after him with all your heart and with all your soul. **James 4:8** Draw near to God, and he will draw near to you. Cleanse your hands, you sinners, and purify your hearts, you double-minded. **John 2:1-25** On the third day there was a wedding at Cana in Galilee, and the mother of Jesus was there. Jesus also was invited to the wedding with his disciples. When the wine ran out, the mother of Jesus said to him, "They have no wine." And Jesus said to her, "Woman, what does this have to do with me? My hour has not yet come." His mother said to the servants, "Do whatever he tells you." **Jer. 29:12-14** Then you will call upon me and come and pray to me, and I will hear you. You will seek me and find me, when you seek me with all your heart. I will be found by you, declares the Lord... **Prov. 8:17** I love those who love me, and those who seek me diligently find me. **Heb. 11:6** And without faith it is impossible to please him, for whoever would draw near to God must believe that he exists and that he rewards those who seek him. **Lam 3:25** The Lord is good to those who wait for him, to the soul who seeks him. **Matt. 7:7-8** "Ask, and it will be given to you; seek, and you will find; knock, and it will be opened to you. For everyone who asks receives, and the one who seeks finds, and to the one who knocks it will be opened. **Isa. 55:6-7** "Seek the Lord while he may be found; call upon him while he is near; let the wicked forsake his way, and the unrighteous man his thoughts; let him return to the Lord, that he may have compassion on him, and to our God, for he will abundantly pardon. **Psalm 119:10** With my whole heart I seek you; let me not wander from your commandments! **1Chron. 16:11** Seek the Lord and his strength; seek his presence continually! **Matt. 6:33** But seek first the kingdom of God and his righteousness, and all these things will be added to you. **Job 5:8-9** "As for me, I would seek God, and to God would I commit my cause, who does great things and unsearchable, marvelous things without number: **Psalm 34:10** The young lions suffer want and hunger; but those who seek the Lord lack no good thing. **Psalm 40:16** But may all who seek you rejoice and be glad in you; may those who love your salvation say continually, "Great is the Lord!" **Psalm 63:1** A Psalm of David, when he was in the wilderness of Judah. O God, you are my God; earnestly I seek you; my soul thirsts for you; my flesh faints for you, as in a dry and weary land where there is no water. **Psalm 9:10** And those who know your name put their trust in you, for you, O Lord, have not forsaken those who seek you. **Col. 3:17** And whatever you do, in word or deed, do everything in the name of the Lord Jesus, giving thanks to God the Father through him. **Psalm 119:2** Blessed are those who keep his testimonies, who seek him with their whole heart, **Heb. 13:15** Through him then let us continually offer up a sacrifice of praise to God, that is, the fruit of lips that acknowledge his name. **2 Chron. 7:14** If my people who are called by my name humble themselves, and pray and seek my face and turn from their wicked ways, then I will hear from heaven and will forgive their sin and heal their land. **John 7:38** Whoever believes in me, as the Scripture has said, 'Out of his heart will flow rivers of living water.'" **Psalm 22:26** The afflicted shall eat and be satisfied; those who seek him shall praise the Lord! May your hearts live forever! **Psalm 34:1,2** Of David, when he changed his behavior before Abimelech, so that he drove him out, and he went away. I will bless the Lord at all times; his praise shall continually be in my mouth. My soul makes its boast in the Lord; let the humble hear and be glad. Oh, magnify the Lord with me, and let us exalt his name together! I sought the Lord, and he answered me and delivered me from all my fears. Those who look to him are radiant, and their faces shall never be ashamed. ... **Jonah 2:2** "I called out to the Lord, out of my distress, and he answered me; out of the belly of Sheol I cried, and you heard my voice.

Shadows

Good Shadows Friday, Better Shadows Sunday!

by Dean L Gossett Feb 23,2014

Shadows are often scary but harmless. They may foreshadow things either good or bad.

Some shadows are sweet, the shadow of a mom about to lift her child in her arms. The shadow of a tree that shades us from the heat of the day. The shadows of a man and wife holding hands as they walk together through joys & sorrows.The good shadow of Christ's cross that dealt out death & removal of our sins. The better shadows of the risen Christ walking with Cleopas and his wife on the road to Emmaus as their hearts burned with joy. The prophetic shadows of the Old Testament that warm our hearts with their blanket of fulfilled truth.

Some shadows are scary like when we walk through the valley of the shadow of death. Yet we need fear no evil for if we know the Lord. His goodness and mercy follow us and the fear of death is gone as we ascend into the house of the Lord forever.

There are shadows that scare and
shadows that bless,
Shadows that warn and shadows that
shade,
Shadows that hover and shadows that
fade.

Whatever their message if we look at
them right,
They'll lighten our load & help win our
fight-
A fight of faith that's good
to help us live as we should.

On earth there are shadows for our
learning.
In God there are no shifting shadows
made by turning.

Friday's shadows were good. He died for
our sin.

Sunday's shadows are better. He arose
so we could win!

God is the same yesterday, today &
forever.
His truth shall never waver.
So let us learn from the shadows of time
Till they flee away in heaven sublime.

There encompassed in light all around
Shadows will never be found.
All will be bright
In our home with no night.

Sing About it. <Click here:
http://www.youtube.com/watch?v=0G3-
KsR9AAI>

Snow White Tale Illustrates My Life

Hello,

Let me share a little about my myself. I am one of those who founded Valley Bible Church at the Crossing over 25 years ago. We started with 39 people, three elders and a few families including many children. Today we are in the thousands.

I retired about 15 years ago but am still active teaching small groups, speaking at Bethesda Retirement Center in Hayward, Calif. I also help lead a small group and do one on ones with 4 or 5 guys and write. I send out emails to about 1000 people often to be of encouragement to God's people and to those who yet need to come to Christ. Quiet a few people tell me they are encouraged by my illustrated emails which are usually about 3 to 5 minutes long. Below is one I just sent out and for your encouragement.

God bless you,

Dean L Gossett, elder servant of Jesus Christ and His people.

PS Someone put a question on Facebook asking, "What Disney Movie is Actually Based on Your Life?'

There is no question but that Snow White and the Seven Dwarves illustrates my life. Like the seven dwarves I am sometimes Grumpy, sometimes Happy. Sleepy, Bashful, Sneezy, Dopey and sometimes helpful like Doc.

Like Snow White I was fooled into taking fruit from a wicked person called The Devil. I found myself like Adam and Eve dead in trespasses and sin. The seven characteristics of the dwarves though meaning well could not give me back my life. Then one day the Prince of Peace came along and gave me a kiss of love. Mercy and truth met together; righteousness and peace **kissed** each other. He kissed me with the kiss of life, forgiveness and joy. And I came to life with a new desire to please the Prince. He kissed me like the prodigal kissed his son and I who was dead came to life. I who was lost was found. Like Mary who kissed His feet continually, I in turn have kissed him back continuously out of gratitude now for over 59 years.

Then at age 24 next to Fairyland in Oakland, with one well placed kiss I began my at present 55 years of married bliss to my precious wife, Gloria. Through her God's Prince also brought life, love joy peace, two children, two grandchildren and many, many spiritual children.

The fairy tale of Snow White and the Seven Dwarves illustrates my real life true story. I suppose the author of Snow White may have had in mind me, my wife and many others. Maybe you too, I hope and pray.

Snow White Tale Illustrates My Life

Let me share a little about my myself. I am one of those who founded Valley Bible Church at the Crossing over 25 years ago. We started with 39 people, three elders and a few families including many children. Today we are in the thousands.

I retired about 15 years ago but am still active teaching small groups, speaking at Bethesda Retirement Center in Hayward, Calif. I also help lead a small group and do one on ones with 4 or 5 guys and write. I send out emails to about 1000 people often to be of encouragement to God's people and to those who yet need to come to Christ. Quiet a few people tell me they are encouraged by my illustrated emails which are usually about 3 to 5 minutes long. Below is one I just sent out for your encouragement.

God bless you,

Dean L Gossett,
elder servant of Jesus Christ and His people.

PS Someone put a question on Facebook asking, "What Disney Movie is Actually Based on Your Life?'

There is no question but that Snow White and the Seven Dwarves illustrates my life. Like the seven dwarves I am sometimes Grumpy, sometimes Happy. Sleepy, Bashful, Sneezy, Dopey and sometimes helpful like Doc.

Like Snow White I was fooled into taking fruit from a wicked person called The Devil. I found myself like Adam and Eve dead in trespasses and sin. The seven characteristics of the dwarves though meaning well could not give me back my life. Then one day the Prince of Peace came along and gave me a kiss of love. Mercy and truth met together; righteousness and peace **kissed** each other. He kissed me with the kiss of life, forgiveness and joy. And I came to life with a new desire to please the Prince. He kissed me like the prodigal kissed his son and I who was dead came to life. I who was lost was found. Like Mary who kissed His feet continually, I in turn have kissed him back continuously out of gratitude now for over 59 years.

Then at age 24 next to Fairyland in Oakland, with one well placed kiss I began my at present 55 years of married bliss to my precious wife, Gloria. Through her God's Prince also brought life, love joy peace, two children, two grandchildren and many, many spiritual children.

The fairy tale of Snow White and the Seven Dwarves illustrates my real life true story. I suppose the author of Snow White may have had in mind me, my wife and many others. Maybe you too, I hope and pray. https://www.youtube.com/watch?v=hQZ6zzLpoNQ> https://www.youtube.com/watch?v=45r2t1pGGyQ&frags=wn> https://www.youtube.com/watch?v=YSnXNHUEodY>

O Great I Am
by Dean L Gossett
(To be Sung to the tune, Jesus the Very Thought of Thee)

O Great I AM I sing to You, O self-existent One.
Your bread ti feeds my hungry soul, Your Light illumines me.

Your life it gives me strength to pray. Eternal joy is mine.
I gaze anew on Your dear face. I see Your Glory shine.

O Christ of God You know all things, God's dove anointed One.
You art a King, a Prophet, Priest. This all your loved ones know.

You are our Father's unique son. both God and man in one.
We rapture in Your O loving One who gave for us Your Son.

You are the Door of Noah's ark, the Door of Israel's Boy.
Our Door in Christ swings open wide. Our hearts all burst with joy.

O Great I AM I love Your name. I love to sing its worth.

Tis music in my needy ears, the sweetest name on earth.

O soon coming One, I wait for You. You are my all in all.
Soon I will hear Your loving shout, respond to Your best call.

And so O Lord, O living Vine, I would abide in Thee.
That what You are, O I may be, through out eternity.

I would be fruitful in every way, in thought and word and deed.
So let Your living sap, O Vine, my empty heart feed.

O Great I AM, I am Your child. I relish You, my greatest Star.
My being melts, it groans to find the fullness of all You are!

Soul Sleep-Dream or Reality
DLG

The story is told that two strong believers in Christ who also believed strongly in soul sleep were killed in an auto accident. The next moment they saw each other in a beautiful city surrounded by many others in a state of peace. They heard beautiful music and could hardly believe their ears for joy. One of the soul sleep believer's says to the other one,   "How can this be? We are suppose to sleep until the resurrection." The other being more entrenched in his adherence to the soul sleep doctrine replied, "No problem. **We're just dreaming!**"

That seemed to satisfy his friend who turned to another person in their supposed "dream world " and said,"You know you are not really here. You're really dreaming."

The person didn't answer him. So he said it again, "'You are not really here. You're just dreaming." Again the person didn't answer him.

So he says,"Why don't you answer me."

Finally the person responds saying, " You can't be talking to me because according to your belief, "The dead know nothing." So you can't be talking to me for you are telling me you know something, that I am just dreaming. Then he smiles at his brother in Christ and says, "Welcome to heaven brother where God's word is forever settled and the complete truth is known. They all smiled and hugged one another realizing that their dream had become a reality.

God is not the God of the dead but of the living. "He that believes in me" said Jesus, though he were dead, yet shall he live and **whosoever lives and believes in me shall never die." To be absent from the body is to be present with the Lord. If I am absent from my body and present with the Lord that means part of me, my soul and spirit, are very much alive. One can be absent from another in body yet present with them in spirit. And that presence is real. Af death a believer realizes that his spirit has been made perfect. First our spirits are made perfect. Then we receive a new perfect body.**

Special Prose, Poetry & Prayer for Eunice Anne Barnett

Eunice, I thought of you today and I want to love God with all my heart and love all His people too. That's why I'm writing this specially for you.

Did you know that your name Eunice means happy and victorious and your name Anne means grace and favor. So as you allow it, you are God's happy, victorious, grace-favored young woman. I understand your name was picked for a special reason when you were born. I know that as you seek God in your life you will find all the meanings of your name coming true. I haven't talked to you in a long time but I was always impressed with your outgoing care to people and to me. You always seemed so happy when I used to talk to or see you at VBC. You Eunice are favored by the Lord and thus enabled to walk with him in one accord. I'm reminded of Enoch who walked with God and was so close to him that one day God said, "We are closer to My House than yours. So come home to stay with me." And Enoch walked with God right into heaven.

Why are we here. Why are you here? We are told the answer in <u>Acts 17:26</u> From one man he made every nation of men, that they should inhabit the whole earth; and he determined the times set for them and the exact places where they should live.

<u>Acts 17:27</u> God did this so that all people would seek him and perhaps reach out for him and find him, though he is not far from each one of us.

So my prayer for you Eunice is that you might find His purity. For it is in His purity that we may be pure. May you find His love for it is in His love we can truly love. May you know His presence for it is in His presence we find true joy. May He help us both set our affections on things above where from glory to glory we bathe in His pure unfailing love!

May God some day say to you, Well done Eunice Anne Barnett, "Enter into the light of My happy, favored, victorious, grace-filled, Rainbow-encircled, Joyous Home!!"
<u>https://www.youtube.com/watch?v=TvThHk-wMRk></u>

Star Wars in the Bible?

Star wars are definitely found in the Bible. One example of this is what happened during the days of a prophetess named Deborah in the Old Testament. The nation of Israel was subjected to the rule of a cruel Canaanite king named, Jabin. The people lived in continual fear of the king and his commander, Sisera.

Deborah, who was both a prophetess and a judge of Israel, tells us what it was like in Israel during those days.

"The highways were deserted,
And the travelers walked along the byways.
Village life ceased, it ceased in Israel,
Until I, Deborah, arose,"..."not a shield or spear was
seen among 40,000 in Israel."Judges 5:7,8
There was even more fear of the Canaanites
than fear today from ISIS.

The great fear lasted for 20 years until God told Deborah that Israel would defeat Sisera and king Jabin. So she gave God's command to her leader husband, Barak, to assemble an army of 10,000 men to go fight with king Jabin's army. Barak said he would only go and fight if she came with him. Deborah told Barak that the glory would go to a woman if she went with him.

After much prayer she did go with him. Sisera, with his 900 chariots and his army, was winning at first. Then the "stars fought in their courses" against Sisera's army. These stars fighting for Israel were angels. The Bible teaches that angels are sent by God to fight and care for his people. The angels sometimes control weather as seen in Revelation 7:1. A big rainstorm flooded the Kishon river and Sisera's chariots got stuck in the mud. Israel army totally defeated them. After the battle Sisera fled on foot to a tent where a woman named Jael lived. He thought she would help him. She gave him milk to drink, covered him up, and when he went to sleep she drove a tent peg through his head and killed him. Let us never put down the ability of women's faith and actions to enable great victories.

After defeating Sisera and king Jabin, Israel had peace for 40 years.

Today we do not **wrestle** against flesh and blood, but in prayer against spiritual hosts of wickedness in the heavenly places. Eph. 6:12 Our nations greatest need today is for Deborahs and Baraks who will wrestle in prayer on God's side enabling angelic help.

I read a true story about 9/11 where obviously the stars were fighting for one couple, Robert Matthews and his wife. They prayed for safety for his wife who was to catch a flight to California. On the way to the airport, they had a flat tire which they stopped to fix. She missed her flight. Later Robert's father who was a retired NYFD firefighter told them the flight she missed was the one that ran into the southern tower on 9/11. Then Robert, his son, shared Christ with his father but got no positive response. His retired father went to help at the 911 crash site and was killed. Robert was angry at God after his father died until a man and wife knocked on his door, and told this story, "The man explained to Robert that his wife had worked in the World Trade Center and had been caught inside after the attack. She was pregnant and had been caught under debris. He then explained that Robert's father had been the one to find his wife and free her. Robert's eyes welled up with tears as he thought of his father giving his life. His visitor then said, 'there is something else you need to know.' His wife then told Robert that as his father worked to free her, she talked to him and led him to Christ. Robert began sobbing at the news."

The stars in their courses fought for Robert Matthews, his wife, and his dad. God had acted on their behalf. As we pray to the true God and Father of our Lord Jesus Christ we too will find the stars fighting in their courses for us. We will all enjoy the Star Wars movie but even more important are the true star wars being fought on behalf of God's people who know and trust Him. This song, *God Will Make a Way* captures what has just been said:, https://www.youtube.com/watch?v=1zo3fJYtS-o>

Storming the Gates of Hell

Jesus tells us that "the gates of hell will not prevail against His church." If it means anything it means that those of us who make up His church have His power available to storm the gates of hell, to break them down and carry them away to the hill called Calvary. Jesus defeated death and the Devil at the cross and rose in triumph over his forces.

Jesus tells us that part of our heritage as followers of Christ is that what we bind on earth will be bound in heaven and whatever we loose on earth will be loosed in heaven. That means we have all power available to defeat the enemies of God. How often do we claim Jesus promise of victory over Satan and the gates of hell?

Jesus said if two of us agree on something we ask it shall be granted. Will you join me in this prayer?

Lord Jesus we ask that Your battering ram of truth, our prayers and songs of faith, and Your Spirit's power will render totally ineffective the power of Satan and hell over the following people: Ashely, Jac, Ken, Tyler, Cody, Wayne, Joan,

Janet, and Greg. Kevin, Tony, David, Barbara, Mike, Jessica, Grace, Devin, and Nate. We ask that you bind Satan and loose them to follow You on earth and in heaven.

It is time for You to work for the forces of evil have made void Your will. They come at us with the arm of the flesh but we come against them in the name of our great God and Savior Jesus Christ. Break down their gates, Lord as you did with Samson. His enemies waited all night at the gate to kill him. But he arose and defeated them, tore down the gate with its doors and bars and carried it 38 miles away to the top of a hill. Even though Samson was a sinful man in too many ways, yet God used him in defeating the enemies of God. So perhaps He will use us as well. Tear out spiritually the gates of the enemy Lord again in the lives of these people for whom we pray In Jesus name, Amen.

Should you wish for me to pray for someone not mentioned here to be set free, send me their names in an email (deanlgoss@att.net) and I will join you agreement for their deliverance daily IF agree to pray daily with me and never give up. It IS God's will that no one perish. We can't lean on our own understanding in these matters, but we can acknowledge Him in all our ways and prayer. We can join Him in the battle for the souls of men and women, for the repentance and regeneration of those we love and He loves even more.

Victory depends our Lord's power not on ours. Here are some songs of victory for you to sing.
<http://www.youtube.com/watch?v=zdAo-qiGG8g>
.

The Lord's Day - Saturday? Sunday?

Saturday is the Sabbath. Today the Lord is our Sabbath, our rest. In him we find rest every day, not just Saturday. Jesus rose the first day of the week, Sunday. He started a new creation made up of all those who trust Him as Savior. With seven cries from the cross Jesus finished the work of salvation, commended His Spirit to the Father, then rose the day after the Sabbath to start a new creation made up of all who trust Jesus as Savior. He finished the work of salvation on the Sabbath when no one was to work. He rose from the dead on the first day of the week, Sunday. Believers met on the first day of the week as we see in Acts 20:7. People set aside their offerings on the first day of the week which was Sunday, not Saturday. Below are scriptures to prove that it is not sinful to remember and worship Christ on the first day of the week, Sunday.

Jesus rose from the dead on the first day of the week, Sunday, not Saturday.

Luke 24:**1** Now upon the first *day* of the week, very early in the morning, they came unto the sepulcher, bringing the spices which they had prepared, and certain *others* with them.John 20:**19** Then the same day at evening, being the first *day* of the week, when the doors were shut where the disciples were assembled for fear of the Jews, came Jesus and stood in the midst, and saith unto them, Peace *be* unto you.The Believers in Christ gathered to remember Christ on the first day of the week which is Sunday. They broke bread which means they ate together and celebrated Christ and preached as is seen here in

Acts 20: **7** And upon the first *day* of the week, when the disciples came together to break bread, Paul preached unto them, ready to depart on the morrow; and continued his speech until midnight.

1Cor 16:**2** Upon the first *day* of the week let every one of you lay by him in store, as *God* hath prospered him, that there be no gatherings when I come.

It is interesting that the Bible teaches us that by the works of the law shall no person be justified in God's sight. It is not law-keeping that saves us but God's grace. The law is good but we are not. Christ died on the Sabbath but arose the next day, the first day of the week. We are only given two commandments to love God first and to love others as we love ourselves. If we do that we automatically do the spiritual and moral requirement of the law not to be saved but because we are saved.

The mark of the Beast is 666 to be shown on the forehead or hand of those who worship Him. Nowhere in the Bible does it say the mark of the beast is Sunday. Show me a verse that says that clearly in the New Testament and I'll eat the Bible.

Jesus was accused numerous times of breaking the sabbath because He did good on that day, healed the sick, raised the dead, etc. The Pharisees condemned those they thought violated the Sabbath but they were wrong. They were not merciful. They put law above grace. That is what those do who say the Mark of the Beast is Sunday. The Bible never says that. Those who seek to be justified by law claim that there meeting on Saturday justifies them, But the Bible says, "by the deeds of the law shall no one be justified in His sight."

I believe that Seven Day Adventists who teach that the Mark of the Beast is not keeping Saturday, and who trust in God's grace and forgiveness for salvation and don't trust in their law keeping, are saved. Those who think they earn salvation by keeping the law are lost. Salvation is a gift. Look on the internet to see all the reasons that the Mark of the Beast is not keeping Sunday. The Bible tells us how to be saved and it is absolutely not by keeping the law. "Not by works of righteousness which we have done but by His mercy we are saved." 1 Cor.15 tells us clearly what the gospel is that saves us and it makes no mention to the ten commandments at all. Read it and see.

If one is saved by keeping the Sabbath on Saturday why does the Bible never say that, not once?

Dean

Surf the Waves With Jesus

When a surfer sees a very large wave coming he knows it may mean the ride of his life or the end of his life. He can catch it right and ride it to the heights or he can catch it wrong and ride it to his destruction. When waves of suffering, affliction, rejection, hurt, and even death enter our life we may catch the waves and ride them high in triumph or we may let them drown us.

We catch those waves the right way by looking to Jesus the author and finisher of our faith who makes us more than conquerors through His love. Take a look at Jesus. From Him we learn to surf the trials and difficulties of life and ride them high to glory.

Jesus overcame all the waves of his suffering, affliction, rejection, hurt and death. As He hung upon the cross He felt all the waves of God's judgment we deserve falling on Himself. Listen to the prophetic words of His feelings as He experienced the feeling of being forsaken and then overcame those feelings through prayerful trust in His Father.

"For the waves of death encompassed me, the torrents of destruction assailed me; the cords of Sheol entangled me; the snares of death confronted me. "In my distress I called upon the Lord; to my God I called....Deep calls to deep at the roar of your waterfalls; all your breakers and your waves have gone over me. Why are you cast down, O my soul, and why are you in turmoil within me? My God, my God, why have you forsaken me? Hope in God; for I shall again praise him... And Jesus did praise Him again. For a moment He felt abandoned but He was heard and with great love restored to His Father's arms. He rode those billows and waves of rejection, hurt, suffering, affliction and death to the heights, overcoming them all as He placed everything in His Father's hand who elevated Him to glory.

We too by God's grace can catch the waves and ride them high. We see this in the true story of Jesus walking on water and then enabling Peter to do the same. Visit this in Matthew 14:22-33: Immediately he made the disciples get into the boat and go before him to the other side, while he dismissed the crowds. And after he had dismissed the crowds, he went up on the mountain by himself to pray. When evening came, he was there alone, but the boat by this time was a long way from the land, beaten by the waves, for the wind was against them. And in the fourth watch of the night he came to them, walking on the sea. But when the disciples saw him walking on the sea, they were terrified, and said, "It is a ghost!" and they cried out in fear. But immediately Jesus spoke to them, saying, "Take heart; it is I. Do not be afraid." And Peter answered him, "Lord, if it is you, command me to come to you on the water." He said, "Come." So Peter got out of the boat and walked on the water and came to Jesus. But when he saw the wind, he was afraid, and beginning to sink he cried out,"Lord, save me." Jesus immediately reached out his hand and took hold of him, saying to him, "O you of little faith, why did you doubt?" And when they got into the boat, the wind ceased. And those in the boat worshiped him, saying, "Truly you are the Son of God."

When Jesus walked on water He enabled Peter to walk on it as well. Keeping his eyes on Jesus he rode the waves in triumph. When he took his eyes off of Jesus and looked at the wind and the waves then he began to sink, but Jesus in grace took him by the hand and walked him back safe and sound to the ship.

When we keep our eyes on Jesus we will rise as He did above the waves of all of our trials. Look to Jesus now and surf the waves of your highest difficulties.

Mightier than the thunders of many waters, mightier than the waves of the sea, the Lord on high is mighty (Psalm 93:4)! He has set a boundary for the sea, a perpetual barrier so they cannot prevail; Look to the wonderful grace of Jesus who even the wind,waves and sea obey! Let His love lift you today. <http://www.youtube.com/watch?v=JQCxJFE-7_E>

Gloria's
Shock & Awe
May-June 2018

8:30 AM a large crash sound in our bedroom. Shocked as I find my wife Gloria lying on the rug. Most pictures on the table near her bed and the lamp were knocked on the floor. Her head was inches from hitting her head on the curved table leg.

I put my arms around her and asked her if she hurt. She said, "Yes." I asked her where? She replied in a sad voice, "I dunno." I tried to lift her. She tried to help but couldn't use her right arm or leg. I prayed and wept trying to help her up. I put a pillow under her head and called 911.

I was told by 911 to unlock the door. She had gotten up to go to the bathroom so I started cleaning her and the rug up. By the time I got to the door the 911 ambulance was there as well as my wonderful neighbors Joe and Rina.

After Gloria was carried to the ambulance we rode to Kaiser in Walnut Creek. They cleaned her up more and checked her vital signs which were ok except she couldn't move her right leg and arm. Meanwhile word had spread in our neighborhood and my daughter came to emergency.

Gloria was given an MRI and it was determined that a bleeding tumor under the skulls dura was pressing against her brain causing her to fall and also was affecting her memory and speech. The tumor was round, about 3 inches across in a circle.

Her caring sisters, our daughter Glenda, son Ken, grandkids, Tyler & Kirsten, friend Mike, and church elders Randy & Dan came to help or pray for her. Most of all our Helper Jesus inspired hundreds to begin praying for her. God's help was with her as evidenced by her sweet smile and gratitude to all as she did recognize them and said when asked, "Hangin in there."

We were told told she couldn't be operated on until about a week later in Kaiser Redwood City. Then we were told she could be operated on in Sacramento in a couple of days. So Gloria was taken by Ambulance to Sacramento while Glenda drove us there in my car. We arrived on Friday. (We stayed at Residence Inn which allowed us to stay for $100 dollars less a night because of Gloria's emergency. Sharing this so if you have an emergency you will know many hotels will help you out financially.)

The day after we arrived she was operated on. Dr. Moller came in looking very young. Gloria's sister said, "Do you think you can do this." But he was 42 and had done brain surgery for 12 years. My son Ken did research on the doctor and found he was rated 5 stars. Also he was teaching others. He told us there was a possibility that her brain tumor might be cancerous.

The nurse Anne was a solid Christian and told us it was not ordinary that people visiting were standing strong for our Savior. One nurse kept singing Amazing Grace and other songs around Gloria. When it was time for the surgery Anne and another nurse and all the rest of us surrounded Gloria and prayed for her. Anne said, "Now she is in the doctors hands but even more she is in God's hands.

The doctor said the operation would take about 3 to 6 hours but it was over a little before three hours. The Dr. Came in beaming. One of the nurses told us there are different kinds of doctors. One kind is excellent in what they do but not in a very caring relationship with patients. Another kind is excellent and caring. Dr. Moller was of the last most desired.

Gloria was moved out of intensive care into another room. Her right arm and leg which didn't work before surgery was restored. The tumor, the Dr. said was fairly certain not cancerous. Nurse Anne came all the way to Gloria's new room to see how she was doing. My daughter Glenda and I wrote special notes commending Anne's love and care.

We got mixed message about what was to occur after the surgery. Some felt she would be taken home by ambulance. One scenario was she would be in Kaiser Sacramento for 10 to 14 days. Another scenario was when she got home she would have to have someone awake 24 hours a day watching her. None of those scenarios were correct.

She was examined the day after the operation. She was able to walk. Much of her memory had returned. She was eating more than me. After mental and physical tests she was released the next day on Monday. She came home with Glenda driving in our car the second day after the operation.

While someone needed to be at our home 24 hours it was not necessary to sit by her bed and watch her. She had an indoor walker and was able to go to the bathroom by herself though I kept watch each time she got up.

Therapists from Kaiser came to our home eventually and after a couple of visits felt she needed no in house therapy mentally, or occupationally. She will have one more visit with the Speech therapist. Then anything required will be done on an outpatient basis.

Melanie Erbil from our church set up for folks to bring food for Gloria, myself and my son every other day. People have brought delicious meals and most always flowers and dessert. We have enough cookies in the freezer to sink a battleship. The whole house is everywhere decorated with flowers. I found out in our married life a sure way to get a kiss from my wife. Just bring her flowers! Voila, there it is!

The prayers, love, care and kindness shown us if phenomenal. We have experienced what Jesus said in**John 13:35,** "By this all will know that you are **My disciples**(learners), if you have love for one another." We have seen   clearly the love others have had for us.

During our trial Gloria and I have felt the shock but seen the awesome hand of God in all the events. Here are a few other awesome things.

In Sacramento while Gloria was in the hospital I had car trouble. Just so happened Gloria's sister Lavona, had a cousin who had a garage about 5 minutes from the hospital. We left our car there and were driven by one of the workers to the hospital. Then when it was finished they drove my daughter Glenda back to pick up the car.

Besides the wonderful care at Kaiser, many came all the way to Sacramento to visit her. Glenda was their night and day to take care of her and me. Our son Ken stayed there also to help care for her. Both Gloria's sisters, Linda and Lavona drove to Sacramento, stayed and visited her many times. Our grandson Tyler brought her beautiful flowers and a caring note. Our granddaughter, drove up to spend time with her and has continued to do so after coming home to Dublin.

Our son Ken got Gloria a special walker and assembled it so she could walk outside and get exercise. Our neighbors across the street, Joe and Rina, visited us and Joe is installing special hand rails in our house to avoid falls.

We have had numerous occasions to share Christ and His love with many people. I don't want to take time to explain ever last thing but I can say that never in my life have I felt such deepening love for my wife and all our friends. It all started with a shock and is continuing with

awe and joy. We have learned afresh that we can celebrate our Father's care and say for certain, "The Joy of the Lord is and has been our strength. "Nehemiah 8:10. Gloria, Glenda and I all sang this song as a trio, proof of our God's great love and care. Listen to it now if you wish. https://www.youtube.com/watch?v=9HLyhEdh92E&index=2&list=RDzY5o9mP22V0>

Talking Sun Flowers

The photo above of the nine sunflowers **growing on one stoc**k in my back yard remind me of the fruit of the Spirit which is love, joy, peace, patience, gentleness, goodness, kindness, faith and self control. Wish you could see them in their actual beautiful color

What makes a sunflower grow? It starts small, a little seed planted in rich soil. Add water, sunshine and time. Those are the simple secrets of its fruitfulness.

I notice if I fail to water it daily it begins to droop. Then when I water it within a half to one hour it completely revives.

He that has eyes & ears let him see and hear the message of the sunflowers.

First, plant your heart firmly in the soil of God's truth. Then go daily to the water of God's word. Don't skip a day lest you begin to droop. Sit expectantly in the light of the Son and slowly, miraculously you will become beautiful and fruitful. People will take note of the fruit of the Spirit in your life and be drawn to its Source, Who is the Creator of both beauty and fruit in plants and in His people. The Sunflowers in my back yard silently shout the secret of a beautiful and fruitful life.

The particular sunflower from which I took the seeds was given to me by a lady who had them growing in her front yard. They grow almost like trees from about 8 to 12 feet tall. Some stocks have just one flower. Some have two or three. The one I show above has at least nine flowers and is still adding more. It is like Christians. Some produce 30 fold, some 60 and some 100 fold. Actually each flower produces hundreds of seeds which can continue to multiply beyond our ability to count them all. Anyone able to tell you how many sunflowers in a seed? Anyone able to tell you how man seeds in all sunflowers since they began? Only God! The rest of us can't count that high.

So who can count the blessings you bring to others by growing and producing spiritual fruit? Never underestimate the flower power in a single seed nor the spiritual blessings your one life can bring to others.

Enjoy The Sunflower Song. <http://www.youtube.com/watch?v=68uq2PW768U>

Below is a poem I wrote for you to enjoy that really happened to me with a squirrel. Then follows an encouragement this Valentine's Day to love God our great Creator and Lover of our souls.

Tame in the Wild
by Dean L Gossett

There's nothing like
  A tame squirrel
    In the wild.

So different
  From a zoo.
    No bars to shut him in.
    No fatness in his chin.

Instead,
  Long,
        Streamlined, Thin,
  With no bars
    To force him to be my friend.

He plays
  And eats
    With me----Free!

Lifting his head
  This way and that,
    Nibbling,
      Soft,
        Awesome,
Unlike the Zoo,
  Being friends for free,
    He touches me!

I know most of you probably love animals and birds. Do you take a moment to thank God for them?

Sometimes I sit in the sun, reading, praying, watching the birds, and thanking God for them. Recently I realized I don't tell God I love Him as much as I should. We all love to be loved. So I decided to take a few minutes each day to tell God I love Him. I suppose He likes to hear that as much as we as we do. I also decided to sing to Him often. I sit in the sun and sing to the Son. I recently sang the song, "How Great Thou Art." No one was around to hear me except God and the animals. so I sang it with all my heart. It brought tears to my eyes.

Someday all of us who know Jesus as Savior will all sing together at Jesus feet!

I think I'll put a tune to John 3:16 and sing it. Join me if you wish. "God so loved the world that He gave His only begotten Son, that whosoever believes in Him should not perish but have everlasting life."

Everlasting life and loved by Christ, yes, alive and loved forever!

Love, Dean

Tea For Three.

A friend of mine was asked why he had such a successful marriage. He said, "Because there is a third person in our marriage." Astonished the questioner asked, "Who?"

His answer, "Jesus!"

Inviting Jesus into all you do makes all you do inviting!

Tea for Three
by Dean L Gossett

Tea for three
Jesus will bless you
Hear you and be near you.
He'll cheer you on all your vacations.
He'll thrill you with spiritual sensations.
He'll fulfill your highest expectations.
Tea for three, that's the way it should be,
The Husband, the wife and Jesus, a Trinity!

Tea for Three

Marriage takes three to be complete;
It's not enough for two to meet.
They must be united in love
By love's Creator, God above.

Then their love will be firm and strong,
Able to last when things go wrong.
When they have God's love they'll know
He's always there, He'll never let go.

As they love God they'll find
He will fill their heart and soul and mind;
In His love they've found the way
To love each other every day.

A marriage that follows God's plan
Takes more than a woman and a man.
It needs a oneness that can only be
with Christ—marriage takes three.

https://www.youtube.com/watch?v=XyT5ICbS0nA>

From Tea for Two to Tea For Three.
A friend of mine was asked why he had such a successful marriage. He said, "Because there is a third person in our marriage." Astonished the questioner asked, "Who?"
His answer, "Jesus!" Inviting Jesus into all you do makes all you do inviting!

Tea for Three
by Dean L Gossett
Tea for three
Jesus will bless you
Hear you and be near you.
He'll cheer you on all your vacations.
He'll thrill you with spiritual sensations.
He'll fulfill your highest expectations.

Tea for three, that's the way it should be,
The Husband, the wife and Jesus, a Trinity!

Tea for Three

Marriage takes three to be complete;
It's not enough for two to meet.
They must be united in love
By love's Creator, God above.

Then their love will be firm and strong,
Able to last when things go wrong.
When they have God's love they'll know
He's always there, He'll never let go.

As they love God they'll find
He will fill their heart and soul and mind;
In His love they've found the way
To love each other every day.

A marriage that follows God's plan
Takes more than a woman and a man.
It needs a oneness that can only be
with Christ—marriage takes three.

https://www.youtube.com/watch?v=XyT5ICbS0nA>

Thank God for Crying Babies
August 30, 2014
by Dean L Gossett

On Sunday at church someone asked a panel of teachers what to do with distractions. Someone mentioned crying babies. I wanted to share a miracle that happened in my life about a crying baby, but I kept quiet and just listened.
But now I will speak up and share that miracle associated with a crying baby.
I was at a large meeting years ago when a preacher was speaking to a great crowd of people. Suddenly a baby started crying very

loudly. The preacher disturbed by it said, "Crying babies are like God's commandments.They should be quickly carried out." The mother got up with her crying baby and left.

Sometime later I was in San Francisco speaking at a church called Parkside. After speaking for about five minutes a young mother came into the service late and sat down. Her baby was crying very loudly and it was kind of disruptive to me. I thought about what the preacher said about crying babies are like God's commandments. They should be quickly carried out.

 I could not bring myself to say that and I am so grateful that I didn't. Soon the baby calmed down. I finished the message and asked if anyone wanted to accept Christ as Savior to come forward.

The lady forward with her baby in her arms with tears running down her cheeks. We sat down and I talked to her and she prayed to accept Christ as her Savior.

She later wrote me a letter telling me how she had missed a bus but caught a second one and that was why she came in late. She then shared how the Lord had changed her life, she was forgiven and so grateful.

So I have never ever been disturbed by crying babies again. When babies are crying God is working. So I look for blessings to come from disturbances and would never ever ask a mother to leave because her baby is crying.

Another crying baby mentioned in the Bible is the baby Moses. When he was born he was supposed to be put to death by the order of the Pharaoh of Egypt. But he was not. His parents Amram and Jochebed loved their beautiful baby boy and hid him for 3 months. When she could no longer hide him she made a little ark of bulrushes, made it water proof and put the child in it. Then she laid it in the water by the reeds by the river's edge. HIs sister stood afar to see what would be done for him. Pharaoh's daughter saw the ark and sent one of her maids to get it. When she opened it she saw the child and he was crying. And she felt compassion for him knowing it was one of the Hebrew's children. Moses sister, Miriam asked her if she would like her to call a nurse to take care of the baby for her. She agreed. So Miriam took him to his real mother and ironically she was paid to nurse him until he was old enough to go live with Pharaoh's daughter. She named him Moses because she drew him out of the water. Of course we know the rest of the story. He grew up and at the age of eighty was used by God to save the whole nation of Israel from slavery. Moses name meant rescued and by God's grace he became the rescuer of a whole nation.

Let us Thank God for crying babies and always show them compassion. Sing about it: <https://www.youtube.com/watch?v=uOXHvnSeoAo> If this song doesn't bring tears to your eyes, especially the part about a baby crying, I'll be amazed!!

Thanksgiving Every Day
by DLG

One of the most encouraging things to me is to sit down and thank God for everything I can think of. If I start out a little discouraged I always end up encouraged. All who read this message have this message have much to be thankful for. Contrast your life with those refugees from war torn countries and from places in the world where many don't know where their next meal is coming from.

There is a song that says "Count your blessings. Name them one by one. Count your many blessings see what God has done. You'll go to sleep counting your blessings." My wife told me about a fifth grader who said, "If you woke up tomorrow and had only things you were thankful for today, what would you have left?"

The Bible says it this way, "In every thing give thanks for this is the will of God in Christ Jesus concerning you." 1 Thess. 5:18. There are many things we thank God for like family, friends, house, home, children, food, clothing but this goes beyond just thanking God for things which of course are good. But it doesn't say "**for** everything but **in** every thing give thanks." We wouldn't give thanks for someone being murdered or assaulted or **for** war breaking out, but we can give thanks **in** those situations. We can be thankful in our trials, suffering, hurts because we can learn from them. Someone said, "Many a roving minstrel among the sons of men have said of their sweetest music, 'I learned it in the night.' And many a rolling anthem that fills the Father's throne, cried at its first rehearsal in the shroud of a darkened room." We learn more from our trials and suffering than from the easy days in our life. So we can thank God for them.

Why not make every day a Thanksgiving Day? Sit down alone and count your blessings. Thank

God for everyone. Then thank him for what you have learned in your trials. If you do this Thanksgiving won't be just one day a year but every day. That is the way God intended our lives to be, thankful every day.

Most important of all, if you are a follower of the Lord Jesus Christ, thank him for your salvation. If you have yet to experience his salvation, you can experience it today. Today is the day of salvation. Thank him for dying for your sins. Thank him for rising from the dead and offering you eternal life. Then clinch your salvation by saying today, "With my mouth I confess you as my Lord and in my heart I receive you as my Lord and Savior." Then you will be able to sing with all of Christ's genuine followers, "Thank you Lord for saving my soul. Thank you Lord for making me whole. Thank you Lord for giving to me your great salvation so rich and free."

Lord, help us to make every day Thanksgiving Day. Amen!

Sing About it! Count Your Blessings. Pick one or more and score!

<http://www.youtube.com/watch?v=wNu9QoNj7Cc>
http://www.youtube.com/watch?v=MlaJaLiGF0g>
<http://www.youtube.com/watch?v=DXKxazgio2s>

Family Thanksgiving Fun
by DLG

1. When the Pilgrims went down to the Beach that first Thanksgiving, what kind of tan did they get? A Puritan
2. What happens if you combine a turkey and a banjo? You get a turkey that can pluck itself.
3. Why can't you take a turkey to church? They use FOWL language.
4. Did you hear about the turkey that wasn't fit to eat? He got the stuffing knocked out of him!
5. Who don't some turkeys eat on Thanksgiving? They are too stuffed.
6. If the Pilgrims were alive today, what would they be most famous for? Their AGE!
7. Why do pilgrims pants keep falling down? Because their belt buckles are on their hats!

8. What pill did the Pilgrims bring with them that helped them not be grim? The "gospill".

Of the eight one liners above two were original by me. Which do you think they are> 1 & 4 or 5 & 8

Get it quite right and win my signed free book.

Laughs, learning and love,
Dean

This is an open letter sent to my neighbor whom I have known for over 23 years. He in construction, is an outstanding builder and did an excellent job remodeling his home redoing and putting in and expanding his drive way, redoing the walls, putting in a new lawn and transforming his back yard. It reminds me of the contrast between our homes now and God's final home for us. Pray for Joe and his family with us, please.

How happy and thankful we should be for our homes and families now. Imagine what a Happy Thanksgiving God's own will have in their new and final home with Him and all His grateful family.

Joe & Rina,
Below is a photo of your Job well done! Sent this to you before but sharing now some new good news. We thank you for kindness and care shown us.

All your beautiful hard work on your house above reminds me of Jesus words about preparing a new and final home for those who come to Him, not to religion. He said, "Let not your heart be troubled. You believe in God, believe also in me. In my Father's house are many mansions. I go to prepare a place for you and if I go away, I will come again and receive you to myself that where I am there you may be also."

When we trust Christ we have the wonderful promise of a final home prepared by Jesus. Joe is a craftsman and has wonderful skills in building. Imagine what a home built by God himself will be like?

Do you know, Joe & Rina, what Jesus profession was before He began his last three years of ministry? He was a carpenter. Then after that he spent His time doing the most amazing preaching, teaching, healing and blessing that ever happened on planet earth? He spent time building in people's lives.

The Bible says, "We know if our earthly house of our present dwelling place were dissolved, we have a building of God, an house not made with hands eternal in the heavens. For in this we deeply long, earnestly desiring to enjoy our house which is in heaven." Also the Bible says the city has eternal foundations. Nothing can ever destroy it. 2 Cor 5:1,2

You can read about this wonderful home in Revelation 21 and 22. It is a shame that more people do not know about this final home being created for all who trust in God's Son as Savior and Lord. The Bible says clearly that God is building a city for all who trust Him which is 1500 miles wide, 1500 miles long and 1500 miles deep by man's measurement.

The Bible in Romans 10:9,10 and John 1:12-14 tells how to be sure that after this life you will have a new grand and glorious home prepared for you by God Himself. I pray you will not miss it and that all your family and ours will be there together to enjoy that home eternal in the heavens.

To remodel or prepare a home on earth for those we love is a wonderful thing. Imagine what it will be like to live in a home prepared by the God who loves us beyond our fondest dreams. This is no pie in the sky by and by. Religion doesn't hack it. Jesus Christ loves you and wants to give you that home as a total gift. Romans 6:23 It is certain! How do I know? Because God who does not lie promises it and He is not like politicians. He keeps every promise He ever makes!

God bless you,

Dean & Gloria<http://www.youtube.com/watch?v=Ame9NzE_2KI>

The Accuser Silenced
Dec7, 2017

In the New Testament book of Revelation, chapter 12 verse 10, Satan is called the accuser of the brethren who accuses Christ's followers day and night. He is continually on the prowl seeking to devour us. He points out our sin but his opposition can be overcome completely!

Joshua in the Old testament book of Zechariah is seen in a vision as Israel's high priest. Satan is standing next to Joshua to oppose him. Satan is rebuked by the Lord. Why? Joshua who represents Jerusalem & Israel is seen in Zechariah's vision as being clothed in filthy garments representing sin, no doubt pointed out by Satan who is the opposer and accuser of God's people. His accusations, while often true, are silenced by

what God does for Joshua and all God's people. Instructions are given to cleanse Joshua and replace Joshua's filthy clothing with clothing that depicts overcoming through perfect forgiveness. Joshua had been plucked from the fire of sin and made perfect. Here is how the Lord made Joshua perfect. Then He, the Lord, answered and spoke to those who stood before Him, saying, "Take away the filthy garments from him." And to him He said, "See, I have removed your iniquity from you, and I will clothe you with rich robes."Zech 3:4,5

This vision in Zechariah has a number of meanings. It means Israel who will be redeemed by Christ some day, and will have her sin removed and be declared a nation rescued, restored and forgiven in one day. 'And I will remove the iniquity of that land in one day. In that day,' says the Lord of hosts,'Everyone will invite his neighbor under his vine and under his fig tree." That restoration of Israel and Jerusalem will be followed by 1000 years of peace represented by everyone sitting peacefully under a vine and a fig tree. Zech 3:9,10

Zechariah's vision also applies to you and me. If we have trusted Christ as Savior and been accused of sin by Satan, he can not successfully lay a charge against you.. Shall God who forgave us condemn us? No!

No one, including Satan, can successfully accuse a true follower of Christ. Romans 8:31-39. Yes, we are sinful but God has plucked us out of the fire of sin, cleansed us and made us pure. That is the rebuke of the Lord to Satan. Yes we had been clothed in the filthy garments of sin but Christ, our great High priest, was made sin for us and defeated it by rising from the dead. Believing Him we are totally cleansed and clothed in the righteousness of God. So the Lord rebukes our adversary the Devil who would devour us silencing him! Christ has redeemed us from the curse of the law and sin and clothed us in His perfection. Heb. 10:14

So Israel as a nation will someday be redeemed and restored to glory. So also shall all of us who truly know Him as Savior and had our filthy garments replaced with robes of righteousness. When Satan reminds you often of your sin call on the Lord to rebuke him. Instead of devouring you he will be made to run away and someday he will be devoured forever in the lake of fire. https://www.youtube.com/watch?v=FY4DCG-nFBl>

The Benefits of Believing God

Do we get benefits for believing God or for just believing in God? The Devil believes in God and trembles but he doesn't trust him. The benefits are for those who believe in him and who also believe what he says. Without faith *it is* impossible to please *him,* for he who comes to God must believe that he is, and *that* He is a rewarder of those who diligently seek Him." Heb. 11:6

One great reward or benefit for believing God is being grateful for all of God's blessings and telling him so. Psalm 103:1 "Bless the Lord O my soul and all that is within me bless his Holy name, **forget not all his benefits** who forgives all your iniquities."

What a fantastic benefit to bless his Holy name. Why bless him? Because one who believes God knows that his or her iniquities and sins are all forgiven. I'm 81 years old so if I sinned against God just once every day that would equal 29,565 sins so far and the Lord has forgiven ALL of them. How do I know that? Because "He who did not spare His own Son, but delivered Him up for us all, how shall He not with Him also freely give us all things? **33** Who shall bring a charge against God's elect? *It is* God who justifies." To be justified is to be counted right, forgiven, perfect. God says so. I believe him. So I know all my sins and iniquities are forgiven,

blotted out just as if I never sinned. What a benefit!

My and your benefit of being forgiven also blesses many others by inspiring us to forgive others, not seven times as the apostle Peter thought, but seventy times seven times. Jesus taught Peter and teaches us to forgive all of another's sins, not seven times when asked to be = forgiven but seventy times seven. In other words be like God who forgives ALL our iniquities. Also, The benefit of forgiveness gives all who believe God a portfolio which includes being made fit for heaven!

Forgiveness of all my iniquities by God is a magnificent benefit. It is possible only because Jesus died to pay the debt of my sin. He died so that none of my sins would be imputed to me anymore. I believe what God says and bless him for forgiving all my iniquities. For by the one offering of his Son he perfects forever those who are set apart to him by believing him. Do you believe God so you can say with gratitude Psalm 103? "Bless the Lord O my soul for ALL his benefits who forgives my iniquities and remembers them no more forever!"

There are many more benefits for believing God besides gratitude and forgiveness based on Psalm 103 & the rest of the Bible. One of them is healing which will be explained next in "More Benefits for Believing God." Meanwhile, if you like, please share with me and others how many benefits you find in Psalm 103 that belong to one who believes God? "Wherefore everyone, be of good cheer; for **I believe God, that it shall be even as it was told me.**" Acts

27:25 By faith, believing in God and believing what he says we are deeply benefited! <https://www.youtube.com/watch?v=JjWV_Kuxd2s>

The Best Body Guards

We are all aware that some people have body guards. Usually they are rich or famous. The presidents have body guards and usually they are protected but sometimes the body guards can't protect them. An example is Ronald Reagan. In spite of his body guards he was shot and badly wounded. He recovered but some presidents' body guards failed them so badly that they were killed. Abraham Lincoln is an example. On the night he was shot his body guard was supposed to be guarding the door to his seat at the Ford Theatre but instead of guarding him he was at a bar drinking. You know the rest of the story.

I'd like to share with you how you can have more than one body guard that will never fail you. The Bible teaches that all who know Jesus Christ as Lord and Savior have angelic body guards who watch over them in life and are with them so they can even be safe in death. " Are not all angels ministering spirits sent to serve those who will inherit salvation." (Heb. 1:13) "For he will command his angels concerning you to guard you in all your ways." (Psalm 91:11)

So through out our lives as followers of Christ angels care for us even though we may not be aware of it. Nothing happens to us that God does not allow and everything is ultimately working together for good because we love God.

Then we have God Himself as our body guard. He is with us when we rest and drink in the green pastures and quiet waters of life. He is with us to lead us in paths of righteousness for His name's sake. When it comes time to die he is with us as we walk through the valley of death. His rod fends off the devil and his staff keeps hold of us.

Then at death angels carry us into the land of eternal love and life where we rest in the everlasting arms of Jesus to dwell in the house of the Lord forever.

When we see the angels and see our Savior we will know for sure that our body guards motivated by goodness and mercy followed us all the days of our lives. And our ultimate body guard, the Lord Jesus Christ never failed us ever! So we shall dwell in the house of the Lord forever to enquire in His presence and to behold his beauty!

Do you have these body guards, the angels and Jesus watching over you? If you don't you can have them beginning right now. Confess Jesus as your Lord and Savior. Believe with all your heart he died for your sins and rose to forgive you. Then he will confess you as his child before the angels filling heaven and your heart with joy. Then you will want to sing with all your heart this wonderful song, *Angels Watching Over Me*. http://www.youtube.com/watch?v=hOFXYXJoE44

The Best News Ever Told
Dec 2, 2015
DLG

Today I shared the best news ever told with my neighbor, Mike. I asked him if his name was in the Book of Life. He said he didn't know. So I shared this with him:

Jesus sent out his disciple who performed many miracles. They rejoiced saying, "Lord, even the spirits submit to us in your name." Jesus said to them, "Do not rejoice that the spirits submit to you but **rejoice that your names are written in heaven.**" **The best news that a person can ever hear is that his or her name is written in The Book of Life in heaven.** If your name stays written in the book of Life it means you will go to heaven and be with Jesus forever.

The Bible tells us of some, that their name was in the Book of Life but was blotted out The Bible clearly teaches that people's names can be blotted out if they never truly believe and so die in their sin.

The best news you will ever hear is that if you truly trust Jesus Christ as Savior you will overcome sin, death, Satan and hell and will **not** have your name blotted out of the Book of Life. Jesus says of His followers, "I will never, never leave you or forsake you." When we trust Him as Savior he blots out our sins and iniquities but will never blot our names out of His Book of Life. **That is the best news possible.**

I know that my name is in the Book of Life. How do I know? Because Jesus tells me it is. He says that whoever believes that Jesus is the Christ is born again and an overcomer and He won't blot that person's name out of the Book of Life. Jesus says, "Whoso overcomes will be clothed in white raiment(God's gift of righteousness)and I will **not** blot their name out of the Book of Life but will I confess their name to my Father in heaven and before the Angels." Rev. 5:2.

I believe that with all my heart! I just shared that with my neighbor, Mike. He said that he didn't know if his name is in the book of life. I prayed with him and if he believed that prayer his name is in the Book of Life and it will stay there. Pray for him. And How about you? My prayer for you is that your name be permanently in the Book of Life because you believe and that it won't be blotted out because you fail to ever believe. "If anyone takes away from the words of the book of this prophecy(In the Bible), God shall take away his part from the Book of Life, from the holy city, and *from* the things which are written in this book. **Revelation 22:19**_ So while the voice of Jesus calls you, come to Him and believe. Trust Him today and your name will stay in The Book of Life!

Sing about it here: https://www.youtube.com/watch?v=HUd8Vb_7o4w>

Lord, I care not for riches, neither silver nor gold;
I would make sure of Heaven, I would enter the fold.
In the book of Thy kingdom, with its pages so fair,
Tell me, Jesus, my Savior, is my name written there? Refrain
Is my name written there,
On the page white and fair?
In the book of Thy kingdom,
Is my name written there?
Lord, my sins they are many, like the sands of the sea,
But Thy blood, O my Savior, is sufficient for me;
For Thy promise is written, in bright letters that glow,
"Though your sins be as scarlet, I will make them like snow."
Refrain
Oh! that beautiful city, with its mansions of light,
With its glorified beings, in pure garments of white;
Where no evil thing cometh to despoil what is fair;
Where the angels are watching, yes, my name's written there.

The Blessings of Erasers, White Out & Blood

I am deeply thankful to God for erasers, white-out and blood. Why? Because they all remove or take away things that are wrong. Which one of has not used an eraser to remove something wrong that we have written? Many of us have used white-out (first called mistake-out) when typing, to cover an error we made and then replaced it with what was right. And all of us every day have the blood in our bodies cleanse us from germs, disease and infections.

Of the three, erasers, white-out and blood, blood is the greatest. Why? Because blood not only removes wrongful things in our body, it also replaces, renews, refreshes and recreates new life every day. The Bible said that "life" is in the blood thousands of years before scientists ever caught up and proved it.

Believe it or not, our taste buds are only ten days old, our lungs are completely replaced and renewed every six years and our whole body every 10 years. And what is the active ingredient in us that does it? Blood!

The greatest application of erasers, white-out and blood is seen in the spiritual realm. O Joy! The Bible says of us who trust Jesus Christ as Savior that our sins are blotted out, erased, removed, omitted. forgiven, lifted off our backs. That is the wonderful good news of the Bible. They are erased. Erasing is good but white-out is even better. Why? Because white-out removes from sight an error and then it is replaced by what is right. When we trust Christ not only are our sins stamped out, they are replaced with right. We are counted righteous! By the one offering of Christ our sins are removed, but more, we are perfected forever! God gifts us with eternal life and counts us as righteous as His Son. It is as if we did no sin just like HIs Son. Of course we did sin but God counts us pure because Jesus paid the debt of our sin and removed it. "Jesus paid it all. All to Him I owe. Sin had left a crimson stain. He washed me white as snow."

When Jesus died on the cross he shouted, "It is finished!" In the original language it is one word which means paid. In ancient times when a debt was fully paid it was stamped with that one word, **"Tetelestai"** So the Bible tells us that "the blood of Jesus cleanses us from all our sin." Since Jesus was God and man His blood shed for us not only takes away our sin but cleanses and renews us. As long as I live my blood keeps me alive and regenerates my body. As long as I live in Christ and Christ lives in me by His Spirit, the blood of Christ continues to renew me day by day. Jesus took away my sin by dying for me and as I partake of His body and blood spiritually I am refreshed, renewed, and recreated in His image.

God in His great wisdom displays in the blood of your own body the message of the greater effectiveness of the blood of His own Son. Thank God He not only erases our sins as we believe but His mercies are new every moment in elevating us to a state of perfection in His Son. Have you experienced that? If you have you will say with me, O Joy, "O love that will not let me go. I rest my weary soul in Thee. I give thee back the love I owe, that in Thine ocean depths my love may richer fuller be." This calls for two songs:

https://www.youtube.com/watch?v=Hs05AtP2wd8>

https://www.youtube.com/watch?v=I-tXgsBq418>

The Christian's Bar of Soap

For many years I taught the Gospel at Kid's Camp at Koinonia Conference ground in the hills near Watsonville, Ca. One lesson was about the importance of using the Christian's Bar of Soap. We passed around a bar of soap with 1John 1:9 carved into it.

The kids were asked how many times a day that they washed. Some didn't care much for washing though their parents required it. Most agreed that they had to wash two or three times a day. When asked how they would like to be around someone who didn't wash hardly ever, most of them said that would be awful because people would start to smell, have dirty hands and faces.

We then talked about keeping clean spiritually. Jesus taught that if a person is bathed he need only have his hands and feet washed daily as he got dirty through living in this world. Of course he was talking about being clean spiritually. When we receive Christ as our Savior our sins are washed away through His blood shed for us on the cross. We are bathed in His forgiving, cleansing love. But we need daily to apply His cleansing blood to our every day life. "If we say we have not sinned we deceive ourselves and call Him a liar and His word is not in us. If we confess our sins He is faithful and just to forgive us our sins and cleanse us from all unrighteousness(I John 1:9,10." "The blood of Jesus Christ God's Son cleanses us from all sin(I John 1:7)"

How am I doing using the Christian's bar of soap, confession and being cleansed from my sin? How are you doing? Do you ever get tired of using soap to keep yourself physically clean? Most of us would agree that to be mature we see the need for continual washing to stay clean. The same is true for us spiritually as Christians.

In the upper room shortly before Jesus went to die he washed his disciples feet. He bowed in love and service to them. He still does that. Peter didn't want Jesus to wash his feet. Peter said to him, "You shall never wash my feet." Jesus answered him, "If I do not wash you, you have no share with me." Simon Peter said to him, "Lord, not my feet only but also my hands and my head!" Jesus said to him, "The one who has bathed does not need to wash, except for his feet, but is completely clean. And you are clean, but not every one of you(1John 13:8-10)."

Judas was not clean because he had never really received Jesus as His Savior. If a person has not accepted Him as Savior confessing sin is worthless because essential bathing, full acceptance of Christ has never occurred. But those who have been bathed
need to confess sin immediately upon realization of sinful failure.

All of our lives we need to wash often. The same is true spiritually. We never get beyond the need to confess our sin and be forgiven and cleansed from ALL unrighteousness. One sign of spiritual maturity is being aware of sin in our lives and to confess it immediately.

Thank God for the Christian bar of soap, IJohn 1:9,10. This side of heaven we need it daily. Never give up using it! If we don't use it as we should people begin to notice that the aroma of Christ in our lives is being covered with a bad smell. People who wash when needed give off the aroma of God's love and life for He always stoops to wash us whenever we need it. What a God of love!

For Younger Folks: (http://www.youtube.com/watch?v=rv16YUTCp9U&feature=related)

Hilarious and Meaningful For Older Folks: ((http://www.youtube.com/watch?v=lYZVwZEn6CQ)

The Lincoln Movie & The Crude, the Rude, the Lewd and the Prude
DLG

:

After seeing Steven Spielberg's movie LINCOLN, I came away appreciating a lot of it. But a number of things said and shown were very offensive. It revises some of history and has Lincoln and many others use profanity, something completely unnecessary which detracted from the excellence of the movie. According to contemporaries of Lincoln's time "Lincoln never

used alcohol or tobacco, and though fond of telling lengthy anecdotes featuring barnyard humor, he always avoided profanity; during Lincoln's Presidency the strongest expletive used in the White House was "By Jingo!" Among the last scenes of the movie Thaddeus Stevens, a strong advocate properly against slavery, is seen in bed with his black housekeeper. Rumors had spread about his having an affair with his housekeeper but there is no proof in history that they were true. Thus a corrupted revision of history.

It is a shame that a movie which has some very good historical truth has to be degraded by revising history and using profanity.

Some of the greatest movies of all time made by Disney's Pixar never use crude, corrupt profanity. Pixar's movies are rated G and have been among the top movies of this century validating that profanity is not needed for excellence. As a teacher for many years profanity was not permissible in most classrooms of my days from 1963 - 1996. Things have changed a lot for the worse corrupting our society with blatant, frequent cursing.

This is a call to those who long for language that builds people up instead of tearing them down. It is a call for not just bleeping out those words but eliminating them entirely. Eliminate the negative "f--- word, the G--D--- and the Sh-- word which were used altogether 33 times in the Lincoln movie. Shame and blame on the writers and users of the script for those who use the sh-- word. They have it on their tongue as well as contaminating others' ears with it.

Once I was a salesman for World Book. They taught us to never use profanity because some people might be offended and turned off by it. Someone has said, "If we don't use profanity but words that build up and encourage people it offends no one and produces a more caring and thoughtful society."

I have noticed that even some who believe that "corrupt communication ought not go out of their mouth" don't seem aware that tacking God's name on their exclamations is hurtful. They use God's name, Jesus' name and even the word Holy in unholy ways. I have spoken for many years before groups. When I first started I often used the exclamation "gee". Someone came up after a message and asked me if I knew what gee meant. Then he told me it was a short curse word for God and Jesus. Some might call him a prude for saying that to me. I did not. I quit using gee because if it offended anyone I should follow scripture which teaches us in Eph. 4:29-31 to "Let no corrupting talk come out of your mouths, but only such as is good for building up, as fits the occasion, that it may give grace to those who hear. And do not grieve the Holy Spirit of God, by whom you were sealed for the day of redemption."

We can all improve in the way we speak to others. One way is to guard our tongues so that we do not corrupt ourselves and others by offending God's Holy Spirit who is grieved by language that does not build up and show grace to those who hear us. Before I came to Christ I used profanity often but usually among guys and not in public. Today many people curse in public, in movies, in mixed company, before children and before God with no apparent care if any one is offended or turned off by it. Christ not only forgave me for such language but changed my heart to desire to say what is right. God changes those who come to Him. They no longer wish to use words that corrupt but rather seek to use words that build others up. One is not a prude who refuses to be crude, lewd or rude.

"Freedom of speech was not added to our Bill of Rights to excuse profanity, bad manners, libel, or outright lying. Our forefathers never meant "freedom of speech" to cover something as base as profanity."
Connie Eccles
Click below to See Connie Eccles excellent article on Freedom of Speech
<http://www.comportone.com/connie/articles/ freespch.htm>

Deception, Downfall & Destruction of the Devil
by Dean L Gossett

The Devil's prideful desire is to go up, up, up. Instead his destiny is down, down, down. Consider the three D's of the Devil, his Deception, Downfall & Destruction. Lucifer started his Deception in heaven seeking to be above God, deceiving 1/3 of the angels to follow him in his lust for glory! Shortly the first stage of his downfall commenced. He was banished from his position and cast down to earth where he became the old Serpent in the garden of Eden.

Using his cunning craftiness he tricked Eve into eating of the forbidden fruit. Her mate, Adam, quickly fell pray to his wife's deception and plunged the world into sin and death.

Since then the Devil has been the constant deceiver who seeks to control and destroy all mankind He sought many times to wipe out Christ's ancestors, Israel, and later Jesus himself. Having failed to stop Jesus birth, he sought to snuff Jesus out in his youth. Then he sought to deceive him as he began his ministry, But the Devil failed and left Jesus presence in defeat. Later Satan inspired the people of Israel and the Gentile Roman powers to sentence Christ to death upon a cross. Satan thought he was winning but actually through death Jesus destroyed him who had the power of death. On the cross Christ was bruised in his feet, then raised Himself from the dead crushing Satan's head and his power in fulfillment of Genesis 3:15.

Soon Satan will fall even further. He will be cast down into the bottomless pit for 1000 years. During his 1000 years in bondage the world will know its most perfect golden age when Christ will rule the world. Peace, prosperity and the knowledge of God will cover the world as the waters cover the seas. At the end of the 1000 years Satan will be released from his prison briefly and go out to deceive the nations for one final time. Surrounding God's Holy city and people, Satan and the deceived nations of the world will seek to wipe them out. Then Christ will have had enough! He will destroy Satan under

His people's feet as He casts him into the lake of fire, his final home prepared for him, the fallen angels and all his followers.

Thus Satan the deceiver, accuser and counterfeiter who sought to be above God was cast down to the earth, then to his defeat at the cross, then to his banishment to the pit of infamy and finally to his eternal downfall and destruction in the lake of fire. He who sought to lift himself up, up, up above God, above His plan and above His people, will find himself cast down, down, down to slither, sulk and wander in the fires of hell. He who has eyes to see look through the 3D glasses of Biblical truth and take to heart the final fate of Satanic Pride's Defeat, Downfall and Destruction. Sing about it:

http://www.praiseinmotion.net/
8_Satan_is_Defeated.html>
<https://www.youtube.com/watch?
v=FY4DCG-nFBI>

The Exodus Movie. What's Right? Wrong? or Left Out?
Be Set Free from the Slavery of Partial Truth.

I went with five other family member to see the Exodus Movie. We didn't expect "Hollywood" to get the story all right but there were a few things that they did get right and many that they either got wrong or left out.

The most important thing that they did get right is that the Hebrews were slaves in Egypt for 400 years and that God used Moses to bring about their freedom. The movie left out the fact that Moses at age forty thought that his people would realize that he was going to deliver them from slavery.

The movie showed correctly that Moses fled Egypt, took a wife near Mt. Sinai, had a son (but left out his second son), and met God on the mountain; however, the God he met was depicted as a young boy who left out most of what God said. Actually God spoke directly to Moses.

Moses was told by God in an epiphany or Christophany that His name is "I AM." He was told to tell the Hebrews that I AM sent him. I AM means He has always exists as the true God, in the past, present and in the future. That pointed forward to Jesus Christ who called Himself the "I AM" many times. God told Moses on the mountain to go back to Egypt and tell His people that I AM has sent me to set you free. Moses asked how he would know it would happen. God told him the proof it would happen would be seen when he returned to the mountain. Do the will of God and you will know it is true!

Left out was Moses objection to God's orders . He told God he was not a good speaker. God told him He made his mouth and assured him his brother Aaron would assist him in speaking. Moses wanted to know what he should do to make the Hebrews believe he was sent by God to free them. God gave him two signs to perform before the Hebrew elders. Both were left out of the movie. Instead it shows Moses supposedly with a sword and untruly organizing the Hebrews to fight the Egyptians.

While the movie showed the plagues, it didn't show Moses telling Pharaoh about each plague before it happened. It did show him hinting about the last plague, the death of Pharaoh's son, and it did show the Hebrews putting blood on the door posts to protect them against the death of a firstborn child. The movie also rightly showed Pharaoh ordering the Hebrews to leave after his firstborn son died.

It rightly showed the Israelites fleeing through the mountains to the sea and Pharaoh changing his mind and taking an army to pursue them. It did not show Moses lifting up his rod to part the sea but showed him wrongly throw his sword into the sea. After the new nation crossed safely, it wrongly showed sea waves engulfing the Egyptians, Moses and Pharaoh. It had Moses and Ramses swimming to safety. Moses was actually safe on the other side of the sea watching Pharaoh's army drowning.

It shows Moses back on the mountain of God carving out the commandments with the "young boy God" nonsense, asking him if he agreed with them. Actually God carved out the commandments shown more accurately in Cecil B DeMille's past movie, THE TEN COMMANDMENTS.

Hopefully many will read the real story of the Exodus in the Bible book of Exodus, chapters 1-15, and compare it with the Exodus movie. Then, If they then apply the door posts of their hearts with faith in God's word and the blood of Christ, they will be kept free from the slavery of partial truth. https://www.youtube.com/watch?v=qtO0RsGF8Ow>

The Face of God & The Internet
by Dean L Gossett

As you sit where you are now
Thousands and thousands of signals
Traveling through space
Bounce off your head, your body, your face
Carrying messages of knowledge increased
And in our days released.

Why are they there? What is there message?
Is it that it all has happened by chance
To give man glory for his advance?

Or is it because God's face is revealed in man's creativity.
Made in the image of God he unlocks what was there
From the beginning, hidden in time and infinity.
Only to reveal a greater view
Of the face of God in what is new.

Man brings out from his mind things both old and new.
Some inspired by an enemy who tells what is untrue.
Others see this increase of knowing power
As prophetic truth unfolded for this very hour.

The internet, knowledge flowing through space
Reveal's God's face.
He made this world and all of space unfurled.
It speaks of Him from big to little.
God plays the music. Creative men dance to His fiddle.

History and all its inventions no matter their intentions.
Speak loudly to those who have ears.
He is the maker of all the heavenly spheres.
Those who can see beyond their noses
See the face of God in the universe and even in roses.

The Word made flesh gives life that's fresh
That In His Son we might mesh.
Faith in Him opens one's eyes to see God's face
In what is happening in earth's unfolding race.

The days run on like a swift unfolding song
Showing forth His glory all day long.
The blind can't see beyond this mystery.
But those whose eyes are open see in it the trinity.

A three-fold-look at Him that is and was and is to be
Is their's to know and set them free.
They see more than an increase in knowledge
They enroll in God's special college.

They learn of Him in the old and new.
They see the face of God in all that's true.
His glory fills the air as hearts leap up.
They drink each day from heaven's cup.

With eyes of affection on things above
They bask in the forgiveness of God's love.
Each day is fresh with living bread
They see His face who once were dead.

He made everything with potential for today.
The space was there for man to explore
For modern day discoveries galore,
For radio, television, and the internet,
For more to come. You bet!

So what do we do with discoveries call
Boast in a primeval cell that planned it all?
The fool may do that if he chooses.
But in the end He loses.

For God made possible all we see
And soon will make a better heaven and earth
For eternity.
And in that day no one will say.
Evolution did it all-Hip Hip Hooray!

No! God will get the credit for what He has done.
All glory will go to Him and His Son.
Those who believe and give Him space
Will ever, always, look adoringly on His face!

<http://www.youtube.com/watch?v=PVCrpGRSlow>

The Final Gates

Earth is fading, Heaven Waits
My outer man is perishing
I glimpse the final gates.

Earths vision weakens,
My inner longings grow
I long to be strong
To release m y grip below.

To grasp and be grasped
By heaven's promises
To lay hold of that
For which God laid hold of me.

To rise above
My tossing restless body,
To soar in Spirit
To ascend to higher love.

The Future of Israel & You

When Jesus was a baby he was taken to the temple in Jerusalem and an honorable man named Simeon foretold of Jesus' impact on the Gentiles and Israel.   Simeon said, "Lord, now You are letting Your servant depart in peace, According to Your word; For my eyes have seen Your salvation Which You have prepared before the face of all peoples, A light to *bring* revelation to the Gentiles, And the glory of Your people Israel." And Joseph and His mother marveled at those things which were spoken of Him. Luke 2:29-33

Then Simeon said to Jesus' mother, "Behold, this *Child* is destined for the fall and rising of many in Israel, ..." Luke 2:34-35

All of these things foretold by Simeon have come true or will come true. Jesus **has** become a light to the Gentiles with millions coming to Jesus for salvation. It is also true that Israel as a nation **has fallen.** Rejecting Jesus as king happened to Israel as was foretold by the prophet in Hosea 3:4,5 "For the children of Israel shall abide many days without king or prince, without sacrifice or *sacred* pillar, without ephod or teraphim. **5** Afterward the children of Israel shall return and seek the Lord their God. They shall fear the Lord and His goodness in the latter days." Part of this prophecy regarding Israel, she has fallen, has come true and part, she will rise again, is yet to come true.

After they rejected Christ their king, God gave them up to be scattered throughout the nations but they will return to the Lord in the latter days. They have already returned as a nation to their land as is foretold by Jeremiah 29:14, and still today they are without a king,   without sacrifice, without sacred pillar, without ephod, which was a garment with 12 stones representing Israel, by which a priest got guidance from God. That guidance is gone for Israel today.   A good thing is that Israel today does not worship teraphim, household gods as they often did in the past. They finally learned their lesson and are no longer worshipping idols. But there is one lesson they have not learned. They still pray for the Messiah to come. They rejected Jesus as their Messiah and continue to pray for their Messiah to come when in reality, He has already come.

Jesus presented Himself to them as their King. They rejected Him so have yet to learn that Jesus is both King and their Messiah. But at some point, in the latter days, Israel will call out to God to rescue them from surrounding enemies who seek to wipe them off the face of the earth. They will learn of God's goodness when He gives them a last chance to believe in Jesus when he returns and defeats their enemies. Then Israel who had fallen will rise and become the head of the nations. Jesus will rule HIs redeemed nation, Israel! Then nations will refrain from war for 1000 years. How amazing and welcome! If Israel's fall has been awful, how wonderful will be her rising again through Jesus to finally be what she should be.

This lesson of Israel's fall and rising again fits you and me. Our future depends on what we do about Jesus. Reject Him and have no glorious King to rule your life, no sacrifice for your sins and no One to guide you. In other words you will remain in a fallen state. The good news is that you can rise from your condition of lostness. Believe in God's Son who loves you so much He died for you and if you trust Him rise out of sin and shame to life everlasting with Him. He will become your Messiah, a light of salvation to Israel and to you. if you haven't come to Him yet, will you come to Him today? This songs highlights the history and future of Israel: The Holy City <https://www.youtube.com/watch?v=tld1MZ2F4GA>

The Glory of a Merciful Heart

Mercy and truth are met together;
righteousness and peace have kissed each other.

Psalm 85:10

O the glory of a merciful heart.
O the joy of a smiling face.
Oh the bliss of a forgiving friend

Who chooses to forget what I did to offend
Who treats me as if it never happened.
O joy without end!
Greeted now by a happy friend lifts my soul
On wings of rapture's bliss,
Lifts me to know and feel God's kiss.
If such feeling sublime can be mine now from a friend,
What will it be like to know
God's smile without end?
No words can tell
No heart express the wonder of God's grace
As seen upon His face
When at last I know
My greatest Friend's smiling embrace!
O that will be glory for me, glory for me
When by His love I look on His face
Then feel His forgiving embrace!
That will be glory for me!
https://www.youtube.com/watch?v=-lOarryn9Ag>

The Greatest Treasure.
Have You Found it?

Many years ago I spoke at a young people's camp. The subject was **The Greatest Treasure. Have You Found It?** That week I listed 25 names of people who said they found The Greatest Treasure.

People will go to a great deal of effort to procure treasure. What would you do to get the greatest treasure of all? First, you need to know what the greatest treasure is. It is not gold or pearls or money. It is a person. His name is Jesus Christ. The Bible says that in Jesus are "hidden all the treasures of wisdom and knowledge."Col. 2:2,3

Jesus, not Solomon, is the wisest man whoever lived. Jesus is not a treasure of temporary valuable things that don't last, but He is a bonanza of wisdom and knowledge that lasts forever.

So how can you get this most valuable treasure of all? The amazing thing is that it can not be bought but it is free, a gift. The gift of God is the gift of gifts, God's Son, all other gifts in one. The gift of God includes love, joy, peace, forgiveness, gentleness, kindness, goodness, self control and eternal life all found in His Son. God so loved the world that He gave His only Son so that whoever believes in Him should not perish but have the life of God living in him or her forever.

God is not only the greatest treasure but He sees you as a great treasure too. He loves you and proved it by dying for you to put away all your sin and to come live in your heart. He becomes yours as a gift as you believe in His love, death and resurrection for you. He comes to live in you by His Spirit. He becomes your treasure and you become His treasure. "O I am my Beloved's and my Beloved's mine." He brings a poor vile sinner into His house divine!

Here's how to receive that greatest treasure right now. With your mouth confess Jesus as Lord and believe in your heart that He is risen from the dead and you will be saved from your sin and have the greatest gift of all. He becomes your treasure forever living in you. Romans 10:9,10

Will you believe in Him today? Will you right now admit your sin and need for forgiveness and accept Him and become a possessor of all the treasure that is in Him. He will give you the certainty that your sins are forgiven and gone, replaced with the knowledge that Christ lives in you and He will never leave or forsake you.

If you truly trust Him you will live the rest of your life on earth and later in heaven to please Him, worship Him, and make Him known to others.

Proof of the reality that you have truly accepted Christ as your Savior will be that you tell someone you have believed. Email me if you wish to confess that you received Christ as your Savior. If you email me I will share with you a further evidence that is expected of all who come to Christ. That evidences is being baptized, immersed in water, which symbolizes your death and burial with Jesus Christ. Coming up out of the water you will symbolize that you have a new life with Christ living in you. https://www.youtube.com/watch?v=LdjcuHb7J7U>

PS Please, if you have already found the greatest gift, pray that 25 or more people will read this and accept the gift.

What is Your Higher Power?

AA teaches people need a higher power to defeat alcoholism. The man who came up with AA actually had the help of the highest power. His higher power was the highest power, a person not a thing or just a force. His highest power was Jesus Christ who said of Himself, " All power is given unto me in heaven and in earth. Go therefore, and teach all nations, baptizing them in the name of the Father, and of the Son, and of the Holy Ghost: Teaching them to observe all things whatsoever I have commanded you: and, lo, I am with you always,... Amen. Matthew 28:18-20 Can you think of any power higher than Jesus who has all power in heaven and on earth?

Jesus Christ is God according to John 1. It says of Him that he is the Word or complete expression of God. In His existence before He was born as a human "all things were were made by Him and for Him and without Him nothing was made that is made." Can you think of any higher power than making all things? It says that He upholds all things by the word of His power. Can you think of a higher power than sustaining the universe and everything in it? That is what Jesus Christ is doing right now!

Jesus says that "whoever believes in Him though he dies, yet shall he live and whosoever believes in Him shall never die again." John 11 After He said that he raised a man named Lazarus from the dead. Can you think of any other one powerful enough to raise and give eternal life to the dead?

The Bible says of Jesus that "in Him are hidden all the treasures of wisdom and knowledge." Col.2:3 Can you think of anyone or anything more wise and knowledgable than Him? Everything he said was totally wise, true and powerful!

I have chosen Him as my highest power, as my Savior, as my Lord, as my forgiver, and as my God. How about you? There are other high powers but He is the only highest power. To fear, respect, trust and honor Him as the highest power is the wisest thing you will ever do.

I trusted Him over 61 years ago and found Him to be powerful, true and with me all these years. When I came to Christ at age 20 I was not an alcoholic but I was a "sinoholic.' He set me free from sins control over me. a chaplain wrote my mom who asked him what happened to me. He wrote her and said, "He has had a deep religious experience. It will all pass away in a little while." Well

sixty-one years later it has not passed away and never will. The Bible says, "He that begins a good work in you will continue it until the day of Christ." Jesus as your highest power will give you salvation from the guilt of sin, save you daily from the power of sin, and rescue you someday from the very presence of sin. How powerful is that! So what are you waiting for? Don't come to a lesser higher power of religion or anything or anyone else. Come to Him now and let Him be your highest power! It will be a day of rejoicing for you. Sing about it! <https://www.youtube.com/watch?v=bmTl9cFrqAk>

The Joys and Costs of Temporary & Eternal Freedom

This morning my wife started playing some freedom songs that she does every year on July 4th. For some reason the patriotic songs touched me more than they have before. I begin to think about the freedom I have had all my life. I just talked to a friend whose husband Chris has bad hearing because when in the service explosions effected his hearing. He like me has a hearing aid which the government gave us because we are veterans. We are free but remember that some paid with their lives that we might have freedom. Some of the songs Gloria played brought tears to my eyes as I thought of all those who did give their lives. It is wonderful to live in the land of the free and the home of the brave but we must always remember it came at a cost. As someone said, "Freedom is not Free." I'm grateful as I'm sure you are for those who paid the ultimate cost for our freedom.

There is another freedom even greater than the freedom we enjoy in America. It is the freedom of knowing you are a citizen of heaven, knowing you are forgiven, knowing the freedom and peace of God, and the freedom of knowing why we exist and where we are going after this life. I am going to the place of which the Lord said I will give it to you. Come go with me. It is the land of fairest day, of everlasting life, of joy without end. It comes to us at a great cost, the cost of God's Son giving His life to set us free from the consequences of our sin and wrong doing. He came and fought the ultimate battle, sacrificing Himself so that by grace we might be free from the bondage of sin.

His sacrifice was the greatest of all because He didn't have to give HIs life. He said, "No one takes my life. I lay it down freely and I take it up again." He proved God's love for us in the highest way. His death is the opposite of terrorist murderers. They give their lives to murder people. Jesus gave His life to set people free to have everlasting life. The terrorists put to death adulterers, gays, and anyone who doesn't subscribe to their Satanic god. Jesus gave His life for adulterers, gays and and all of us who are sinners. He waits with great patience desiring everyone to come to Him for forgiveness. and change. Terrorists take life. Jesus gives life. That is true freedom.

There's a joy to natural freedom but a greater joy to spiritual freedom. To live in America where we are free is wonderful but it isn't the best. The best is to live in heaven where freedom will never end, where those who practice terrorism will be excluded. Jesus is the answer to true, eternal freedom. To reject Him is to reject freedom. Jesus does not want anyone to die without being free spiritually.

The joys of American freedom are wonderful but temporary. The joys of heavenly citizenship are forever. It is all a matter of choice. Choose you today whom you will believe and serve. As for me and my house we have chosen the Lord Jesus Christ. Why? Because His freedom is true and best. Can anything be better than the best? Have you chosen the best?

Thank you Lord for the temporary joys of freedom in America but thank you most for the eternal joys of freedom which you have bought with your death and resurrection! Amen!

https://www.youtube.com/watch?v=ZsmdRsJ6BYw>

The Lessons of Affliction

As I look back over my 60 years of life as a follower of Jesus Christ, I find that I agree strongly with Psalm 119:67 which says, **"Before I was afflicted I went astray: but now have I kept thy word."**

There are many kinds of afflictions. I just want to share one kind, the afflictions caused by sin. Aren't you grateful that when you do things that displease God they eventually cause you misery and grief. And when we wise up we finally learn the lesson to refrain from those things. We went astray until we were afflicted. Thank God for the consequences of our behavior.

The apostle Paul in Romans tells us that those who continue to reject a true relationship with God finally get to the point that He gives them up to uncleanness, lusts, sexual sin, envy, murder, strife, deceit, hate, violence, pride, evil, disobedience to parents, and lack of love, mercy and forgiveness. Deep down they know the consequences of their behavior but instead of renouncing it they encourage others to join them in their rebellion and rejection of God and right.

Those who admit their sinfulness and come to Christ for forgiveness find a new desire born in them to please God. But it doesn't mean we always succeed. In Psalm 119 the one who loves and seeks God strongly still realizes that their is a tendency to go astray. After showing his longing to please and walk with God throughout the Psalm he ends by saying, "I have gone astray like a lost sheep; seek your servant; for I do not forget thy commandments." He realizes that God must seek him and bring back his wandering heart to Himself. The wonderful thing is that He does exactly that.

Before I became a Christian I sinned a lot. After I became a Christian I sinned less but I am not sinless. I thank God that sin has consequences which make me miserable and afflict me. So when He seeks me out through affliction I do what He says, "If we confess our sins and He is faithful and just to forgive us our sins and cleanse us from all unrighteousness."(1John 1:9) Praise God that sin afflicts my conscience and heart driving me into the forgiving arms of my Savior.

Over the years Jesus in grace has helped me learn from my afflictions. I haven't arrived yet but there has been progress and I have learned through His forgiveness to keep His word. We won't be totally freed from our old nature which causes us to go astray at times until we meet Jesus in heaven. God's purpose for us now is to become more and more like His Son. He will finish what He started in us and someday present us faultless before His throne of glory. The final transformation will be when we shed our old nature, when we see Jesus face to face and we will be like Him in sinless character forever.

Meanwhile, thank you God that afflictions and your seeking us bring us to the point of keeping your Word in this life. We relate and care for others needing to be restored by the seeking Savior. Song, help for those Prone to Wander. <https://www.youtube.com/watch?v=ax NMWLEb6U>

The Lessons of Affliction

As I look back over my 60 years of life as a follower of Jesus Christ, I find that I agree strongly with Psalm 119:67 which says, **"Before I was afflicted I went astray: but now have I kept thy word."**

There are many kinds of afflictions. I just want to share one kind, the afflictions caused by sin. Aren't you grateful that when you do things that displease God they eventually cause you misery and grief. And when we wise up we finally learn the lesson to refrain from those things. We went astray until we were afflicted. Thank God for the consequences of our behavior.

The apostle Paul in Romans tells us that those who continue to reject a true relationship with God finally get to the point that He gives them up to uncleanness, lusts, sexual sin, envy, murder, strife, deceit, hate, violence, pride, evil, disobedience to parents, and lack of love, mercy and forgiveness. Deep down they know the consequences of their behavior but instead of renouncing it they encourage others to join them in their rebellion and rejection of God and right.

Those who admit their sinfulness and come to Christ for forgiveness find a new desire born in them to please God. But it doesn't mean we always succeed. In Psalm 119 the one who loves and seeks God strongly still realizes that their is a tendency to go astray. After showing his longing to please and walk with God throughout the Psalm he ends by saying, "I have gone astray like a lost sheep; seek your servant; for I do not forget thy commandments." He realizes that God must seek him and bring back his wandering heart to Himself. The wonderful thing is that He does exactly that.

Before I became a Christian I sinned a lot. After I became a Christian I sinned less but I am not sinless. I thank God that sin has consequences which make me miserable and afflict me. So when He seeks me out through affliction I do what He says, "If we confess our sins and He is faithful and just to forgive us our sins and cleanse us from all unrighteousness."(1John 1:9) Praise God that sin afflicts my conscience and heart driving me into the forgiving arms of my Savior.

Over the years Jesus in grace has helped me learn from my afflictions. I haven't arrived yet but there has been progress and I have learned through His forgiveness to keep His word. We won't be totally freed from our old nature which causes us to go astray at times until we meet Jesus in heaven. God's purpose for us now is to become more and more like His Son. He will finish what He started in us and someday present us faultless before His throne of glory. The final transformation will be when we shed our old nature, when we see Jesus face to face and we will be like Him in sinless character forever.

Meanwhile, thank you God that afflictions and your seeking us bring us to the point of keeping your Word in this life. We relate and care for others needing to be restored by the seeking Savior. Song, help for those Prone to Wander. <https://www.youtube.com/watch?v=ax NMWLEb6U>

The Mystery of God Finished
Encouragement for the Finishers

Jesus was a carpenter. Surely he had a feeling of accomplishment every time he made a table or finished a project. Aren't we that way also? Finished is a word we like to hear. We use it many times in our life. When one task is finished we start a new one. That is also true of God!

Revelation 10:7 tells us " when the seventh Angel blew his trumpet, which he was about to do, the Mystery of God, all the plans he had revealed to his servants, the prophets, would be completed."   Each   plan had a starting and finishing point. God started and finished His work of creation in six days and rested the seventh day. What he had done He saw as good. Then the Devil threw a serpent's fang into the mix and messed up Adam & Eve and everyone born since except for Christ. God's first work of creation was marred by sin which continues to this day.

But God had a better idea. "Man has plunged the world into sin. I'll take the sin away for all who receive My Son. He will be made sin for them." So God sent His Son to make a new creation composed of the newborns of His kingdom. In six cries from the cross Jesus carved out His new creation. His sixth cry was, "It is finished." Then after His seventh cry he rested saying "Into Your hands I commend my spirit,"

The price of salvation was finished, paid for by Christ in full. But He wasn't through. He started a new work, the building of His church against which the gates of hell cannot prevail. God's building of the church goes on victorious until now. Someday when the last convert receives Him that work will be finished.

After that God will begin a new work against Satan. His Son Jesus will outwrestle the Devil binding him so he is unable to influence the world for evil.

That binding of Satan will be part of keeping His promise to Israel thousands of years before when He promised them a King to sit upon their throne forever. When Christ returns that will happen. Israel who had been the tail of the nations will become the head under their newly received Savior. Since God always keeps His promises and finishes what He starts, Israel will be born again spiritually in one day and Christ's 1000 year rule shall begin!

After the thousand years, Satan will be released from his prison and deceive the nations to go fight against God and His people. Then Christ will wipe out the Devil and all evil. He will make a new heaven and earth. Thus the mystery of God will be finished as told throughout the Bible.

It is done, finished! But the joy isn't over for his people. It has just begun. God will do new things on a new earth and heaven. Throughout eternity those who know Jesus will start and finish new songs, eat new food from the tree of life, and have new conversations with heaven's occupants.

With such a glorious finish line before us ought we not run with patience here the race that ends at the ribbon line of eternity. God help us to keep the faith, to fight the good fight, to finish well.

God begins a good work in all who trust Him and He will finish it! That is part of the wonderful mystery of God which He will also finish someday. But the best, the surprises of eternity, the unrealized mystery, is yet to finish!

Thoughts to Help Us Wise Up
The Mystery of Wisdom Revealed

There are two categories of wisdom. One is fleshly, sensual, philosophical and foolish, filled with enticing guesses and opinions. The other is spiritual and factual imparted by God. It is revealed by God as we get to know Him and His Son through His word and Spirit. It is varied and multiple in nature. It is gracious and powerful based on God's will. It is found in the Bible, and understood by those who have the Spirit and base their understanding on what the Spirit teaches. 1 Cor. 2:7 "But we speak the wisdom of God in a mystery, even wisdom that had been hidden which God determined before the world began to bring about our glory. Our glory is His perfect purpose for us both now and forever.

Christ is God's wisdom. When we hear Christ's words and see his works we view God's wisdom. For in Him are found all the inexhaustible treasures of wisdom and knowledge. Some say Solomon was the wisest man that ever lived. The Bible doesn't say that. He was the wisest of his day but the wisest man who ever lived is our Lord Jesus Christ for He practiced perfectly what He preached. Solomon did not. Like everyone else except Christ, Solomon was a sinner.

Unlike Solomon, Christ exercised His wisdom before he was born. As the Christ he created the world. All things were made by Him and for him. He was there before

Abraham, before Adam and Eve, before the world began. He gave man light and life and physical breath. He was the word that spoke from Mt. Sinai, the power behind Moses, and the force that set Israel free from slavery. He was the Rock that followed Israel in the wilderness from which they drank and the one who enabled Israel's victories in the promised land. He was the guide that enabled David to kill Goliath, empowered Him as King, and forgave him for his terrible sin.

Then born of a woman, the Christ became a human. He grew in wisdom and stature and in favor with God and man. As a man Christ Jesus astounded people by His wise, authoritative teaching and mighty works. His character was flawless. He thought no sin, did no sin, knew no sin nor did he speak anything sinful. He was from above, pure, full of peace, gentleness, joy, and mercy. He was fruitful, impartial and without hypocrisy. His wisdom led Him to the cross where he confounded Satan, paid our debt of sin, and overcame death.

His wisdom enables us to be like Him in character. As we learn His wisdom we are filled with love, patience, goodness, kindness, faith, humility, grace and self control. His wisdom now is shown to the world clearly by those in His church who walk according to the Spirit's power and wisdom. His wisdom and power will enable all who know Him to overcome sin, death and hell and rise to be with Him forever. Do you know Him? You can by reading and believing John 3:16.

Eternity will unfold His wisdom forever and we shall never be able to exhaust it. Romans 11:32-36 Have you ever come on anything quite like this deep, deep wisdom? It's way over our heads. We'll never figure it out. Is there anyone around who can explain God? Anyone smart enough to tell him what to do? Anyone who has done him such a huge favor that God has to ask his advice? Everything comes from him; Everything happens through him; Everything ends up in him. Always glory! Always praise! Yes. Yes. Yes.

The Never Ending Song
Sung to the Tune of Doe a Dee
by Dean L Gossett

C for Christ, the Christ I love
D He Died upon a tree
E Eternal life is mine
F By Faith I have been saved
G My God is on my side
A Assurance now is mine.
B Be sure you know my Lord
That will bring you back to C

When you know my Lord and King
How can you do less than sing: C for....

The Power of Encouragement
by Dean L Gossett

As you think back on your life would you say that those who have encouraged or discouraged you have made the greatest impact on your life? This is an open letter of gratitude to those whose encouragement has changed my life for the better. Encouragers have driven me to action and praise to God.

In school I had only two teachers that I can remember who encouraged me. One of those encouragers came right after a most discouraging year. My sixth grade teacher dwelt on my faults of which there were many so I had a terrible year being given the benefit of the doubt and promoted to seventh grade by the skin of my teeth. My seventh grade teacher Mr. Manford was so different. He built me up by dwelling on my strengths. He encouraged me at a baseball game and I hit three home runs in one game. The contrast in seventh grade with my sixth grade was so memorable that on the last day in his class I stood at the door of his room with tears in my eyes not wanting to leave.

In high school a coach named Mr Murphy encouraged me in high jumping rubbing down my legs and telling me I was clearing the bar by a foot but needed to kick my trailing leg. I jumped my highest that day and went on to win 4th place in the California State meet in Davis, Ca.

When I became a teacher later in life those two teachers who encouraged me made me make up my mind to seek to encourage every kid in my class.

I was encouraged by a Chaplain speaking on board a ship to Japan in 1954 to believe in Christ as my Savior. From that time on I began to seek God asking Him to move His hand and give me a clean heart.

Three years later I was encouraged by a man named Jim Murdoch who invited me to come to church and lunch with him and his family. I had never been a church goer but I went with him four times that day in 1957 and at the last meeting was encouraged by the speaker, Mr Hollingsworth, to come to Christ. I prayed and asked God to help me accept Him and He did. I went forward and prayed to receive Christ.

My first request after conversion was thinking, "How can I live this new life?" A man answered my question without my asking it out loud. He encouraged me telling me how go grow in faith telling me "Faith comes by hearing and hearing by the Word of God. So read God's word to have faith to live for Christ." That is what I did beginning 58 years ago and continue to do today. It worked.

At age 24 I married my wife who has encouraged me in teaching & preaching and raising our family. She has been a faithful helpmate to me for 54 years now. We have been encouraged by over 40 clear answers to prayer, including the strong spiritual growth of my daughter, Glenda, and complete and spiritual transformation of my granddaughter at age 20.

I have been encouraged by my son Ken's success as a high school teacher for over 17 years.

I have been encouraged by my cousin Marsha Christian on numerous occasions.. Marsha helped me overcome some deep struggles in my life and was a prayer partner for years.

In the 1970s I was encouraged by a writer, Bill McDonald to also become a writer. He helped send me to the Billy Graham school of writing after which I had my first book published in 1973 called *A Journey Through the Bible*. It is a correspondence course. To date over a million people have completed it. By God's grace three more of my books were published. All four are listed here: <http://www.ecsministries.org/159972.ihtml> Journey Through the Bible <http://www.amazon.com/The-Royal-Ride-Esther-Acts/dp/1420842374>The Royal Ride, Esther in VII Acts<http://www.amazon.com/The-Hair-Angel-Dean-Gossett/dp/1425976778> The Hair Angel (for those 5-105)<http://www.amazon.com/BEAUTY-FOR-ASHES-Life-The-Beautiful/dp/

1418451029> BEAUTY FOR ASHES, My Life,the Bad and the Beautiful

Since the Internet arrived I was encouraged by a friend, Martha Giggleman to send articles of encouragement to people via special illustrated emails which now go out to over 1000 people.

During the course of my writing one of the most encouraging feedbacks I got was from a friend named Evie Dopart who told me my writing was "excellent and my poetry was exceptional." How deeply Evie you encouraged me to keep on keeping on.

Another friend, Mike Teauge encouraged me to write a blog on the Internet. I started on the blog a little more than a month ago and have been getting some good feedback. Martha Giggleman who encouraged my first email articles also wrote and encouraged me to write a blog or create a daily devotional. Her encouraging words were an added blessing to me giving me assurance that having begun a blog was a good thing. I'm hoping it will live on after I die to encourage others. The address of the blog and its Photo created by Matt Pine is <https://deanslifelifters.wordpress.com>. So I told Martha I am doing a blog now and the articles I do are on Wordpress, Twitter, Google and Facebook. Martha replied, "Excellent. Many will be blessed." May her words come true. **I thank God for all my encouragers especially The Lord Jesus Christ who gives words of life in unending supply and deserves all the glory for anything good in my life.**

God is an encourager whose plans for you are good, not bad. I hope and pray that these words may be used of God to unleash the power of encouragement in your life.

PLease write me if you wish and share how encouragers have made an impact on your life. Thank you, Dean
<http://www.youtube.com/watch?v=SBs7-crFAKQ>

The Power of Encouragement
by Dean L Gossett

As you think back on your life would you say that those who have encouraged or discouraged you have made the greatest impact on your life? This is an open letter of gratitude to those whose encouragement has changed my life for the better. Encouragers have driven me to action and praise to God.

In school I had only two teachers that I can remember who encouraged me. One of those encouragers came right after a most discouraging year. My sixth grade teacher dwelt on my faults of which there were many so I had a terrible year being given the benefit of the doubt and promoted to seventh grade by the skin of my teeth. My seventh grade teacher Mr. Manford was so different. He built me up by dwelling on my strengths. He encouraged me at a baseball game and I hit three home runs in one game. The contrast in seventh grade with my sixth grade was so memorable that on the last day in his class I stood at the door of his room with tears in my eyes not wanting to leave.

In high school a coach named Mr Murphy encouraged me in high jumping rubbing down my legs and telling me I was clearing the bar by a foot but needed to kick my trailing leg. I jumped my highest that day and went on to win 4th place in the California State meet in Davis, Ca.

When I became a teacher later in life those two teachers who encouraged me made me make up my mind to seek to encourage every kid in my class.

I was encouraged by a Chaplain speaking on board a ship to Japan in 1954 to believe in Christ as my Savior. From that time on I began to seek God asking Him to move His hand and give me a clean heart.

Three years later I was encouraged by a man named Jim Murdoch who invited me to come to church and lunch with him and his family. I had never been a church goer but I went with him four times that day in 1957 and at the last meeting was encouraged by the speaker, Mr Hollingsworth, to come to Christ. I prayed and asked God to help me accept Him and He did. I went forward and prayed to receive Christ.

My first request after conversion was thinking, "How can I live this new life?" A man answered my question without my asking it out loud. He encouraged me telling me how go grow in faith telling me "Faith comes by hearing and hearing by the Word of God. So read God's word to have faith to live for Christ." That is what I did beginning 58 years ago and continue to do today. It worked.

At age 24 I married my wife who has encouraged me in teaching & preaching and raising our family. She has been a faithful helpmate to me for 54 years now. We have been encouraged by over 40 clear answers to prayer, including the strong spiritual growth of my daughter, Glenda, and complete deliverance from addictions and spiritual transformation of my granddaughter at age 20. I have been encouraged by my son Ken's success as a high school teacher for over 17 years.

I have been encouraged by my cousin Marsha Christian on numerous occasions.. Marsha helped me overcome some deep struggles in my life and was a prayer partner for years.

In the 1970s I was encouraged by a writer, Bill McDonald to also become a writer. He helped send me to the Billy Graham school of writing after which I had my first book published in 1973 called *A Journey Through the Bible*. It is a correspondence course. To date over a million people have completed it. By God's grace three more of my books were published. All four are listed here: <http://www.ecsministries.org/159972.ihtml> Journey Through the Bible <http://www.amazon.com/The-Royal-Ride-Esther-Acts/dp/1420842374>The Royal Ride, Esther in VII Acts<http://www.amazon.com/The-Hair-Angel-Dean-Gossett/dp/1425976778> The Hair Angel (for those 5-105)<http://www.amazon.com/BEAUTY-FOR-ASHES-Life-The-Beautiful/dp/1418451029> BEAUTY FOR ASHES, My Life, the Bad and the Beautiful

Since the Internet arrived I was encouraged by a friend, Martha Giggleman to send articles of encouragement to people via special illustrated emails which now go out to over 1000 people.

During the course of my writing one of the most encouraging feedbacks I got was from a friend named Evie Dopart who told me my writing was "excellent and my poetry was exceptional." How deeply Evie you encouraged me to keep on keeping on.

Another friend, Mike Teauge encouraged me to write a blog on the Internet. I started on the blog a little more than a month ago and have been getting some good feedback. Martha Giggleman who encouraged my first email articles also wrote and encouraged me to write a blog or create a daily devotional. Her encouraging words were an added blessing to me giving me assurance that having begun a blog was a good thing. I'm hoping it will live on after I die to encourage others. The address of the blog and its Photo created by Matt Pine is <https://deanslifelifters.wordpress.com>. So I told Martha I am doing a blog now and the articles I do are on Wordpress, Twitter, Google and Facebook. Martha replied, "Excellent. Many will be blessed." May her words come true. **I thank God for all my encouragers especially The Lord Jesus Christ who gives words of life in unending supply and deserves all the glory for anything good in my life.**

God is an encourager whose plans for you are good, not bad. I hope and pray that these words may be used of God to unleash the power of encouragement in your life.

Please write me if you wish and share how encouragers have made an impact on your life. Thank you, Dean
<http://www.youtube.com/watch?v=SBs7-crFAKQ>

The Rainbow's Meaning
DLG

The recent rainbow coloring of the White House made me rethink the meaning of the rainbow. After the world wide flood was over Noah left the ark with his rescued family. A rainbow appeared in the sky and God Himself tells us the meaning of the rainbow, "This is the sign of the covenant I am making between me and you and everything living around you and everyone living after you. I'm putting my rainbow in the clouds, a sign of the covenant between me and the Earth. From now on, when I form a cloud over the Earth and the rainbow appears in the cloud, I'll remember my covenant between me and you and everything living thing, that never again will floodwaters destroy all life." (Gen. 9:12-15)

The rainbow represents the glory of God's grace as a symbol of His promise not to destroy life with a world wide flood ever again. He has kept His promise as He keeps all His promises. He doesn't destroy our country even though we break His laws and will. He is patient desiring that all Americans admit their sin and come to Him for forgiveness, and help to change from doing wrong to doing right.

Rainbows have been changed by some to stand for liberty to sin while in reality they

represent God's grace putting up with evils that deserve His wrath. We are all guilty as the Bible makes clear. We have all sinned and come short of what God expects. The good news is that he doesn't deal with our sin right away but patiently waits desiring us to have a change of heart that we might find forgiveness now. Jesus died for everyone of us to set us free from condemnation. Instead, He waits for us to turn from our sin to Himself for salvation. Once that happens our behavior changes as we seek. to obey and please Him. After forgiving a woman caught in adultery Jesus told her, "Go and sin no more." Having forgiven her and rescuing her he expected her to stop her sin.

The reality of true conversion will be seen in that once forgiven, a person no longer promotes or practices sin as an acceptable way of life. Receiving Christ's forgiveness, a person is created new in Christ to do good instead of sin. (Eph. 2:8-10) Let's pray for all people to come to appreciate God's rainbow which means he patiently refrains from punishing sin now. HIs desire for you and me is to accept His forgiveness and be given a new life dedicated to doing right. Failure to ever admit and turn from our sin will someday end not in a flood of water but in a lake of unquenchable fire. The rainbow tells us that God does not desire us to perish.

This song believed will remove you from any harm to come:
https://www.youtube.com/watch?v=IofNq0U2xk0>

The Reason For Everything
by DLG

Is it possible that God could take a mere mortal like me and enlighten me as to His reason for planning and creating everything? Why not? The tiny but full image of the sun can be viewed in a drop of dew. So God can reveal in me and you His glorious wisdom and purpose for everything.

Here it is! God created everything, angels, Satan, the heavens and earth, mankind to teach one great eternal lesson to everyone.

First He created angels. One of those angels named Satan rebelled against Him seeking to exalt himself above God. He deceived 1/3 of the angels to follow him. The result was that God would use his rebellion to teach us all to chose wisely rather than exercise our free will to go against God.

God prepared a final destiny for the Devil and his angels and all who would follow him. That destiny is eternal death in a lake of fire. But before that awful destruction, God would teach a lesson to angels and mankind that would be demonstrated through time and eternity.

He created a heaven and earth, and a man and woman endowed with His likeness but made lower than the angels The man and woman and their offspring, though lower than angels could be exalted above the devil and the. fallen angels. How?

Those humans deceived by Satan who turned from him and exercised faith in the true God and His plan of forgiveness would humiliate Satan. They would be exalted above him, So God in His infinite wisdom devised a plan to rescue those who would trust Him.

He humbled himself by taking a human body, made lower than the angels so that through the suffering of death He could win the hearts of all mankind who would trust Him. He came a tiny babe grown to manhood to live a perfect life of trust in contrast to Satan's rebellion. Then in love He died for us to bring us back to His father and exalt us above the angels.

Satan who wished to exalt himself above God lost his place in heaven, was cast down to earth, then to the bottomless pit and finally into the lake of fire with his followers.

Meanwhile the righteous curious angels and mankind could learn God's highest lesson. That lesson is the reason for everything, that we might make the wise choice of trusting and honoring God and not the foolish choice of trying to exalt ourselves above Him,

Throughout eternity the wise angels and wise exalted mortals will still have free will. The lesson of trust and its joyous consequences will have been so ingrained and learned that no one will ever again lift their heel against God! The reason for everything is that you might seek God, trust Him, love Him and obey Him forever. Have you learned that lesson? Have I?

God help us to really learn that lesson.

Love to you,

The Rest of the Story

In the Bible there are a number of stories that leave it up to our imagination to decide the rest of the story. One such story is about a man named Hobab, Moses' father in law through marriage.

Hobab came to Moses when he was leading the nation of Israel in the wilderness toward land that God had promised Israel. Moses invited Hobab to join him in traveling to that land.

Moses said, ""We are setting out for the place of which the Lord said, 'I will give it to you.' **Come with us**, and we will treat you well; for the Lord has promised **go**od things to Israel." Numbers 10:29 Hobab refused at first and said he was going to go back to his home.

Then Moses sought Hobab's help. He asked him to be eyes for the children of Israel to help guide them in the wilderness. Hobab's response is left open ended. We don't know for sure the rest of the story. Did he go home or join them? We can only guess.

This story applies to us, too. God invites us to receive His Son as our savior. He died for us and is now is in heaven. He invites us to come to Him for He has good things for us. He is preparing a place for all who will trust Him which is filled with glorious things. He has a heavenly home for us filled with love and endless joy.

I have heeded His call and received Him as Savior. I am going to the place of which Jesus spoke when he said, "In My Father's house are many mansions. I go to prepare a place for you and if I go I will come again and receive you to Myself that where I am there you may be." I have accepted Christ's offer, believed Him and received Him. That is part of the rest of my story.

What will will be the rest of your story? If you haven't yet, will you join me and accept God's love as shown by His promise to take His own to His Father's house? He died for your sins so you can be with Him forever. If you believe Him you will go the place God has for you, not only a new home in heaven but a new earth to enjoy always. The rest of the story depends on you. How will you finish it? https://www.youtube.com/watch?v=o2aLSat3h0w>

If you receive God's Son you will gain a compassionate heart to share the good news with others and see them forgiven and on their way to heaven,. If you trust Him you will find your heart rejoices when the lost are found. If not you will find no joy in seeing other prodigals found who have been lost. If not you will know the sorrow of those who have no compassion. The rest of the story depends in your decision whether or not to receive God's wonderful invitation. How will the rest of this story end for you? It's your choice! Choose wisely for your whole future good or bad depends on the rest of your story. Amen!

The Rope of Love

A harlot's life was at stake. Her name was Rahab. Her city, Jericho, was about to be attacked and destroyed. Two men from the attacking army came into her city to spy it out. Word got out that the spies were there and they sought protection which they found at Rahab's place. Of all the people in the city, Rahab the harlot had insight into the fact that the God of Israel was the true God. She had come to believe in Him. So she rescued the two men by becoming a rope of love helping them escape death. She hid them on her roof. Then she helped them escape on a scarlet rope hung from her window. Before the men left they told her to hang the scarlet rope in her window which when seen by the advancing army would save her and those with her from sudden destruction. The scarlet rope did its job. All the people in her town of Jericho perished except for her and family members who joined her. Thus she became a rope of salvation to whoever joined her in her home on the wall.

Rahab rescued the men. They in turn rescued her. When the attacking army of Israel marched round the walls she remembererd their promise that if she put the scarlet rope in the window she and those with her would be saved. God caused the walls of her city to tumble down except for where she lived. Then the troops came and delivered Rahab and those who were with her inside her home. Her life of harlotry was over. Rahab then married Salmon probably one of her rescuers. So she was not only saved from death but also became a bride, loved by Salmon. Her rope of love became a line of life and joy. Rahab had a son with Salmon named Boaz. Boaz was the father of Jesse who was the father of the great King David, ancestor of the greatest King, Jesus Christ the Lord.

There is still a scarlet rope let down from the window of heaven that runs all through the Bible. That rope is the love of God, seen by eyes of faith. Those who lay hold of that scarlet rope escape eternal death which is replaced by eternal life. That eternal life comes through the forgiving, scarlet blood of God's love. It is experienced through heart belief in the death & risen life of His Son. It is a love to which I daily cling lifting me above all problems, sin, failure, suffering, discouragement, sorrow, loneliness, rejection, hurt and pain. It is a love that will not let me go nor will I let go of it. It makes me more than a conqueror through Him who loved me and gave Himself for me.

People still need a life line today provided by God. He gives us that life line through His beloved Son who lived and died for us. All we have to do is reach out and take Him as our Savior. He shed His scarlet blood that we might experience God's greatest cord of love. He continues to love us like a faithful husband to a joyful wife. God seeks today to win mankind with a rope of love. He calls to all to come to Himself, find forgiveness, life, love and victory over death. He still throws out the life line today. Will you take hold of it? If you have not taken hold of it why not do it now while you listen to this Song: <http://www.youtube.com/watch?v=PjXr9tQT6bU>

The Movie Noah and The Ships of Faith

The Hollywood version of Noah's ark has Noah saving the innocent animals to start them afresh in a new cleansed earth. It leads us to believe that Noah sees not only those who are part of a corrupted evil world to be put to death but also even himself and his family. He plans to kill female twin babies born to his son Shem on the ark thus leaving only "evil" males who won't be able to repopulate the world again. In the end he finds a sudden compassion and love for Shem's twin baby girls and can't bring himself to kill them. He feels he failed and gets drunk. But in spite of him feeling he failed it turns out that not only the supposed innocent animals are saved but so is mankind. Thus to Hollywood Noah's motive to save only the animals fails. Of course the whole Noah movie is full of contradictions, corrupted facts and fails to present Noah as a preacher of righteousness whose main goal was to save both the animals and mankind.

Most of us know the real story of Noah, his preaching, his warning, his invitation to a lost world that was soon to perish unless they believed his message of coming destruction and joined him in the ark, the ship of faith. Only the animals and eight people, Noah, his wife, his three sons and their wives listened to the point of believing and entering the ark. The rest of the people rejected the offer of God's saving grace, refused to believe Noah's warning and invitation and perished in a world wide flood. In contrast to the Hollywood version of Noah, the Bible portrays him as a man of grace, love and righteousness whose motive for building an ark was to save as many as would join him. Only seven people and the animals joined Noah and survived the flood. In Noah's day there was only one way of salvation, the ship of faith, the ark designed by God and built by Noah and his family,

Today the world faces an even greater final coming destruction. It faces the judgement of God in destroying not just human and animal life by a flood of water but the destruction of the whole universe by fire which will melt the present earth and heavens. As in Noah's day there was only one way to escape so in our day there is only one way to escape. That way is the Lord Jesus Christ.

As their was a message of grace in Noah's day, a ship of faith to save those who would believe, so there is an ark today into which those who listen can enter and go through the coming universal explosion and fire unscathed.

in the Old Testament three men were thrown into a fiery furnace. They came through the fire unharmed! Why? Because they had an ark of protection through the Son of God whose care and presence saved them.

Today God calls out for all who will to come to His Son. The Lord Jesus Christ is the ark, the ship of faith into which we must enter to be saved from the coming Big Bang that will melt the elements of heaven and earth and destroy those who reject Him by relegating them to the lake of fire.

We are warned now of that coming destruction and offered a place of eternal refuge in the ark of God's Son. By faith you can enter in to Him today and be spared from the destruction to come. If you believe in God's Son given to die for your sins and risen to give you life eternal, you will be placed in Him. He is God's final and only ark of salvation. He is the door of salvation, the only One through whom you can be saved.

He stands at the door of your life and knocks and says, "If anyone hears my voice and opens the door I will come into Him ..." If He comes into you and you come into Him you are in the ark of salvation and all that the ark is becomes yours!

Recently I shared this story of the two life saving arks, Noah's ark and the Saving ark of God's Son, with a man named Mike. He responded by saying that when I shared with him it was like God came into the room. He told me he got goose bumps, was scared and asked, "What shall I do? I told Him and he responded thoughtfully to the grace of God.

So what is your response? In Noah's day most of the world rejected his life saving message. Today there are still those that mock that Jesus is coming back to melt the present creation and make a new heaven and earth. Nevertheless, He is coming to save those who trust Him and to take vengeance upon those who will not receive His

message of life saving love. What about you? What will you do about Jesus' invitation to come to Him? If you do come to him you will step out on a new earth and heaven infinitely more wonderful than the new earth of Noah's day. It will be no small step but one giant leap into glory. Sing this song and mean it & you will never perish.
<http://www.youtube.com/watch?v=LUK6P_QmGjM>

The Star of Jacob
by Dean L.G.
Merry Christmas

A Star Shall Come Out of Jacob
(Numbers 24:17)
Star Out of Jacob bringing peace and love and light.
Star that leads me through earth's night.
O'er the hills of earthly ills
To the place his beauty fills,
To the baby gently sleeping
In the golden hay
While angels round you
Gather to your side and pray;
Long awaited Star of Jacob,
Star of old,
Star that led me to his fold.
In your light
My darkness is made bright
Humbling me in adoration
Finding there God's salvation.
Gazing on his gentle face
I find my joyful place,
Before the King of earth and sky and seas
Adoring now on bended knees.
<http://www.youtube.com/watch?

v=q5n6X9sUznl

The Stranger

I didn't write this. If anyone knows the author please let me know. Couldn't find who wrote it on the internet. Whoever wrote it, I am including it because it has a powerful, surprising end.

"A few months before I was born, my dad met a stranger who was new to our small Tennessee town. From the beginning, Dad was fascinated with this enchanting newcomer, and soon invited him to live with our family. The stranger was quickly accepted and was around to welcome me into the world a few months later. As I grew up I never questioned his place in our family. Mom taught me to love the Word of God. Dad taught me to obey it. But the stranger was our storyteller. He could weave the most fascinating tales. Adventures, mysteries and comedies were daily conversations. He could hold our whole family spellbound for hours each evening. He was like a friend to the whole family. He took Dad, Bill and me to our first major league baseball game. He was always encouraging us to see the movies and he even made arrangements to introduce us to several movie stars. The stranger was an incessant talker. Dad didn't seem to mind, but sometimes Mom would quietly get up - while the rest of us were enthralled with one of his stories of faraway places - and go to her room read her Bible and pray. I wonder now if she ever prayed that the stranger would leave. You see, my dad ruled our household with certain moral convictions. But this stranger never felt an obligation to honor them. Profanity, for example, was not allowed in our house - not from us, from our friends, or adults. Our longtime visitor, however, used occasional four-letter words that burned my ears and made Dad squirm. To my knowledge the stranger was never confronted. My dad was a teetotaler who didn't permit alcohol in his home - not even for cooking. But the stranger felt he needed exposure and enlightened us to other ways of life. He offered us beer and other alcoholic beverages often. He made cigarettes look tasty, cigars manly, and pipes distinguished. He talked freely (too much too freely) about sex. His comments were sometimes blatant, sometimes suggestive, and generally embarrassing. I know now that my early concepts of the man/woman relationship were influenced by the stranger. As I look back, I believe it was the grace of God that the stranger did not influence us more. Time after time he opposed the values of my parents. Yet he was seldom rebuked and never asked to leave. More than thirty years have passed since the stranger moved in with the young family on Morningside Drive. But if I were to walk into my parents' den today, you would still see him sitting over in a corner, waiting for someone to listen to him talk and watch him draw his pictures. His name? We always called him TV. Time after time, he opposed the values of my parents, yet he was seldom rebuked."

The Strongest People in the World

The strong people in the world are those who have the greatest trials and still trust God through them all. No matter their trial(s) they believe God is using it to bring about their own good eventually. They believe the sufferings of their lives are light in comparison to the glory and weight of blessing to come either in this life or the next. Job who lost everything except his wife and life sums it up, "Though he slay me yet will I trust Him." He was strong!

He lost his children, wealth and health and trusted God through it all. He got his health, wealth and wife's respect back with many more children than they lost. His final blessing outweighed his suffering in this life. Some never get their reward until after they die. They find that faith and love are stronger than death. They are the strongest people in the world. Listen to Andrea Crouch's song, "Through it All".

<https://www.youtube.com/watch?v=Bo-mp_m3nj8>

The Three Tenses of Salvation

Not long ago I shared with someone the Bible verse, "Now is my salvation nearer than when I first believed." My statement was based upon the Bible verse, Romans 13:11 which gives the final of three tenses of salvation. Since I already experienced salvation why did I say my

254

salvation is nearer than when I first believed? Many are not aware that salvation is in three tenses in a person's life when he or she trusts the Lord Jesus Christ as Savior. I experienced the first tense of salvation when I first accepted Christ as my Savior at age 20. At that time I experienced salvation from the penalty of sin. Then I explained that since then, for 62 years now, I've been experiencing salvation from the power of sin, learning to be saved from the practice of sin by having victory over it in two ways. The first way and the best victory comes through God's Spirit enabling me to defeat sin. Romans 8:11 Second, should I fail, I confess my sin and He is faithful and just to forgive my sin and cleanse me from all unrighteousness. 1John 1:9 Last, I will soon experience final salvation, saved from the very presence of sin forever.

Salvation is a gift that God gives in three tenses, salvation from the penalty, power and finally from its presence to perfection. Scripture tells us that after this life we are transported to the heavenly Jerusalem where we are part of and among those who are made perfect. So the final step in salvation is being made perfect forever. It happens completely when we see Jesus Christ. When we see Him we shall be like Him for we shall see Him as He is. 1John 3:2 Salvation starts with a partial but saving vision of Christ dying and rising for us and is completed when we get a total vision of Him face to face. So, final salvation means I, and all who trust Jesus, will be eternally perfect in body, soul, spirit, love, worship and holiness, doing only right forever. What a joy that will be in contrast to the growing evil on this present earth. God starts salvation past, present and completely finishes it in the future. God always

finishes what He starts. Phil. 1:6 I'm counting on it. How about you?

Salvation is nearer now than when I first believed. Sing about it.
<https://www.youtube.com/watch?v=rwLl5nY5WPI>

Star Wars in the Bible?
Star wars are definitely found in the Bible. One example of this is what happened during the days of a prophetess named Deborah in the Old Testament. The nation of Israel was subjected to the rule of a cruel Canaanite king named, Jabin. The people lived in continual fear of the king and his commander, Sisera.
Deborah, who was both a prophetess and a judge of Israel, tells us what it was like in Israel during those days.

"The highways were deserted,
And the travelers walked along the byways.
Village life ceased, it ceased in Israel,
Until I, Deborah, arose,"..."not a shield or spear was
seen among 40,000 in Israel." Judges 5:7,8

There was even more fear of the Canaanites than fear today from ISIS. The great fear lasted for 20 years until God told Deborah that Israel would defeat Sisera and king Jabin. So she gave God's command to her leader husband, Barak, to assemble an army of 10,000 men to go fight with king Jaban's army. Barak said he would only go and fight if she came with him. Deborah told Barak that the glory would go to a woman if she went with him.

After much prayer she did go with him. Sisera, with his 900 chariots and his army, was winning at first. Then the "stars fought in their courses" against Sisera's army. These stars fighting for Israel were angels. The Bible teaches that angels are sent by God to fight and care for his people. The angels sometimes control weather as seen in Revelation 7:1. A big rainstorm flooded the Kishon river and Sisera's chariots got stuck in the mud. Israel army totally defeated them. After the battle Sisera fled on foot to a tent where a woman named Jael lived. He thought she would help him. She gave him milk to drink, covered him up, and when he went to sleep she drove a tent peg through his head and killed him. Let us never put down the ability of women's faith and actions to enable great victories.

After defeating Sisera and king Jabin, Israel had peace for 40 years.

Today we do not **wrestle** against flesh and blood, but in prayer against spiritual hosts of wickedness in the heavenly places. Eph. 6:12 Our nations greatest need today is for Deborahs and Baraks who will wrestle in prayer on God's side enabling angelic help.

I read a true story about 9/11 where obviously the stars were fighting for one couple, Robert Matthews and his wife. They prayed for safety for his wife who was to catch a flight to California. On the way to the airport, they had a flat tire which they stopped to fix. She missed her flight. Later Robert's father who was a retired NYFD firefighter told them the flight she missed was the one that ran into the southern tower on 9/11. Then Robert, his son, shared Christ with his father but got no positive response. His retired father went to help at the 911 crash site and was killed. Robert was angry at God after his father died until a man and wife knocked on his door, and told this story, "The man explained to Robert that his wife had worked in the World Trade Center and had been caught inside after the attack. She was pregnant and had been caught under debris. He then explained that Robert's father had been the one to find his wife and free her. Robert's eyes welled up with tears as he thought of his father giving his life. His visitor then said, 'there is something else you need to know.' His wife then told Robert that as his father worked to free her, she talked to him and led him to Christ. Robert began sobbing at the news."

The stars in their courses fought for Robert Matthews, his wife, and his dad. God had acted on their behalf. As we pray to the true God and Father of our Lord Jesus Christ we too will find the stars fighting in their courses for us. We will enjoy the Star Wars movie but even more important are the true star wars being fought on behalf of God's people who know and trust Him. This song, *God Will Make a Way* captures what has just been said:, https://www.youtube.com/watch?v=1zo3fJYtS-o>

Choose God's Door
March 12, 2013

There ia a way that seems right to a man
but ends in death.
God grant he may abandon that way
before he takes his last breath.
Jesus said, "I am the way the truth and
the life. No man comes to the
Father except by me."
It cost Him his life. He is the true way
for you and it's free.
The gate is wide and the way broad that
leads to death and destruction.
The gate is straight and the road narrow
that lead to life's and salvation.
Christ is the door that leads to paradise
and the river of life.
Satan's way ends in the lake of fire and
endless strife.
So chose wisely while it is possible today.
The time will come when your choice will
pay.
Choose God's Door, His beloved Son.
Then in life and death you will have won!

The Ultimate Home
Throughout our lives we all have experienced many homes. Every home is filled with memories, some good, some bad. I spent an hour in my mind going through all the homes of my life, the lay out of each home, and the experiences there. You may want to take a moment and reflect on some of your homes.

Then ponder this thought. This world is not our final home. We are just passing through. All who follow and trust Jesus will inherit an ultimate home some day. Jesus spoke of that ultimate home when he said, "Do not let your hearts be troubled. You believe in God believe also in me. My Father's house has many mansions; if it were not so, I would have told you. I am going there to prepare a place for you. And if I go and prepare a place for you, I will come back and take you to be with me where I am." John 14:1-4

The apostle Peter also tells us of that ultimate home in his New Testament letter. He tells us us in 2 Peter 3:10-13 that "the day of the Lord will come like a thief (unannounced)...That day will bring about the destruction of the heavens by fire, and the elements will melt in the heat. But in keeping with His promise we are looking forward to a new heaven and a new earth, t**he home of righteousness.**

So our best and final home, as those who believe in God and in His Son, is yet to be when God takes us to our final home in a new heaven and earth which will be our home of righteousness. Everything will be right then. We will have new bodies not made of flesh and blood, bodies incapable of doing anything wrong. We will love God and each other perfectly without any hidden wrong motives and we will be loved by God and His people perfectly. No more sin, no more sorrow. All will be joy on that tomorrow. Our new home will have everlasting foundations since its builder and maker is God. Looking forward to that day when we will live together forever in the land of love..

I am going on 81 years of age now so I think more of that ultimate home and I seek to share the perfect hope of being

there with others. Do you have that perfect hope? If so, it will motivate you and I to live and love one another honorably and purely now and to care for and share our hope with others who may not yet have it. That hope and home is actually marvelous but as free as the sunshine. It is a gift. "The wages of sin is death but the gift of God is eternal life." Rom. 6:23. It is a gift to all who will admit their need and accept it. Jesus promises to never cast out anyone who comes to Him and believes and receives Him which includes an eternal home prepared by God, **John 6:37** "All that the Father gives Me will come to Me, and the one who comes to Me I will by no means **cast out**." God's word in the Bible is astonishingly good news . If you haven't will you receive that good news today? It is such a wonderful offer. Come to Him today and be made ready for God's new heaven and earth, the ultimate home of righteousness?

For a single blessing listen to this:https://www.youtube.com/watch?v=4ndMZqT6i4I>

For a double blessing listen to this: <https://www.youtube.com/watch?v=ZNrVed6dP6s&ebc=ANyPxKoK0ro_Hb Y-knWO1RFnsYrF1Ewill7TOSVzDqQk40Dp2fDCw7HrtAYWISt8JkDha9hwlDq3W491tS5iJpocnXUzlvgPsg>

The Ultimate Passover Lamb

The true story of Israel being set free from slavery in Egypt took place thousands of years ago due to the slaying of and application of the blood of a lamb to the top, and sides of Israelite doors. That application, called the Passover, saved the Israelites firstborn because the messenger of death passed over the homes of those who had blood on their doors, while at the same time killing

Pharaoh's firstborn which persuaded him to let all Israel go free. The Passover was the beginning of Israel's spiritual calendar to be celebrated each year at the beginning of Israel's first month called Abib or Nisan. It was to be a national-perpetual-reminder-celebration of how God kept His promise to free Israel from Egyptian slavery and bondage.

The Ultimate Passover story is in the New Testament. Jesus is called the Lord our Passover because He shed his blood to forgive and remove our sin. Today He can free both Jewish and Gentile people(non-Jews) from bondage to sin? There is a marvelous correlation between the first Passover and the final Ultimate Passover in the New Testament when Jesus shed His blood. So now all who believe in Jesus death have His blood applied to the doors of their lives and are set free forever from a greater bondage than Egyptian slavery. All are forgiven and freed forever from personal bondage and slavery to sin?

Israel as a nation no longer offers a sacrificial lamb nor applies the blood to their physical homes. Why not? Because that first Passover in Egypt is finalized in the last Passover. Jesus is a believer's Ultimate Passover Lamb. Behold, He is the Lamb of God who takes away the sin of the world.

Hosea 3:4,5 tells us that Israel will go many years without sacrificial lambs, without a king, and without priestly guidance.Then Hosea says Israel will in the latter days return to honoring and worshiping the Lord. The whole nation will be born anew spiritually some day when Jesus returns, rescues them and they realize Christ really is their Messiah. In that final time they will trust Jesus,

God's ultimate Passover Lamb. Then they who had been the tail of the nations shall become the head of the nations as they and all God's people rule and reign with Christ for a thousand years.

Sixty years ago I believed in and received God's Son who took away my sin and set me free to love and serve Him. That reception of the Lord, my Passover, was the beginning of my spiritual calendar a grand moment in my life! Soon I will shed this life and enter the final promised land where I'll never grow old. That is as sure as the fact that God's Ultimate Passover Lamb shed his blood for me and I am free.

If you, as an individual Gentile or Jew receive Jesus today, it will be a grand event in your life which, like me, you will celebrate forever. If you haven't received Him, do it today and God will pass over you and set you free forever! Sing and believe about it here: https://www.youtube.com/watch?v=w2VrRk4pZHY> & rejoice about it here: https://www.youtube.com/watch?v=hhxolymJ11Q>

Threads
March 12, 2013

Years ago I memorized a poem which sums up the life of one who knows the Lord. It goes like this:

The Weaver
by B.M.Franklin.

My life is but a weaving between my Lord and me.
I cannot chose the colors He works steadily.

Oft times he weaves sorrow and I in foolish pride
Forget he see the upper and I the underside.

Not till the loom is silent and the shuttles cease to fly
Will God unroll the canvas and explain the reason why.

The dark threads are as needful in the weavers skillful hand
As the the threads of gold and silver in the pattern He has planned.

I recently shared The Weaver poem at a memorial service of a lady named Dorothy Bailey. She had years of gold and silver experiences when her mind was intact and she walked with God. In those days the dark threads of sin in her life were replaced by the silver and gold threads of God's forgiveness. She experienced silver and gold threads of success in those days as a witness and seamstress. Then Alzheimer's took over and for many years she could not remember anything or anyone. Those were years of dark threads with no seemingly clear explanation.

What helps? The Bible tells us that people who know Jesus and suffer more have a greater release at death. Their reason is totally restored and enhanced. The silver and gold threads are seen in the risen perfection of their spirit and soul. Dorothy is now fully whole.

Though I have not known the threads of Alzheimer's disease, I too have experienced the dark threads in God's pattern for my life. Like the moon we all have a dark side. We are born with it. It is called sin. It manifests itself in many ways from rejection of God and mistreatment of others to lying, stealing, cheating, sexual sin, greed, selfishness , hatred, anger that is sinful, covetousness, self righteousness, religious pride, non-Biblical life styles. and hatred.

Coming to Christ as Savior forgives those dark threads and replaces them with God's gold and silver threads of love. He then begins to weave new patterns mixed with the old dark threads. We still have failures that are put to rest by our God who does not deal with us as our sins deserve but through the redemption of His Son removes them and replaces them with new desires to please Him.

The canvas of our lives takes on many forms but always Our Weaver works steadily in our lives to fill it with gold and silver threads. He entwines our sickness, our sorrows and even our death with joyous strands of beauty. He gives us beauty for our ashes. Then finally the day comes when the canvas is complete. At that moment we will see the Master's skill in shaping the patterns of our life for final glory(3). And we will say, "Well done good and faithful Savior!" All is perfect at your feet. We are complete! Your thoughts and plans for us who trusted You were for our eternal benefit. Thank You for the dark threads that led us to you. Thank You that when You unroll the canvas then we will know as we are known. We rejoice in You and thank you for both the dark threads and the gold and silver threads in the pattern you have planned. Hebrews 11:35 (2) Hebrews 12:23 (3) Jeremiah 29:11

The Woes of Self Exaltation-The Exaltation of Humility

Nothing is more clear in the Bible than the fact that pride destroys and humility exalts a person. The Pharisees in the Bible were proud, self exalting, blind leaders of the blind. In contrast Jesus showed humility more than any person who ever lived and He clearly taught the results of a person exalting himself verses the results of a person humbling himself: "And whoever exalts himself will be **humble**d, and he who **humble**s himself will be exalted." (Matt. 23:12) Nothing displays Jesus humility more that his Christmas birth, his life and his death. Then he was exalted from His humble death to the position of King of Kings and Lord of Lords.

Pride is spoken of in the Bible as being the "condemnation of the Devil." That condemnation follows all who follow the Devil to endless destruction. So it is best for us all to humble ourselves under the mighty hand of God and be forgiven to escape the final end of pride.

Pride is at the top of the list of the things God hates. One of the worst ways pride is seen is in believing we are good enough to earn God's forgiveness, God's heaven, God's love and God's presence. In the Bible Babylon the Great is shown as the ultimate in religious pride. People who think they can reach God through self effort as attempted by the builders of the Tower of Babel, display self righteousness which is abhorring to God. The Lord says of such people, "All their righteousnesses are as filthy rags."

On the other hand God says of those who humble themselves and believe in His unmerited grace reaching down to them so save them, "Who ever comes to Me I will in no way cast out." And He says of them, "All their righteousnesses are of Me." The Bible says it clearly, "For by grace(undeserved favor) are you saved and that not of yourself. It is the gift of God, not of works lest any man should boast." It goes on to say that good works are the result of God working in a humble person, not to save them, but as a result of God saving them. "For we are His workmanship, created in Christ Jesus for good works which God has prepared beforehand that we should walk in them." (Eph.. 2:8-10)

Pride says "I am as good or better than anyone else so God will accept me and let me in heaven because of my good works." Jesus response to that is, "I never knew you! Depart from me."

So where do you and I stand? Do you admit your utter and complete need of God's mercy and grace. Do I? My answer is in the song, "My hope is built on nothing less than Jesus blood and righteousness!" When I came to Christ at the age of twenty, fifty-nine years ago, I cried out to God and said, "I can't come to you without your help." He heard my prayer and enabled me to receive Him as my Savior.

Will you humble yourself if you have not yet received Him as your Savior? He will hear your cry for help and save you. He promised, "Whoever humbles himself will be exalted." What higher exaltation is there than being accepted, forgiven, regenerated, loved and kept by God forever! None that I know of. So please come to Him today if you haven't. If you have come to Christ, please pray for anyone who reads this and has not yet come to Him, to do so now. https://www.youtube.com/watch?v=mqnbLkSgMOY>

There's Love in the Air
(For All My Friends in Christ)

There's love in the air
So you need not despair
There's love in my heart for you.

There's joy up above
From the God of love
There's room in His heart for you.

You need not be blue
Our love's ever true
There's room in our hearts for you.

Soon we'll fly on a Dove
To the land of His love
There's room in His home for you.

There's a song in the air
It rides on each prayer.
Each answer means love for you.

Our song never ends
As we go on our way
There's Love in our hearts to stay.

So rejoice by His side
With your arms open wide.
Make room in your heart for love.

Theory of Everything or Revelation about Everything

Stephen Hawking has been working on a *Theory of Everything* for years. So far he thinks he has proven that the universe was created by a big bang. Whether or not the heavens and the earth started with a big bang we can be sure that **they will end with a big bang**. "...the day of the Lord will come as a thief in the night, in which the heavens will pass away **with** a great noise, and the elements will **melt with fervent heat**; both the earth and the works that are in it will be burned up... Nevertheless we, according to His promise, look for **new heavens and a new earth** in which righteousness dwells." 2Peter 3:10,13

Personally I prefer the revelation of everything we need to know more than a theory of everything. The Bible reveals clearly the birth of the universe, the stars, the earth and even you and me. It tells us that all things were created by God, the Word who spoke everything into existence and continues to uphold it all today. "In the beginning God created the heavens and the earth. The earth was without form, and void; and darkness *was* on the face of the deep. And the Spirit of God was hovering over the face of the waters. Then God said, "Let there be light"; and there was light." Genesis 1:1-3 "All things were made by him; and without him was not any thing made that was made." John 1:3 For of him, and through him, and to him, are all things: to whom be glory for ever. Amen. Romans 11:36 "The celestial realms announce God's glory; the skies testify of His hands' great work." Psalm 19:1 All of creation daily & silently shouts out the reality of God. To reject the reality of God, the Bible says twice, is to be a fool.

Life is more than evolution's cool-aid-drink,
for truly missing is the missing link.
Dig in the ground and find each fossil, God
still stands infinitely colossal.
Check with your instruments & microscope,
leave God out and you have no hope.
Ok, measure the light of a sunlit streak but
God alone makes the rainbow speak.
Make an A Bomb, a hydrogen and a cobalt,

Such power to God is weak as a drink of
malt.
Give Him a straw. He'll drain it dry.
After all, He just spoke and Jesus made the
sky.
Disprove the maker of the universe? Never
says the Bible's first verse.
In the Beginning God created the heaven
and the earth. He caused the world's birth!

Believe in Him. Seek Him until you find Him.Then He who commanded the light to shine out of darkness will shine in your heart to reveal the light of the glory of God in the face of His Son, Jesus Christ. He who created the world's birth will create in you a new heart of endless worth. 11Cor.5:17 Sing about it here: <https://www.youtube.com/watch?v=u5Or_gP_3ql&spfreload=10>

Three Rs for Our Nation

When I was in grammar school 71 years ago I was taught reading, writing and arithmetic but the school did not teach me to remember the original foundation upon which our nation was built. That foundation at first in the 1600s was religion, meaning belief in the God of the Bible and in His Son, Jesus Christ. It meant **remembering** morality, and doing **right** from God's perspective as clearly taught in the Bible. That included admitting that one was a sinner, **repenting**, calling wrong, wrong and trusting in God's forgiveness which enables and creates a desire to **return** to right by learning to love God and man.

Early American schools, churches and families were encouraged to teach the three Rs of **remembering** what God says, **repenting** from sin and **returning** to and believing the one true God. It did not mean any religion is good or productive. Since those early days revisionism has changed freedom of religion to mean any religion which is far removed from its original meaning.

Religions that do not support our constitution but teach its okay to take others lives who don't believe as they do, is the opposite of what freedom of religion means. People who come to our country need to be vetted and clearly reject any religious beliefs that seek to put to death those who don't believe as they do.

As a Christian I am glad to vet myself. Christianity teaches me to love others even though they may not believe as I do. That does not mean i have to agree with everyone about marriage, morality, politics, but I am to love them with the hope and prayer that they might adopt truth about God. God today is patient, desiring that men, women, boys and girls might come to the knowledge and acceptance of God's will and plan for their lives. Though failing to do right deserves death from God's standpoint, He still allows people to live as they wish with His desire for them to come to repentance and faith in His will and way for them. He sends his rain on the just who trust Him and the unjust who don't trust Him. So I too should be kind to both those who trust Him and to those who don't. I should love the stranger and the immigrant but that person must put himself under our constitution and laws of our land. If he clearly rejects our constitution and laws that are just then he must not be allowed in our land. Immigrants should be required to vow to uphold our constitution. They should agree to the fact that we in America are given the rights to life, liberty and the legitimate pursuit of happiness. But woe to them or any of us who violate laws that are clearly right. Authorities of the state do not carry weapons against wrong and the right to arrest without reason.

Swift justice is right against anyone of us who acts unjustly. We have freedom of speech but vile cursing, rioting, robbing, murdering, and burning and destroying property, should be justly punished and stopped by those delegated authority by God. Freedom of speech should not include vile language against authorities and leaders.

Let us as a nation **remember** and return to the days in our country when right ruled more clearly, when people were willing to **repent** of wrong doing and **return** continually to the true God to whose authority we must all give account. Let's remember that whether one believes it or not, all who have been delegated authority will answer to the Highest Authority, to the judge of all the earth, to the Father of Lights who shall eventually banish all darkness.

Through Flood, Fire, Blood to Freedom?

There are many heart breaking things going on today which often bring tears to my and other people's eyes. I'm reminded of the behavior of mankind during the time of Noah mentioned in Gen. 6:5 "God saw how great the wickedness of the human race had become on the earth, and that every inclination of the thoughts of the human heart was only evil all the time."

We are told that this evil grieved God. Finally, God had enough evil. Most of us know the story about the world wide flood God sent upon the earth. Everyone drowned except for a man named Noah, his wife and their three sons and their wives. They found freedom in a God-designed -ark that carried them safely through the flood.

After the flood God promised to never again wipe out all mankind with a world wide flood. He then put the rainbow in the sky to remind Himself and us of His promise. The rainbow represents His glory which reminds us still that He has kept His promise for many thousands of years.

How do you suppose God feels about what is going on in the world today? Once Jesus, during his life on earth, observing what was going on among most people said, "How often I would have gathered you as a hen gathers her chicks under her but you would not come to me." Again God says, "All day long I have stretched forth my hands to a disobedient and contrary people." He still reaches out today to everyone desiring all to come to Him to escape a worse catastrophe than the world wide flood.

God has kept his promise about not destroying the world with a flood but most don't realize that some day God is going to send something worse than a flood. A day is coming when God will destroy not just the earth but both heaven and earth. How will he do it? By a huge explosion and fire! The Bible tells us this in 1Peter 3:10-12, "But the day of the Lord will come like a thief. The heavens will disappear with a roar; the elements will be destroyed by fire, and the earth and everything done in it will be laid bare. **11** Since everything will be destroyed in this way, what kind of people ought you to be? You ought to live holy and godly lives **12** as you look forward to the day of God and speed its coming. That day will bring about the destruction of the heavens by fire, and the elements will melt in the heat."

Today the place of safety and freedom is not in an ark but in a person, in God's Son. If you come to God believing in His Son's death for you to take away your sin and forgive you, He will save you through the final explosion of heaven and earth. If you confess with your mouth that Jesus is Lord and believe in your heart that God has raised him from the dead, He will save you from being wiped out on the day of His judgement when he destroys all who reject Him by fire. Instead of being blown away, you will go through that day unscathed, unshaken, saved forever to walk on the shores of a new eternal heaven and earth.

How about it? Will you or have you come to Christ today and been set free from cataclysmic destruction?.

John 3:16 "God so loved the world(that's you) that He gave His only begotten Son, that whosoever(that could be You!) believes in him, should not perish but have everlasting life." That is real freedom! If the Son shall set you free, you shall be free indeed! He leads His own on to freedom through flood, fire and His blood. Sing about it here:
<https://www.youtube.com/watch?v=AMU0G7pTeLo>

To Bow Or Not to Bow

There are those who for one reason or another will not now believe that Jesus Christ is Lord. Some argue that Jesus was

1. a great teacher but not the Lord to whom belief, obedience and worship is due. 2. just one of many ways to heaven all religions being equally acceptable thereby rejecting Jesus as Lord. 3. a myth who never really did the miracles attributed to Him, nor did He defeat death rising from the dead. 4. a person who lived but man's "higher textual criticism" proves the Bible unreliable and full of contradictions.

Here's the good news for some and the bad news for others: Every knee shall bow and every tongue confess that Jesus Christ is Lord to the glory of God the Father.

The four false reasons given above for not believing in Jesus fail the test of time and truth.

Ever one who does not believe and receive Jesus now as Lord will bow their knee and confess with their mouth that He is Lord after they die. Only it will be too late! Jesus said, "il you don't believe that I am he(the Lord, the way, the truth, the life, the Christ, the Son of God & only Savior) you will die in your sins and cannot come where I am" You can reject the One who loves you and died and rose to save you from your sins BUT you will believe, bow and confess He is Lord in eternity! Their will be no reason, purgatory or higher court of appeal to opt out bowing. That's the bad news.

The good news is that it is not to late now to bow your knee to Jesus. If you confess with your mouth that He is Lord and believe in your heart that God has raised Him from the dead now, you will be saved from your sin and raised at death to be with Him forever. It's your choice to believe the good news and bow now or you can bow too late and experience the bad news. Don't be among those of whom Jesus said, "You won't come to me that you might have life."Be among those who come to Him and find life abundant both now and forever.

If you haven't believed the good news and bowed to Jesus as Lord, will you do it now? That's Jesus' desire and my prayer for you. Love to you, Dean.

Here this Song in Cambodian and then in English and believe it and you will know the truth that sets you free from the lies of man: <http://www.youtube.com/watch?v=JBys0_rlxoo>

Letter to Kirsten

Kirsten,

Here is a poem by Sandra Goodwin which really touched my heart. I think it will touch yours too. It is called TRAVELING ON MY KNEES. Though I can't be with you there I can by prayer. Here it is:

Last night I took a journey
To a land across the seas.
I didn't go by ship or plane--
I traveled on my knees.

I saw so many people there
In bondage to their sin,
And Jesus told me I should go,
That there were souls to win.

But I said, "Jesus I can't go
To lands across the seas."
He answered quickly, " Yes you can-
By traveling on your knees."

He said, "You pray, I'll meet the neeed.
You call, and I will hear.
Its up to you to be concerned
For lost souls far and near."

And so I did, I knelt in prayer,
Gave up some hours of ease,
And with the Savior by my side
I traveled on my knees.

As I prayed on, I saw souls saved
And twisted persons healed.
I saw God's workers' strength renewed
While laboring on the field.

I said, "Yes Lord, I'll take the job.
Your heart I want to please.
I'll heed Your call and swiftly go
By traveling on my knees.
Remember that your mom, Grandma and Grandpa and many others are traveling with you every day with our prayers. And we are asking Him for great and mighty things for you and all your team. May you be spiritual mothers and fathers to nations!
Love, Grandpa

There's Treasure in the Lord

There's Treasure in the Lord my friend-
He gave His life to save your soul,
He rose to live again.
He's coming soon to claim his own,
Won't you believe, believe in Him today?

There's power in the Lord my friend
He holds the world in its place.
He set the stars in space.
He"ll lift your load of sin today.
Won't you believe, believe in Him today?

There's grace in the Lord my friend.
He left the glory of His throne
He died for you alone,
He showed His love in every way
Won't you believe, believe in Him today?

There's truth in the Lord my friend.
His words are sure; they will endure.
Though heaven and earth will pass away.
Won't you believe, believe in Him today?

There's life in the Lord my friend
He conquered death; he split the tomb.
He lives in heaven for you.
Won't you believe, believe in Him today?

There's growth in the Lord my friend
He wants to live His life anew; He wants to
grow in you.
So listen and do His word , my friend.
And you will grow, will grow in Him today.

There's glory in the Lord my friend
He's gone away to prepare a place for those
He loves my friend.
He's coming soon to take them home.
Won't you believe, believe in Him today?

There's Treasure in the Lord my friend
I know the riches of His grace, I've seen the
glory in His face
He is the Rock full of precious jewels.
I have believed, I have received Him, today!

Trip to Two Cities. One Great, the other Greatest!

My last trip took those who went with me on a ride to The Land Of Beginning Again. Today we are headed to two great cities. They are far away so join me in my private plane. We fly first over the sea of humanity to a city set on seven hills. It is called Babylon the Great. It is a city admired and thought great by many.

At first this city was economically and religiously great. It was ruling over kings and rulers throughout the world. In fact the city was seen as a woman who thought herself a Queen who would never be a widow nor ever see sorrow. Yet in reality she was the mother of whores and her offspring were full of all the abominations, idolatries, adulteries and evils of the earth.

She got her inspiration from a scarlet beast, Satan, upon which she rode, and she was supported by a false prophet, and an anti-Christ whose evil kings and rulers gave her power and authority. She was clothed in purple and scarlet and covered with gold and precious stones. In her hand was a golden cup raised in a toast to fulfill her drunkenness on the blood of righteous saints, men and women who stood up for Jesus and rejected her self righteous glory   She enjoyed being

drunk with the blood of the called, chosen and faithful followers of Jesus who worshipped the true God.

On that first trip I heard a voice from heaven calling out to all of God's people to come out of her, the city of evil so that they will not share in her sins and and her coming plagues.

Forward to the future: We see the site of that great city. Looking down we see it has been utterly destroyed. On one day in one hour all has been lost. All that can be seen is smoke rising up from where she had once been. I wondered at it all. What happened? Then I heard a voice from heaven explain it. A greater city with a Greater Ruler and a greater offspring had totally defeated Babylon the Great. That Ruler is Jesus. The city is Jerusalem the Golden. She is Jesus' Bride.

Babylon the Great, bride of Satan and her inspirers had made war with Jesus, the Lamb. He conquered them all. In one day and one hour He wiped out Babylon the Great. As quickly as one can throw a large stone into the sea so Babylon is gone, out of sight, drowned in her sea of sin. Thrown into the lake of Fire, never again shall the dethroned Queen rule over the earth.

Let's leave this sight. Come, let us fly to a greater city. There we see from my plane a new scene. Below us is a new Jerusalem, a Golden City which will never pass away. It is the Bride of Christ. She and all that trust God will reign over the earth first for a thousand years and then forever.

Babylon the Great will lose everything. Jesus and His Bride will win everything. Are you today a part of Babylon the great which is yet to fall, in which never again will there be singing, music, riches and wealth? Or are you part of the New Jerusalem whose music will never end, whose spiritual riches and wealth shall endure forever?

It all depends on whether or not you hear God's call to come out of Babylon to believe in the grown Babe of Bethlehem who died for your sins and arose to give you eternal life and make you part of His eternal city. Come out now if you haven't to Jesus the author and finisher of faith and salvation. If you do, you will understand and enjoy our trip to these two cities, Babylon the Great and Jerusalem, the Greatest!

This trip was inspired by Revelation, chapter 17 to 21. Sing about it. Click here: <https://www.youtube.com/watch?v=54jXxagNjvU>

A True Pet Story About a Cat Named Tripod

Dear Dana,

You might like this story my granddaughter shared with me. She lives with three young gals, 21,22 and 23 years old. She was totally delivered from addictions at age 20 and now has an amazing love for people. The three girls recently adopted a stray cat with only three legs they named Tripod.

The cat was sickly. One girl who is not a pet fan didn't welcome Tripod at first. Then one day the other two girls were at work and she was home with the cat. As she looked at it she felt the Lord was telling her Tripod was going to die. She talked to my granddaughter on the phone about it who advised her to wrap it in a warm blanket. A few hours later Tripod did die.

When my granddaughter came home and after they took care of its "funeral' she said to the other girl who has had a hard time believing God will take care of her needs, "You know that Jesus says he values animals noticing every sparrow that falls to the ground as well as the lilies of the field and He provides their needs. Jesus says you are more valuable than many sparrows and flowers. That means cats too. He values them all and He values you more and will take care of you. The girl lit up and responded by believing, "He will take care of me. I

need not worry about how much I have as long as I have Him to care for me."

The result was a changed and peace filled heart.

Being a dog lover yourself I'm sure Jasper appreciates your love and I hope you believe the love God has for you even beyond your love for Jasper. God proved His love for us that even while we were weak, helpless and falling short of what we should be, He died for us and rose again to offer us life eternal, love and grace forever as a gift. The gift of God is eternal life. Have you received that love, Dana? I hope so and pray for you.

Triumph Over Tragedies

In life people experience all kinds of tragedies. Some examples are the loss of a love, or a loved one, a dying marriage, divorce, unruly children, moral failure, bankruptcy, blindness, deafness, a crippling car accident, paralysis, and cancer. All of these cause grief and pain. Yet there have been folks who triumphed over them. Examples are **Helen Keller and Fanny Crosby** whose blindness led to fame, **Joni Eareckson Tada** whose paralysis has led to the blessings of millions, the **Apostle Paul,** who forgiven for murdering Christians, became one himself and blessed the world. They all triumphed over tragedies.

Of all the tragedies we must face in life, death is the greatest. Not long after we are born we realize that someday we have to die. So what can we do about it? Some refuse to acknowledge it. Randolph Hearst would not allow people to use the word death in his presence. While people don't like to think of death, any sane person knows it is a reality we must all face. The Bible says, "It is appointed to us once to die and after that the judgement." People might argue about the judgment that follows death but no one can deny that it is "appointed to man once to die..."

The fool does not face reality. The wise man and woman face it head on and ask the question, "How can I triumph over death?"

The answer is that Jesus died for us, the just for the unjust, that He might bring us home to God through death. He died then arose from the dead three days later. He was seen after he rose from the dead by over 500 witnesses on ten different occasions.The evidence for Christ's triumph over death is overwhelming. What jury in the land would not accept the agreeing, eyewitness account of over 500 people? Not one! Unless they are brain dead.

That which makes true Christianity different than religion is that Jesus defeated death, came back to life and He offers all who come to Him the blessing of eternal life . Here are His words, "I am the Resurrection and the life: he that believes in me though he were dead, yet shall he live and whosoever lives and believe in me shall never die(John 11;25,26)."

What did he mean? When we trust Christ death loses its sting. The grave loses its victory. Our mortal bodies will put on immortality. We are more than conquerors through Jesus. A conqueror may win a great battle but afterward die. If he dies not knowing Christ as His savior, He is a loser in the end. So we who trust Christ are more than conquerors because our victory goes beyond the battle with death into life eternal in God's new heaven and on His new earth.

When I die I want this written on my tombstone, "When you pass by don't bother to cry. Lift your head up high and look into the sky. Because Jesus rose, so will I."

What about you? No matter how hard our life now, if in the end we triumph over death we will be more than conquerors through Him who loves us. Jesus Christ wants you to be triumphant in life and death. He wants to be your Savior from both physical and spiritual death. Here's how to receive Him if you haven't: Romans 10:9,10. Read it. Believe it. Settle it. Rejoice in it. Share it. Sing It! <http://www.youtube.com/watch?v=0JMiUT6btb4&feature=related>

by DLG

I am a great fan of real evolution. By evolution I mean a process of change. No one can deny that change takes place. But we must examine that change and determine if it is real. For example, no one can't deny that changes have taken place within species. Horses have changed through time. But they are still horses. Humans have changed through time but they are still humans. I have changed through time from a baby to a child, to a teen, to an adult, to an older adult. But I am still a person. I haven't evolved into another species.

While I believe in evolution as I have just explained it, I reject with all due disrespect those pseudo scientists who have flooded our schools and world with the false and utterly ridiculous notion that one species evolved into another, and it all happened by chance. The Bible says in Psalm 100:3 says, "Know that the LORD he *is* God: *it is* he *that* has made us, and **not we** ourselves; *we are* his people, and the sheep of his pasture."

It is total nonsense to think and teach that man came from a cell floating in the sea. Then the cell changed into a creature that migrated to land. Then it turned into modern man. The missing link is still missing!

"A million years before our time,
Some protoplasmic cells-just listen now-
First got their heads together, anyhow,
There wasn't any conscious plan or scheme
of any kind,
The cell contained the ooze, the ooze the
plan,
The plan grew restless and the game began!
Oh omnipotent cell of which the sages tell,
Progenitor of worlds and all this bloomin
universe that whirls,
Of all that was or is or is to be,
Let all the fools bow down and worship thee."

I am not the author of the poem above.

But there is a wonderful,, marvelous evolution that has taken place through time in the lives of many humans. It is the most glorious change a   person can experience this side of heaven. The Bible tells about it clearly. It says in "2Cor. 5:17 Therefore **if any man** *be* in Christ, *he is* a new creature: old things are passed away; behold, all things are become new. 2Cor. 5:17 Therefore, if anyone is in Christ, he is a new creation; the old has gone, the new has come!"

Being in Christ brings about the greatest change a person can experience now. He or she knows in whom they have believed. His name is Jesus Christ who is the way to God, the truth of God and the life of God. Those who know HIm know where they came from, why they are here and where they are going. They have passed from spiritual death to life. Because they believe in God's Son who died for them, they are born anew. They have become new creations. That is the true triumph of real evolution!

Since Jesus came into their hearts old attitudes, old ways of thinking, old sinful behavior change.. And as they renew their minds and hearts through Christ they change even more. All who put their trust in Him will have a final triumphant evolution as they shed the old life down here and get a new body and endless life in heaven. Praise God for that kind of evolution. Have you experienced it?

Here is a song that shows the joy of having Christ in one's life. Listen to it and rejoice if it is true of you.   <http://www.youtube.com/watch?v=QqN7qeuy9K4>

May love and real evolution be yours, Dean

True Friendship

Perfect Friend, the Lord Jesus, Best Friend and lover... my wife.

Other Friends.......They love you, but they're not your lover. All care for you, All sharpen you, All share your joys and your sorrows. All weep with you when you weep. All rejoice with you when you rejoice. All forgive and forget your sins & mistakes. All encourage you by keeping in touch. All respond to your questions if they can. All listen to what you share.All pray with and for you regularly. All help lift you when you're down. All like to talk to you and be around you. All are ready to share their hearts. All Laugh with you. All Protect you like a DAD. All Care for you like a MOM. All Tease you like a SISTER. All joke and kid with you like a BROTHER. All play with you like a Cousin. All love you like God

A nice place to be is in the THOUGHTS of All! A nicer place to be is in the the PRAYERS of All! All my friends are in my thoughts and prayers continually. My desire for them all is to be in the best place- In................. God's Hands!
This is sent to you In our Perfect Friends love,
Dean

What Is A True Friend Like?
DLG

Consider 10 characteristics of a true friend. A true friend: 1. shows   love to you whenever possible.   2. is a good listener. 3. answers your questions. 4. takes the initiative to share their heart. 5. isn't too busy to respond to your concerns & helps you when asked 6. only wounds you with words   in love that you might heal. 7. keeps promises. 8. overlooks or forgives your faults. 9. helps you up if you fall & is willing to die for you. 10. prays for you and with you and wants to be around you.

On a scale of 1-10 with 10 being highest how would you rate yourself as being a true friend to someone? How would you rate someone you consider being a true friend to you?

Jesus is a 10 as a friend because He fulfills all of the characteristics of a true friend. 1. Having loved His own which are in the world, he loved them to the uttermost. 2. His ears are attentive to our cry. 3. In Him are hidden all the treasures of wisdom and knowledge. 4. I have made known to you all things the Father has told me. 5. Whoever comes to me I will not cast out & I will ever live to make intercession for you. 6. I am the good shepherd. I give my life for you. 7. The promises in 'Christ are yes and amen. He keeps his promises to you. 8. He said to a sinner,"Your sins are forgiven friend." 9. Take up you bed and walk. 10. I pray for them that they may be kept from evil and the evil one. I will never leave you or forsake you. I go to prepare a place for you that where I am you may be also.

The perfect 10 was made sin for us that we might be with Him forever. We are his friends if we do what He asks and He asks us to love Him and others. To be a true friend is to be like Jesus and to be a friend to Him and others.

Listen to the song about Jesus being a friend. What Ia A True Friend Like? Listen to the song about Jesus being a friend. <http://www.youtube.com/watch?v=KM2kbogwgBM>

Truth & Lies -The Truth Test!
DLG

Jesus was confronted by Israel's governor Pilate with a question, Pilate therefore said to Him, "Are You a king then?" Jesus answered, "You say *rightly* that I am a king. **For this cause** I was born, and **for this cause** I have come into the world, that I should bear witness to the truth. Everyone who is of the truth hears My voice." Pilate said, "What is truth?" Jesus answers that question later. Not only was everything Jesus said the truth, He is truth! As He said it , "I am the way, the truth and the life. No one comes to the Father but by me."

To know Him is to know truth! It is to be set free from the consequences of sin, to be forgiven and to have eternal life.

To reject Him is to be a recipient of a lie. Who is A liar but he who rejects Jesus as truth. Truth sets us free. (1John 2:22,23) "Whoever denies that Jesus is the Christ is a liar and the truth is not in him or her! "Whoever denies the Son does not have the Father either; he who acknowledges the Son has the Father also.

If you do not believe in Jesus you could remain a liar. Of course you don't have to remain a liar. In Hebrews 4:7 God says, "**Today**, **if you** will hear His voice, Do not harden **you**r

hearts." If you open your heart to Him, You can pass the truth test today. Who do you believe Jesus Christ is? Peter got it right as have all His true followers saying and believing, "You are the Christ, the Son of the living God."

He that has the Son has life. He that does not have the Son does not have life but the wrath of God remains on him! Read John 3 and believe verse 16. "God so loved the world(you) that whosoever(you) believes in Him shall not perish but have eternal life." If you open your heart now to Him you will pass the truth test and have both the Son and God the Father.

Have you passed the truth test? Is Christ now, today your truth and life? Sixty one years ago I heard the good news I have just shared with you. He kept His promise and I believed and passed the truth test. Have you? Once you come to Him, He will never let you go nor ever forsake you. When I came to Christ a chaplain told my mom. "Your son has just had a deep religious experience. It will all pass away in a little while." How wrong he was. Over sixty years have gone by and it has not passed away and never will because He that began the good work of salvation in me will complete it. Sing this song now and believe it and He will never let you go either! Amen1

<https://www.youtube.com/watch?v=nt69WDtYNLo>

Turning Shortages into Surpluses
Trials into Triumphs
by DLG

What did Mary in the New Testament have in common with Pharaoh in the Old Testament? In a time of shortage they both advised the people wisely to go to a man in tune with God for help. Mary told the servants, at the wedding of Cana, when there was a shortage of wine, to "go to Jesus and do whatever He says."

Pharaoh in a time of shortage of food in Egypt told the people to "go to Joseph and do whatever he says."

In both cases in Cana and Egypt the shortage problem was solved. Why? Because the people went to the Lord or Jesus who turned water into wine and the trial was turned into a triumph. In Egypt the people went to Joseph who had prepared for a shortage of food by storing up food in preparation for a famine. So a shortage was also turned into a surplus and the trial was turned into a triumph.

We learn from this to go to Jesus and to those God blesses with wisdom in our times of trials and. shortages. Got any shortages of patience, love, joy, peace, kindness, goodness, faith, humility, self-control, food, forgiveness, fellowship, fun, wisdom, unbelief, worship, purpose? Take your burden to the Lord and leave it there. Do I hear an Amen out there?

< https://www.youtube.com/watch?v=kHzIKHsAsB8>

Two Kinds of Blindness

The Bible teaches clearly that their are two kinds of blindness. One is physical. The other is spiritual. A group of us were sitting around talking at my house when the subject of God speaking to us came up. One guest said, "God doesn't speak to anyone." Most in the room did not agree with him. Actually, God is speaking all the time. It is just that some folks are spiritually blind and deaf and do not hear Him.

For those who have eyes to see and ears to hear creation silently shouts the reality of God. The heavens declare the glory of God and the firmament shows his handiwork. Day to day lectures on the reality of God. Night to night gives us lessons on His creative power. There is no place on earth where there voice cannot be heard. Yet, many do not hear the voice of God speaking through His creation. Why not?

They have ears but they can't hear, eyes but they can't see. Jesus says, "You will not come to the light that you might have life." The light shines in darkness, but the darkness does not comprehend it. Who ever comes to Jesus, the Light of the world, finds new spiritual eyes and new spiritual ears.

Jesus tells us that if we admit our spiritual blindness and come to Him, He will open our eyes to see and our ears to hear. He said, "I am the light of the world. Whoever comes to Me shall not walk in darkness but shall have the light of life."

God speaks to us through the book of creation, nature, and through the book of revelation, the Bible. If you want to hear God speak, seek Him in both creation and in the inspiration of His word. When on earth Jesus opened the eyes of the blind and the ears of the deaf many times. He still does that today. We all need to go to Jesus and say, "Lord I would like to receive my sight. I want to see spiritually. Lord I would like to receive my hearing. I want to hear your voice spiritually."

Jesus promises to hear you and answer that prayer for He said, "Whoever comes to me I will in no way cast out." His promise is as real today as it was when he first uttered the promise on earth to receive whoever comes to Him. At the age of 20 I was standing in a church holding a hymn book. The song being sung was "Be in time. Be in time. While the voice of Jesus calls you be in time." I asked God to help me come to Him and He did. My life has never been the same since. Once I was blind. But now I can see. The Light of the world IS Jesus! Will you come to Him? If you do you will never regret it. Listen to this song on You Tube and believe it and God will give you spiritual eyes to see and spiritual ears to hear: <http://www.youtube.com/watch?v=ovYPQI93zro>

Ultimate Self Esteem

These days there is a big emphasis on having and imparting self esteem to ourselves and others. By self esteem we mean having a feeling of self worth, that we are valuable and important.

Certainly we all want to feel worth something. How do we get that feeling? We can get it from our parents who show us love and care or we can get the opposite if our parents don't show us love and care. We can get it from a job well done, from a victory won, even from a spouse we call hon.

I'm reminded of a true story about a man who was sent to San Quentin for crimes he committed. He had never felt loved by anyone. But his father visited him in jail and changed his whole attitude. For the first time in his life his dad told him he loved him. That so gave him a sense of his self worth that he decided to be a model prisoner, which he was. Then he got news that his dad had died. He fell apart. He began misbehaving and getting in all kinds of trouble. The warden at the time, Warden Duffy was a compassionate carrying person. He visited the man in his cell and asked him what happened. When told about his dad dying who loved him and no one else was cared for him, Warden Duffy said, "I love you." He helped the man and the man changed again. After getting out of prison his feeling of self worth intact, he spoke to young people and sought to help them by showing them love.

When we feel we are worth something we show it in the way we live. This is an example of the power of love to give someone self worth.

The ultimate sense of self worth comes from a relationship with someone who can love you forever. Only one person now qualifies for that position. His name is the Lord Jesus Christ. He gave himself for you to takes away the guilt of any faults or failures you have so that you can be free from them. He imparts to you new life and love and instills you with character as a gift from Himself. His love is the greatest because it not only takes away our failures but imparts a new ability to be spiritually, mentally, and socially acceptable.

His love gives me ultimate self worth because it also frees me from the fear of death and guarantees me life beyond the grave.

Fame, fortune, romance, human success may give a temporary sense of self worth but only God's eternal love as shown in His Son's love for me guarantees me eternal self worth. He wants me to be with Him forever. And He has made it possible because He lives forever and I shall live forever with Him in heaven.

God's love for me gives me my ultimate feeling of self worth. It is the best. God gave the best so we could be at our best.

Here is a song that can give you a sense of your worth: Just click on it and in a couple of minutes it will come up for you to enjoy.

<http://www.youtube.com/watch?v=mHQQ7PomylE>

Love to you,
DUnited Forever

Wayne,

I was thinking about when you and I took Dad's and Mom's ashes out that day and spread them in the river. These are my thoughts, about that day and a final day to come.
Dean

My Hope and Confident Trust For a Final Day

No grave stone for my mom and dad
On earth they were together while I was a little lad.

Then divorce took them apart for many years.
When they died and turned to ashes my brother and I shed tears.

Together we mingled their ashes in a crystal stream's flow
Saying a prayer together as we watched them go.

As I thought about it deeply today
My thoughts and hopes lept forward to a brighter day-

A day when men and women will no longer be married as on earth.(1)
When all who trust Christ will rise to a new birth.

It will be a birth like a dream where no sin, hurt or pain can divide His own
When lost loves and broken friendships are banished by His throne!

But it is more than a dream for it will really come true
When God in eternity makes all things new!

The dead in Christ will rise first as Christ enjoined
Then we who are alive and remain with them will be rejoined.

This hope is surer than the rising sun
For we have the promise of the truthful One!

He is the way, the truth and the life.
We who believe His promise will see the end of strife.

God saves the best until last.
And sure as God lives and breathes all that hurts will be past!

We will live again on a new heaven and earth
After death leads us on to our final birth.(2)

All tears will be wiped away and love will finally come to stay
As God unites us all in that final day!(3)

Jesus clearly teaches that when men and women leave this life
they are no longer married nor are they given in marriage. This is
contrary to some false teaching but solves the great problem of
banishing the results of earthly divorce, and broken friendships.
Proof of this is found in Matthew 12:25

UP
My Poem For Forever Friends

Up, up, up we shall fly
Higher than a bird through the sky
We will meet the LORD in the air
So long earth's sorrow and care

Up, up, up we shall arise
Say good bye to earth's demise.
Gaze on the glory of His face
Say goodbye to earth's dark place.

Up, up, up to lift love's cup
Drink it anew with our King
Dance with Him and sing
Raptured to heaven's startup fling

Up, up, up to His city fair
Built by Jesus flying through the air
To a city with a jeweled foundation
With new bodies matching His creation

Like Abraham we looked for a City
Whose builder and maker is God
Gone, cities made of sod
We've golden streets to trod

Up, up, up when we hear his shout
When faith stamps out all doubt
We'll fly so free to join Him there
O blessed UP, when we meet Him in the air.

<https://hymnary.org/text/
in the land of fadeless day>

Valentine
Reflection for Gloria from Dean

You've come away to be my love
And we have shared the things above,
Where heights and depths of love divine,
Unite our hearts as they entwine..

We''ve rested in Him our true Rock
Who gently leads and feeds His flock.
By still waters where He leads
We''ve joyed in Him who meets our needs.

Though trials came and trials have gone
Our love in Him has thrived and grown.
And when we breathe our last on earth
We'll rise rise to heaven's final birth-

A new birth of love and grace
Ours as we gaze upon His face.
Love will come full circle with no delay
In our final home in God's eternal day!

So come away once more and still be my love
And we will exalt in heaven above.
Where heights and depths of love entwine
Uniting our hearts with joy divine!.

Victoriously Handicapped

Jacob wrestled with God and both he and God won. I had a discussion with a friend who disagreed with me and said Jacob didn't win but got a bad case of sciatica. While getting sciatica may be true we need to look at the rest of the story in Genesis 32.

Jacob was about to have a fearful meeting with his brother, Esau. At one time Jacob feared his brother would kill him because he stole their Father's blessing through deception. He also stole his brother's birthright. Jacob was a supplanter, a trickster who was out for himself at the cost of others. After 20 years being away from home, he returned with a big family and lots of live stock and wealth.

Jacob knew he was going to meet his brother and was troubled about it. So he put all of his family and goods on one side of a river in an orderly fashion. He planned on giving his brother many gifts to appease him.

But Jacob had a greater problem on his hands. He needed to deal with his life before God.

We are told that Jacob went across the Jabbok river to be alone. There he was met by a man (actually an angel, a man and God as we read later). He wrestled with Him all night till dawn was about to break.

Scripture says that the One Jacob was wrestling with "saw that he could not defeat him(Jacob) and he touched the joint of his thigh." What? God could not defeat Jacob? If he wanted to He could defeat him in a second. Instead, God humbled Himself by letting Jacob's tenacity pay off though it cost him pain. God touched him and dislocated his hip. He became handicapped but his pain was accompanied with victory. While God put his hip out of joint and he limped, He still won.

God said to Jacob, 'Let me go for dawn is breaking.'

Jacob said, "I will not release you unless you bless me."

Then the One he was wrestling did bless him. He renamed Jacob telling him, "You shall no longer be called Jacob but rather Israel (Prince of God) for you have struggled with God and with man and you have prevailed and been victorious." While Jacob was given a handicap he was victorious in his struggles with himself, his brother and most importantly with God.

There are a few lessons to apply to us in this story. We too wrestle with ourselves, others and God. By holding on to God fervently in prayer we may and will often suffer but in the end we will be victorious. Also, if we are strong we need to bear the infirmities of the weak. God in strength let Jacob prevail. As parents we need to let our children win sometimes even though we are more powerful than they. The day my son beat me in chess was a day of triumph for him. It built his confidence. In life we do not always win by winning. Sometimes we win by letting the other guy win. Perhaps it might best be said that both Jacob and God won because Jacob was a better man after that, a Prince of God, and surely God was pleased that Jacob became His Prince instead of a supplanter and trickster of others.

When my friend disagreed with me it caused a struggle which was painful. But in the end it led me to see God in a new way. So Lord, help us see that holding on to you in the midst of struggling is the secret to developing princely character. Hear it sung about by clicking below.

<http://www.youtube.com/watch?v=rQG5wHWGsM0>

Visions of God Change Us Life's Greatest Transforming Vision

March 14, 2011

One morning I woke up thinking, "What I need most is a vision of God." I then opened a book by C. H. Spurgeon. The reading for the day was titled "Seeing Him." He mentioned that we can endure in this life as we "see Him who is invisible."

People in the Bible who had a vision of God were amazingly changed. We are told that "The LORD would speak to Moses face to face, as a man speaks with his friend." The result was that Moses helped set a nation free and endured great trials because by faith he saw Him who is invisible.

Job experienced catastrophic experiences losing his children, livestock and health. Though his friends didn't help him, as they spoke to him face to face, God did. God spoke to Job asking him all kinds of questions he couldn't answer. Finally Job says, "My ears have heard of you but now my eyes have seen you. Therefore I despise myself and repent in dust and ashes." Though Job was a man of integrity he learned his greatest lesson when He saw God. It was a moment that led to the reversal of his destiny. His life, wife, and fruitfulness after His vision of God led to blessings far greater than anything he had ever experienced in his earlier life.

Isaiah describes a vision of God he had in the year that king Uzziah of Judah died, "I saw the Lord sitting on a high and lofty throne. The bottom of his robe filled the temple." Uzziah had died but the King of Heaven was very much alive. "Angels were standing above Him. Each had six wings: With two they covered their faces, with two they covered their feet, and with two they flew. They called to each other and said, "Holy, holy, holy is the Lord of Armies! The whole earth is filled with his glory."

Isaiah's response brought about his forgiveness and a task God assigned him: The angel voices shook the foundations of the door posts, and the temple filled with smoke. So I said, "Oh, no I'm doomed. Words that pass through my lips are sinful. I live among people with sinful lips. I have seen the king, the Lord of Armies!" Then one of the angels flew to me. In his hand was a burning coal that he had taken from the altar with tongs. He touched my mouth with it and said, "This has touched your lips. Your guilt has been taken away, and your sin has been forgiven." After the vision Isaiah was commissioned to speak for God to the nation.

In the New Testament we are told that seeing the glory of God changes us. All who experience a vision of God realize and experience their own need to be forgiven. Then their lives are changed forever: "And all we, who with unveiled faces reflect the Lord's glory, are being transformed into his likeness with ever-increasing glory, which comes from the Lord, who is the Spirit. " To see Jesus in action and listen to His words is to see God. It is not religious rules that change us but seeing who God is. He reverses our destiny like Job, cleanses us and fits us for service like Isaiah, and transforms us into the image of His Son.

Our final total transformation will come when we go to be with Jesus. Then we will see Him fully as He really is and that vision will change us to be like Him forever. Meanwhile, Lord help us here on earth to see more and more of your glory, to capture visions of who you really are, so that we may know you and reflect your glory on earth as we will in heaven.

Love to you,

Dean

For further visions of God in the New Testament: John 14:9; Heb. 1:3; Rev. 19:11; 2Cor 12:1-3; Heb. 2:9; Heb. 12:1-3; Rev. 1:1-20

Walking and Talking with God
A Modern Day Psalm #1 of Dean

1.The Lord, my delight,
Gives me songs in the night.
2.The Lord, my hope
Helps me cope.
3.Because He is my peace
My praise to Him will never cease.
4.Because He loves me truly
I'll seek to trust Him fully.
5.Whenever I look up
He fills my cup.
6.When I face a hard task
He helps me if I ask.
7.When I feel very low
His presence makes me grow.
8.When I feel faint
He hears my complaint
9.When I say my prayers
I know He cares.
10,When I ask and receive
He renews what I believe.
11.When I confess my sin
He revives my soul again.

12.When I wander and go astray
He helps me turn back to His way.
13.When my heart feels grief
He hears and grants relief.
14.He loves me when I'm good
And do the things I should.
15.He loves me when I'm bad
And make Him sad.
16.When I draw near He always hears
HIs presence banishes all my fears.
17.Like Enoch of old
I'll walk with Him
'Til He takes me home
To stroll on streets of gold!

Walking on Water Days

Followers of Christ, like Peter, have their walking on water days. Here in the Bible is Peter's walking on water day!   "Now in the fourth watch of the night Jesus went to them, walking on the sea. And when the disciples saw Him walking on the sea, they were troubled, saying, "It is a ghost!" And they cried out for fear. But immediately Jesus spoke to them, saying, "Be of good cheer! It is I; do not be afraid." And Peter answered Him and said, "Lord, if it is You, command me to come to You on the water." So He said, "Come." And when Peter had come down out of the boat, he walked on the water to go to Jesus. But when he saw that the wind *was* boisterous, he was afraid; and beginning to sink he cried out, saying, "Lord, save me!" And immediately Jesus stretched out *His* hand and caught him, and said to him, "O you of little faith, why did you doubt?" And when they got into the boat, the wind ceased. Then those who were in the boat came and worshiped Him, saying, "Truly You are the Son of God." Matthew 14:25-33

Every miracle for a follower of Christ is like a "walking on water day." I've had quite a few "walking on water days" since coming to Christ 61 years ago. After my conversion at age 20 my joy in Christ was like walking on water. For a while I thought I'd never sin again. Then I sinned and felt deeply sorrowful. Peter sank after walking on water when he took his eyes off of Jesus. I sank as I failed the Lord. He lifted me up when I obeyed 1John 1:9 and confessed my sin.

Since then I have found that all followers of Christ will have walking-on-water days and rescue-from-sinking days.

I prefer to think more about the days of Christ's triumph in my life rather than the days I failed to focus on him. One of my greatest walking on water days occurred at a family reunion. My wife, my children and I were invited to a family reunion because my uncle was dying. I asked God to please work it out so I could share the Lord with all my extended family.

After arriving my aunt, who was a follower of Christ, asked us all on Sunday to go to Minnie haha Covenant church. I had prepared a message to share with everyone about God's ability at death to transform my uncle's humble body into a new glorious body like his risen Son's body. I also planned on using the Monarch Butterfly as an illustration of the resurrection.

When we arrived at the church at the door that Sunday, July 21,1974, I was handed the church bulletin . No one knew what I had planned except God.   He miraculously caused someone to put my verse on the bulletin cover. It was the verse I had prepared to speak on.   Also there was a photo of the Monarch Butterfly on the bulletin. A joyful thrill filled my body as I looked at the bulletin. Then came an even greater thrill. The pastor of the church whom I had never met before came up to me and said, "Would you like to take the message today?" What are the odds? Would I? Yes! I was "walking on water" as I gave God's message and illustrated it with the Monarch butterfly. The Monarch starts out as a worm crawling on the ground then spins a cocoon emerging as a soaring butterfly. So all who trust the Lord will come out of the grave with a new body flying to meet the Lord in the air.

Afterwords back at the house a holy quietness seemed to fill the room. Members of the family asked me questions. My mom said that she was nervous when I got up to speak. Then she said she forgot it was me. Best compliment I ever had. She changed her attitude toward me which before had been somewhat hostile. The next day at a fair she went forward to receive Christ at a Moody Bible Science presentation, but no one talked to her. However, later at age 59 she accepted Christ on the beach in Hawaii and was baptized.

So followers of Christ should expect "walk on water" type miracle experiences and also sinking event rescues. Sink or swim depends upon our focusing on Jesus in faith or looking away from him to circumstances. If you follow Christ you should expect "walking on water days" but also some sinking days when Jesus will lift you up again. Then some day when life is over and we've sunk into the ground we will feel Jesus hand lifting us upward. We'll be equipped to fly away to be with Jesus to enjoy "walking on water" days forever! Please don't skip these two songs which add joy to all you have read. Click on them below.

https://www.youtube.com/watch?v=5OLwCk4Jw-4>
https://www.youtube.com/watch?v=PYyyfw349Fl>

Walls

Walls in the Bible are full of interesting and helpful lessons. The city of Jerusalem was at one time surrounded with walls built by the people to keep enemies out and to protect and unite those behind the walls. Because of lack of trust on Israel's part, the walls were eventually torn down and the people taken away captive to Babylon.

Years laster, after many years in captivity Cyrus, king of Persia, made a law that the people could return from captivity to Jerusalem and rebuild the wall and the city. His law ordering their return is in the Bible and also found in archeological evidence in the 9 inch Cyrus Cylinder.

Ezra and Nehemiah are the ones who were in charge in the refurbishing of the city and its walls. As they worked together their unity and purpose became a great defense against those who would like to have destroyed them.

Today we still deal with walls, good and bad. I had a friend for many years with whom sharing prayers, sharing our lives and unity existed. Then something happened. My friend became my enemy and will no longer communicate with me. The wall of unity has been broken down between us. I don't really understand why. But I know it hurts! And I pray continually that the wall of rejection might be replaced with the rebuilding of our friendship. I know that forgiveness and restoration IS God's will. And I know my friends bitterness is causing much hurt to many.

But I have hope. God is able to order us to forgive and forget and rebuild the wall of friendship. How? By putting away all bitterness and replacing it with kindness as the Bible says, "Be kind toward one another, tender hearted, forgiving one another even as God has for Christ's sake forgiven you."

In America a lot of its original foundations and walls have been torn down. That is bad but to rebuild foundations and walls that unite are a necessary requirement for our country to grow and thrive.

The return of Israel from Babylon was brought about by God after much prayer. We should not give up hope for our relationships and national well being. As long as we can pray and ask God to move the hearts of our leaders to restore foundations and remake walls together we can be victors.

The greatest foundations and walls are found in Revelation 21. It tells of a city, with gates, walls and lasting foundations, whose builder and maker is God. Our greatest hope is that such a city might be reflected in our country in the hearts of those who know and seek to know God.

Let's pray that God might pour out His Spirit on our leaders, families and nation so that they allow us to build on solid foundations and to rebuild walls of peace and unity. The gates of hell cannot prevail against God's church, nor can they prevail over a nation of people whose Lord is the true God who made heaven and earth and who can remake and revive the foundations and walls of our country.

What A Saint Ain't and What a Saint Is
(Put A Little Joy in Your Day)

Walking around my block I bumped into my neighbor Gwen outside combing the long hair of her daughter. I commented, "Boy, your girl is sure getting big. How old is she now?" She said, "Six and a half and my other daughter is eight." I said,"I taught children her age in 3rd grade for many years."She said, "You're a saint."

First time anyone called me a saint for teaching kids. I told her that actually I had taught teens for a while but liked teaching 2nd and 3rd graders better because they are eager to learn." She agreed.

So my question is, "What really is a saint and what ain't a saint?

The word saint has been corrupted by many from its original meaning in the Bible. Some think a saint is someone who has been declared a saint by a hierarchal church of some kind. Such a person must be responsible for two miracles after their death or have died as a martyr for their faith. Some people venerate saints on a level above ordinary Christians based on the idea of the superiority of the "clergy" over the "laity." These are all man made inventions. They are not found in the Bible.

In the Bible everyone who trusts the Lord as their Savior is a saint before they die. The word saint or saints is found 98 times in the Bible. It means someone set apart to God by His grace as sacred, holy and clean. The apostles Paul and John in writing to the existing churches of his day addresses all believers as saints over and over and they were not yet dead.

The New Testament Bible has no rules for canonizing or beatifying anyone. It recognizes every true born again believer in Jesus Christ as a saint. In the New Testament a person becomes a saint by admitting he or she is a sinner, by turning to and trusting Jesus Christ as Savior. I am a saint, not because of my goodness but because of the gift of God which is His righteousness bestowed upon me. God makes a person a saint or saint he ain't!

The Bible does not exalt a group of "clergy" over a group called "laity" which is believed by many Bible scholars to be an error hated by God and practiced in the Bible by a group called Nicolaitans(Rev. 2:6.15). The Bible clearly condemns comparing ourselves with each other and exalting or lowering our view of each other on that basis.

When someone bowed to Peter to exalt him Peter took him up saying, "Stand up. I myself also am a man." He did not exalt himself as the supreme head of the church nor did anyone else in the Bible. Jesus was the Rock on which the church was built and Peter was one of the living stones as are all members of God's church. We are all equal as children of Christ for "there is neither Jews nor Greek, their is neither bond nor free, there is neither male nor female; for we are all one in Christ Jesus(Gal.3:26-29). In Paul's letter to the Philippians he even mentions saints in Caesar's household very much alive and honoring God.

To be greatest of all is to take a lowly position as a servant and not to lord oneself over others. We are to be humble not exalting ourselves over others in dress, food, position or service. The apostles wore ordinary garb not calling to others mind their position or appearing preeminent over others.

So to all saints. This is your day and it is not just delegated to a special group of halo encircled folks but to all sinners saved by the grace of God.

Put a little joy in your day. Sing About It:
<http://www.youtube.com/watch?v=cCuK8nfupwQ

What a Wonderful God
This song with new words unfurled
Is set to the tune
What a Wonderfful World

I see skies at night
I see Birds in flight
I say to myself
What a wonderful God

I see roses in bloom
Jesus risen from the tomb
I say to myself
What a wonderful God

I see answered prayer
I see people who care
I say to myself
What a wonderful God

I see skies of blue
I see fresh morning dew
I sing aloud
What a wonderful God

I see rainbows in the sky
I see raindrops dropping by
I sing to myself
What a wonderful God

I see beautiful girls
I see cute little squirrels
I sing to myself
What a wonderful God

I hear poems of praise
Songs that amaze
I think to myself
What a wonderful God

I see sins forgiven
Kirsten Godlike driven
I think to myself
What a wonderfful God

I have a wife who cares
With hugs to share
I think to myself
What a wonderful God

I have a wonderful son
Whose teaching's well done.
I think to myself
What a wonderful God

I see Tyler having Pinata fun
I thank God for my grandson.
I say to myself
What a Wonderfful God!

I have a beautiful girl
Who shines like a pearl
I say to myself
What a wonderful God

I walk my daily mile
I see friends who smile
I say to them
What a wonderful God

I see texts on my phone
I'm not alone
I think to myself

What a wonderful God

I feel joy in my heart
Love that will never depart
I think io myself
What a wonderful God

I lift my words to heaven
My sins are all forgiven
I sing to myself
What a wonderful God

I see people born again
I see new life begin
I think to myself
What a wonderful God

I have a mom and dad In heaven
where there's real Livin!
I say to myself
What a wonderful God

I sing my song to the wonderful tune by Louis Armstrong: https://youtu.be/q6sbz8u_MCs>

What are You Looking for?
How About a City whose builder and maker is God?

Bible characters, Abraham, Isaac, Jacob and all who trust God throughout their lives are looking for something? Is it a job that would pay for their living expenses? Is it earthly riches? Is it Romance? Is it fame! Is it power over others? Is it respect? Is it a nice home or homes on earth? Is it lots of children? Is it retiring & partying?

Most of us sometimes look look for things in life that are not best for us, but if we become people of faith we look for what is lasting and eternal. It is summed up this way, You are not come to the mountain of law that kills but to the mountain that gives life "But you have come to Mount Zion and **to the city of the living God**, the heavenly Jerusalem,... "Heb. 12:22-24

While Abraham lived in or passed through 17 cities in his life, they will all pass away for the day is coming that the present heaven and earth with all its cities and inhabitants will disappear, melted in a giant explosion to be followed by a new heaven and earth including God's true heavenly eternal city, the new Jerusalem. All who trust and follow God are looking and waiting for what Abraham looked for, "By faith Abraham dwelt in the land of promise as *in* a foreign country, the land of promise as *in* a foreign country, dwelling in tents with Isaac and Jacob, the heirs with him of the same promise; for **he looked for and waited for the city which has foundations, whose builder and maker is God.** Heb. 11:9,10. Beyond the temporary, he looked for an eternal home with lasting foundations made not by men but by God Himself. That is what I also look for. What about you?

God says to those who died trusting him, " These all died in faith, not having received the promises, but having seen them afar off were assured of them, embraced *them* and confessed that they were strangers and pilgrims on the earth. For those who say such things declare plainly that they seek a homeland. And truly if they had called to mind that *country* from which they had come out, they would have had opportunity to return. But now they desire a better, that is, a heavenly *country.* **Therefore God is not ashamed to be called their God, for He has prepared a city for them." Heb. 11:13-16**

___Abraham never returned to the wicked city,Ur, out of which God called him. It was a city that worshipped the male moon God called Sin and the female goddess who was supposedly married to him called Allah. Abe gave up and left idol worship! That is true of those who truly follow God today.

We live on earth in various temporary cities where we learn of Him but which we look beyond to the city built by God whose foundations are eternal. Revelation speaks of that eternal city and tells us its foundations are made of precious stones, its streets of gold, its doors of pearls. Its inhabitants are called, chosen, holy, worshipful, and glorified. Its splendid Savior is our Lord Jesus Christ, grand center of it all.

I have now lived in Dublin, Calif with my wife and family for 48 years. We have learned many lessons in our home. However, we look forward to our final home made by God Himself. It will be perfect and eternal. No tears, sins, parting or failures. Our home is wonderful but is far inferior to our eternal home. For a Ssingle blessing sing about it here:https://www.youtube.com/watch?v=OaOIdhPLqeQ> For double blessing sing about it here: https://www.youtube.com/watch?v=-15v9iworAU>

Abdullah, Thank you for your helpful service. I tried to call you at the Att store in Stoneridge mall and thank you on the phone but they have the place set up so you can't get anyone who works there on the phone. Anyhow, thank you. I have enclosed an article I wrote sent out to over a thousand people. Hope it will be a blessing to you.
Dean L Gossett

Easter Thoughts for Thinkers
What If the Dead Are Not Raised?

In the Bible the apostle Paul asked the question, "What if the dead are not raised?" 1 Corinthians 15:32 He had risked his life many times and by this time in his life had almost died on numerous occasions. If the dead are not raised then his life of sacrifice and preaching would amount to nothing. Also, the future of everyone else would also be doomed. Why? Because "it is appointed once to die" for all of us. You may argue about what happens after you die but you cannot argue with the fact that you will die. However, there is good news possible for many. Paul and the Bible give us a multitude of facts that everyone after death will rise again. That is good news for many **but not for all.**

There are clearly two kinds of resurrections in the Bible. Daniel tells us so in the Old Testament in **Daniel 12:2.**"**Many of those who sleep in the dust of the earth shall awake, some to everlasting life, and some to shame and everlasting contempt.**"

Many people think there is only one resurrection of the dead for everyone. Not so! Those who have faith in the true God and His Son are resurrected to glory and everlasting life and will reign with Christ. Then later the resurrection of those who have not trusted God and rejected Jesus as Savior takes place. They will be awakened to death and everlasting shame. Here is proof in clear and easy to understand words: **"I also saw the souls of those who had ...their testimony to Jesus and for the word of God....They came to life and reigned with Christ a thousand years. 5 (The rest of the dead did not come to life until the thousand years were ended.) This is the first resurrection. 6 Blessed and holy are those who share in the first resurrection. Over** them the second death has no power, but they will be priests of God and of Christ, and they will reign with him a thousand years." Rev. 20:4-6 The thousand year reign of resurrected believers is a prelude to reigning with Him forever on a new heaven and earth.

So when you are resurrected what will follow, eternal life, peace and joy, or everlasting shame, death and misery? It all depends upon what your reaction is to God's free gift offer of salvation through His Son. The Bible says clearly, "This is **life eternal** that you might know the true God and His Son whom He has sent." To **not** have the Son is to not have life eternal but to have **death infernal**. So if you know the true God and His Son, you will be a part of the resurrection to life instead of to death and shame? The Bible tells us clearly how to be saved from the second death. **"The word is near you on your lips and in your heart"(that is, the word of faith that we proclaim);** because **if you confess with your lips that Jesus is Lord and believe in your heart that God raised him from the dead, you will be saved. For one believes with the heart and so is justified, and one confesses with the mouth and so is saved."** The scripture says, **"No one who believes in him will be put to shame. For there is no distinction between Jew and Greek; the same Lord is Lord of all and is generous to all who call on him. For, "Everyone who calls on the name of the Lord shall be saved." Romans 10:9-13.** Because Jesus Christ took your sin and death upon Himself and arose **He proved that the dead will be raised!** These Easter thoughts enable you now to confess Him with your mouth and believe in your heart that He arose from the dead. If you do believe God you will know that the dead really are raised! Sing and believe this song and you will find Him and rise from the dead to eternal life and joy. <https:// www.youtube.com/watch?v=nLoYv_LIVQ4>

Abdullah, Thank you for your helpful service. I tried to call you at the Att store in Stoneridge mall and thank you on the phone but they have the place set up so you can't get anyone who works there on the phone. Anyhow, thank you. I have enclosed an article I wrote sent out to over a thousand people. Hope it will be a blessing to you.
Dean L Gossett

What is Love?
Love Strong, Greater and Longest
by DLG

In my life I have experienced love in a number of ways. First, as a child I knew love for my mother. It meant to value her, to appreciate and care for her. Then I experienced puppy love at age 13. Most of us have experienced that kind of love as a young person. You want to be around that other person. Often you may not know what to say. You just want to be with them. Some people undervalue puppy love but we must remember it is at least temporarily real to the puppy. The flames of puppy love live on in our memory.

Then their is love for a brother or sister, or a relative. You enjoy their company. You do things together. You learn to appreciate them. I have fond memories of my brother and most of my cousins.

Then there are friends that we learn to love. They are enjoyable to be with, helpful, forgiving and kind. Some times you may love someone as you get older so much you are obsessed with them. You think of them continually, you like to be with them, and even feel a little sick at heart when you part. That kind of love can sometime be dangerous. You may find yourself saying or doing the wrong thing because of your obsession. We need to learn to confess our obsession and seek forgiveness and change. We are to have godly love which rejects anything immoral.

Then you may meet that special one you want to marry. You marry and show love to your partner giving yourself emotionally heart, soul and body to one another, You enter into love that binds you together. I often sign my letters or cards, Love, Dean and Gloria. Why? Because the Bible says that married love makes two people one. She is part of me and I am part of her.

What really is love? The Bible tells us, "God is love." He is the source of all true love. Even people who are evil give good gifts to their children. Why? Because they are created in the image of God.

Then there is greatest love being willing to give your life for another. "There is no greater love than this that one lay down his life for another." That of course is what Jesus did for us. He died for us, the just for the unjust that He might bring us to God and win our love. "We love Him because He first loved us." Our love turns into a returned love to our Savior. And we begin to lay down our life for Him. We lay down our life by pleasing Him or by actually dying for Him. Divine love is the highest form of love. We are to love God first and to love others as we love ourselves.

I have experienced all of the different kinds of love I have just shared. Sometimes i have violated love and felt miserable because of it. But God has forgiven me and taught me how to give real love to others. Because God has forgiven me most, I love Him most and also love most those who have forgiven me.

There is one kind of love I have yet to experience. In eternity I will see Jesus as He fully is and then I will know perfect love, love that is stronger than death and lasts forever. The Lord says, " I have loved you with an everlasting love." Though we have never completely seen Jesus, if we know him, in eternity when He is fully revealed to us, at that moment, in the twinkling of an eye, just seeing Him will change us forever. We will be like Him in love, purity, and character without end.

Do you know His love? If not read John 3:16 to John 3:20. Find the love there that lasts forever. Trusting Jesus fully will transform you totally to love purely. There are many kinds of love but the greatest will be total love at our first visual sight of Jesus. Then we will know the longest love being loved by Christ and enjoying Hie everlasting love forever!!

Sing about it. O love that will not let me go: <https://www.youtube.com/watch?v=nt69WDtYNLo.>

What's Your Favorite Rock?

While watching a movie called Planet Earth, I enjoyed a strange and unusual sight. A fresh water Dolphin emerged from the water with a large rock in its extended mouth. The narrator told why it had the rock in its mouth. Fresh water male dolphins when seeking a female go to the bottom of the Amazon river where they find a large rock which they put in their mouth, then emerge a few feet above the water to wave the rock around which mysteriously attracts a female and they mate.

As I read that I thought about a famous rock that attracted me. It is my favorite rock found in the Bible called the Rock of Ages. God and Jesus are both often spoken as a Rock. In the Old Testament Moses who wrote the first five books of the Bible once asked God to see His glory. God answered his request and told him that he would come stand by him upon a rock. He told him that he would make a cleft in the rock and cover him there with his hand. Then as God passed by he would be able to see God's glory but only his back parts. No one could look at God's front at that time and live.

So God put him in the cleft of the rock and the Lord passed before him and proclaimed, "The Lord, the Lord God, merciful and gracious, long suffering, and abounding in goodness and truth, keeping mercy for thousands, forgiving iniquity and transgression and sin, by no means clearing the guilty...Exodus 34:6-7.

What Moses saw was God's character, merciful, gracious, patient, full of goodness and truth but not bestowing it upon the guilty who won't admit their guilt but reject God's mercy and forgiveness.

Moses rock experience became mine as at the age of 20 I was invited to come to God's Son, the Lord Jesus Christ who is called The Rock Upon Which he builds his church. Jesus asked all his disciples one day, "Who do men say that I, the Son of Man, am?" So they said, "Some *say* John the Baptist, some Elijah, and others Jeremiah or one of the prophets."

He said to them, "But who do you say that I am?"

Simon Peter answered and said, "You are the Christ, the Son of the living God."

Jesus answered and said to him, "Blessed are you, Simon Bar-Jonah, for flesh and blood has not revealed *this* to you, but My Father who is in heaven. And I also say to you that you are Peter, and on this rock I will build My church, and the gates of Hell shall not prevail against it."

Peter's name means little rock. He had rightly said that Jesus was the Christ, the Son of the living God. Upon that fact that Jesus was the Christ, the Son of the living God, Jesus said he would build his church. In another passage of scripture we know Jesus is the rock because when Israel rejected him it is said, "The rock that was rejected is become the corner stone, the head of the corner.."

So when at age 20 when I did not reject Christ but accepted him as the Christ, the Son of the living God, I became part of his church against which Satan and the gates of hell can not prevail. He is my favorite Rock because he is the one who showed me mercy, forgiveness of my sin, goodness, and truth, and has given me eternal life. No one else could do that for me. That is why Jesus is my favorite Rock. Their is so much more about God and Jesus in the Bible about them as the Rock.

He is called the Rock of Ages cleft for me in whom I have been hidden. God told Moses he would show him his back parts. When we see Jesus I believe we see his front parts. Jesus totally reveals God. He said so, "He that sees me sees the Father."

Jesus is the embodiment of truth, love, goodness, mercy, forgiveness and eternal life. That is why he said, "I am the way, the truth and the life. No one comes to the Father but by me. " He became my Rock at age 20 and now at age 81 he is more than ever my favorite Rock! "On Christ the solid Rock I stand. All other ground is sinking sand." Have you come to the Rock? Why not do it now as you listen to this song? <https://www.youtube.com/watch?v=gM7gt_cSxjw>

When we meet someone new we often ask, "What kind of work do you do? Dare we ask God what kind of work He does? Jesus disciples asked Him what they should do to do the works of God? Jesus answered, "The work of God is this: to believe in the One he has sent." Why? Because believing that Jesus is the Christ glorifies God and imparts eternal life to the believer.

In response to Jesus question to Peter asking Him who He was, Peter said, "You are the Christ, the son of the living God. And upon that truth Jesus said He would build His church and the gates of hell would not prevail against it." Peter and the disciples and apostles believed on the One God sent and thereby were given the ability to do the work of God which is getting others to believe. Christ is building only one church made up of all those who believe in His Son whom He sent. So God's work is not establishing a bunch of religions or denominations?

God's work is based on a belief in a person not faith in traditions, religions and rules. Most of us have heard the statement, "Religion is the opium of the people." Carl Marx who said that was right but terribly wrong because he included Jesus Christ in his statement. Religion is a drug that addicts people convincing them that belief alone in God and keeping a set of rules and traditions is enough. To believe in God falls far short of the work of God. The Devil believes in God and trembles but it does him no good. One must go beyond belief in God to **believing** God. And to believe God is to believe in the one whom He has sent, His Son the Lord Jesus Christ.

Believing God about His Son enables forgiveness, eternal life. overcoming death, and overcoming the world, the flesh and the Devil. Religion overcomes none of these. In fact religions team up with traditions and the philosophy of men, and the misleading rudiments of the world's religious and non religious systems.

At age 20 I believed in Jesus as God's Son whom He sent. The result was a rebirth, the coming into my life of His Spirit who enabled me to perceive, understand and enter the kingdom of God over which His Son rules.

Once a person sees and enters His kingdom he or she than begins to share in the work of God. God works through them to make Christ known so that others also might believe Him.

Belief in Christ gets past religion to regeneration. to imparted righteousness, to spiritual reproduction.

Ask yourself. Am I religious or regenerated? Am I religious or born again through belief in God's Son.

Exchange your rags of religious self effort for the joy of believing the record God has given us of His Son. Give up addiction to religion and accept the freedom found in Christ. Rely on the power of God and not the religious efforts of mankind.

Here is a song to encourage you in your journey:
<http://www.youtube.com/watch?v=mqnbLkSgMOY&feature=related>
Love to you, Dean

What Will Eternity Be Like?

Heaven and the new earth will be experienced by all who have believed in Jesus as Savior. Here are some of what is ahead to look forward to for all who truly believe God about His Son. It is just a little of what to look forward to experience for all who set their affections on things above.

So---Look forward to getting new eyes with no glasses or cataracts, only cataracts of water to swim in. Look forward to new ears without hearing aids. New hands with no ET, essential tremor. New body that doesn't bleed. New food, at least 12 kinds, to be perfectly digested. No waste so no bathrooms!

No tendency to do anything wrong. New love free from lust but filled with grace toward everyone. New glorious body like Christ's risen body in exchange for my earthly body to never die or wear out.

Never ever have to sin because Jesus died for sin, forgave it and washed it all away.

No more trials, tears, suffering, pain or death which will be swallowed up in the victory of eternal life. A new transforming vision of Christ who is our life and continual joy. New elevated pure fellowship and learning with friends and family.

New understanding of all the realities of heaven. New feet to walk on streets of gold. New eternal home whose builder and maker is God! New, glorious ability to sing and worship God. New appreciation, without jealousy for the rewards and blessings of others. New eternal friendships! New joys with animals and plants and all of heaven's creations.

New absence of any arguments about the authenticity of God's Word. Forever O Lord, is your Word settled in heaven! Amen!

No evil, only right will rule. Satan banished! Fear gone forever! War exterminated! No marriage among men and women but we will know spiritual marriage to our Savior loving Him and being loved by Him forever!

These are just a few of some of the things revealed to us about our future through God's Word and His Spirit, but there are many new things we will experience that are beyond our ability to know now! The new heaven and earth though mind boggling is all true!

Love to all! If you haven't yet, trust Jesus today!!The results will be what I just shared and more of the glories of the new heaven and earth. Let's do what the Bible says whether old or young "set our affections on things above, not on things of the earth." Col. 3:2-4 Praying I will see you there!

This old song gives us a little more of a glimpse into our glorious future which is a gift to all His saved people. <https://m.youtube.com/watch?v=-lOarryn9Ag->

Unfortunately those who reject Jesus as Savior will not experience heaven's glories. Sadly, my next article will tell what eternity is like for rejectors of God and His Son but it will also tell how to stop being a rejector.

Love to All. Dean

What We Will Look Like and Be Like in Heaven?

Dear Shirley,

There is a young lady who drew a picture of Jesus which she says she saw in a vision. It is the most beautiful picture of Jesus I have ever seen. The 4 year old boy who had the out-of-body experience says he saw Jesus. His parents kept showing him pictures people had drawn of Jesus asking him if that is what he looked like. He always said "No." until he saw the picture of Jesus done by Akiane Kramarik. She is a child prodigy who painted Jesus picture at age 9. . When he saw her picture of Jesus he said, "That's Him."

I put a link below which will take you to her other remarkable artistic accomplishments.

We can be sure in heaven that we will be recognized and we won't be in a wheel chair. There will be no sickness or death or tears in the new heaven and earth. More than likely we will be able to think ourselves from one place to another. The Bible says that the Lord calls every star now by name. Perhaps we will be able to explore the universe and learn why he named each star as he did.

We will eat and drink at the marriage supper of the lamb. We will be able to pluck fruit from the tree of life which produces 12 kinds of fruit each month. We will be able to drink from the river of life. Most likely our food will be 100% used by our body so there will be no waste nor necessity for going to a rest room. Also, our spiritual bodies will be more tangible even than our present bodes. Our capacity for enjoyment will be at its absolute highest.

There will be no marriage in heaven proving the Muslim and Mormon religion wrong regarding marriages in the next life. Jesus says we will not give or take in marriage but be like the angels. That eliminate any possibility of problems over who is married to who in the next life. We won't be angels but we will be like them. Angels are swift and beautiful. So shall we be. Someone might wonder how we will all be different and recognize each other. We are different on this earth and can recognize those we know. So why should we doubt that reality in heaven?

Some say we sleep until the resurrection. That is true of our bodies but not our spirits.

We find many people who have died very much alive in Spirit mentioned in the gospels, in the letter of Hebrews and in the book of Revelation.

I believe that we may have a spiritual DNA which we take with us at death enabling at a future date our bodies to be reunited with our souls and spirits in a new and glorious state, this mortal putting on immortality, the perishable putting on the imperishable. It will be glorious and while we cannot know a lot about it now, we will rejoice in that day and no one will be able to take away our joy. We will be in the place the Lord has prepared for us, enjoying the New Jerusalem, the new heavens and the new earth.

Scripture says that it has not entered the heart of man regarding the glories and surprises to come but it also tells us that He has revealed much to us by His Spirit. We can know enough now to rest in the fact that heaven is for real and we who know Christ will enjoy it, the Lord, His people, the angels, the heavenly city, the new earth and the stellar beauties of the new heavens. For the believer in Christ, the best is yet to come. .

May God bless you with these thoughts.

See you there soon, Shirley,

Dean

<http://www.godvine.com/12-Year-Old-Prodigy-Paints-her-Visions-of-Heaven-43.html>

<http://www.youtube.com/watch?v=49wut32Cguw>

What's In a Name?

"**A rose by any other name would smell as sweet**" is a commonly quoted part of a dialogue in William Shakespeare's play _Romeo and Juliet_, in which Juliet argues that the names of things do not matter, only what things "are" sounds good but names represent who someone is or what something is. Try getting a rose in a flower shop by asking for it by its smell or calling it a lilac. Won't Work. Names are important.

The Bible has at least 200 amazing names for just Jesus. There are more than 900 names for God in the Bible. Each of these name reveal different aspects of God's nature and or actions. Learning them is truly sweet like Jesus which means "He will save his people from their sins." That is fragrant news.

For Thinkers! What's the Best Reason for Living?

DLG

I recently asked a family member "What is your greatest desire or greatest desires in life?"

He told me he didn't understand the question. So I wrote him back, "Sorry you didn't understand my question. What I meant is what, if any, desires, reasons or purposes to live for are **most important** to you?" To make money? To be kind to others? To give to help others. To help your children and grand children? To have fun? To please God? To prove that that the Bible isn't true. To scan the internet for interesting stuff. To prove God doesn't exist? To be politically correct? Of course if you don't have any reasons or don't care to share any with me, I'll accept that. Just trying to bless you by challenging you to zero in on what you think is important.

A wise person lives by wise planning.

Until I came to know Christ my reasons for living were to just mainly satisfy myself,
to live for pleasure, to get along in life by doing what ever I wanted. That probably defines most people's plans for living.

The Bible describes clearly what most people live for. It tells of two different men, one was Solomon, thinking about why most people live from a seemingly wise but really empty point of view. The other is about a rich man who tells his point of view about living. After the rich man's conclusion he is given God's evaluation of his decision about what is important in life. Both men give their reasons for living saying, "Eat, drink and be merry". You may want to read both men's conclusions about life in Ecclesiastes 8:15 and Luke 12:19 and think about them. Were their plans for living wise?

God tells the rich man what he thinks of his plan. You might want to look up what God says to him in Luke 12:19, and then ask yourself, "What would God say to me about my reasons for living? For the best reason to live read Acts 17:26 and especially verse 27.

Where Are the Nine?
July 4, 2011

One attitude often missing in the lives of people is an attitude of gratitude.

As Jesus entered a village, ten men, all lepers, met him. They kept their distance but raised their voices, calling out, "Jesus, Master, have mercy on us!" Taking a good look at them, he said, "Go, show yourselves to the priests." They went, and while still on their way, became clean. One of them, when he realized that he was healed, turned around and came back, shouting his gratitude, glorifying God. He kneeled at Jesus' feet, so grateful. He couldn't thank him enough— and he was a Samaritan. Jesus said, "Were not ten healed? Where are the nine? Can none be found to come back and give glory to God except this outsider?" Luke 17:12-18

I'm sure that all ten lepers who were healed were happy that their leprosy was gone but only one came back to give thanks and glorify God. I need to ask myself, "Am I grateful, thanking God for what He has done in my life?

There is a song that goes like this, "When I'm weary and I can't sleep, I count my blessings instead of sheep. I go to sleep counting my blessings." Do you and I count our blessings and thank God for them?"

A few people are encouragers and full of gratitude and thanks while many are not. I am thankful for the people during my 33 years of teaching who went out of their way to say thank you. I've taught from the pulpit, written articles, and books. While I should not seek the praise of men, I find it encouraging when someone thanks me and says they were uplifted by what I said or wrote.

I believe we need to cultivate a thankful heart. And when people encourage me I almost always write and thank them. I need to improve in being grateful to others and to God. I notice not many people go out of their way to be thankful. I think it needful to be reminded about practicing this virtue. The Bible says, "In everything give thanks for this is the will of God in Christ Jesus concerning you."

Do you and I go to church or other places with a main purpose to encourage someone else? "Let us not give up meeting together, as some are in the habit of doing, but let us encourage one another—and all the more as you see the Day (of Christ's return) approaching.(Heb. 10:25)" Shouldn't we make a habit of encouraging others. I find that when I encourage others I am always encouraged myself. When we draw out our souls to others then our light rises in darkness and our darkness becomes filled with the light of the noonday sun.

Someone said,"I can live a month on a good compliment." Think back on your youth. Two kinds of people stand out. Those who insulted you and those who complimented you. I remember in high school a girl insulted me by saying, "Your hair is hanging in your face." I never forgot it. I was shy when I was in high school. I remember someone rebuffed me because I was quiet. My mom defended me and said, "Still water runs deep." I never forgot my mom's uplifting words.

At my grandson's graduation this week, the Superintendent said something I've never heard before. He encouraged all the graduates to go to someone and thank them for encouraging or helping them. What a great idea!

One's altitude is lifted by gratitude. Go for it. Here is a song to reinforce our gratitude to god and others. <http://www.youtube.com/watch?v=lBpv-ZzcQD8>

Where Was God?
DLG
November 16,2017

Many sympathized but a few people mocked those who were murdered in Texas by the rifle of Devin Kelley. They asked, "Where was God? The Lord Jesus Christ answered that question long ago. "Whatever I tell you in the dark, speak in the light; and what you hear in the ear, preach on the housetops. **And do not fear those who kill the body but cannot kill the soul. But rather fear Him who is able to destroy both soul and body in hell**. Are not two sparrows sold for a copper coin? And not one of them falls to the ground apart from your Father's will." Matthew 10:27-29.

God takes into account even the death of sparrows. How much more the death of those babies, children and all those in the Texas church who trusted Him. Where was He? He was there ushering them into life eternal. "He who believes in **the Son has** everlasting **life**; and he who does not believe **the Son** shall not see **life**, but **the** wrath of God abides on him."John 3:36 These words from the Bible tell us clearly what God did for those who had the great privilege of being martyred for their faith. Sadly it also tells what will happen to their atheist killer.

God saw the death of all those murdered, who trusted Him, as precious.Psalm 116:15 Why? Because they are with Him in heaven more alive than ever. But God is sad about the death of their killer. Ezekiel 33:11 Why? Because He wanted him to trust Him but he never did. So he will not see life but will have both his soul and body destroyed in hell. We should be sad for him and for those who lost their loved ones but glad for them who have entered into the joy of life eternal. **God was there for sure!** God is a very present help in times of trouble. Death to a believer is but a shadow of evil through which they pass. Though scary, it is after all just a shadow, which can hurt no one who trusts in the Lord Jesus Christ, for He is with them saving and comforting them forever. Where was God? He took them to dwell in the house of the Lord forever!

May the Lord help you believe today In the Lord Jesus Christ if you haven't. Sing these songs below and you may, like me, cry tears of joy for all who died knowing Jesus and sadness for all their loved ones.

<https://www.youtube.com/watch?v=8XUYZoguhEQ>
https://www.youtube.com/watch?v=rwLl5nY5WPI>

Who Is Jesus?
October 9,2011

When Jesus came to the region of Caesar Philippi, he asked his disciples, "Who do people say the Son of Man is?" They replied, "Some say John the Baptist; others say Elijah; and still others, Jeremiah or one of the prophets." "But what about you?" he asked. "Who do you say I am?" Simon Peter answered, "You are the Christ, the Son of the living God." Jesus tells us that Simon Peter was right and that His answer was revealed to Him by God His Father.

Let's think further about who Jesus is from the lips of God His Father, from Jesus Himself, from the Holy Spirit and from me and you.

Three times God the Father spoke aloud from heaven telling us who Jesus is. According to the Father, Jesus is His beloved Son who pleases Him and we should listen to Him. The Father calls Him God and speaks of His throne as being forever. He also tells us we should listen to Jesus who glorified Him through His life and death,

What about the Spirit of God? Who does He say Jesus is? The Spirit authenticated the words of the Father at Jesus' baptism by descending on Him in bodily form and later declaring Jesus to be the Son of God with power shown by His resurrection from the dead. He reveals clearly who Jesus is.

What about Jesus? Who does He say He is? He says he is the complete expression of the Father, and that whoever sees Him sees the Father. He tells us that He and the Father are one. He said everything He said was the Father saying it through Him. He claimed to always please His Father and that there was no sin in Himself. He claimed to have all power in heaven and on earth. He forgives sins because He died for them and has the power to forgive them. He claimed to be the the only Savior even as God the Father made the same claim in the Old Testament. So Jesus is God who receives worship and does not refuse it as his disciples and angels did. He said he lived before he was born and revealed to John that He created everything. Contrary to some who say Jesus was God's first creation, Jesus actually created everything. If Jesus created everything He had to have existed before he created it all. He always was, is and shall always be.

He existed as the Son before He was born as is revealed in Psalm 2. Later He became a man and was born of Mary. He was put to death in the flesh but made alive in the Spirit. He spoke as no one else who ever lived and did works and amazing miracles unmatched in history. He told us who He was and is and proved it by His amazing life, death and resurrection.

Who is Jesus to me? He is the One who changed my life forever. He forgave and forgives my sin. He is my Savior. I believe in who He is from the witness of the Father, the Spirit and Himself. I love Him because He loved me first. I worship Him because He deserves it. I serve Him out of admiration. That is who Jesus is to me. Who is Jesus to you?

Love to you, Dean

Who Suffers the Most?
September 10, 2017

When a powerful hurricane kills hundreds of people who suffers the most? When thousands die due to war, who suffers the most? When a mom and dad lose a son or a daughter who all of their lives heard about God's love and forgiveness but died rejecting Him, who suffers the most? God! When a sister loses her brother and father within a few weeks of time, who hurts the most? God! When someone I have prayed for all my life dies rejecting Jesus, the kindest, most caring, most forgiving, most honorable man that ever lived, who suffers the most? I suffer but God suffers more.

You ask, "Well why does God allow bad things to happen?

The reason He allows them is because He loves more deeply and truly than anyone else. He is good, pure, perfect all knowing, all caring full of desire that no one perish but that all come to His perfectly just Son who visited our planet. God became flesh and walked upon this earth and did nothing but good all His life. He was just and He died for us who are unjust that we might be counted right as a gift. That is the good news of the Bible. False religion says, "If you do good and keep the commandments perfectly, God will love you and take you to heaven." God says, "You have broken my commandments but if you admit it and trust My Son who died for your sins, I will give you the gift of forgiveness and eternal life. God the Father forsook His Son as He hung there upon the cross and heard Him cry out, "My God, why have you forsaken me?" Why? So that if you trust Him, you will be forgiven and never forsaken. Jesus says to all who accept his Son, "I will never leave you or forsake you."

I trusted Him 62 years ago and He has kept His promise. He has loved me with an everlasting love and if you have not believed and trusted Him yet, He waits with outstretched arms, putting up with your sin and all the evils of the world so that you might call upon Him and be saved from all sin including your own. Jesus says to you, "Come to me all you who labor and are heavy laden and I will give you rest." He says, "Come and receive the gift of God without money or good works. Believe Me and I will forgive you and give you eternal life. I will come by My Spirit and live inside you. The penalty of your sin is death but the gift I will give you is eternal, joyous, unending life."

I came to Him 62 years ago and He kept His promise. He forgave me and gave me eternal life. He allows evil and horrible things to happen not willing that anyone should perish. If He wiped out all evil today there would be no one left to forgive. Do I understand it all like God does? No. If I did I would be God. But this I do know, a human father and mother hurt over the wrong their children do. How much more does God as a Father hurt over us and provide forgiveness. He puts up with wickedness and sin because He is patient. And his patience causes Him to suffer more than anyone else.

When a wicked person dies, God says, "I take no pleasure in the death of a wicked person." Why not? Because He grieves over that person who isn't forgiven because he rejected His forgiveness. He suffers over every lost person more than anyone else. On the other hand when someone dies who believes and receives His forgiveness and love that person's death is precious in His sight. The Bible says, "Precious in the sight of Lord is the death of His saints." All believers are saints. No church can make anyone a saint. Only God makes saints as His gift to all who believe and trust His Son who died for them. He suffers far more than anyone else and proved it by becoming one of us and suffering the ultimate hurt for our sin. <u>God suffers most so we can be forgiven the most!</u> . if that makes you mad it is because you rejected His Son. If it makes you glad it is because you right now accept His Son. He that has the Son has life. He that does not believe the Son, the wrath of God abides upon that person. Be wise! Choose God's Son and life.

Who Will Roll Away the Stone?

As I write this I know that many who read it may be beset by some difficulty that seems impossible to solve. Like the women who came to Jesus tomb to anoint the body of Jesus, you face a seemingly impossible situation. The tomb of Jesus had been sealed with a stone so heavy, probably 1 1/2 to 2 tons, that humanely speaking it would be impossible to move by a few women. Those women's concern is seen in their words, "Who will roll away the stone?"

The answer was that an angel had rolled it away so when they arrived they could see inside that Jesus was gone. He had risen from the dead, triumphing over sin, death and hell.

As you approach your own dilemma that seems impossible to solve, the same God that used an angel to roll the stone away from Jesus tomb is able to roll away your stone of grief, stone of sin, stone of rejection, stone of sorrow, stone of estrangement.

Lord Jesus roll away the reproach some may be feeling as they read this. Help them overcome estrangement from You or from another.

God's Word tells us angels are sent to minister to His people who are heirs of salvation. So Lord, grant reconciliation between those estranged. Grant your people the removal of heavy barriers that they might be able to see that you are alive, risen and all powerful to remove their reproach.

When the Israelites finished their forty years of wandering in the wilderness, they approached the Jordan river which was at flood stage. It seemed impossible for them to enter the promised land but God that day removed the reproach from them. The priests went ahead, and as soon as they put their feet into the river it dried up. The people were told to take twelves stones from the river Jordan and put them on the other side of the Jordan river in a place named Gilgal. Gilgal meant "rolled away." All the Israelites went across on dry ground and once everyone was across, the Jordan returned to flood stage. What the Israelites could not do, God did for them. He sent His angel before them to rescue and minister to them. He rolled away the reproach of Egypt that day. The stones at Gilgal became a lasting reminder of what God did for them that day. The reproach of the world, the flesh and the Devil was taken away.

Our God whom we serve still sends His angels to help do the impossible. Today I presented to God a request. Roll away any weighty stone of rejection, sin, sorrow, trials, temptation and failure from my life and the life of each person who reads this. Then in memory let them sing one or both of these songs with me:

Just click on the triangle in the middle of the black circle: A deep song-<http://www.jwpepper.com/The-Stone-Is-Rolled-Away/10340292.item#.Uy3v21zolFw>

Rolled Away, a simple illustrated song for the young at heart-<https://www.youtube.com/watch?v=CK7XjP0jl0M>

Why Do We Suffer? Why Do We Die?

One thing is certain. No one can argue that suffering and death don't exist. Where do they come from? Is it a product of chance evolution which tells us everything is getting better and better. Really? Open your eyes and you will see plenty of grief for you and me. And it hasn't changed in thousands of years.

Interestingly enough we find the first answer to the reason for suffering in the first book of the Bible. When Adam and Eve broke God's one command and ate from the tree of the knowledge of good and evil God Himself says to Adam, "Because you listened to your wife and ate from the tree about which I commanded you, 'You must not eat of it,' "Cursed is the ground *for your sake*; through painful toil you will eat of it all the days of your life."

The ground was cursed for man's sake as was the woman in bearing children. God did it for our sake. While work is gratifying to some extent we all admit it can cause troubles and suffering. While one of a woman's greatest joys is bringing a child into the world, it comes about through suffering.

Why does the body get old and wear out? Why are there earthquakes, tornadoes, lightning storms, disasters at sea, and on the land? Why do some people kill other people? In the midst of our living we often suffer and are on a course to meet death.

Facts from nature and God's Son give us the reason for suffering and dying. Nature shows us that a seed can not reproduce and bring about new life unless it falls into the ground and dies. God the Father shows us that the death of His Son can produce new life. In the Bible His Son is called His "seed." He died on the cross but rose to give all who trust Him forgiveness, eternal life and endless joy. This world is not the end. Death is but a stepping stone for those who believe God, a step into the "Aha!" of eternal life where death and suffering will be gone forever. It is leaving the wilted flowers of earth for flowers forever fresh.

Do these thoughts satisfy you regarding the reason for suffering and death? Then what will you replace them with? Nothing else really makes sense.

When we suffer it leads us to one of two reactions. We can run to God for help and understanding or we can get mad at Him, or say He doesn't exist and run away. If God didn't give us the blessings of suffering in this world would any of us seek Him?

Another reason we suffer is that we might be a help and be a blessing to others who suffer. God comforts us in our suffering if we seek Him so that we might comfort others. One who suffers because he stands for God is able to comfort another who suffers in the same manner.

In life there is physical death none of us choose nor do we know when it will take place. There is another kind of death which **we can choose**. Christ chose to give up His life and suffer Jesus said, "No man can take my life from me. I lay it down freely and I take it up again." With Christ's help **we can choose every day to die to self.** As we, like Christ, give up our life now for God and others we really begin to live. If we don't choose to give up our life we lose it. This is a great mystery but it is true in nature and in the clear teaching of Christ. If we suffer for right Jesus said, "Rejoice!" Why? Because suffering willingly for Jesus produces eternal, fruitful results.

May it be so for you. God bless you as you take in this song below which shows the reason for Christ's suffering. Dean <http://www.youtube.com/watch?v=1TjUsi7X28U&feature=related>

Why Does God Allow Bad Things To Happen?
July 15,2016

Let's think about some things God disproves but allows to happen. One thing He allows but doesn't approve is atheism. He is patient letting atheists go on rejecting Him desiring that someday they will have a change of heart, repent, and acknowledge Him. Some do eventually accept His existence and their responsibility to Him. They are converted and change. When I was converted to Christ at the age of 20, one of the first people I heard preach was an ex-atheist named Worth Ellis. He told how he had mocked God even though he didn't think He existed. If he saw lightning and heard thunder he lifted his arm toward the sky and shouted, "Shoot her again Pete!" Then he came to Christ and the God he had rejected became the theme of his preaching for the rest of his life.

Recently I heard a doctor speak who studied 4,000 near death experiences. He said that no atheist who had the near death experience stayed an atheist. All near death atheists then quit being atheists! They returned to their child like faith and belief in God.

How does that relate to me in my relationships with atheists? Well, To be like God I do not approve of atheism but like Him I show love to atheists, help him when they need help, eat with them and share truth with them, praying for their enlightenment and salvation.

We could deal in detail with all kinds of bad things God doesn't approve, like idol worship, adultery, disrespect for parents, murder, homosexuality, lying, stealing, pride, covetousness, sorcery, and unbelief. The good thing to remember is that He allows our bad behavior because He loves us, is patient and wants us to turn to Him before we die. Many people who practiced such sins later admitted their sin, were forgiven and changed.

I was one of them. I once practiced bad things God disproves like sexual sin, lustful thoughts, fornication, bad language, lying and others of which I am now ashamed. At the age of 20 God showed me love and forgiveness for my sins. He changed my life forever. Though I sin less, I am not sinless. This year I celebrate over 60 years of working at sinning less.

To be wise, seek God, find Him, and exchange the wages of your sin, which is death, for the gift of God which is eternal life! These Bible verses tell how to make that exchange now: Romans 10:9,10, Ephesians 2:8-10 John 1:12 and John 3:16. If you haven't come to Him, find and believe those verses. Give him your sins and He will give you His forgiveness. You may want to make that trade now while you sing these songs:. https://www.youtube.com/watch?v=w2VrRk4pZHY> https://www.youtube.com/watch?v=n2-WA_HQ_A4>

Why Pray for Great Things?
Let's Pray for Folks to Come to Christ
February 18, 2013

He is able to do exceedingly, abundantly, above all that we ask or think.

Once when giving a message at John Malliaris' memorial service I asked that my granddaughter pray for some to come to faith in Christ. She said, "No, grandpa. I'll pray that ALL will come to faith." So I changed my prayer. I still pray that all in John's life will come to faith as he did and be with him in heaven.

The Psychiatrist & A Troubled Man

July 12,2011

A troubled man comes to a psychiatrist for help. His problem is that he has a terrible fear every night that someone is under his bed. He is told that he can be cured by coming to the Psych three days a week for a year for $90 a visit. The man leaves and never comes back. A year later the Psych sees him on the street and inquires as to how he is doing.

The man says, "Well I thought about what you said. Then I read a verse in the Bible that says Jesus is a Wonderful Counselor, the Mighty God, the Prince of Peace and that the government of my life can be on His shoulder.

So I prayed for help to get rid of the fear of someone being under my bed. Suddenly the answer came to me.

""Oh, how is that," said the Psych?"

I got me a Japanese futon which has no legs. I haven't had any fear of anybody being under the bed since I got it.," said the ex-troubled man.

Then he smiled and said, "By the way. I bought a new car with the money I saved by not going to you.

The moral of this parable is, "Before you try other approaches which may or may not help to solve your problem, seek the Wonderful Counselor and let him govern your life. Let Him by his might help you cut out of your life anything that robs you of peace. Before all else may fail, try prayer to the Greatest Counselor and trust the Prince of Peace."

The Lord hear and grant all your petitions and give you peace.

Dean

The Wisest Man Who Ever Lived

Who is the wisest man who ever lived? Today I heard two famous men say Solomon was the wisest man who ever lived. That is a mistake that people often make. Actually the Bible says Solomon was wiser than the men of his time but not the wisest person that ever lived. Solomon said many wise things but God was angry with him because he failed to act on his wisdom by taking multiple wives who led Israel to idolatry and the demise of their kingdom. Read 1Kings 4:29-34; 9:9-12

In contrast, Jesus never failed. The Bible says of him, "In him are hid all the treasures of wisdom and knowledge." Col. 2:3. So in reality Jesus is the wisest man who ever lived.

Some will say, "Well, they are just talking about men."

Okay. Jesus was God in the flesh but he was a man, a real man." He said and did always those things that pleased his Father. He knew no sin, did no sin and in him there was no sin. HIs success, in dying for our sin and rising to give us life, led to the establishment of His impregnable church and eternal kingdom.

Unlike Solomon, Jesus alone was filled with ALL the treasures of wisdom and knowledge. We learn from Solomon but only Jesus deserves our worship. Do you worship Him?

Sing about it here: <https://www.youtube.com/watch?v=OaRwD2Y7C0s>

Will You Be A Designated Survivor?

I just learned something new to me. When the president of the U.S. gives a state of the union address someone on his Cabinet is designated to hide out away from the Capitol. Should the Capitol be attacked the designated survivor would have to take over. This has happened ever since the 1960s.

I know of others designated to be survivors of something far worse than a possible attack on our Capitol. It is the day when heaven and earth will pass away. This event is clearly described in the Bible in 2 Peter 3:10, **"But the day of the Lord will come as a thief in the night, in which the heavens will pass away with a great noise, and the elements will melt with fervent heat; both the earth and the works that are in it will be burned up."** Then 2 Peter 3:12 further explains this catastrophic event when it says, **"the heavens will be dissolved, being on fire, and the elements will melt with fervent heat?"** Some mock this coming event saying all things have continued on for thousands of years and it won't happen. They forget that the people of Noah's day heard that the world would be flooded. They mocked him but 120 years later it happened. So will the present earth be destroyed as God promises. Those who mock will be destroyed. Those who trust will be designated survivors. 2 Peter 3:13 makes a wonderful promise to those who are designated survivors, **"Nevertheless we, according to His promise, look for new heavens and a new earth in which righteousness dwells."**

The "we" mentioned in verse 13 are the definitely designated survivors! All of them will be like Shadrach, Meshach and Abed-nego in the Old Testament who trusted the true God and survived being thrown into a super hot fiery furnace. Because the furnace was so hot their enemies, who threw them in the burning furnace, were burned up. But those three who trusted the true God were not even singed nor were their clothes affected. Even the smell of the fire was not on them. So it will be for all of us who trust the living God. We will pass through the heat and melting earth unscathed!

John the apostle in The Bible also mentions the demise of the first heaven and earth in Revelation 21:1, **"Now I saw a new heaven and a new earth, for the first heaven and the first earth had passed away."**

Will you be a designated survivor? If it happens while you are alive, will you pass through the melting fervent heat and join John and Peter and all true followers of Christ in the new heaven and the new earth? You can for sure be a designated survivor if you know Jesus Christ as your Savior. You will survive if you die knowing Him or if you happen to be here when He wipes out this present earth and creates a new one.

Be wise and come to Jesus Christ today. Respond to His call, **"Come to Me, all *you* who labor and are heavy laden, and I will give you rest. Take My yoke upon you and learn from Me, for I am gentle and lowly in heart, and you will find rest for your souls."** Here's how to come. Come by believing with all your heart God's promise in this verse,**"For God so loved the world that He gave His only begotten Son, that whoever believes in Him should not perish but have everlasting life."John 3:16**

http://hymnbook.igracemusic.com/hymns/jesus-i-come>

Will You Take Up Your Cross? Will I?

Then Jesus said to them all, "If anyone desires to come after Me, let him deny himself, and take up his cross daily, and follow Me. For whoever desires to save his life will lose it, but whoever loses his life for My sake will save it. For what profit is it to a man if he gains the whole world, and is himself destroyed or lost? For whoever is ashamed of Me and My words, of him the Son of Man will be ashamed when He comes in His own glory, and in His Father's, and of the holy angels." Luke 9:23-26

What is my cross? It is losing my life Jesus, for your sake. It is not being ashamed of you and your words. It is suffering for the sake of others. It is enduring pain to benefit others in your name. It is bearing someone else's burden. It is weeping with those who weep. It is going on in the trials and pains of life to bring about blessings for others. It is realizing that my life should be like yours Jesus, putting others welfare above my own.

It is realizing that you were both a man of sorrows acquainted with grief and a man of joy because what you did for others to save them has brought millions of people to trust you, be forgiven, have eternal life, have peace and purpose, know they are loved and be with you forever on earth and in heaven.

Can I really take up my cross Lord Jesus? Since your callings are your enablings, I know you would not ask me to do something I can't do. So yes with your help, right now I deny myself, cling to my cross and trials and follow you.

Far from being ashamed of you, you are my hero, my Savior, my joy, my crown, my love, my peace, my hope and my eternal glory. With your help I will gladly endure my cross daily. Going on in the pain for you and the benefit of others is life's greatest challenge and grandest accomplishment.

Let us lay aside every weight, and the sin which so easily ensnares us, and let us run with endurance the race that is set before us, 2 looking unto Jesus, the author and finisher of our faith, who for the joy that was set before Him endured the cross, despising the shame, and has sat down at the right hand of the throne of God. Heb.12:1-3

May I and others who read this today respond to your challenge, accept your help to deny ourselves, take up and endure our cross, follow you, bear one another's burdens and learn as you did to find joy and gain through Godly pain. In Jesus name, Amen!

————

Wings
O Lord who made the wings of every bird
To Catch the winds and ride them high,
To dip and soar in every sky,
To rise in Thee
and fly!
Let me
On unseen wings
Rise high in Your embrace
To catch the currents of heaven's Dove
On wings of faith to soar in higher love!

"They that wait upon the Lord shall renew their strength. They shall mount up with wings..." Isaiah 40:31

Women I Have Loved

The first woman I loved was my mother.
I loved her 'til the day she died and I cried.
I still love her.

Then there was Mary in eighth grade.
It was a case of puppy love,
but it was real to the puppy.
She died also this last year.
i never got to tell her how I felt in those young years.
Then I had a dream and she told me she loved me in the dream and kissed me.
I said and did the same and the dream was over.

Then there is Gloria whom I still love.
Our love bloomed at 24
And has lasted now till 74 .
i still love her and like to be around her.
i like it when we do things together.
And when our love is intimate all problems and trials disappear when we become one.
We still love each other and we still have fun.
God in heaven has kept us together all these days.
And filled our lives with both the sorrows of night and the sun's golden rays.

There is Glenda my daughter who is such a blessing to me.
From the time she was a little girl till now she is one I have loved and will always be.
Her heart has been broken by sorrows in life.
But God has healed her and helped her grow through all the strife.

Then there is Kirsten my granddaughter of nineteen..
Whose life is filled now with joy and Godly esteem.
She is full of life and spontaneous combustion
And on the move now for God I'm trusting'.
She doesn't do slow and is always on the go.
But now thank the Lord she is going for Him
To be a missionary with Youth With a Mission.
And that's no fiction but is a fine addiction!

I trust she is on her way
to maturity as a young woman
And she'll remember she is loved as my granddaughter
who needs always to honor her heavenly Father!

Then there is Marsha, my cousin and close friend.
I've shared with her and she with me the hurts and joys that came to be.
I've told of my faults confessed to the Lord and to her.
And she has stayed a friend that is pure.
I pray for her and she for me.
She has known the hurts of disharmony
Her married life has been to often a start and a fall.
But her trust in God has kept her through it all.
My prayer is for the day that she and John's life
Will grow together in grace and closeness and banish all strife.

These are a few of the women for whom I have felt love.
It has been hard for me figure it all out.
But I'll end this with a shout!
For I'm learning more and more to love everyone as Jesus did
Not shelving my love nor keeping it hid!
Expressing it without doing wrong, for love is of God
And if we can't love those we see
Then love for God can never be!

Your Body Is Shouting

Please think about the amazing facts I share that follow. What do they indicate about your body. Check them out to see how well you hear your body?
1. Your body has a built in heating system that keeps you healthy around 98.6 and if it gets too low or high let's you know you are sick? 2. Your body has a built in cooling system that sweats to keep you cool? 3. Your body has a built in healing system that heals minor cuts? At a Jr. high camp one

year we had a contest with an award to the one with the most scars. The winner had 74 scars. Every cut had been healed by his marvelous built in blood healing system. 4. Your body has a built in oxygen supplying and nourishing and disease fighting systems inside your bones, your blood. It provides you nourishment daily and kills germs. 5. Your body has a built in thinking system which allows you to figure out and learn reading, writing, and arithmetic. Your system that helps you think may shout something amazing to you.

I have included only 4 of the 12+ amazing scientific facts about your body. But Scientists leave out a lot such as explaining our unity of body, soul and spirit. The Bible does not leave out what scientists leave out. Psalm 139:14 says, "I will praise You, for I am fearfully and wonderfully made; Marvelous are Your works, And that my soul knows very well." That includes not only our physical body but our whole being which most scientists don't deal with.

Notice that the Bible doesn't say, as some scientists say, that we are marvelously made by chance evolution. Psalm 100:3 says, "it is He that made us and not we are ourselves," and John 1:1-3 says, "All things were made by the Word, who is God, both by him and for him and without him nothing was made that is made."

Scientists don't deal with it but the Bible clearly tells us what happens to our bodies after we die. After death the Bible says comes the judgement. All whose names have stayed in God's book of life will go to be with Jesus Christ in heaven. All who reject Jesus will go to be with Satan in the lake of fire. That is why Jesus said, "Don't fear him who can kill your body but fear him who can kill both body and soul in hell." That is very clear isn't it.

Do you believe your Creator or man-designed-chance-evolution? It is the Creator who became a man who gave His life for you. Christ Jesus died out of love for you to redeem your body that will die someday. Then if you have believed in Him as your Savior who arose from the dead and afterword appeared to over 500 people, so will you also rise from the dead someday. He will raise your temporary body to be with him in heaven with millions who have eternal bodies perfect in every way!

So don't be a fool! Believe the God who gave you your amazing present body so you can get an even more magnificent body after you die! Believe God's promise today which is that He gave His only begotten Son for you so that if you believe you will not perish but have eternal life in a new, never ending, never dying body. Good news! You better believe it!

Almost Persuaded was a song God used to help me believe. I pray that you will be persuaded & believe so that someday your present temporary body will be exchanged for a glorious eternal body? Your body, soul and Spirit are shouting out for you to be persuaded!

"Almost persuaded" now to believe; "Almost persuaded" Christ to receive;
Seems now some soul to say,"Go, Spirit, go Thy way, Some more convenient day on Thee I'll call.
Almost persuaded," come, come today; "Almost persuaded," turn not away;
Jesus invites you here. Angels are ling'ring near, Prayers rise from hearts so dear; O wand'rer, come!
Oh, be persuaded! Christ never fails—Oh, be persuaded! His blood avails—
Can save from every sin, Cleanse you without, within—
Will you not let Him in? O pen the door!
"Almost persuaded," harvest is past! "Almost persuaded," doom comes at last;
"Almost" cannot avail; "Almost" is but to fail!
Sad, sad that bitter wail—"Almost—but lost!"
Be now persuaded, oh, sinner, hear! Be now persuaded, Jesus is near;
His voice is pleading still,Turn now with heart and will,
Peace will your spirit fill—Oh, turn today!

Your Value

Someone said to me with tears in her eyes, "Sometimes I feel worthless and it makes me angry." I assured her of her great value and it made me realize that many people struggle with not having any feeling of self worth. If you struggle at all with that problem or know someone who does, this may help.

First, God says of you and I that we are made in His image. That means we are special to Him. it means we have god-like characteristics. Your image is so valuable to God that He is displeased with anyone who misuses his tongue to curse others made in His likeness. Though we have all in some way devalued and distorted the image God gave us, He made it possible to restore and enhance that image. Our image is so valuable that God has gone out of His way to show your true value to Him. His Son, Jesus Christ displayed perfectly all the characteristics of God and gave Himself in death to remove your sins and shortcomings so you could be created anew in His likeness. If you believe God you will come to realize that He has done two wonderful things for you because you are so valuable. He put away everything in your life that does not reflect His perfection. How did He do it? His Son died for you once for all, the just, perfect man for the unjust, imperfect you and I, that we might be counted perfect. Believing God about the gift of His Son for us is counted to us for righteousness, His perfection.

If you believe what He did, dying for your sin He has "perfected you forever through the one offering of His Son for you." You are so valuable that He made it possible to not only take away all that is wrong in your life but rising again from the dead

He made it possible to replace all that is wrong with all that is right. When you believe what He did for you, He removes your sin and give you His perfection as a gift. That is good news! Can you be valued anymore by God than His making you perfect in His sight?

When you realize your value to Him you really begin to live. Jesus said it like this, "I am come that you might have life and have it more abundantly." In a way, it is an insult to God to think you have no worth. Don't insult Him. Believe Him and rejoice in your new found worth!

Above is a photo of a bird rescued by our good friends, Byron and Sharon Lance. Someone was going to euthanize it. Sharon and Byon rescued it. This shows it 10 days after they got it. As Sharon said, "Chirp, Chirp. More feathers. I thank God for all creatures large and small. God makes all things beautiful in His time.

It is still doing well now after a couple of weeks. Being in caring hands it has hope for life. Reminds me of nurse Anne who prayed with us before my wife's miracle successful brain surgery. She said, "She is in the doctors hands but more than, she is in God's hands." How true and sweet is that!

Gloria, My Mate Update
Shock & Awe
May-June 2018

8:30 AM a large crash sound in our bedroom. Shocked as I find my wife Gloria lying on the rug. Most pictures on the table near her bed and the lamp were knocked on the floor. Her head was inches from hitting her head on the curved table leg.

I put my arms around her and asked her if she hurt. She said, "Yes." I asked her where? She replied in a sad voice, "I dunno." I tried to lift her. She tried to help but couldn't use her right arm or leg. I prayed and wept trying to help her up. I put a pillow under her head and called 911.

I was told by 911 to unlock the door. By the time I got to the door the 911 ambulance was there as well as my wonderful neighbors Joe and Rina.

After Gloria was carried to the ambulance I rode with her to Kaiser in Walnut Creek. They checked her vital signs which were ok except she couldn't move her right leg and arm. Meanwhile word had spread in our neighborhood and my daughter came to emergency.

Gloria was given an MRI and it was determined that a bleeding tumor under the skulls dura was pressing against her brain causing her to fall and also was affecting her memory and speech. The tumor was round, about 3 inches across in a circle.

Her caring sisters, our daughter Glenda, son Ken, grandkids, Tyler & Kirsten, friend Mike, and church elders Randy & Dan came to help or pray for her. Most of all our Helper Jesus inspired hundreds to begin praying for her. God's help was with her as evidenced by her sweet smile and gratitude to all as she did recognize them and said when asked, "Hangin in there."

We were told told she couldn't be operated on until about a week later in Kaiser Redwood City.

Then we were told she could be operated on in Sacramento in a couple of days. So Gloria was taken by Ambulance to Sacramento while Glenda drove me there in my car. We arrived on Friday. (We stayed at Residence Inn which allowed us to stay for $100 dollars less a night because of Gloria's emergency. Sharing this so if you have an emergency you will know many hotels will help you out financially.)

The day after we arrived she was operated on. Dr. Moller came in looking very young. Gloria's sister said, "Do you think you can do this." But he was 42 and had done brain surgery for 12 years. My son Ken did research on the doctor and found he was rated 5 stars. Also he was teaching others. He told us there was a possibility that her brain tumor might be cancerous.

The nurse Anne was a solid Christian and told us it was not ordinary that people visiting were standing strong for our Savior. One nurse kept singing Amazing Grace and other songs around Gloria. When it was time for the surgery Anne and another nurse and all the rest of us surrounded Gloria and prayed for her. Anne said, "Now she is in the doctors hands but even more she is in God's hands.

The doctor said the operation would take about 3 to 6 hours but it was over a little before three hours. The Dr. came in beaming. There was no cancer. One of the nurses told us there are different kinds of doctors. One kind is excellent in what they do but not in a very caring relationship with patients. Another kind is excellent and caring. Dr. Moller was of the last most compassionate.

Gloria was moved out of intensive care into another room. Her right arm and leg which didn't work before surgery was restored. The tumor, the Dr. said was fairly certain not cancerous. Nurse Anne came all the way to Gloria's new room to see how she was doing. My daughter Glenda and I wrote special notes commending Anne's love and care.

We got mixed messages about what was to occur after the surgery. Some felt she would be taken home by ambulance. One scenario was she would be in Kaiser Sacramento for 10 to 14 days. Another scenario was when she got home she would have to have someone awake 24 hours a day watching her. None of those scenarios were correct.

She was examined the day after the operation. She was able to walk. Much of her memory had returned. She was eating more than me. After mental and physical tests she was released the next day on Monday. She came home with Glenda driving in our car the second day after the operation.

While someone needed to be at our home 24 hours it was not necessary to sit by her bed and watch her. She had an indoor walker and was able to go to the bathroom by herself though I kept watch each time she got up.

Therapists from Kaiser came to our home eventually and after a couple of visits felt she needed no more in house therapy mentally, or occupationally. She had one last visit with the Speech therapist.

Melanie Erbil from our church set up a meal train for folks to bring food for Gloria, myself and my son and daughter, every other day. People brought delicious meals and most always flowers and dessert. We had enough cookies in the freezer to sink a battleship. The whole house was everywhere decorated with flowers. I found out in our married life a sure way to get a kiss from my wife. Just bring her flowers! Voila, there it is!

The prayers, love, care and kindness shown us is phenomenal. We have experienced what Jesus said in **John 13:35,** "By this all will know that you are **My disciples**(learner. followers), if you have love for one another." We have seen clearly the love others have had for us.

During our trial Gloria and I have felt the shock but seen the awesome hand of God in all the events. Here are a few other awesome things.

In Sacramento while Gloria was in the hospital I had car trouble. Just so happened Gloria's sister Lavona, had a cousin who had a garage about 5 minutes from the hospital. We left our car there and were driven by one of the workers to the hospital. Then when it was frepaired they drove my daughter Glenda back to pick up the car.

Besides the wonderful care at Kaiser, many came all the way to Sacramento to visit her. Glenda was their night and day to take care of her and me. Our son Ken stayed there also to help care for her. Both Gloria's sisters, Linda and Lavona drove to Sacramento, stayed and visited her many times. Our grandson Tyler brought her beautiful flowers and a caring note. Our granddaughter, drove up to spend time with her and has continued to do so after coming home to Dublin.

Our son Ken got Gloria a special walker and assembled it so she could walk outside and get exercise. Our neighbors across the street, Joe and Rina, visited us and Joe is installing special hand rails in our house to avoid falls.

Gloria was released by her Dr. Moller to a normal life again. He told us originally that it could take 3 to six months to recover. She is pretty much back to normal after a month and a half. She even drives our car. And I know she is really doing well because she is telling me what to do around the house again.

We have had numerous occasions to share Christ and His love with many people. I don't want to take time to explain every last thing but I can say that never in my life have I felt such deepening love for my wife and all our friends. It all started with a shock and is continuing with awe and joy. We have learned afresh that we can celebrate our Father's care and say for certain, "The Joy of the Lord is and has been our strength. "Nehemiah 8:10. Gloria, Glenda and I all sang this song as a trio, proof of our God's great love and care. Listen to it now if you wish. https://www.youtube.com/watch?v=9HLyhEdh92E&index=2&list=RDzY5o9mP22V0>

This book I have written really has no end because all who believe God and are rescued and saved will live for ever in His hands. Sing about it by clicking on it below.

<https://www.youtube.com/watch?v=hXrqnfcW_Y8>

Goodbye for now. See you soon together in the land where we will know love forever and never grow old.

Take a minute to bathe in God's love in anticipation of our final home. https://www.youtube.com/watch?v=LmtFxnQsl6Q>

The Beginning!

Printed in the United States
By Bookmasters